Dynamics of Virtu

Series Editors
Ursula Huws
De Havilland Campus
Hertfordshire Business School
Hatfield, United Kingdom

Rosalind Gill
Department of Sociology
City University London
London, United Kingdom

Technological change has transformed where people work, when and how. Digitisation of information has altered labour processes out of all recognition whilst telecommunications have enabled jobs to be relocated globally. ICTs have also enabled the creation of entirely new types of 'digital' or 'virtual' labour, both paid and unpaid, shifting the borderline between 'play' and 'work' and creating new types of unpaid labour connected with the consumption and co-creation of goods and services. This affects private life as well as transforming the nature of work and people experience the impacts differently depending on their gender, their age, where they live and what work they do. Aspects of these changes have been studied separately by many different academic experts however up till now a cohesive overarching analytical framework has been lacking. Drawing on a major, high-profile COST Action (European Cooperation in Science and Technology) Dynamics of Virtual Work, this series will bring together leading international experts from a wide range of disciplines including political economy, labour sociology, economic geography, communications studies, technology, gender studies, social psychology, organisation studies, industrial relations and development studies to explore the transformation of work and labour in the Internet Age. The series will allow researchers to speak across disciplinary boundaries, national borders, theoretical and political vocabularies, and different languages to understand and make sense of contemporary transformations in work and social life more broadly. The book series will build on and extend this, offering a new, important and intellectually exciting intervention into debates about work and labour, social theory, digital culture, gender, class, globalisation and economic, social and political change.

More information about this series at
http://www.palgrave.com/series/14954

Stephanie Taylor • Susan Luckman
Editors

The New Normal of Working Lives

Critical Studies in Contemporary Work and Employment

Editors
Stephanie Taylor
School of Psychology, Faculty of
Arts and Social Sciences
The Open University
Milton Keynes
United Kingdom

Susan Luckman
Hawke EU Centre for Mobilities,
Migrations and Cultural Transformations
University of South Australia
Adelaide, South Australia, Australia

Dynamics of Virtual Work
ISBN 978-3-319-88160-7   ISBN 978-3-319-66038-7   (eBook)
DOI 10.1007/978-3-319-66038-7

© The Editor(s) (if applicable) and The Author(s) 2018
Softcover reprint of the hardcover 1st edition 2017
This work is subject to copyright. All rights are solely and exclusively licensed by the Publisher, whether the whole or part of the material is concerned, specifically the rights of translation, reprinting, reuse of illustrations, recitation, broadcasting, reproduction on microfilms or in any other physical way, and transmission or information storage and retrieval, electronic adaptation, computer software, or by similar or dissimilar methodology now known or hereafter developed.
The use of general descriptive names, registered names, trademarks, service marks, etc. in this publication does not imply, even in the absence of a specific statement, that such names are exempt from the relevant protective laws and regulations and therefore free for general use.
The publisher, the authors and the editors are safe to assume that the advice and information in this book are believed to be true and accurate at the date of publication. Neither the publisher nor the authors or the editors give a warranty, express or implied, with respect to the material contained herein or for any errors or omissions that may have been made. The publisher remains neutral with regard to jurisdictional claims in published maps and institutional affiliations.

Cover credit: © Georgijevic/Getty

Printed on acid-free paper

This Palgrave Macmillan imprint is published by Springer Nature
The registered company is Springer International Publishing AG
The registered company address is: Gewerbestrasse 11, 6330 Cham, Switzerland

Contents

Collection Introduction: The 'New Normal' of Working Lives   1
Stephanie Taylor and Susan Luckman

Part I   Creative Working   17

Online Selling and the Growth of Home-Based Craft Micro-enterprise: The 'New Normal' of Women's Self-(under)Employment   19
Susan Luckman and Jane Andrew

Hope Labour Revisited: Post-socialist Creative Workers and Their Methods of Hope   41
Ana Alacovska

From Visual Discipline to Love-Work: The Feminising of Photographic Expertise in the Age of Social Media   65
Karen Cross

Creative Labour, Before and After 'Going Freelance': Contextual Factors and Coalition-Building Practices   87
Frederick Harry Pitts

Searching, Sorting, and Managing Glut: Media Software
Inscription Strategies for 'Being Creative' 109
Frédérik Lesage

Part II Digital Working Lives — 127

Negotiating the Intimate and the Professional
in Mom Blogging 129
Katariina Mäkinen

Vlogging Careers: Everyday Expertise, Collaboration
and Authenticity 147
Daniel Ashton and Karen Patel

From Presence to Multipresence: Mobile Knowledge
Workers' Densified Hours 171
Johanna Koroma and Matti Vartiainen

Affectual Demands and the Creative Worker: Experiencing
Selves and Emotions in the Creative Organisation 201
Iva Josefsson

Coworking(s) in the Plural: Coworking Spaces
and New Ways of Managing 219
Silvia Ivaldi, Ivana Pais, and Giuseppe Scaratti

Part III Transitions and Transformations — 243

'Investment in Me': Uncertain Futures and Debt
in the Intern Economy 245
Kori Allan

Letting Them Get Close: Entrepreneurial Work
and the New Normal 265
Hanna-Mari Ikonen

Self-Employment in Elderly Care: A Way to Self-Fulfilment or Self-Exploitation for Professionals? 285
Elin Vadelius

Creating Alternative Solutions for Work: Experiences of Women Managers and Lawyers in Poland and the USA 309
Ingrid Biese and Marta Choroszewicz

Beyond Work? New Expectations and Aspirations 327
Stephanie Taylor

Index 347

List of Figures

Fig. 1 Established maker interviewees' income from creative practice 23
Fig. 2 Established makers currently receiving financial support from partner or family 31
Fig. 3 Established makers supplementing income with other paid work 33
Fig. 1 Different types of communication and collaboration events in mobile multilocational work 193

Collection Introduction: The 'New Normal' of Working Lives

Stephanie Taylor and Susan Luckman

Introduction

Lauren Berlant (2011) has written of the need to understand the problem of living contemporary lives, including the 'new normal' and 'new ordinary' (p. 261). This critical international and interdisciplinary collection investigates the new normal of work and employment by examining the viewpoints and experience of the workers themselves, and the privilege or disadvantage they experience. The book includes contributions from academics in 7 countries, presenting research conducted in 11 national contexts and also the 'between' spaces of online communications and mobile working. The 15 chapters in the body of the collection look in detail at new work and work activities in a range of occupations and locations in

---

S. Taylor (✉)
School of Psychology, Faculty of Arts and Social Sciences,
The Open University, Milton Keynes, UK

S. Luckman
Hawke EU Centre for Mobilities, Migrations and Cultural Transformations,
University of South Australia, Adelaide, South Australia, Australia

© The Author(s) 2018
S. Taylor, S. Luckman (eds.), *The New Normal of Working Lives*,
Dynamics of Virtual Work, DOI 10.1007/978-3-319-66038-7_1

the global workforce, exploring changing forms of governance, the coping strategies adopted by the workers in order to manage difficulties and life circumstances, and their understandings of the possibilities, trajectories, identities and potential rewards that they accept as the new normal. Drawing upon empirical research, the collection explores how contemporary work is marked, even for the privileged 'middle class', by the 'ordinary as an impasse shaped by crisis in which people find themselves developing skills for adjusting to newly proliferating pressures to scramble for modes of living on' (Berlant, 2011, p. 8).

In the chapters in this collection, unsurprisingly, no single feature dominates the new normal of contemporary work and employment. Instead, many changes contribute to the shifting work experiences discussed in the research studies, from the use of digital technologies, with the ever-expanding possibilities these offer, including for mobilities and potentially limitless locations of work, to the rise in 'own account' working (International Labour Organisation, 2015), and the associated entrepreneurial and creative values which have become a prescribed coping mechanism around contemporary work and work arrangements. However, perhaps the most significant feature to emerge in these studies is the affective weighting attached to personalised and increasingly individualised work, and the motivation this provides for a shift in how people *want* to work and how they organise their lives. Moreover, this motivation has repercussions for the difficulties that people accept, such as the ways in which organisations are increasingly operating in the name of giving staff 'what they want', for instance, by winding back infrastructure and placing greater emphasis on shared and/or flexible work patterns in order to decrease running costs. These affective aspects of the new normal, and the subtle forms of self-exploitation and exploitation they give rise to, are yet to receive the critical attention they warrant.

A number of themes cross the various studies. Inevitably, there is a strong **temporal** focus in accounts of change. Academic studies of work and employment have labelled many of the transitions linked to new work and employment, for example, as millennial or twenty-first century, post-Fordist or neo-liberal. Those accounts often have a negative emphasis, as if the experience of contemporary working lives continues to be defined by what has been lost, including (ideals of) experience-linked remuneration, predictable career progression and the benefits of secure employment. In contrast, policy and media accounts tend to be highly positive about work today, invoking progress, including through the future focus of the contemporary model figures of the entrepreneur and the creative worker. For example, a recent UK government review on working practices commends 'the UK's successful record in creating jobs, including *flexible jobs which open up work to people with different needs and priorities*' (Department for Business, Energy and Industrial Strategy, 2017, p. 7: emphasis added). Within this collection, workers' own experiences of pathways of change are the particular focus of Part III on transitions and transformations, but the temporal theme appears throughout.

In keeping with the near constant and contingent negotiations of Berlant's new normal, there is also a theme of **context**. Some chapters discuss the impacts on individuals of changes occurring at the level of the state, such as austerity policies and reduced spending on welfare. For example, the privatisation of formerly state-provided services has produced new social service entrepreneurs (see Vadelius, this collection). The relevance of context has of course been transformed by the digital technologies that are central to so much contemporary work. Although **digital working** is implicated with almost every occupation (Huws, 2013), its subtler effects are still being explored, including the emergence of digital occupations, like blogging and vlogging, that are so new they are not always recognised as work. The possibilities of digital working include the interconnection, and separation, of virtual and physical spaces, such as in mobile working and new forms of workspace sharing, like coworking spaces. Yet, despite its ubiquity and acceptance as part of the new normal, digital working has not erased the importance of more conventional **sites** of work. For example, home-based employment exploits the affordances of the online marketplace and is sought out by many workers, especially women, for the work–life flexibility it offers, despite the relatively low income that it usually provides. But conflating the site of paid work with home potentially comes at the cost of the work intruding into the still-relevant physical spaces of domesticity and personal life. Site is also relevant to creative workers outside the 'advanced economies' (International Labour Organisation, 2015) who do jobs which are defined by an international creative sector, and probably exist because of the global reputation and celebration of that sector. Their working conditions are still set by their national locations, including within the 'radically tumultuous and uncertain institutional and societal contexts' of post-socialist nation-states' (Alacovska, this collection).

Another strong theme in the collection, linked to the previously identified affective weighting, is the **personalisation** of work. Older boundaries between a worker identity and a private self or subjectivity are eroded when work entails **emotional and affective labour** (Gregg, 2011; Luckman, 2015) and when formerly personal and private areas of life become monetised in new forms of 'social reproduction' (e.g. Jarrett, 2016; Weeks, 2011). A number of chapters look at the implications of transforming amateur engagement into professional work, or home life into business. The normalising of connections between work and non-work, professional life and formerly personal aspects of people's lives is of course central to academic accounts of **creative working** (the focus of Part I). Creativity is both an economic 'good' associated with the global sector of the cultural and creative industries, and an aspiration for workers in many new occupations. The compass of the creative sector is widened by broad definitions (e.g. Fuller, Hamilton, & Seale, 2013), with the resultant near-impossibility of specifying all the occupations which belong within it. Digital working has also given rise to new understandings of creative practices and creativity. In addition, Taylor (2015) discusses a recent discursive drift through which creativity has become more generally associated with 'own account' working (self-employment, freelancing, etc.) through the model figures of the entrepreneur (Bröckling, 2016) and the creative maker or auteur. As a consequence, creative work practices potentially appear desirable for freelance or self-employed workers in any area or occupation, shaping their working lives. Chapters in this collection show how the affective discourses of creative and entrepreneurial work, and the identities they make available, drive many of the choices workers make, and are being increasingly exploited as motivators, for example, to maximise worker productivity.

The collection shows how the aspects of new working lives encompassed in these themes are engaged with and negotiated, managed or lived around as the new normal of workers' experience. Transitions have indeed occurred within various research participants' working lives—for instance, from employment to self-employment, leisure pastime to work, or almost work—but they are often accepted as unremarkable by individual workers themselves, even though for an academic observer the details may be strikingly worthy of comment, and the socio-economic implications still to be fully drawn out. One indication of workers' increasing acceptance of change is through their take-up of education and training in new skills, including self-study materials, like 'how to' guidance (discussed by Cross, Lesage, and Ashton and Patel, this collection). These processes of upskilling themselves contribute to different criteria for expertise, creativity and professionalism, and even wholly new occupations.

Arguably, however, the ultimate theme of the collection is the patterns of **advantage and exclusion**, which operate around work today. The chapters show the discursive and organisational persistence of the division which characterised an earlier 'normative model' of work (Huws, 2013) distinguishing masculine activities of paid employment in a formal workplace from the unpaid activities of social reproduction historically carried out by women in the home. The division remains relevant to women attempting to combine home-based working with family life, for example, and more broadly to the feminised emotional labour entailed in communicating and relating to others, as Cross notes (this collection).

Some chapters suggest that new occupations and work arrangements do offer advantages, like a sense of control and achievement through different working arrangements (Vadelius, this collection) and even a successful blurring of life–work boundaries to the extent that the claims of family life can take precedence over those of work (Biese and Choroszewicz, this collection). However, the inequalities of contemporary labour markets are well recognised (e.g. Oakley, 2013), and it is important to acknowledge that the collection is dominated by the experiences of middle class people from advanced economies whose privilege continues to advantage them in the world of new work, including through the choices that are available to them regarding how to manage the interface between paid work and life. Clearly, this privilege is not distributed evenly and the collection explores some of the forms that it takes. For example, Allan (this collection) discusses the new 'classed privilege' which provides more access to debt, including student loans, which is justified as an investment in the future. Like the unpaid internships, with their widely acknowledged problems, which have become common in the current context of high unemployment (and especially youth unemployment) in many countries, such debt is an example of the difficulties faced by career entrants, and the young more generally. Other chapters question the misleadingly 'democratic' associations of digital working, challenging the common assumptions that there are low entry barriers to new digital occupations like blogging (Mäkinen, this volume) and vlogging (Ashton and Patel, this volume).

The situations presented through the studies in this collection are still in progress, and those positive experiences that are discussed have been achieved through struggle. Most of the workers are qualified professionals in high earning fields who have some options and more room for compromise as they navigate the new normal. Their decision-making, however, does indicate that even the privileged are not always happy with the status quo or the changes occurring as a result of larger shifts in working lives. That these relatively advantaged workers are still operating in a world of substantial trade-offs can only start to offer some insight into the pressures of the increasingly stressful, uncertain and intrusive experience of the new normal of work for those with less wriggle room to negotiate it more on their own terms. Thus, what starts to emerge clearly here in the pervasiveness of increased self-employment and the widened uptake of entrepreneurial identities is that, rather than individualistic responses to the grind of the new normal, new forms of collective identity and action are clearly required, perhaps driven by greater mutual consciousness-raising and sharing of disappointments and desires.

The sections and chapters

The collection is organised into three sections corresponding to key themes and aspects of the workers' experience. The chapters in Part I centre on **creative working**, the chapters in Part II discuss **digital working lives** and the chapters in Part III explore **transitions and transformations.**

The chapters in Part I approach creative work and creativity from a range of theoretical and disciplinary positions and draw upon empirical data to critically analyse what is at stake now as a result of the maturation, or 'settling down', of creative working lives. In Chap. 2, 'Online selling and the growth of home-based craft microenterprise: The "new normal" of women's self-(under)employment', Susan Luckman and Jane Andrew find Berlant's 'cruel optimism' in play within the craft economy in the situation of Australian women who run craft micro-enterprises, selling their products online and face-to-face. In a discussion of empirical data generated by a three-year study of design craft micro-enterprises, the authors suggest that at a time of growing employment uncertainty, shrinking arts funding and widespread governmental policy emphasis on encouraging small business, the development of creative micro-enterprises can be seen as part of a wider pattern of the privatisation of responsibility for a worker's economic position. The research indicates that the growth of craft self-employment is masking considerable un-and under-employment, especially among women. The ease of establishing a professional business profile and the ability to network via social media as a marketing tool provide nascent craft entrepreneurs with a sense of being real, sustainable, significant and justified in continuing down this path. However, the social and economic costs to individuals, families and the wider society of all this effort and risk-taking are profound and, the chapter argues, require greater attention as part of wider cultural and economic policy making.

In Chap. 3, 'Hope labour revisited: Post-socialist creative workers and their methods of hope', Ana Alacovska draws on sociological and anthropological theories of hope and hope labour to understand how creative workers manage their lives in the precarious post-socialist economies of Macedonia and Albania. She argues that hope entails more than future-oriented instrumentalism and dream-like optimism. Hope is not only found in 'postalgic' circumstances but also amidst conditions of hopelessness, because hope is needed to endure hardship. Alacovska outlines a theoretical framework for capturing the performative role of hope in sustaining creative careers amidst widespread precariousness and work casualisation. The chapter approaches hope as an experiential category of being-in-the-world and hoping as a practice of getting through the hardships of the concrete realities of work–life. The research discussed in the chapter is an interview study conducted with fashion designers, musicians, actors and new media workers in Macedonia and Albania.

Chapter 4, 'From visual discipline to love-work: The feminising of photographic expertise in the age of social media', by Karen Cross, approaches the gendering of labour through a discussion of amateur and professional photographic practice. Taking up the concept of 'free labour' from Maurizio Lazzarato (1996), in the Italian postoperaist tradition, and also Tiziana Terranova (2000), the chapter discusses the trend towards relationality now defining digital labour. It looks at the shifting gender dynamics in a new aesthetic reframing of photography in recently published photography training manuals. The chapter adopts the formula of 'love-work' to compound the previously neglected concerns of the amateur with professional values, and to express the new terms of social media practice as it promises to mitigate historical losses, especially those relating to the domestic and familial concerns of women.

Chapter 5, 'Creative labour, before and after "going freelance": Contextual factors and coalition-building practices', by Frederick H. Pitts also looks to postoperaist accounts, using the work of Sergio Bologna. In his discussion of freelance creative workers in the UK and the Netherlands, Pitts presents empirical findings to oppose the resonant discourses of liberation in postoperaist accounts of 'immaterial labour' and their modern proponents. He suggests that struggle is necessary to recapture creative activity from its imbrication in capitalist social relations. The chapter presents a case study to explore the movement of creative workers from formal employment to freelancing. It examines the struggle they wage to secure conditions within the commercial contractual relationship of freelance work which enable them to be creative in the way they initially desired. The chapter also explores the emerging forms of coalition-building in evidence among the freelancers.

Chapter 6, 'Searching, sorting, and managing glut: Media software inscription strategies for "being creative"' by Frédérik Lesage looks ahead to the digital focus of Part II. The chapter adopts Angela McRobbie's (2016) concept of the 'creativity dispositif' in an account of how media software enables and constrains contemporary creative practice. The chapter explores how the software used for creating, editing and sharing media content can both enable and constrain what it means to 'be creative'. The chapter introduces 'glut' as a software inscription strategy, examining how glut is operationalised for the widely used software Adobe Photoshop, and for instruction about the software in an online learning platform.

Continuing the technological focus, the chapters in Part II explore new occupations, work arrangements and workspaces which are being normalised through digital working. 'Mom blogging' is a growing field of women's work, in which motherhood and personal narratives intersect with paid work and micro-entrepreneurship. In Chap. 7, 'Negotiating the intimate and the professional in mom blogging', Katariina Mäkinen investigates how mom bloggers in Finland build personal brands that rely on their lives and identities as mothers, and also their skills and experience as professionals. Presenting research findings from interviews and a virtual ethnography, the chapter addresses the 'new normal' of blogging, investigating how the monetisation of everyday life, the construction of public displays of subjectivity and the dissolving of parenting into work, and vice versa, are negotiated by the bloggers themselves as an everyday part of living, working and parenting.

In Chap. 8, 'Vlogging careers: Everyday expertise, collaboration and authenticity', Daniel Ashton and Karen Patel discuss a variation on blogging, vlogging, as an increasingly visible and normalised form of cultural work. They argue that how-to guidance and journalistic coverage overstate the accessibility of vlogging careers and obscure the various forms of expertise required, including the underlying strategies vloggers use to engage their audiences, for instance, by interacting with fans and collaborators, and the skills they require to stage a relatable authenticity. The chapter analyses the social media presence of four prominent vloggers.

The focus of Chap. 9 is the mobile information and communication technologies (mICT) that enable knowledge workers to be available 24/7, wherever they are. In this chapter, titled 'From presence to multipresence: Mobile knowledge workers' densified hours', Johanna Koroma and Matti Vartiainen introduce the concept of 'multipresence' to describe how workers on the move can be simultaneously present in different physical, virtual and social spaces. Exactly how multipresence is experienced depends on the specific technology, context and situation involved. The potential benefits are increased flexibility and more efficient use of time, while the costs include interrupted concentration, stress, reduced productivity, and problems with life management and work–life balance.

In Chap. 10, 'Affectual demands and the creative worker: Experiencing selves and emotions in the creative organisation', Iva Josefsson discusses the emotion talk of workers at a video game development studio in Sweden, examining the affectual demands of their jobs. Such demands may serve organisational interests, functioning to discipline an organisationally desirable committed and engaged worker, but at times they prove problematic for the workers. The chapter shows how the creative discourses in play in this context collapse the distance between self and work. This not only heightens the sense of personal meaningfulness for the workers but also disables their attempts to keep some distance from their working lives.

Coworking spaces first appeared in San Francisco in 2005 but are now found all over the world. In Chap. 11, 'Coworking(s) in the plural: Coworking spaces and new ways of managing', drawing upon research in Italian coworking spaces Silvia Ivaldi, Ivana Pais and Giuseppe Scaratti critically examine this form of workspace organisation and its associated values and practices, such as collaboration, reciprocity, community and sustainability. Identifying multiple types, rather than a singular model, of coworking, they trace out four predominant forms of organisational structure and culture, suggesting that coworking is giving rise to new ways of working and managing organisations.

The chapters in Part III explore trajectories of change within some contemporary working lives, and the extent to which the transitions are establishing new relations to work, including new occupations. The first chapter in the section, Chap. 12, '"Investment in me": Uncertain futures and debt in the intern economy', by Kori Allan, looks at the situation of people who are still at the point of career entry. Presenting findings from ethnographic fieldwork with interns in Canada's publishing and journalism industries, the chapter argues that the promissory value of meaningful work facilitates enthusiastic self-exploitation despite low or no wages. While interns resent 'grunt work' as just free labour that should be waged, they view meaningful work as a future-oriented investment in their networks and skills. Interns also recognise, however, that only the privileged can afford unpaid internships. As contingent work has spread to the middle classes, privilege is not necessarily constituted through secure employment, certain futures or higher wages, but rather through differential access to opportunities for self-appreciation.

The next two chapters look at novel forms of entrepreneurship. 'Lifestyle-based entrepreneurs' are self-employed people who work from home and have moved into entrepreneurship to live a certain lifestyle and escape insecure wage work. In Chap. 13, 'Letting them get close: Entrepreneurial work and the "new normal"', Hanna-Mari Ikonen looks at the example of home-based businesses in Sweden and Finland that host the 'dog hobbyists' who participate in dog training in rural settings. In this new entrepreneurial work, production, reproduction and consumption blur together as the hosts' entire lifestyle becomes commercialised. Despite individualised risk, the entrepreneurs remain optimistic that they have the resources to make real their fantasies of living the 'good life'.

In Chap. 14, 'Self-employment in elderly care: A way to self-fulfilment or self-exploitation for professionals?', Elin Vadelius looks at the situation of people who were previously employed in large health and social care organisations and who now run small or medium-sized businesses in the elderly care sector in Sweden. The chapter investigates their reasons for becoming private providers of publicly financed and regulated welfare services, and their experience of this situation. The political arguments for creating markets in public services are that competition and entrepreneurship contribute to greater innovation, diversity and freedom of choice for the elderly, and that deregulation can provide women with better opportunities to realise their visions and ideas by starting own businesses. The chapter explores the participants' experiences of success, or non-success, as self-employed and private providers of home care, and their feelings about the transition, which include pride and achievement but also defeat and failure.

In Chap. 15, 'Creating alternative solutions for work: The experiences of women managers and lawyers in Poland and the USA', Ingrid Biese and Marta Choroszewicz suggest that mainstream career models no longer correspond to how contemporary individuals want to live and work. The authors argue that for women who attempt to combine a career with family or care responsibilities, prevalent masculinist career models are especially problematic. The chapter presents the stories of two women, a lawyer from Poland and a manager from the USA, who questioned traditional definitions of success in order to create lifestyles that provide them with a greater sense of authenticity and control. The women left mainstream career models to take up alternative work arrangements that combine different areas of their lives while still drawing on their skills and potential. The chapter suggests that these life changes were successful and that by opting out of an established way of working, the women adopted new mindsets and practices that better accommodate their wants and needs.

In the final chapter of this section and the whole collection, Chap. 16, 'Beyond work? New expectations and aspirations', Stephanie Taylor discusses the possible emergence of new norms, aspirations and expectations attached to work. She presents an analysis of interviews with UK artist-makers which suggests that these people value their creative practices as 'not work' and as offering personal associations and forms of fulfilment which they regard work as unable to provide. The chapter argues that earlier understandings of work based on a masculinist 'factory' model not only persist but also have extended into all occupations, reinforcing negative associations of meanings and affects, so that even the educated and qualified middle class do not expect to find self-actualisation and personal reward through working.

Whose 'new normal'?

The craft makers discussed by Luckman and Andrew (in Chap. 2), the creative freelancers studied by Pitts (Chap. 5), the bloggers and vloggers in the chapters by Mäkinen (Chap. 7) and Ashton and Patel (Chap. 8), the professional hosts researched by Ikonen (Chap. 13), the satisfied welfare entrepreneurs in Vadelius' study (Chap. 14) and the professional women discussed by Ingrid Biese and Marta Choroszewicz (Chap. 15)—what these and other contemporary workers all appear to have in common is an ambition to follow their own values and, even more, to organise their own lives in their own ways. This freedom is prioritised over the more conventional rewards of financial success, to the extent that, for Taylor's participants (Chap. 16), it prompts a turning away altogether from work in order to pursue an alternative practice. That ambition is, of course, the dream of the privileged. Their advantage is relative but the collection reasserts that privilege in contemporary life is gendered, (middle) classed, (middle) aged and geographically circumscribed. In the small number of studies that explore the normality of those outside these privileged positions, it does not seem to be a coincidence that Alacovska, discussing the workers in failing post-socialist economies (Chap. 3), and Allan, considering the circumstances of younger people who are struggling to begin a working life (Chap. 12), both centre their accounts on 'hope' as almost the converse of possibility. The remainder of the research participants inevitably experience some constraints, but their dreams of control and freedom at least seem achievable. As Laurent notes, 'norms of self-management … differ according to what kinds of confidence people have enjoyed about the entitlements of their social location' (p. 5).

Without wanting to universalise middle class experience and aspirations, we suggest that this privilege can reveal more widely and deeply held aspirations around, and deficits within, the contemporary experience of work. Indeed, what emerges from these rich and varied empirical studies is precisely a picture of Berlant's 'cruel optimism' (2011); that is, a picture of paid work as increasingly organised around new normals of hope and promise that become an 'obstacle to flourishing' (p. 1) as within different employment arrangements the promise promotes the intensification of labour and, too often, an acceptance of limited reward for large effort. Like Berlant, we have found that the 'subjects of precarity' tracked here in terms of their experience of work 'have chosen primarily not to fight, but to get caught up in a circuit of adjustment and gestural transformation in order to stay in proximity to some aspirations that had gotten attached to the normative good life' (Berlant, 2011, p. 249). Negotiating both practical and affective relationship to this tension is the new normal of work.

Acknowledgements This collection originated in the conference streams that the editors led at the New Meanings of Work Conference WORK2015, University of Turku, Finland, 19–21 August 2015. We would like to thank all the stream participants and the conference organisers. Our thanks also to Professor Lisa Adkins, consultant for the conference, for her assistance with setting up the streams, and the Hawke EU Centre for Mobilities, Migrations and Cultural Transformations at the University of South Australia, for editorial funding. We are grateful to Miranda Roccisano for her editing work and Louis Everuss for his initial copy checking of the chapters. Finally, we thank the editors of the Dynamics of Virtual Work series in which this collection is published.

References

Berlant, L. (2011). *Cruel optimism*. Durham and London: Duke University Press.

Bröckling, U. (2016). *The entrepreneurial self: Fabricating a new type of subject*. London: Sage.

Department for Business, Energy and Industrial Strategy. (2017). *Good work: The Taylor review of modern working practices*. gov.UK. Retrieved July 13, 2017, from https://www.gov.uk/government/publications/good-work-the-taylor-review-of-modern-working-practices

Fuller, G., Hamilton, C., & Seale, K. (2013). Working with amateur labour: Between culture and economy. *Cultural Studies Review, 19*(1), 143–154.

Gregg, M. (2011). *Work's intimacy*. Cambridge: Polity Press.

Hochschild, A. (2003). *The managed heart: Commercialization of human feeling*. Berkeley, CA: University of California Press.

Huws, U. (2013). Working online, living offline: Labour in the Internet Age. *Work Organisation Labour and Globalisation, 7*(1), 1–11.

International Labour Organisation. (2015). *World employment and social outlook: The changing nature of jobs*. Geneva: International Labour Office, ILO Research Department.

Jarrett, K. (2016). *Feminism, labour, and digital media: The digital housewife*. New York and London: Routledge.

Luckman, S. (2015). *Craft and the creative economy*. Hampshire: Palgrave Macmillan.

McRobbie, A. (2016). *Be creative: Making a living in the new culture industries*. Malden, MA: Polity Press.

Oakley, K. (2013). Absentee workers: Representation and participation in the cultural industries. In M. Banks, R. Gill, & S. Taylor (Eds.), *Theorizing cultural work: Labour, continuity and change in the cultural and creative industries* (pp. 56–67). Abingdon and New York: Routledge.

Taylor, S. (2015). A new mystique? Working for yourself in the neoliberal economy. *Sociological Review, 63*(SI), 174–187.

Weeks, K. (2011). *The problem with work: Feminism, Marxism, antiwork politics and postwork imaginaries*. Durham, NC: Duke University Press.

Stephanie Taylor is Senior Lecturer in Social Psychology at the Open University, UK. Her research investigates a complex gendered subject and contemporary identification, including identities of creativity, creative work and own account working. Her recent books are *What is Discourse Analysis?* (2013) and *Contemporary Identities of Creativity and Creative Work* (2012) (with Karen Littleton), and the co-edited collections *Gender and Creative Labour* (2015) (with Bridget Conor and Rosalind Gill) and *Theorizing Cultural Work: Labour, Continuity and Change in the Cultural and Creative Industries* (2013) (with Mark Banks and Rosalind Gill).

Susan Luckman is Professor of Cultural Studies and Associate Director of Research and Programs at the Hawke EU Centre for Mobilities, Migrations and Cultural Transformations, University of South Australia. She is the author of the books *Craft and the Creative Economy* (Palgrave Macmillan 2015) and *Locating Cultural Work* (Palgrave Macmillan 2012), and the co-editor of *Craft Economies* (2017), *Craft Communities* (2018) and *Sonic Synergies: Music, Identity, Technology, Community* (2008).

Part I

Creative Working

Online Selling and the Growth of Home-Based Craft Micro-enterprise: The 'New Normal' of Women's Self-(under)Employment

Susan Luckman and Jane Andrew

In her 2011 book *Cruel optimism*, Lauren Berlant identifies the return of 'DIY practices' of making do and getting on—of holding onto dreams and persisting even in the face of their costs—as emerging from people's 'hope that changing the white noise of politics into something alive right now can magnetise [in them] to induce images of the good life amidst the exhausting pragmatics of the ordinary's "new normal"' (Berlant, 2011, p. 261). At a time of growing employment uncertainty, shrinking arts funding, and widespread governmental policy rhetoric on encouraging small business, the exponential rise in the number of creative micro-enterprises across much of the industrialised world is clearly part of this 'new normal' as we 'transition from the liberal to the post-neoliberal world' (Berlant, 2011, p. 261). Within wider patterns

---

S. Luckman (✉)
Hawke EU Centre for Mobilities, Migrations and Cultural Transformations, University of South Australia, Adelaide, South Australia, Australia

J. Andrew
School of Art, Architecture, and Design, University of South Australia, Adelaide, SA, Australia

© The Author(s) 2018
S. Taylor, S. Luckman (eds.), *The New Normal of Working Lives*, Dynamics of Virtual Work, DOI 10.1007/978-3-319-66038-7_2

around the privatisation of individual responsibility for one's economic position, creative self-employment remains a financially risky undertaking, often pursued at the expense of financial security. The ease of establishing a professional business profile and the ability to network and market via social media provide nascent creative entrepreneurs with a sense of being real, sustainable, and significant, and function as a justification to self and others for continuing along this path. But for many, social media is less a miracle promotional tool and more an expected baseline requirement in maintaining professional self-branding without necessarily leading to any significant sales or financial return for effort (see Luckman & Andrew, 2017).

In this chapter, we argue that the growth of design craft self-employment is masking a 'new normal' of considerable unemployment as well as under-employment, especially among women. In this way, for many makers, pursuing a craft-based creative micro-enterprise can thus be seen as the epitome of Berlant's 'cruel optimism', whereby that which we may desire 'is actually an obstacle to [our] flourishing' (Berlant, 2011, p. 1). What emerges is a balancing act, whereby the perceived non-economic rewards gained from pursuing life in the creative risk economy are seen to be worth the economic trade-offs involved. The social and economic costs to individuals, families, and the wider society of all this effort, risk-taking, and sublimation from public debate of larger issues around family friendly employment are profound and require greater attention as part of wider cultural and economic policy making.

The empirical data informing this chapter are drawn from a three-year study investigating how online distribution is changing the environment for operating a creative micro-enterprise, and with it, the larger relationship between the public and private spheres. A key research question is: What are the 'self-making' skills required to succeed in this competitive environment? The project focuses on the contemporary Australian designer–maker micro-economy, which is at present experiencing unprecedented growth as part of the larger upsurge of interest in making as a cultural and economic practice. It aims to:

- identify the attitudes, knowledge, and skills required to develop and run a sustainable creative micro-enterprise;
- analyse the spatial and temporal negotiations necessary to run an online creative micro-enterprise, including the ways in which divisions of labour are gendered; and
- examine how the contemporary creative economy contributes to a growing, ethics-based micro-economic consumer-and-producer relationship that privileges small-scale production, environmentally sustainable making practices, and the idea of buying direct from the producer.

We recognise that not all handmade micro-entrepreneurs are at the same stage of their career or have the same origin story; hence, this qualitative, mixed methods national research project consists of three parallel data collection activities: semi-structured interviews with established makers; a three-year longitudinal mapping of arts, design, and craft graduates as they seek to establish their making careers; and a historical overview of the support mechanisms available to Australian handmade producers. At the time of writing, the project had interviewed 18 peak and/or industry organisations (involving 22 people) and 59 established makers, and had almost completed the second round of interviews with emerging makers (Year 1/'1-Up' = 32; Year 2/'2-Up' = 25). The project employs this phenomenological approach to offer a rich 'insider' perspective on creative micro-enterprise. Semi-structured interviews of this kind are the best tool available for capturing the work–life stories of creative practitioners in their own words. People are asked to identify key personally and professionally decisive moments in their life histories, enabling us to identify the kinds of skills and personal qualities that makers draw upon, and the impact of wider entrepreneurial and other discourses that impact upon the decision-making of individual makers. Many of them identify creative micro-enterprise as a work–life model they believe to be personally and environmentally (if not economically) sustainable and located within the growing alternative economic networks afforded by the growth of the Internet (Anderson, 2006; Gibson-Graham, 2006).

Making (as) a living?

Within our cohort of research participants, both emerging and established, we are finding a wide variety of interests, work experiences, and career development motivations. The career profiles of Australian makers parallel the four key profiles identified in the UK in the Crafts Council *Craft in an Age of Change* report (BOP Consulting, 2012), namely:

> *Craft careerists*: committed to the idea of craft as a career, they move to start their businesses shortly after finishing their first (or second) degrees in craft-related subjects [34% of our established makers]
> *Artisans*: do not have academic degrees in the subject but nevertheless have made craft their first career [40% of our established makers]
> *Career changers*: begin their working lives in other careers before taking up craft as a profession, often in mid-life [19% of our established makers]
> *Returners*: makers who trained in art, craft or design, but who followed another career path before 'returning' to craft later on [7% of our established makers]. (p. 5)

What unites these diverse experiences, however, are relatively low levels of financial return for effort. For despite the popularity of handcrafted bespoke objects around much of the industrialised world, and the ease of setting up a business identity and launching it online, the vast majority of both our emerging and our established maker research participants are not generating significant net income from their creative practice (see Fig. 1 for the established maker income). One of our participants reflected on this issue and recalled conversations she had with a number of fellow stallholders at a major design craft market:

> *PK*: Oh I've had some funny discussions with people who, and I know it's not all about this, but they make no money and now I still see them back the next time and the next time and the next time, and there's just this idea that there are so many markets everywhere and

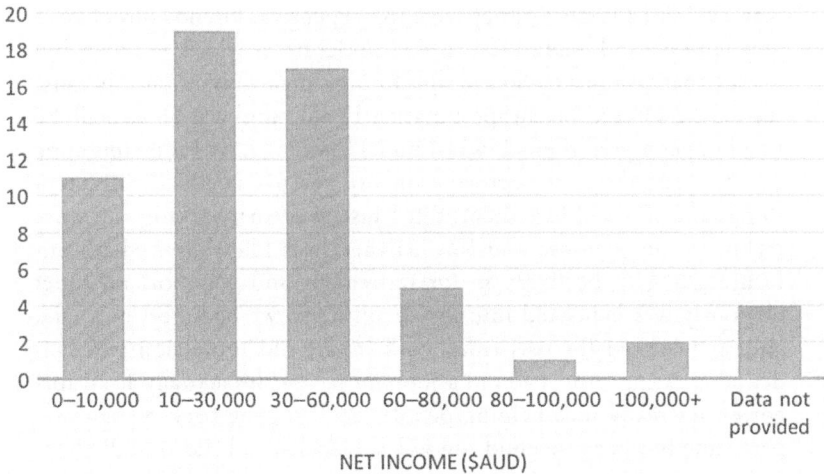

Fig. 1 Established maker interviewees' income from creative practice

people must be making money from them that's why there are so many markets, but it's not really the case. I think people are using them as promotion as well. (Pip Kruger, Emerging Maker, http://www.pipkruger.com)

The financial precarity of craft making is a recurring issue in our interview discussions:

CD: it's not all about money but you don't make much money.
Q: You didn't get into art to make money?
CD: No if I wanted to make money I would do a job. (Christina Darras, Established Maker, http://christinadarras.com)
PM: Now she probably is the only one I know about, who is surviving or still making money just out of her art work. ... I don't make a lot of money out of my craft. (Pip McManus, Established Maker, http://members.ozemail.com.au/~pipmcmanus/mainpage.html)
Q: So in that year, has your involvement in the creative sector changed?
A: It's collapsed (Laughing). ... No it ... changed, oh I tried really hard, we did, I did a number of markets, different types of markets, selling online, all that stuff. I just think no one wanted

scarves, I don't know, or they were too expensive, I'm not sure. I got a few requests, so I made a few scarves under order which was nice, but it was, that was just 2. So actually I didn't make any money, because the markets were, the cheapest market I could find was $65 a stall. So I had to get myself there, it was 4 hours [away]. … So I was siphoning money basically, … I borrowed off my parents $6000 for different things and so I still owe them. But I just, it wasn't working and we're trying to buy a house and [my partner] was like, 'Well what's our future going to be like?' So for retirement and whatnot, no super obviously was being fed into my account. So we had a bit of a talk, and so I looked for part-time work in my old profession which is dental assisting. And I found a job and it, and it's actually I, I'd forgotten it's really nice helping people. So I've gone back to that and part-time but because childcare was so expensive, I did initially have 2 days where I was going to concentrate on [my business] and that childcare was so expensive it went up to $120 a day. (Emerging Maker, Victoria)

But it is not all 'doom and gloom', with some of our makers engaging in economically successful—or at least sustainable—self-employment and small business. Defying many traditional narratives around artistic careers, what is seen as key here is making the call to take oneself seriously as a creative professional, and willingness to work the hours and engage in not just the creative side of things, but the things required to run a small business:

while you know it's really ingrained that you can't make money as an artist, I've always been able to say, well actually my parents are artists and they have been full-time artists you know now for about 20 years. [So] I'd really like to be able to say that to people and say, it's perfectly possible don't say it's not. But you have to … I think one of the problems is people actually don't work hard enough, and I know that sounds a bit cynical but, and I say it a little bit I guess from my own point of view, I think you can have this idea of, 'oh I'm going to be an artist and it will be so lovely, and I'll do a bit of work and I can sell at exhibitions'. Anyone who's making full time money at art is working full time at least. (Established Maker, Queensland)

Modest incomes are being made by some participants in our study (see Fig. 1); our suspicion is that that those people offering no response to the question regarding income represent mostly makers with such a small turnover that they are effectively either just breaking even or perhaps running at a loss. A few may also be those doing okay, but feeling sectoral discursive pressure not to disclose exactly how well.

These income figures need to be considered not only through the lens of traditionally low-paid artistic work, but also in terms of the gendering of the designer–maker micro-economy. While inclusive sampling techniques seek to get a geographic and practice-based spread of research participants, our research participant cohort still tends to reflect the gender biases of the sector, with women constituting 82% of our peak and/or industry organisation interviewees, 82% of our established maker interviewees, and 81% and 84% (Year 1 and Year 2) of our emerging maker interviewees. Furniture making is one of the areas that tends to have a higher income return, and this sector also tends to be one of the few with greater numbers of men than women. Reinforcing this precarity, only five of the (so far) 59 established makers we have interviewed have income protection insurance, and only 24% are in a position to contribute to a superannuation account from their creative income (though some have limited superannuation savings from previous employment while others referred to their owned home as their superannuation strategy, property prices in Australia being among the highest in the world). Or, as one of our makers said when asked if she was in a position to contribute earnings from her creative business to a superannuation fund, 'this is my super fund. I'll be doing it [working] until I die'. This all begs the question: if generating a sustainable income from your creative enterprise is so difficult, what are people's motivations for persisting in this endeavour?

One clear contributing factor remains the unfinished business in Australia of more family friendly work practices and workplaces, alongside the need for greater provision of quality, affordable childcare. In such an environment, when a second family income can be largely swallowed up by the cost of childcare, many women and a few men see working from home as the answer to their work–life negotiations. With its success enabled by social media marketing and networking and the growth of global long-tail (Anderson, 2006) online distribution networks, the design craft marketplace is dominated by female-led micro-enterprises, frequently based on models of self- and home-based employment. Many, but certainly not all, of these makers have gone down this path to accommodate caregiving commitments. For example, glass bead artist Julie Frahm reflects on the impact of motherhood and her thought process and changes to her world that life with children brings.

> *JF*: [Bead making] is my only income activity at the moment. What happened was … I got pregnant, so I was still a project manager and then went on maternity leave for a year, they gave me 12 months off; I honestly thought I would go back to work and just keep the creative stuff as a part-time option. But when you have a baby … it's like oh, my god your whole world changes. … There were a lot of things going on in my head: 'life's so short', 'what am I?', 'why would I work for someone else?', that doesn't make any sense. Why would I put my child in care four days a week because that's what they want me to do? I want to be in control of my life, they're not going to tell me how to manage my life. (Julie Frahm, Established Maker, http://www.aussiejules.com)

The challenge of balancing full-time employment with children was a recurring motif in many of our interviews:

> Well I worked, I was teaching for about 10 years and then I got the position at the gallery. There was a public education program which I loved, best job I loved it, but then going back it was full time, very full time plus. So it wasn't practical with the kids until they get older, but now this has happened so it's a good thing. (Kate Hard, Sage and Pepper, Established Maker, https://www.etsy.com/au/shop/SageandPeppa)

> So I remember the really early days when it was kind of all on paper, and I was saying I'm going to get going because the idea for the business, for Worth Gallery, that it would be an online presence and that I would work from home, whatever hours I chose to work so that I could be available to

my children, and that I would represent a bunch of artists, have their work on the site, and try to market that outside of South Australia. So that I could represent Adelaide to beyond Adelaide and make direct sales. (Amy Sierp-Worth, Established Maker, http://www.worthgallery.com/)

So I take my kids to school and I pick them up—we've never done day care because this is what my business has paid for me being able to do, that so that's another great thing with having my own business. (Gill Cordiner, Established Maker, http://www.gillcordiner.com/)

Well you see my daughter, she used to come in to [the studio] and she used to sit in the little play pen in the workshop and, yeah, she was a constant in the room. (Established Maker, Victoria)

Well the first workshop, we ended up living above, so that I could work and [my son could] come home from school, and because it was a warehouse space in the middle of city, all his friends came as well, they loved hanging out. So that's what worked until he left school. (Established Maker, Victoria)

One of our younger emerging makers yet to start a family contemplated the future with children:

[….] there's always this little thing in the back of my head, I think, 'Oh, when I—if I have children one day I don't want to stop doing what I'm doing', and I like to have this idea that that's something that I can combine with motherhood in the future without having to go back to a workplace and putting them in childcare—that's not something that I plan to do. (Pip Kruger, Emerging Maker, http://www.pipkruger.com)

We have also interviewed a number of couples who work together in a family making business as a means by which to flexibly share family responsibilities, with a focus on both parties being around and available to children in ways many professional and other careers do not always allow for:

Q: Now you've got children, was working, your work from home, was that a factor in your decision to pursue this kind of practice and business?

WP: It's certainly more a lifestyle choice than a financial one!

AS: Yeah, well, we've both talked about when, you know, when they asked you what you want to do at the school, I mean both of us always said artist, so it's kind of been a lifelong goal really for both of us, to be practising artists, so that's just, we're doing what we want really.

WP: Which wasn't the most, wasn't the kick start, you know. I got told to sort of grow up really and find a 'proper job' when I was at school. But I mean that was the mid-80s, so when I said I want to be an artist they sort of laughed and went 'Yeah but what do you really want to do?' So it wasn't until I hit nearly 40 that I actually managed to start believing that we could do that as a living.

AS: Yeah and it is a lifestyle thing, we like to be able to pick our kids up [from school]. (Anna Small and Warren Pickering, A Small Art Factory, Established Makers, http://www.asmallartfactory.com.au/)

Meanwhile, other makers have long pursued craft as a career; setting off along this path long before the challenges of balancing work with partners and children were ever on their horizons.

Supporting a making enterprise

We recognise that the terms 'successful' and 'sustainable' are subjective and do not necessarily reflect an income that many others living in a high-cost-of-living country like Australia would consider worth the effort. Often what success looks like, even when making money from making, involves a trade-off between creative, original, or gallery work, and reproducible production lines. Designer and maker Christian Hall reflects upon this balance:

CH: I mean research is the thing, research and development [of new works/products] is the thing that dies in this process, and that's what burns so many people out that they went into wanting to be a creative practitioner and they become a small-scale manufacturer for not very much money. It's not hugely lucrative to only be able to make money from the stuff that you make, I think that's hugely problematic to be honest. (Christian Hall, Established Maker, http://www.christian-hall.com.au/)

In this environment 'success' is frequently determined by the individual practitioner, and this is where other benefits from the making business beyond income are factored in by individuals when they evaluate the viability of their practice. Benefits such as being available to children at the end of the school day, as well as, clearly, the fulfilment people receive from the creative act of making:

> *TVB*: I think it just happened. I first started learning jewellery making when I was at university, living in Sydney, and I just did it as a hobby while I was studying, and it was something that was practical and tangible and I really enjoyed the process. Then I went and worked and did quite a few different jobs and sort of walked away from all of it, and then came back to study. So coming back to study for me was more about the fact that I'd missed having that tactile outlet, and also it's just a really nice balance with the rest of life. But I never did the course thinking: 'okay I'm going to turn this into a business, I'm going to make lots of money'. I just did it because I enjoyed it and at the time I wasn't sure where else to go, and then it's evolved from there. (Tanja Von Behrens, Established Maker, https://www.tanjavonbehrens.com/)

Others expressed the pros and cons of running your own business as the ability to:

> *NL*: [….] prioritise family or friends when you need to. But it also means that your business can be sacrificed easier … no one's working on it while you're not. (Natalie Lane, Corner Block Studio, Emerging Maker, http://www.cornerblockstudio.com/)

For James Young, his foray into shoemaker and outfitter (mostly working with leather) was born out of his passion for the desert. It grew from a part-time interest with very little financial return, to a making practice that now is his occupation. The pursuit of his making practice, instead of what he regarded as a physically and mentally exhausting job that required lots of travel, was done with the full support of his designer partner, yet James expresses a self-consciousness about the opinion of others in his ability to make a living for his family out of his making practice:

> Q: So at what point were you able to say, or what was the moment when you said: 'This is it, we're going to go for it', 'This is going to be our focus professionally?' Because I imagine it wasn't a single decision in a relationship.
>
> JY: Yeah, well, I mean a lot of people, … they sort of assume, you know, 'What does your wife say?', you know, and really like [she's] more of a creative lunatic than me in terms of like supporting me to do something that might be [economically] marginal or whatever ….
>
> Q: Was it tied with your plans around wanting to start a family and making a more sustainable balance?
>
> JY: I think that's an added benefit, and I mean I think that the other factor is, you know, was a financial one … the benefit of having that career where you're working really hard and you're too busy to spend any money. … it is expensive to live in Central Australia, and so having a house that we basically own in a place where it's really expensive to rent, it's kind of, it gave us a bit more confidence and freedom to do something that … you know is going to be, always going to be financially kind of marginal. … But then with a family, you know having the integrated kind of life, Elliat and I work together, we share a workspace. It's really good because having kids, like as you may well know, puts a lot of pressure on your relationship, and we've always enjoyed having creative projects together. So it means for us, we get this great professional interaction that's totally aside from who's cooking and dropping the kids off and all that sort of stuff, and so that's a real benefit, and then also the flexibility which is, you know I mean we can work any 60 hours a week each that we want. (James Young, Established Maker, http://www.jamesbyoung.com.au/)

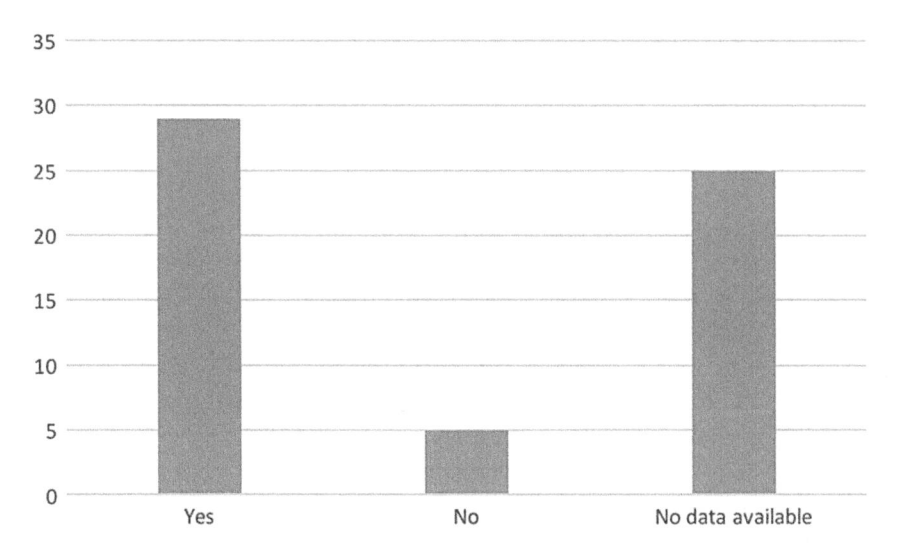

Fig. 2 Established makers currently receiving financial support from partner or family

James' reflections above illustrate that, like women, men working this sphere encounter many psychological and spatial contestations and economic challenges, indeed possibly more than women do, because gendered expectations about being 'breadwinners' for their family place additional social pressure on getting a 'real job'.

Clearly much weighing up of the pros and cons of designer–maker micro-enterprise also needs to factor in the overall household income, with much craft micro-enterprise, at least in its establishment stage, being underwritten by support from a partner or other family member (see Fig. 2). Some of our younger emerging makers have chosen for this reason to live at home. As Emma Young reflects:

> *EY*: [it] just gives me freedom to not need to be stressed about paying bills and rent and food, and I'm barely at home at the moment. I'm here [in the studio] every single day almost. … It will allow me to focus on my artwork and building my business. (Emma Young, Emerging Maker, https://www.facebook.com/emmayoungglass/)

Either by good management or, as Claire Poppi acknowledges, her good fortune, many of our interviewees are grateful to have or to have had a supportive partner, personally and financially, when setting up their practice:

> *CP*: I was very lucky because my partner at the time supported me through that sort of first year where you just weren't making any money, and it would be really difficult if people didn't have that. (Claire Poppi, Established Maker, http://www.clarepoppi.com/)

Although, in principle, supported by their partner for choosing to establish a making enterprise rather than working part-time for an employer to supplement family income while raising young children, some of our participants have shared that there is pressure to generate the same income from their making practice as they did in other waged work, and therefore made clear their making practice did not draw on the family income at all. Some stress the legitimacy of the pursuit of their craft enterprise:

> If it was just a hobby I would do it at night-time when the kids are in bed, I wouldn't have invested in childcare or anything like that if I didn't take it seriously; I take it really seriously and I'm trying to grow it as much as I physically can without losing integrity like going off shore for example. (Established Maker, Tasmania)

Often too, as our findings clearly indicate, given that many of our research participants are not earning an independently sustainable living wage from their creative enterprise they are also having to support themselves with other employment, either linked to their practice (e.g., teaching or running classes, selling DIY kits, curation, or creative retail), or work part-time elsewhere beyond the arts, cultural, and creative sector (see Fig. 3). These findings correspond with other studies of creative workers and represent instances of Taylor and Littleton's 'double life', whereby across their careers, artists and other creative practitioners find themselves having to combine creative work with another source of income (Taylor & Littleton, 2012). Those of our makers who formerly worked in a trade can often effectively run two different small businesses.

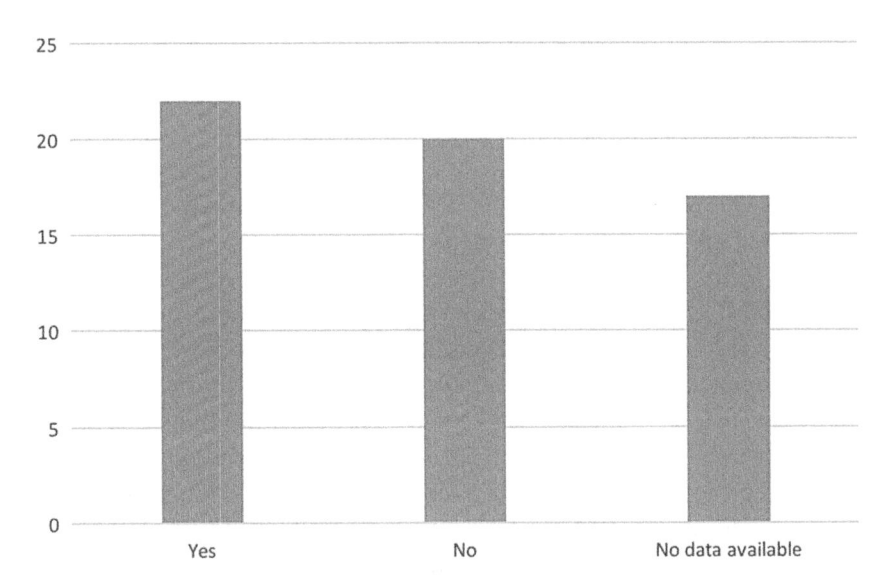

Fig. 3 Established makers supplementing income with other paid work

For one maker, while he is establishing his bespoke furniture/object practice, the trade jobs he undertakes enable him to fund the outsourcing aspects of his production as well as the renovation of an inner-city shop into a studio/apartment for his family. As he said in our recent 2-Up interview:

> I'd love to be just [making] but you have to fund—it's just to have that money each week to actually fund the build, not to have any worries and stress about when you go to the laser cut option—'where am I going to get that five hundred dollars from?' … it's just easier to work and get the money in than to stress about selling lights for me at the moment. (Emerging Maker, Tasmania)

But for some, being a maker does seem to come at a cost above and beyond the economic trade-offs; it is sometimes expressed as a contestation between being a good mother/parent and being good at what you do—the reality of 'being your own boss' not always being as amenable to 'being there' for children as ideally anticipated.

Self-employment and making: Conscription or choice?

The experiences emerging in this research support arguments we have made elsewhere (Luckman, 2015a, 2015b); namely, that the growth of home-based creative self-employment needs to be accounted for at least partly in terms of inequalities within contemporary workplaces, especially when it comes to accommodating creative employment alongside caregiving responsibilities. With women continuing to bear disproportionate responsibility for caregiving, especially of children, the growth of Internet-enabled home-based self-employment is plainly being embraced in our research by mostly women (and just a few couples and men) as a way to keep a foot in the world of creative employment, alongside family and domestic labour in the home. In this way, self-employment is operating as a magical solution, a symbolic if not always ideal making do in the face of ongoing workplace inequality, especially in terms of desires for family friendly employment (Luckman, 2015b) and the wish of educated, professional women previously employed outside the home to maintain an identity beyond 'mum' or 'homemaker'. Crafting self-employment thus becomes a vehicle for also crafting a professional creative identity. Like other worker identities, this also facilitates access to networks and friendships that, in the face of family commitments, can be defended and indeed legitimised as more than social (as men have long done in socialising and networking outside their paid working hours). Plainly, many deeply affective as well as practical decisions are being negotiated in the choices being made here by our research participants, within a field of possibilities circumscribed by Berlant's '"cruel optimism" as a relation of attachment to compromised conditions of possibility' (Berlant, 2011, p. 24). Certainly, even when things may be going well, if not perfectly, in the life worlds of our interviewees, the discussions can be highly emotional, touching on their deeply held understandings of personal identity, and not only personal risk but also partner and family risk. This is where the 'new normal' can be a particularly cruel negotiation to make:

What's cruel about these attachments, and not merely inconvenient or tragic, is that the subjects who have x in their lives might not well endure the loss of their object/scene of desire, even though its presence threatens their well-being, because whatever the *content* of the attachment is, the continuity of its form provides something of the continuity of the subject's sense of what it means to keep on living and to look forward to being in the world. (Berlant, 2011, p. 24)

For these reasons, however, the issue of 'choice' needs to be revisited here; how 'free' are many of our research participants to make other choices—such as staying in or starting other employment and having children? Indeed, how many are 'necessity entrepreneurs'? (Senior, 2015). Despite the highly masculinised, 'big end of town' image of the entrepreneur, throughout much of the industrialised world today, the figure of the entrepreneur should just as likely be conceived of as female, but, as Taylor has written, we need to be wary of the new female mystique on offer here:

this feminized figure [who works on a small scale, mostly alone and from home, motivated by the hope of self-fulfilment and freedom as alternative rewards to a steady income and secure employment] … is part of a 'new mystique', resembling the 'housewife trap' made famous by Betty Friedan (1963), which invited women to move back from the paid workforce to the home and domesticity. The new mystique attached to working for yourself is part of a process of exclusion by which increasing numbers of workers, both male and female, are encouraged to accept a marginalized position in the neoliberal economy. (Taylor, 2015, pp. 174–175)

Conclusion

Craft work, especially when pursued via self-employment, remains a financially risky undertaking that is often pursued at the expense of the individual's own financial security. This situation today is considerably exacerbated by the much lower barriers to entry for creative self-employment enabled by the Internet as a promotional and distribution tool that makes starting up easy, but achieving financial success, or at least sustainability, a challenge. Especially in an increasingly saturated online global marketplace for the handmade, perhaps what we see is the tip of the iceberg—the evocative profile of the successful in-demand creative. Ironically and increasingly, however, the new normal of creative micro-enterprise lies beneath the surface—lots of presence on top but little financial substance underneath, with the actual craft practice/practice in reality on a scale far smaller and less extensive than that indicated by the promotional front.

The richly affective and enabling personal and collective structural frameworks that today not only encourage but also valorise precarious self-employment and 'being in control of your own life' operate in the design craft economy as a powerful 'economic imaginary' (Jessop, 2004, cited in Campbell, 2014):

> As practices in the economic sphere are currently sufficiently complex that their entirety cannot be adequately grasped, Jessop (2004) argues that 'economic imaginaries' (p. 162) arise and gain traction which enable coherent and convincing accounts of economic activity to be made. Whilst inherently partial, these 'imaginaries' do have some correspondence with real economic processes, but serve to privilege some activities over others. (p. 995)

This is how Berlant's 'cruel optimism' is in play within the craft economy. For, as she writes, at the centre of her thinking:

> is that moral-intimate-economic thing called 'the good life'. Why do people stay attached to conventional good-life fantasies—say, of enduring reciprocity in couples, families, political systems, institutions, markets, and at work—when the evidence of their instability, fragility, and dear cost abounds? Fantasy is the means by which people hoard idealizing theories and tableaux about how they and the world 'add up to something'. (Berlant, 2011, p. 2)

For while many will succeed—and it is important, as we have stated, to recognise that success here is not always about financial sustainability, it can also be about quality of life and achieving a work–life balance while staying connected and sane—many others will fail. The potential rewards of successful design craft self-employment are considerable: making money doing what you love, on your own schedule, being your own boss, and importantly, having the flexibility to organise the working day around the needs of significant others. For some, this dream is one they seek to pursue with a life partner as a 'back to the future' family workshop way of reconfiguring an idealised work–life balance in the twenty-first century. Such a vision of 'good work' at the heart of a holistic 'good life' (Hesmondhalgh & Baker, 2011) speaks especially to middle-class, first world aspirations for 'something better' than the grindstone of unfulfilling and also often family unfriendly employment. But as is emerging in our empirical findings, an ever-present new middle-class normal of economic precarity underpins this sector. It may be 'cruel', but this optimism is what people hold on to precisely, as Berlant argues, as a means by which to 'stay in proximity' to aspirations for the good life in the face of not only work's, but life's precarity (Berlant, 2011, p. 249).

What is noticeably emerging in our empirical findings is that an ever-present new middle-class normal of economic precarity underpins this sector, as it does other parts of the middle-class 'gig economy'. For example, the so-called sharing economy of Uber and Airbnb is propped up financially by various means—family savings, partner earnings, retirement or redundancy packages, multiple jobs, and/or a willingness to make the financial trade-off to live with less. Precarious employment is the new normal, and not just for the young, disadvantaged, or de-skilled. Writing more broadly in terms of the 'Uberisation' of employment, Trebor Scholz argues:

> Continued employment with social security and legally regulated norms is no longer the rule. Digitization is making work increasingly dense. Casual work, part-time or freelance, is the new normal. Full-time jobs are fragmented into freelance positions, turning workers into 'micro-entrepreneurs' who are competing under conditions of infinite labor supply. Increasingly, companies retain a small number of core employees, making up the rest with temporary contract laborers. It echoes from all corners: don't romanticize employment. (Scholz, 2017, p. 13)

In such a socio-economic landscape, the 'rhetoric of the enterprising individual is meant to make people feel optimistic about a "liberation" from career and employment and a forced entry into the world of entrepreneurship. Just check in with your "inner entrepreneur" and "do what you love!"' (Scholz, 2017, p. 14). Online platform economies offer dreams of meaningful, effectively full-time (or whatever you want) self-employment, but the business models that underpin them remain controlled by the few and are not run ultimately for the many. But while we must be critically attentive to the wider socio-economic context within which the craft economy operates and thus also the larger structures which the economic imaginary of self-employment sustains, part of the cruelty is how this effectively further disempowers the agency of the individuals who have made a very deliberate decision to pursue craft work—to their minds, the best option as part of a larger 'new normal' life experience of precarity and insecurity.

Acknowledgements This research was supported under the Australian Research Council's Discovery Project funding scheme (project number DP150100485 'Promoting the Making Self in the Creative Micro-Economy). We thank Belinda Powles and Kam Kaur for their invaluable input and assistance with the research project and, as always, the makers who have generously shared their stories with us.

References

Anderson, C. (2006). *The long tail: How endless choice is creating unlimited demand*. London: Random House.

Berlant, L. (2011). *Cruel optimism*. Durham: Duke University Press.

BOP Consulting (Commissioned by Crafts Council, Creative Scotland, Arts Council of Wales, and Craft Northern Island). (2012). *Craft in an age of change*. London: BOP Consulting.

Campbell, P. (2014). Imaginary success? The contentious ascendance of creativity. *European Planning Studies, 22*(5), 995–1009.

Friedan, B. (1963). *The Feminine Mystique*. New York: W. W. Norton & Company.

Gibson-Graham, J. K. (2006). *A postcapitalist politics*. Minneapolis: University of Minnesota Press.

Hesmondhalgh, D., & Baker, S. (2011). *Creative labour: Media work in three cultural industries*. London and New York: Routledge.

Jessop, B. (2004). Critical semiotic analysis and cultural political economy. *Critical Discourse Studies, 1*(2), 159–174.

Luckman, S. (2015a). *Craft and the creative economy*. London: Palgrave Macmillan.

Luckman, S. (2015b). Micro-enterprise as work-life 'magical solution'. In L. Adkins & M. Dever (Eds.), *The post-Fordist sexual contract: Working and living in contingency* (pp. 91–108). Basingstoke: Palgrave Macmillan.

Luckman, S., & Andrew, J. (2017). Establishing the crafting self in the contemporary creative economy. In S. Luckman & N. Thomas (Eds.), *Craft economies*. London: Bloomsbury.

Scholz, T. (2017). *Uberworked and underpaid: How workers are disrupting the digital economy*. Cambridge and Malden: Polity Press.

Senior, J. (2015, January 6). What do we give up when we become freedom-seeking entrepreneurs? A lot, actually. *New York Times Magazine*. Retrieved June 30, 2017, from http://nymag.com/scienceofus/2014/12/what-we-give-up-when-we-become-entrepreneurs.html

Taylor, S. (2015). A new mystique? Working for yourself in the neoliberal economy. In B. Conor, R. Gill, & S. Taylor (Eds.), *Gender and creative labour*. Sociological Review Monographs (pp. 174–187). Chichester: Wiley-Blackwell.

Taylor, S., & Littleton, K. (2012). *Contemporary identities of creativity and creative work*. London: Routledge.

Susan Luckman is Professor of Cultural Studies and Associate Director of Research and Programs at the Hawke EU Centre for Mobilities, Migrations and Cultural Transformations, University of South Australia. She is the author of the books *Craft and the Creative Economy* (Palgrave Macmillan 2015) and *Locating Cultural Work* (Palgrave Macmillan 2012), and the co-editor of *Craft Economies* (2018), *Craft Communities* (2018) and *Sonic Synergies: Music, Identity, Technology, Community* (2008).

Jane Andrew is a Senior Lecturer at the School of Art, Architecture, and Design, University of South Australia, where she is also the Director of Matchstudio, an interdisciplinary research and professional practice studio that supports students' transition from university to work through participation in client-based project activity.

Hope Labour Revisited: Post-socialist Creative Workers and Their Methods of Hope

Ana Alacovska

Introduction

Creative work has been celebrated with 'star struck optimism' (Pratt, 2011, p. 128). A grand, utopian narrative promulgated in policy documents, media accounts, and management textbooks has jargonised creative work as a harbinger of future work: cool, hip, fun, self-realising, autonomous jobs-nirvanas *promising* 'pay for play' and 'payment for doing what you love' (Gill, 2002; McRobbie, 1998; Ross, 2003; Taylor & Littleton, 2012). This grand utopian narrative has fuelled desires for a creative job (Alacovska, 2013). Creative work has thus become a magnet for flocks of 'hopefuls'—a multitude of passionate 'wannabes' enthusiastically disposing of their free labour in the *hope* of attaining their (inevitably scarce) 'dream job' in the future (Menger, 1999).

Indeed, what has most notoriously perplexed researchers into creative work is the disproportionate number of people (variously dubbed 'flocks', 'fish tanks', 'reservoirs of labour', etc.; see Hesmondhalgh,

A. Alacovska (✉)
Copenhagen Business School, Frederiksberg, Denmark

2002) seeking entry into creative industries despite abounding evidence that labour supply outstrips labour demand. Why do so many *aspire* to become artists when failure, job scarcity, and precarity are the norm? Sociologists have elegantly resolved this conundrum by depicting creative work as inevitably forward-looking, involving a strong temporal orientation: becoming a creative worker entails performing free or discounted labour in the present *on the speculation of future* payment and *in anticipation of future* greater artistic autonomy, fame, and bounties. Unsurprisingly, creative industries are awash with unpaid internships— the uncompensated pathway to an anticipated creative job (Siebert & Wilson, 2013). Habitually, creative work (of both traditional and digital kinds) has been framed essentially as 'hope labour' (Kuehn & Corrigan, 2013), 'aspirational labour' (Duffy, 2016), 'provisional labour' (Frenette, 2013), or 'sacrificial labour' (Ross, 2003), whereby a creative workforce is predisposed (often self-exploitatively) to accept non-monetary rewards 'on the promise of deferred bounties' and 'future career rewards' (Ross, 2003, p. 142).

The future-orientation of creative workers has most notably been studied 'at the threshold of a creative career' (Taylor & Littleton, 2012, p. 47), and so it has been approached mainly as a tactical entry strategy into the industry and thus as a relatively unproblematic matter of aspiration, mental gambling, cold calculation, and grandiose phantasy of stardom, all of which nonetheless constitute a powerful disciplining tool in the hands of managers who take advantage of a cheap, aspiring workforce. But, what would desire, ambition, and aspiration look like, we must ask, if they are not seen as disciplining devices that lock aspiring creative workers into an endless future-oriented quest for becoming 'the next big thing'? Should we approach creative workers' future-orientation as merely self-exploitative and grandiose, or as enterprising? In this chapter, I argue for a more nuanced analysis of creative workers' future-orientation. To this end, I elaborate on the notion of hope as the primary operational mechanism and method (Miyazaki, 2004, 2006) employed by creative workers in adjusting to and building a work–life in highly precarious and contingent creative industries and labour markets. Hope is not here apprehended in its deferrable quality or grandiose intentions; hope is not about a deluding belief in the myth of progress, upward mobility, or future bounties, but rather about the ordinariness of daily struggles—about the possibility of living a 'sane life' in spite of precarity (Berlant, 2011; Zigon, 2009). The analytical propitiousness of the notion of hope has not yet been fully explored in studies of creative labour. Hope, in itself a vague, elusive, and experiential category, is still not an operational category of social science (Crapanzano, 2003), and therefore sociological studies of creative work substitute hope with a variety of analytical proxies that are traditionally better established in sociology, such as investment (Bourdieu, 1998), projections (Mears, 2012; Neff, 2012), aspiration (Hesmondhalgh & Baker, 2011; McRobbie, 1998), or speculation (Menger, 1999).

This chapter, in contrast, makes an argument for hope as a lens through which to understand creative workers' moral attachment to the present contingent conditions of work rather than a postalgic and therefore self-exploitative projection of 'golden future' (Neff, 2012; Ybema, 2004). Drawing on anthropological theories of hope, this chapter refuses to approach a worker's future-orientation merely as a self-delusional, self-commodifying imprisonment in a continual state of becoming, which is, as I show below, the predominant mode in which creative work has been interpreted so far. Instead, this chapter examines how hope provides the minimum necessary propensity to imagine the future, even under conditions of constant adversity (Lindquist, 2006). Striding with this approach to hope and future-orientation, I examine here how creative workers mobilise hope when construing their imaginary professional selves amidst 'the new normal' of work; that is, in times when intermittent, insecure, undercompensated, and casualised work are normalised and stabilised as an inevitable and permanent part of precarious everyday life. This chapter essentially asks how and why creative workers uphold a hopeful attitude to work in spite of deteriorating work conditions and discouraging work experiences. In answering this question, I focus on the meaningful, daily struggles of creative workers rather than on their grandiose fantasies and utopian desires of good, autonomous, and well-paid future creative jobs (Hesmondhalgh & Baker, 2011).

The chapter is based on some 160 qualitative, in-depth interviews with creative workers in the post-socialist Balkan countries of Macedonia and Albania, including musicians, actors, fashion designers, and new media workers. Post-socialist creative labour is especially pertinent to the re-examination of hope, since post-socialist creative work is 'doubly insecure' (Primorac, 2006). For, in addition to the precarious and casualised nature of creative labour that has been already theorised, creative work in post-socialism also happens in radically tumultuous and uncertain institutional and societal contexts. These are contexts characterised by a notorious absence of the rule of law, lacking a reliable and well-functioning public sector, with high unemployment rates, flourishing clientelism, and a rudimentary and exploitative private sector. In such places, where economic hardship, precariousness, and institutional dysfunctionality are the natural and ordinary setting, hope is what carries people through the day, since hope makes life liveable while alleviating the constant pressures of daily survival (Berlant, 2011). Expressions of hope are indeed ever more accentuated in times of post-socialist transitional breakdown, adversity, and destitution (Verdery, 1995; Zigon, 2009).

The temporal orientation of creative work: 'Deferred economy', 'aspirations', 'cruel optimism', and 'methods of hope'

Creative work as it is currently conceptualised is essentially work executed on the basis of a promise: a promise of future payment, future employment, future social and economic capital, and future recognition (Duffy, 2016). Aspiring, 'wannabe', and hopeful labourers are genuinely entrepreneurial and enterprising—adopting a calculative attitude and working in the name of a brighter, better, and richer future. Creative work thus entails a strong future temporal orientation.

Bourdieu (1998) had early defined artistic work as a 'deferred economy'. The rules of cultural production presuppose an art-for-art's-sake game that requires the short-term creation of an illusion of disinterestedness in money matters. In the short run, artists deny their own economic interests. They become content with low pay, long and unpaid hours, and dismal working conditions, while garnering social and symbolic capital so as to 'make a name for themselves' through enhanced exposure, prestige, and reputation. Such accumulated symbolic capital is to be converted, *hopefully*, on the long run into economic, monetary, capital. As Frenette (2013, p.372) put it, creative work is 'provisional labour'; it is 'temporal, conditional, and ambiguous', oriented towards the prospect of future 'delayed' work and professional success.

Rather than being irrational or foolish agents working for free and aspiring to enter a contingent and competitive marketplace, artists have been found to be 'risk-lovers', often harbouring strong superstitious beliefs in genius, talent, and stardom that help them 'maintain for so long the hope that they will eventually become famous' (Menger, 1999, p. 561). Artists entrepreneurially accept the 'temporary' hardship of overcrowded labour markets in exchange for the *promise* of *future* success. Hence, all artists are gamblers—genuinely hoping to *eventually* hit 'the jackpot in the lottery called creative work' (Menger, 1999, p. 568). The critical sociology of creative labour has identified precisely this deferred economy of creative work as the paramount cause of self-exploitation, burnout, and 'bulimic' work-lives (Gill & Pratt, 2008; Hesmondhalgh & Baker, 2011; McRobbie, 1998).

As currently presented in creative work studies, hope possesses an instrumental, cognitive, and teleological dimension. The creative work studies' conceptualisation of hope thus entails 'projecting a golden future' or what Ybema (2004, p. 832) calls 'postalgia' (a mirror concept of nostalgia), which inherently presupposes 'a longing for a heavenly future'. Endorsed by policy rhetoric as a radiant model of future work, creative work is forward-looking, infused with optimism and projected positive states in the future. As such, it is linked to the 'aspirational normativity' of contemporary capitalism, encompassing 'an evolving and incoherent cluster of hegemonic promises about the present and future experience of social belonging' (Berlant, 2011, p. 167). This is a projective attachment to something 'yet-to-become' or 'yet-to-occur'—or what Bloch (1986, p. 7) calls the 'Not-Yet' (*Noch-Nicht*); that is, 'expectation, hope, intention towards possibility that has still not become'. According to Bloch, the Not-Yet always exists in anticipation of a future momentum of exhilaration, good life, and happiness. However, such overconfident attachment to the grand vision and fantasies of the good life—upward mobility, lasting intimacies, and a good stable job—represents a double bind, or what Berlant (2011) calls 'cruel optimism'. Fantasies of the good life are 'idealising theories and tableaux' about how people and the world 'add up to something' (Berlant, 2011, p. 2)—theories and tableaux which, although neither sustainable nor tenable in present real life, nonetheless convince people to make further affective investments in fantasies of 'the good life', in part so as not to lose the possibility itself of fantasising about it. These postalgic factors account for how people get caught in the daily impasse and suffering of self-destructive jobs. When a job is infused with one's affective narratives, images of coherence and sense of being, then no matter how painful or injurious it may be, the work nonetheless makes it possible to keep imagining a good life, driving people to develop the skills and knowledge needed to adjust to precarious conditions while keeping alive the project of good-life building. 'Cruel optimism' is thus contradictory: both an incentive to actively participate in the building of alternative life-worlds or 'modes of living' and an obstacle to one's flourishing (Berlant, 2011, p. 1). Through this perspective we can say that creative workers develop relations of 'cruel optimism' towards their work: on the one hand, they forge damaging (self-exploitative) relations with 'compromised conditions of possibilities' and unsustainable 'clusters of promises' (Berlant, 2011, p. 24) about creative work as 'good work' (Hesmondhalgh & Baker, 2011), while on the other hand they persistently and actively nourish and maintain imaginative and resilient relations with their day-to-day work–life in spite of its precariousness.

The critical sociology of creative work has so far judiciously studied one side of this double bind of cruel optimism; that is, the forward-looking abusive attachment to futurity and the utopian fantasies of good work. The projection of a golden, upbeat future, of achieving stardom, wealth, fame, and success—or what Ybema (2004) calls 'postalgia' and Miyazaki (2006) terms an 'economy of dreams'—propels creative workers to invest in their future-oriented, imagined artistic selves while consenting to their own present precarity and contingency. Premised upon an incessant process of *becoming,* or on the normalisation of the Not-Yet, creative work becomes subjugating and (self-)exploitative (Gill & Pratt, 2008; McRobbie, 1998; Neff, 2012; Ross, 2003), much akin to chasing the illusory proverbial pot of gold at the end of a rainbow.

However, sociologists of creative work have tended to neglect the other side of this double bind of hope—the hope that is ordinary, linked to the actual present and not to futurity—hope understood as 'the negotiated sustenance that makes life bearable as it presents itself ambivalently, unevenly and incoherently' (Berlant, 2011, p. 14). Hope entails more than future-oriented instrumentalism, dream-like optimism, and buoyancy of action. Hope is ultimately an experiential category of being-in-the-world, and hoping is a practice for getting through the despair of the concrete realities of work–life (Zigon, 2009). In this sense, hope also involves a moral calling, a 'strenuous moral project' (Mattingly & Jensen, 2015, p. 38) that presupposes the negotiation of what defines a good life and what it means to be a good worker. In the daily, precarious conditions of work, hope transpires as contradictory: on the one hand, it involves an active redefining of one's career dreams; on the other hand, it induces a sense of passivity and resignation, as well as illusion about divine powers of salvation (Crapanzano, 2003). Anthropologists, however, refuse to accept that hope is passive or illusionary. For the anthropologists of hope, hope is 'an existential aspect of agency'; that is, hope furnishes the capacity to act consciously and morally upon the world 'even under the direst privations' (Lindquist, 2006, pp. 7–8). Accordingly, Miyazaki (2006, pp. 16 and 9) defines hope as 'a method of engagement with the world' and as 'a common operative in all knowledge formation'. Through this prism, hope becomes a method of engagement with a troubled present during 'bad times'. Hope, then, is 'a method of radical temporal reorientation of knowledge', especially in contexts in which uncertainty, turbulence, and rupture are given conditions (Miyazaki, 2004, p. 5). Hope is a modality of moral/ethical engagement with the world and with self-knowledge.

In what follows I provide empirical analysis of some of the 'methods of hope' of post-socialist creative workers, that is, of their modes of hopeful engagement with work-related self-knowledge. In doing so I concentrate on the ways in which creative workers animate hope and maintain a hopeful yet moral attachment to their work, even when evidence abounds of contingency, precarity, and fragile fiscal economies. I further examine how nostalgia, informal economic practices, and progressive social art-based action serve as sources of hope.

Sources of hope: Post-socialist modalities of hopeful engagement

> I desire many things [...][1] success with my band, a fully booked festival roster, giving up my steel factory job [...]. But, all my desires would become irrelevant if I lose health. Therefore health! The hope is health first, and then everything will fall into place. (35-year-old rap musician, Albania)

Many sociologists of post-socialism have pointed out that transition has incapacitated post-socialist labourers in their ability to plan meaningfully for the future or to self-imagine with confident optimism (Burawoy, Lytkina, & Krotov, 2000). The institutional failure and industrial collapse have aborted workers' sense of initiative and individual enterprise. As a consequence, post-socialist workers have developed a radical faith in 'chance-based miracles'—a paralysing belief in divine powers of salvation (Verdery, 1995, p. 668). Above and beyond a blissful belief in promises of fairy-land miracles, however, the post-socialist condition of hopelessness propagates vernacular (often unimpressive and mundane) types of hope, and this because hope is requisite to enduring the everyday hardships, instability, and hopelessness of post-socialist conditions. Hope in post-socialism is a 'background attitude that allows one to keep going or persevere through one's life' in the face of hopelessness (Zigon, 2009, p. 258). Hope is the urge to live 'sanely' and 'acceptably' in the social world (Zigon, 2009).

Through this prism, post-socialist creative workers' future-orientation has little to do with either 'postalgia' or 'dream economies' (Miyazaki, 2006; Ybema, 2004). Nor does the future-orientation need to posit fantasies of the 'good life' or 'good work' (Berlant, 2011; Hesmondhalgh & Baker, 2011). Post-socialist creative workers harbour more mundane aspirations of attaining what are commonly referred to as a 'normal life' and a 'normal job'. (On the salience of 'normal life' hopes among post-socialist workers, see Zigon, 2009 on 'the sane life'; Burawoy et al., 2000.) For post-socialist creative workers, the aspirations for a good job that is autonomous, self-gratifying, and self-expressive (Hesmondhalgh & Baker, 2011) are dwarfed by the nagging daily pressures of economic hardship, lacking infrastructure, absent public arts subsidies, and capital investment. Hope for a normal life is then modestly associated with the morality of a healthy and uneventful life devoid of daily economic struggles and survival dramas (Zigon, 2009). This was hope that a creative job will provide stability and a steady family life, often non-grandiosely 'imagined' by the informants as 'the possibility to have a one-week sea vacation in the summer' or of 'sipping a glass of wine after work with your partner on the couch while watching TV'. For post-socialist workers, a hopeful outlook on the future entails acknowledgement of the hopelessness of present unbearable conditions. Given the long working days, the juggling of multiple jobs, and low pay, such otherwise unimpressive hopes may indeed represent a dream of 'a better life […] that might be possible' (Bloch, 1986, p. 1).

The many and heterogeneous objects of hope are irrelevant, however, if we approach hope as a method, as a hopeful engagement with the present. What interests me here is, indeed, what keeps hope in living a normal life alive. To explore that I consider the phenomena of nostalgia, waiting, and the creation of 'spaces of hope' (Mattingly & Jensen, 2015) (passive methods of hope prevalent among an older generation of creative workers), as well as informal economic activities and social-change art practices (more active methods of hope common among a younger generation).

Backward-looking hope: Nostalgia, God's blessing and spa-going

A method of hope typically observable with an older generation of creative workers (above 50) is that of nostalgia—a longing for working practices and work-lives experienced in the old socialist system. Such retrospective utopia should not always be understood as lamenting or glorifying the 'socialist paradise lost' (Velikonja, 2009). Rather, this retroactive reassessment of the past is less an exercise in romanticising and idealising the past than it is an effort to revive past hopes while trying to 'reorient knowledge' towards the possibility of a good life, a safe world, fair working conditions, solidarity, and prosperity (Velikonja, 2009, p. 538) (even if these possibilities were only imaginatively lived in the past). Nostalgia recuperates hope in the present post-socialist condition through the detour of imaginary memories of a hopeful socialist past. According to Anderson (2014, p. 453), nostalgia represents 'disappointed hope', which provides the method of adjusting to living in conditions that continually defy the possibility of existence of any 'audacious hope' as promised by past ideologies. 'The memories of the future unfulfilled' or nostalgia therefore help creative workers recast their orientation from bold projections of golden future to daily struggles in order to keep going.

However, backward-looking hope has not itself become ideological or progressive. On the contrary, it has rendered hope-fulfilling action delusional: 'hope depends on [...] a god, fate, chance, an other for its fulfilment' (Crapanzano, 2003, p. 6). Nostalgia, in this sense of 'resigned hope' (Crapanzano, 2003, p. 27), had its upshot in 'the abeyance of agency' (Miyazaki, 2015)—the capacity to suspend one's agency while delegating responsibility to others (such as God).

Consider the following excerpt from an interview with a low-level fashion designer in her late 50s, conducted while she was having a late-afternoon break in the corporate backyard before continuing her work until midnight with no paid overtime:

> It was better in [a socialist fashion company]. We all went to work with joy. It was friendlier. We all went on workers' holidays on the Adriatic coast. Eh … Now, the pay is low [150–200 EUR], we work late … everything's changed. See there? [She points to a decrepit building behind her]. There was the gynaecological practice where we got free contraception every Friday. A nursery for the kids. A restaurant as well. We had a dentist unit over there [points to the left]. … Now we work in three shifts. The boss calls us mad cows any time we want to go to the toilet. But God will help. Nothing's greater than God. … I hope everything will work out in the end.
>
> Interviewer: What do you do to combat this? Are you a member of a union?
>
> No, not at all. That's such a throwback to the past. That does not exist today. Now is capitalism.

Post-socialist creative workers typically resign themselves to the fact that not much can be done in the present except to hope. They do not merely succumb to fear or despair, however. Despite the 'abeyance of agency', the need to hope—to cherish abstract hope in God's power—is not simply a sign of denial or deceit. Hope possesses restorative power in the midst of embittered everyday work realities, managerial abuse, and overwork. By regularly invoking God's assistance, our informants tried to repair their broken hopes. In this way they expounded the necessity of hope in order to endure, stoically and patiently, the toil of working life 'under capitalism' (Zigon, 2009). Yet their invocation of God may be a manifestation of 'abstract hope' (Crapanzano, 2003, p. 10), hope which, while invoking an ever unreachable and remote horizon of accomplishment, is nonetheless expedient for the pursuit of daily survival. Many workers indeed professed vague yet trustful hope: 'I hope everything will work out in the end'. However, the possibility of a 'concrete' change-inducing agency in the form of unionisation or organised resistance lies outside this hoping horizon. The majority of our informants were not members of any union and commonly regarded unions as anachronistic. Unions constitute another referential and unfulfilled hope of the past—desirable, but incongruous with the present.

Spaces of hope: Working on the self

Outside of the workplace, where any hopes of unionisation and collective action have been cancelled out, post-socialist creative workers create semi-private solidaristic leisure 'spaces of hope' (Mattingly & Jensen, 2015, p. 39). In these spaces, hope—however, miniscule or mundane—is not passively received but 'actively cultivated, practiced' (Mattingly, 2010, p. 4). The above-mentioned fashion designer, like many other female fashion designers interviewed in the Macedonian fashion cluster of Stip, gathered enthusiastically after work in a post-socialist, inexpensive, decrepit, and run-down working-class hot springs spa adjacent to the fashion cluster factories. In communist times, health spas were far removed from today's media-perpetuated attractive images of wellness, wholesome lifestyle, and luxurious consumer choice; instead 'the spa was both a reward for hard work and was part of an economic rationale of extending the productive life of the worker' (Naraindas & Bastos, 2011, p. 2). Even when the trade unions formerly awarding workers with spa vacation vouchers (hard-work tokens) collapsed, the workers individually preserved spa-going as an essentially self-congratulatory, hope-restoring practice. A seamstress with 30 years of working experience, whom I interviewed at the spa, told me:

> The only thing that keeps me going is this spa. I work hard bent over the machine, go home and make dinner for the kids, and the next thing I do is come here. This is a little time for me. I believe really that the waters here have healing properties. I forget about all my problems here. I get to talk to other seamstresses and share the tribulations. This place eases the pain, and gives hope.

The spa represents an informal yet powerful, gendered space of personal but also social and occupational sociality and solidarity—a sheltered, bounded place of hard-earned comfort. In accordance with Miyazaki's (2015, p. 214) theory of hope, fashion workers carve out 'a space for resting in the midst of a crisis' which restores a new 'hopefulness of a rested body and mind'. Hope becomes an ethical imperative to make seriously disadvantaged and exploitative work-lives habitable, to 'keep going' indeed (Zigon, 2009). Spa-going, as a method of hope, makes otherwise underpaid and disillusioned fashion workers capable of positively embracing failure and enduring managerial harassment.

To prevent hope from morphing into hopelessness, creative workers value meaningful action, practise everyday care for themselves, and actively cultivate hope, or, in Zigon's words (2009, p. 261), pursue 'work on the self'. This focused and meticulous work on one's self also takes the form of intense spirituality and religiosity in specially carved, sacred spaces of hope. Disenchanted with her job at a public theatre in which she was consistently harassed and denied roles on the grounds of her age, a 54-year-old actress whom I interviewed in Skopje found refuge in 'an alternative evangelical congregation', her alternative space of hope ('This is my only island of hope … the rare ray of light'). Many of our interviewees viewed hopeful and restorative work on the self through religious communities and spaces (such as monasteries and church-run rehab clinics) as a prerequisite for ultimate sublime, authentic, and enhanced artistic performance.

'Waiting for a job': Daydreaming, escapism, and micro-politics

Another method of recuperating hope and reorienting knowledge towards the future is evident in escapist daydreaming and fantasies of fleeing the Balkans. This includes the dream of supplanting the clientelistic and nepotistic nature of creative work in the Balkans with an idealised version of labour in the West. 'Normal jobs' and 'meritocratic work' in which, as one informant put it, 'you succeed because you are good at what you do, not because of your uncle', and where there is 'no interpersonal favour-swapping', are just a few of the discursive idealisations in which the post-socialist creative workers we interviewed enshrined neo-liberal creative work.

While such escapist dreams may fuel the stamina to endure present precarious work conditions, however, they rarely trigger active hope fulfilment. When I followed up my initial interviews a year later, not one of the informants who had been hoping to emigrate to Western Europe had undertaken any concrete hope-fulfilling actions. One unemployed academically trained violinist justified her inaction as follows: 'I am waiting for a job. I have been promised a job at a state-funded symphony orchestra.' 'Waiting for a job' in publicly subsidised cultural institutions is the pervasive mode of forward-looking. It reveals the entrapment of creative workers in an inherited ill-fated hope in state paternalism, which in turn nurtures clientelism. Many creative workers perceive 'waiting' as an inevitable hope-enduring method that entails long-term nudging and sweet-talking of local political party officials into the micro-politics of state-job allocation, as the party officials are in charge of the employment and human resource policies of state cultural institutions. In turn, party officials inveigle unemployed creative workers into posing as alleged political supporters who (often grudgingly) perform at electoral rallies, promotions, and party banquets or feasts.

Amidst a generalised feeling of hopelessness, a creative job in the public sector represents a 'dream job'; and thus capitalising clientelistically on the hopes of creative workers is not difficult. Political parties trade long-hoped-for jobs in state-funded orchestras, opera houses, and theatres in exchange for electoral support. In most of the transitional and subaltern world, workers share a profound 'just waiting' engagement with futurity (Jeffrey, 2010). According to Jeffrey (2010, p. 3), such future-orientation represents a 'timepass', a '[form] of "waiting" wherein people have been incited by powerful institutions to believe in particular visions of the future yet lack the means to realize their aspirations'. In timepass, people read just their hopes by repurposing their actions, knowledge, and time-horizons.

In such prolonged and abusive waiting for *formal employment*, creative workers are neither inert nor completely submissive. While 'waiting', as I will show in the next section, dispossessed creative workers resort to an elaborate assortment of *informal* economic activities by which they reorient their dis-trust in public institutions towards (1) reciprocal trust/hope in interpersonal relations and (2) social practice art.

The flourishing of informal work is the logical outcome of clientelistic and inefficient creative labour institutions, policies, and markets. Hope for a normal life has been recuperated through entrepreneurial informal work practices—through 'getting your own gigs on the side'. As trust in institutions is eroding, interpersonal trust and relations of mutual aid are proliferating. The mutuality of informal economic relations is based entirely on reciprocity; that is, *hope* in future affirmative action—moral obligation and not deflection.

Even when hope proves itself unrealisable or untenable, creative workers still do not lose hope. This is because not-fulfilled hope presupposes that hope is still possible. They replace unfulfilled hope with newly reinvigorated efforts at knowledge reorientation. This is not a repetitive self-deception or self-defeat but a practice of 'enduring hope' (Miyazaki, 2004), whereby the question of temporality (knowledge of the self) is recast as a problem of agency (the practical realisation of the self).

Among post-socialist creative workers, hope has been the oxygen of perseverance and the *spiritus movens*. Hope instils the determination to fight honourably in life, to never give up. 'Hope dies last' is a phrase that kept recurring in all our conversations with creative workers in the region (see also Zigon, 2009). But hope requires action for its fulfilment—an active engagement with self-knowledge. In its active status, hope influences the disposition to act by breeding trust in interpersonal, collegial, and kinship relations (Raffnsøe, 2013), which in turn recuperates hope, however fleetingly, for progressive politics and social change in general, which Banks (2006) asserts represents the basis of the understanding of creative work as 'moral work'. Next, I briefly examine each of these distinct but interrelated methods of hope.

Hope in action: Informal economic practices, art for social change, and the 'NGO-isation' of creative work

In a context of paralysing systemic conditions—including weak creative labour unions, restricted access to loans, fragile intellectual property protection, corrupted public cultural management, and unreliable welfare protection—post-socialist creative workers revitalise hope in their work through engagement with a wide spectrum of informal labour practices and coping strategies, all of which are deeply embedded in local relational infrastructures (kinship, family, neighbourhoods, and colleagues). The hope-inducing informal labour practices that our informants most commonly referred to in interviews were barter, in-kind payments, favour-swapping, gratuities, and envelope wages. Future work should examine in more detail the multifarious and relational informalities and infrastructures of creative work. Here I would like to briefly elucidate the relationship between informal labour activities and hope.

Many creative workers engage in informal labour practices to 'keep their work' going. Such informal engagements represent 'the only hope' for surviving and persisting in an otherwise unsustainable creative career. In the absence of liquid cash, creative workers maintain work relations through a range of non-monetary exchanges. Many informants confided that they were engaged in chains of repeated barter and favour-swapping, exchanges involving the moral imperatives of trust, fair dealing, personalised ties, and enjoyment, so as to obtain expensive equipment (such as a guitar) or software packages, to cover expenses for rehearsal space, to settle foreign rights and copyright, or similar. One musician had bartered 'a dog, two pigeons, and a wedding party' in exchange for a guitar. Another musician had his album recorded in an improvised recording studio in exchange for his old car. Favour-swapping was also a common mode of survival; for example, a rock musician playing at a fashion designer's show in order to get 'free clothes'. A new media worker reported having designed a full digital web presence for a travel agency, together with an original logo design; in return, the agency reimbursed him with an 'all-inclusive' sea vacation on the Adriatic coast instead of a pay cheque.

All of these multifarious activities bear witness to workers' hopeful and innovative attempts to stay employable by disentangling creative work from direct money investment and, instead, infusing it in elaborate interpersonal infrastructures. Indeed, the above-mentioned assortment of practices is based on a moral contract—a contract that involves the mutual trust and hope immanent in the temporal dimension of gift-giving. The informal exchanges are based on 'hopeful' relationships of trust immanent in the reciprocal relations of gift-exchange (Miyazaki, 2015; Raffnsøe, 2013). According to Raffnsøe (2013, p. 253), hope is 'to be understood as actively trusting the new and unknown'. To en-*trust* one's work or possessions in the hands of others requires hope that the others will fulfil their deferred obligation and reciprocate. Hope becomes thus a matter of ethical practice and moral obligation (Zigon, 2009). In this sense, hope also leads to redefinition of creative work as 'moral work', work predicated on 'new social and economic relations based on sustainability, mutuality and a sense of moral obligation' (Banks, 2006, p. 462).

Informal labour activities are not simply oriented towards enclosed collegial communities. Rather, creative workers engage hopefully with post-socialist societies at large through socially useful creative work taking place under the auspices of countless non-governmental organisations or NGOs operating in the region. The increased 'NGO-isation' (Stubbs, 2007) of cultural work marked a transition towards the prominence of social change values, which economically but also morally monopolised 'art-for-art's-sake' values. Creative work thus has become 'an implausible palliative to exclusion and poverty' (McGuigan, 2005, p. 238). Banks (2006, p. 463) also notes that creative work in Manchester more often than not takes on a socially responsible non-governmental form, requiring a hopeful artistic engagement with impoverished locales through 'helping the community' and 'improving the neighbourhood' initiatives.

Yet, for the creative practitioners themselves, art for social change has become a resource for sustaining both their own creative careers and local communities. To this end, artists have refashioned themselves into informal social entrepreneurs. 'Peace coaches', 'ethnic dialogue facilitators', 'same-sex marriage evangelists', and 'transition psychology art therapists' were just a few of the labels with which creative workers hopefully reimagined themselves.

Many informants were actively engaged in pro-bono creative work, mostly in fundraising events to create spaces of hope, mutuality, and help:

> If I am a famous musician or actor and can make two hundred people come to my concert or performance and pay for a ticket, then I can give a humanitarian concert and gather that money needed for that poor sick-child family that cannot afford the expensive medical treatment. We are people. We artists have social responsibility. When our state is nonfunctional, we are obliged to give these people hope.

Following Bloch, Miyazaki (2004, pp. 14–15) argues that to actively hope actually means attempting to change the world. Through the hopeful engagement in progressive social action, creative workers preserve the economic sustainability in their own creative work while cherishing the moral obligation for social change.

Emboldened hope

In a context of institutional malfunctioning and protracted fiscal crisis followed by long-term unemployment—conditions that would normally be paralysing for most people—I have indeed registered some of the most radical expressions of hope: hopes that not only fuel the quest for a normal or sane life but also rekindle confidence in action for near-utopian social change. Consider the following story.

Martin, a 40-year-old games developer, abandoned a well-paid and secure job in Germany to 'come back home to Macedonia' and set up a game-developing studio. In the course of our conversation, Martin openly decried what he missed of 'the normal life' he used to live abroad, while constantly nourishing a hopeful engagement with present post-socialist conditions by vigilantly adjusting his daily practices and purposefully reorienting his self-knowledge:

> *Martin*: I miss a reliable postal system that will deliver the books I order online and not steal them. Now I order only ebooks or get them through friends in Western Europe. I miss a reliable Internet provider. The connection, and we need superpower, is slow during the day but we come to work during evenings, so it works out somehow … I miss more governmental control over food in supermarkets, but my family and I have now trusted farmers who deliver food directly to us. … I miss also the clean air. It is very polluted here ….
>
> *Interviewer*: I admire your staunch hope in life! But you cannot do much about the air pollution, can you?
>
> *Martin*: (Laughs) No no, we can. We have done the research. What causes the pollution is the thousands of old cars on the streets. … We started developing prototypes for cheap sun-powered vehicles. … I really do have faith that our vehicles will see the light of the day and will save the city!

Driven by necessity, shortages, and instability, post-socialist creative workers not only dare to imagine but also inhabit alternative worlds of informal work relations, progressive social art, and utopian development projects, where not everything pertains to market rationality and economic instrumentality. While striving for a future of not only personal enrichment but also a mutually shared eco-conscious, institutionally, and economically stable environment, creative workers frame their work as essentially 'moral work' (Banks, 2006)—work executed in contradistinction to markets and direct monetary value.

Conclusion

This chapter tried to integrate the concept of hope in the theorisation of the temporality of creative work. It by no means sets out to be a well-rounded or complete attempt to tease out the role of hope in creative work; rather, it is an initial step towards the development of a full-blown analysis of hope in the sociology of creative work more generally. The concept of hope is still not an accepted analytical category in sociology, if only because hope points always in a prophetic and subjunctive 'what if' direction of knowledge. Sociologists of creative work, however, should pay more attention to the empirical unfolding of hope, as it is a prominent indigenous, emic concept with which our informants repeatedly refer to their ethical, moral, and everyday projects of being-in-the-world. In cultural geography, Ben Anderson (2006, p. 733) had already convincingly argued that 'thinking through hope touches something that remains elusive to an act of explanation or description', as the focus on hope makes explicit those modes of operation that are so ingrained and taken-for-granted as to become hidden from analytical scrutiny. *Thinking through hope* in creative labour studies promises to alert us to this taken-for-granted, ordinary, and modest, but nonetheless crucial dynamic of working lives in creative industries.

This chapter has resisted the all-too-prevalent sociological reading of hope in creative work as a form of false consciousness in which 'wannabe' creative workers, mesmerised by the promise of future success, pay and fame, fail to detect the present conditions of their own exploitation. While unravelling workers' complacency is no doubt of political importance, close attention to hope as a mode of existential engagement with everyday work and working conditions will allow us to better appreciate the endurance and persistence of creative workers—not least their moral attachment to work above and beyond bold projections of wealth, success, and fame.

Hope and the hopeful behaviour patterns of post-socialist creative workers are of course path-dependent on the socialist past. This is seen, for example, in the way creative workers in the post-socialist Balkans have inherited from the communist era of shortages a valuable skill set for negotiating informal economic relations of favour-swapping and barter

(Burawoy et al., 2000). It is also seen in the impact of the increased post-socialist NGO-isation of civil society (Stubbs, 2007) and in nostalgia for the socialist 'paradise lost' (Velikonja, 2009). Expressions of hope become more evident in times of transitional breakdown and hardship (Verdery, 1995; Zigon, 2009). However, 'wounded' dismissed Western managers giving away hope 'to return to former glories' (Gabriel, Gray, & Goregaokar, 2013, p. 63) and Japanese security traders disenchanted with the 'Big Bang' financial reforms and 'hoping for early retirement' (Miyazaki, 2006, p. 159) have also been found to harbour a more modest hopeful engagement with their professional futures. The category of hope is thus well poised to help elucidate the complexities of work experiences in 'bad times', not only in times of transitional raptures but also in the West, which is currently ailing due to protracted austerity crises, volatile financial markets, increased unemployment, political instabilities, and economic breakdown. When bad times become instituted as 'the new normal' of life and work, then informal and socially proactive economic activities emerge as new spaces of hope. In this sense, the emphasis on workers' hope also revitalises the hope in creative work as a site and arena of 'moral work' (Banks, 2006).

Last, but not least, the focus on hope opens up potentially rich and relatively underexplored directions in creative work studies. The urge of creative workers to create casual spaces of hope and to pursue dedicated work on the self has to be studied in all its psychological complexities, including religiosity, spirituality, and mental health. The multifarious and relational informalities of creative work deserve more sustained attention from research, if only because they represent a renewed hope-driven attachment to otherwise unsustainable creative careers. The increased NGO-isation of creative work (see Lingo & Tepper, 2013 on the growing trend of social practice art in the USA) begs for immediate scholarly attention, since creative workers' hope in common good, community organising, and local social change is susceptible to abuse by international and corporate actors.

Acknowledgements Work on this chapter has been supported by grant number MK_211 (2014–2016), awarded by the Swiss Agency for Development and Cooperation (SDC) in the framework of the RRPP Programme coordinated and operated by the Interfaculty Institute for Central and Eastern Europe (IICEE) at the University of Fribourg, Switzerland. The views expressed in this study are those of the author and do not necessarily represent the opinions of the SDC and the University of Fribourg.

Note

1. Transcription style: … indicates words have been omitted in a sentence, often just the repetition or a word or two; […] indicates a sentence or more has been omitted; [words in brackets] are inserted to clarify meaning.

References

Alacovska, A. (2013). 'Parachute artists' or 'tourists with typewriters': Creative and cocreative labour in travel guidebook production. *Communication, Culture and Critique, 6*(1), 41–63.

Anderson, B. (2006). Becoming and being hopeful: Towards a theory of affect. *Environment and Planning D, 24*, 733–752.

Anderson, B. (2014). Affect and emotion. In N. C. Johnson, R. H. Schein, & J. Winders (Eds.), *The Willey-Blackwell companion to cultural geography*. London: Wiley.

Banks, M. (2006). Moral economy and cultural work. *Sociology, 40*(3), 455–472.

Berlant, L. (2011). *Cruel optimism*. Durham, NC and London: Duke University Press.

Bloch, E. (1986). *The principle of hope*. Cambridge, MA: MIT Press.

Bourdieu, P. (1998). *The rules of art*. Palo Alto, CA: Stanford University Press.

Burawoy, M., Lytkina, T., & Krotov, P. (2000). Involution and destitution in capitalist Russia. *Ethnography, 1*(1), 43–65.

Crapanzano, V. (2003). Reflections on hope as a category of social and psychological analysis. *Cultural Anthropology, 18*(1), 3–32.

Duffy, E. B. (2016). The romance of work: Gender and aspirational labour in the digital culture industries. *International Journal of Cultural Studies, 19*(4), 441–457.

Frenette, A. (2013). Making the intern economy: Role and career challenges of the music industry intern. *Work and Occupations, 40*(4), 364–397.

Gabriel, Y., Gray, E. D., & Goregaokar, H. (2013). Job loss and its aftermath among managers and professionals: Wounded, fragmented and flexible. *Work, Employment and Society, 27*(1), 56–72.

Gill, R. (2002). Cool, creative and egalitarian? Exploring project-based new media in Europe. *Information, Communication and Society, 5*(1), 70–89.

Gill, R., & Pratt, A. (2008). In the social factory. Immaterial labour, precariousness and cultural work. *Theory, Culture and Society, 25*(7/8), 1–30.

Hesmondhalgh, D. (2002). *Cultural industries*. London: Sage.

Hesmondhalgh, D., & Baker, S. (2011). *Creative labour: Media work in three cultural industries*. London: Routledge.

Jeffrey, C. (2010). *Timepass: Youth, class and the politics of waiting in India*. Palo Alto, CA: Stanford University Press.

Kuehn, K., & Corrigan, T. F. (2013). Hope labour. The role of employment prospects in online social media production. *The Political Economy of Communication, 1*(1), 9–25.

Lindquist, G. (2006). *Conjuring up hope: Magic and healing in contemporary Russia*. London: Berghahn Books.

Lingo, E. L., & Tepper, S. J. (2013). Looking back, looking forward: Arts-based careers and creative work. *Work and Occupations, 40*(4), 337–363.

Mattingly, C. (2010). *The paradox of hope: Journeys through a clinical borderland*. Berkeley, CA: University of California Press.

Mattingly, C., & Jensen, J. U. (2015). What can we hope for? An exploration in cosmopolitan philosophical anthropology. In S. Liisberg, O. E. Pedersen, & A. L. Dalsgård (Eds.), *Anthropology and philosophy: Dialogues on trust and hope* (pp. 24–54). New York: Berghahn.

McGuigan, J. (2005). Neo-liberalism, culture and policy. *International Journal of Cultural Policy, 11*(3), 229–241.

McRobbie, A. (1998). *British fashion design: Rag trade and image industry*. London: Routledge.

Mears, A. (2012). *Pricing beauty: The making of a fashion model*. Berkeley: UCP.

Menger, P.-M. (1999). Artistic labor markets and careers. *Annual Review of Sociology, 25*, 541–574.

Miyazaki, H. (2004). *The method of hope: Anthropology, philosophy and the Fijian knowledge*. Palo Alto, CA: Stanford University Press.

Miyazaki, H. (2006). The economy of dreams: Hope in global capitalism and its critiques. *Cultural Anthropology, 21*(2), 147–172.

Miyazaki, H. (2015). Hope in the gift—hope in sleep. In S. Liisberg, O. E. Pedersen, & A. L. Dalsgård (Eds.), *Anthropology and philosophy. Dialogues on trust and hope* (pp. 209–219). New York: Berghahn.

Naraindas, H., & Bastos, C. (2011). Healing holidays: Itinerant patients, therapeutic locales and the quest for health. *Anthropology and Medicine, 18*(1), 1–6.

Neff, G. (2012). *Venture labour: Work and the burden of risk in innovative industries.* Cambridge, MA: MIT Press.

Pratt, A. (2011). The cultural contradictions of the creative city. *City, Culture and Society, 2*, 123–130.

Primorac, J. (2006). *The position of cultural workers in the creative industries: The South-Eastern European Perspective.* Amsterdam: European Cultural Foundation.

Raffnsøe, S. (2013). Beyond rule, trust and power as capacities. *Journal of Political Power, 6*(2), 241–260.

Ross, A. (2003). *No collar: The humane workplace and it hidden costs.* New York: Basic Books.

Siebert, S., & Wilson, F. (2013). All work and no pay: The consequences of unpaid work in the creative industries. *Work, Employment and Society, 27*(4), 711–721.

Stubbs, P. (2007). Community development in contemporary Croatia: Globalization, Neoliberalisation and NGOisation. In L. Dominelli (Ed.), *Revitalizing communities in a globalizing world* (pp. 161–174). London: Ashgate.

Taylor, S., & Littleton, K. (2012). *Contemporary identities of creativity and creative work.* Surrey: Ashgate.

Velikonja, M. (2009). Lost in transition nostalgia for socialism in post-socialist countries. *East European Politics and Societies, 23*(4), 535–551.

Verdery, K. (1995). Faith, hope and caritas in the land of the pyramids: Romania 1990 to 1994. *Comparative Studies in Society and History, 37*(4), 625–669.

Ybema, S. (2004). Managerial postalgia: Projecting a golden future. *Journal of Managerial Psychology, 19*, 825–841.

Zigon, J. (2009). 'Hope dies last'. Two aspects of hope in contemporary Moscow. *Anthropological Theory, 9*, 253–270.

Ana Alacovska is an Assistant Professor at the Copenhagen Business School, Denmark. Her research interests are the sociology of culture with an emphasis on the power of genres to influence institutional and social relations, the creative labour studies with a special accent on gender inequalities, and the critical studies of media organisations.

From Visual Discipline to Love-Work: The Feminising of Photographic Expertise in the Age of Social Media

Karen Cross

Introduction

Being in service to social networks has for many become an accepted part of daily life. The payoff for this is the sense of social integration that is experienced from interacting with others online, for example, through the creation and uploading of snapshots or the exchange of other forms of personal and more public information. Although considered largely 'amateur' in status, these also represent a form of individualised affective and immaterial labour that is being increasingly capitalised on by new media industries. Most obvious in this respect is the monetising of user-generated content, especially for sales and advertising, but there is also a growing field of expertise linked to the use of social media and the new modes of work that this entails.

This chapter explores the significance of these changes for the new normal of working lives by focusing on photographic practice, particularly

K. Cross (✉)
Department of Media, Culture and Language,
University of Roehampton, London, UK

the gendered nature of the new forms of expertise in this field. I consider the recent re-emergence of how-to training manuals relating to the use of the camera phone, and look at how these involve the adoption of a conceptual artistic use of the amateur lens (signified mainly through the analogue 'snapshot aesthetic'). The chapter considers how this allows for reconfiguration of the amateur/professional divide in photography and also becomes a way of establishing a new form of expertise reflective of feminine 'other-orientated' forms of relating and communication. On the one hand, this represents a shift away from a form of 'visual discipline' and masculine technical and aesthetic mastery. On the other, it extends a form of feminised labour—or 'love-work'—which is today associated with the wider creative and cultural industries.

The chapter opens with a brief discussion of recent theories linked to the concepts of 'immaterial' (Lazzarato, 1996) and 'free' (Terranova, 2000) labour. It also considers recent criticisms that theory fails to take into account women's experiences and the feminisation that new processes of labour involve (e.g., Fantone, 2007; McRobbie, 2010). New forms of creative work arguably involve what recent feminist scholars describe as a 'new sexual contract' (Adkins, 2008; McRobbie, 2007), wherein women's lives become the zone and horizon for the articulation of new forms of labour. Linked to this is the 'new mystique' (Taylor, 2015) of working for oneself within the neoliberal economy, which rationalises certain forms of culturally privileged, yet economically devalued, forms of work. Moreover, work today can be seen to orientate increasingly towards domestically located, amateur, and DIY forms of practice, and in doing so invites an emotionally driven and 'other-centred' approach. With this emerges a new kind of expertise, which eschews the definition of 'the professional' and focuses attention instead on the social dimensions of communication and interaction within online worlds and visual networks. The question I raise here is, what kind of possibilities can this extend to women attempting to configure new modes of work that fit with new technologies of communication and social engagement? I seek to understand this from the point of view of contemporary forms of aesthetic renewal that deploy the amateur popular past, and especially signifiers of domesticity, as a means of manifesting social change.

Network culture and the limits of 'immaterial labour'

The concept of 'immaterial labour' proposed by Maurizo Lazzarato (1996) and Tiziana Terranova's (2000) notion of 'free labour' have been particularly prolific within critical discussions relating to the Internet and contemporary processes of labour. As Lazzarato describes, labour has increasingly become defined by a form of 'intellectuality' (p. 134) demanded by new forms of communication and network exchange. This involves a form of 'self-valorisation' (p. 134) that serves to elevate the working class, but it also opens up the worker's life to capitalism's command over labouring identities. This can be seen particularly in the contemporary media industries, where work takes on a more autonomous feel and allows the individual a deeper sense of personal control. However, working lives today involve an adaptation to certain conditions that effectively erode the structures of institutional support and provision of organised care seen in the past.

According to Lazzarato (1996), established forms of media production (e.g., photography, audiovisual, and software) and practices of cultural mediation (e.g., advertising and fashion) provide the model for newer kinds of work emerging in recent years within which industry simply relies upon socially independent sources of labour that are organised around self-governing practices of work and consumption. The precarious nature of such employment and the fear of not being employed means that it is increasingly difficult to distinguish between leisure time and work—'life becomes inseparable from work' (p. 138). Yet, for Lazzarato, this represents the new political horizon, wherein contemporary forms of labour power can be understood as 'the product of a "silent revolution" taking place within the anthropological realities of work and within the reconfiguration of its meanings' (p. 140).

The conditions of production today also foreground the shifting relationship between production and consumption, and the fact that consumption is 'no longer the "realization" of a product, but a real and proper social process ... defined with the term *communication*' (Lazzarato, 1996, p. 141). The focus of many forms of work today is upon the production of social relations, and within this, Lazzarato argues: 'the "raw material" of immaterial labour is subjectivity and the "ideological" environment in which this subjectivity lives and reproduces' (p. 143). This is what allows social identities or 'forms of life' (p. 146), especially those connected with the working class, and its more generalised signification through the domain of 'the popular', to be foregrounded as a source of innovation. I suggest, moreover, that there is a particular valourising of the position of those who were previously referred to as 'the audience' and who are now considered the more active 'amateur' producers of media. Linked with this is also Terranova's (2000) concept of 'free labour', which similarly highlights the way in which social relations (i.e., the relations of production and communication) become the privileged 'quality' (48) that animates commodities today. As Terranova describes, the digital economy is one that translates consumption into a set of productive activities via processes of pleasurable cultural experimentation. Her discussion of 'the gift' economy and development of open-source software offers a quite specific insight into online activism, which brings into relief the way in which the network can form a space of radical participation. However, it is important to recognise, as Terranova does, that power and privilege continue to frame the use of the Internet in spite of its greater inclusivity of non-institutionally defined forms.

Moreover, as we can also see, inclusivity is manifest in new ways through the new field of consumption. The value of a product today is increasingly defined in terms of 'the quality of labor behind it' (Terranova, 2000, p. 47). This can be seen, for instance, through popularising of environmentally friendly and 'fair trade' products, along with the wider support for local and small businesses led by individuals seeking a more flexible and self-governed forms of work. Yet, in spite of representing a seemingly more diverse field, it is also the case that such newer, and supposedly more ethical, frames of consumption are often constructed via intensely limited horizons of social experience, and these cannot always be accounted for by undifferentiated theories of class. As I wish to consider here, women's experience, and the feminising of contemporary forms of labour, have until recently largely remained marginal within the broader discussions of labour and its shifting forms, but are important to recognise for more than just the simple reason of accounting for the broader spectrum of different experiences. The question of women's work and the feminine framing of labour remains deeply significant for understanding mediations of work, and the way that work is represented in and through the media.

Women's work and the legacy of 'post-feminism'

Recent theories naming new forms of labour have an important role to play, but in order to fully acknowledge any remaining inequalities it is important to engage with the question of gender at every level. Laura Fantone (2007, p. 9) argues, for instance, that it is often the single, male, urban artist or creative worker who is idealised as 'the vanguard of the *precariat*', yet it is apparent that recent shifts in labour conditions and activism that relate to precariousness are equally important to women. As she suggests, more recent struggles revive issues of the failure to take account of women's experience, raised by feminists during the 1970s. In relation to this, Angela McRobbie (2010, p. 60) also urges the re-prioritising of gender within the discussions of labour practices. Her view is that there is a need for a more historically grounded perspective that pays attention to the 'micro-activities' of earlier generations of feminists who combined job creation with political activity. Recent writings on post-Fordism, which include Lazzarato's and other writings from Michael Hardt and Paolo Virno's (1996) *Radical Thought in Italy*, offer a limited perspective on the position of women, and the meaning of the feminisation that recent reconceptualisations of work have involved. Precarious and creative labour represents a highly feminised space of work, yet there has been barely any recognition of the different experiences of women and the kinds of labour that have long remained relegated to the feminine sphere.

Furthermore, new theories of labour must take into account what McRobbie describes as the legacy of post-Fordism, and the way in which women have come to embody 'processes of mobility and transition' (2010, p. 68) within the new labour market. This links with consumer culture and the rise of aspirational forms of femininity, which offer working class women the chance to gain middle-class respectability (see also Skeggs, 1997). However, this transition often involves a disavowal of working class identification and modification of other class-bound, racial, and ethnic experiences that are not foregrounded within mainstream media or within the proliferation of social networks that seek to represent diversity of experience. McRobbie's (2007) own research on young women in the UK points towards the emergence of a new 'sexual contract' that forms the basis of women's work today, and its contemporary forms of visual media representation. Opportunities for financial independence and increased consumer power suggest liberation, but also entail the performance of what McRobbie describes as a 'post-feminist masquerade' (722). Within this, young women are positioned as gender-aware subjects who nonetheless are required to maintain normative standards of femininity. Labour and women's work predominantly require a hyperactive engagement with consumer culture, which is particularly focused upon the fashion and beauty industries. Women both labour and consume within these markets as a way of maintaining gender-appropriate boundaries. The 'masquerade' that this involves forms a way of redirecting aggression away from masculinity and male dominance within the wider labour market. The focus upon bodily forms of self-actualisation becomes the biopolitical force through which 'post-feminism' orientates women to new work-related expressions of femininity. McRobbie has extended this concept more recently to 'the new 'mediated' maternalism' (2013, p. 119), which involves the spread of neoliberal forms of self-governance to fertility and parenthood. This rearticulates the 'post-feminist' transference (and arguably dilution) of politics through purchase power and the whole field of body care, exercise, and pampering, that is now extended to mothers. The plethora of self-help literature also points towards the growing 'professionalisation of domestic life' (p. 130), which is increasingly coming to govern public representations of and debates on motherhood. The ubiquitous figure of the middle-class professional wife and mother offers the new construction of the sexualised 'maternal–feminine' (p. 119), described by McRobbie as a legacy of 'post-feminism'.

An even further condensed social type is found in the figure of the 'yummy mummy', who, as Jo Littler (2013, p. 227) argues, enacts a 'hyper-individualized psychological "maturity"' through a pro-corporate no-nonsense stance to motherhood. The battle of an earlier generation has become replaced by an intensive form of mothering, which provides a setting for both the articulation and containment of maternal–feminine interests. Such figures as Sheryl Sandberg, Chief Operating Officer at Facebook in California, are cited as examples of a public figurehead for the working mother who renews a feminist discourse. Sandberg's organisation, Lean In, and a book of the same name, encourage women not to step away from work after becoming a mother. Her success and celebration reveal 'the extent to which corporate values have achieved a fundamental centrality and seemingly incontestable as well as uncontroversial status' (McRobbie, 2013, p. 133). It also highlights the disambiguation of feminism from class politics and reveals how 'non-elite' (p. 135) or culturally valued types of labour continue to remain absent from public debate.

What we are seeing are essentially conservative versions of feminism. On the one hand, they fetishise the maternal, but on the other, they also operate according to the laws of a vigilant monitoring of social class boundaries, which excludes, for example, the supposedly irresponsible parenting of the single mother or the mother who chooses not to return to work. And yet, the corporate setting is not a purely exclusive zone. It flows out beyond the boundaries of work and into the management of the everyday lives of women and is displaced right through the self-governing practices of family and home. Identification with more long-standing political struggles and strategies linked with post-war social democracy and maternity are effectively forgotten within a system that transfers responsibility from state to individual.

There is a sense in which the reconfiguration of the 'sexual contract' cuts much deeper than the absence of diversity within the popular field of mainstream media. In addition, it is also important to consider the changing arrangements of labour and the way that this involves a temporal shift, which Lisa Adkins argues challenges the idea of the 'sexual contract' (2008, p. 182). More specifically, as Adkins' research shows, value is no longer about the past, 'dead' (p. 195) labour sealed within the commodity. It is much more open; it is 'vital and alive' (p. 195), which is signalled by the emphasis that is now placed upon the future, and the yet-to-come markets of labour. For this reason, theorists of work need to consider the currency of embodied labour power precisely at the moment when value has transitioned beyond the labouring subject and the commodity form. The value of the work that women have tended to perform, and the corporeality upon which their labour power has thus far been premised, is placed in question, especially within today's future-orientated markets that represent the digital economy. What scope then is there for women to identify as self-governing creative subjects within the currently shifting arrangements of labour? Answers to such questions lie in the empirical work that has begun to describe the gender dynamics of contemporary forms of work, especially those that connect into the transformations of network culture and the valorisation of the so-called creative identities that this involves.

Feminine and 'other-centric' creativity

Although online networks involve the intense proliferation of what McRobbie (2013, p. 122) calls the 'the visual media governmentality', which she sees as defining representations of the maternal, they have also become spaces for the articulation of feminist concerns and a departure from mainstream media representations. Additionally, they form resources of hope for women (and men) seeking to redefine the terms of work and labouring identities. This can be seen, for instance, through the rise of such figures as the 'mumpreneur', recently described by Carol Ekinsmyth (2011, 2013a, 2013b) as women who cross the boundaries between the position of the 'mother' and 'businesswoman' (2013b, p. 326). The women in Ekinsmyth's research find that a part of their work involves 'the creative management of time-space' (2013b, p. 533), which necessitates organising work around the daily routines and rhythms of motherhood.

'Mumpreneurship' can be a site of gendered conflict, which is apparent in the way that the division of labour within the family often falls to the mother or caregiver who has chosen to work from home. Work conducted under this category tends to be deemed less important, or 'not proper work' (Ekinsymth, 2013b, p. 540), even by the women who undertake it, and yet as Julian Ann Wilson and Emily Chivers Yochim (2015) have recently argued, the entrepreneurial frame of mothering is today crucial in stabilising the family during times of financial precarity. The 'mumpreneur' is generally considered to be a privileged middle-class position, but it offers evidence of the wider exploitative mechanisms of today's precarious labour market and the way that mothering today necessitates an engagement with the individualising transitional strategies of digital media. It also points towards the emergence of a new work ethic, or what Wilson and Chivers Yochim call a form of 'rationalised happiness' (p. 682), which they say is representative of the 'cruel optimism' identified by Lauren Berlant (2011) as governing the public sphere.

The position of the 'mumpreneur' offers the advantages of blurring the boundaries between motherhood and business, but also idealises the intensive forms of mothering, connecting into a 'post-feminist masquerade' and contemporary mediations of the maternal–feminine, which McRobbie (2013) describes. The gender conflicts relating to the figure of the 'mumpreneur' are also ones that are reflected more broadly across the wider field of cultural and creative work, which entails the promise of the 'good life'. There is not scope here to fully explore all the literature relating to this issue. For the purposes of my argument, however, I wish to draw attention to an aspect of this debate. Stephanie Taylor's research in particular (2010, also see Taylor, 2015; Taylor & Littleton, 2012) shows that it is important to look more broadly at creative and cultural work and the growing prominence of a discourse of relatedness within this field. This is because there is evidence to suggest that new working identities are becoming deeply rooted in individualised forms of innovation aligned with the figure of the creative artist and designer. As Taylor (2010, p. 367) warns, there is a need to be attendant to the gender inequalities that reside within this configuration. Unbounded forms of creative practice often associate with 'the masculine selfishness of the conventional creative artist'. This remains contradictory to the 'other-directedness' (p. 368) of work and forms of affective labour, which are prevalent within the field of cultural work.

As Conor, Gill, and Taylor (2015, p. 14) state:

> The 'boundary crossing' potentialities of creative labour may be a potential attraction for women, both as a turning away from the perceived banality or suppression of individuality associated with the conventional workplaces, and also as an unconfident response to anticipated difficulties.

This is connected to Mark Banks' (2007, p. 185) description of cultural work as representing the outlet for new forms of institutionalised rebellion, and yet often women are simply not afforded the opportunity to fully immerse themselves in their art in the same way as men. This is often due to life commitments, which include caring for children and parents, but it is also to do with the undervaluing of women's work more broadly.

As Taylor (2015, p. 174) also identifies, there is a wider 'discursive drift' involving the convergence of an entrepreneurial and creative frame, which places a high value on working from home. Within this setting, the creative worker becomes a largely feminised 'low-status worker', who is service-orientated and other-focused. Taylor argues, moreover, that the aspiration of working from home represents a 'new mystique resembling the 'housewife trap' (p. 174) previously described by Betty Friedan in her 1963 book, *The feminine mystique*. Home becomes the aspirational site of freedom from 'dreaded professionalism' (Friedan, [1963]1971, p. 348), but it is also that which leads to economic exclusion and the marginalising of women from the main activities of the market. And yet domestically grounded subjectivities are not necessarily to be dismissed as retrograde femininities that simply serve to position women in precarious positions of employment. Arguably, recent identifications with the housewife of a bygone era can be understood as both a consequence and a strategy, emerging within the framing of an austerity culture situated at the margins of political critique (see Bramall, 2013, p. 123). Understanding this is important if we are to grapple more fully with the wider cultural dynamics of gender inequality as it infuses daily life and as it is worked through the dynamics of contemporary labour and work-related cultures. Recourse to past identities and cultural practices today constructs a landscape of quasi-politicised memory. This is certainly evident in the context of the attachment to analogue forms and the desire to manifest a new level of 'authentic' creative practice, which I am describing here. Added to this is the rise of interest in traditionally hobbyist domestic forms of craft now being transmuted within the creative entrepreneurial frame of the Internet, and new creative sites of consumption, which have been explored recently by Susan Luckman in her book *Craft and the creative economy* (2015).

Newer forms of craft, especially those visible in social media, recall a history of women's exclusion from work. However, their reappearance suggests more about present-day concerns to resolve the modes and methods of the past rather than to necessarily revive social life as it was once lived. Returning also to an earlier point made in this chapter, labour is no longer a category that simply refers to the process of intensified forms of commodity production. Labour can be understood as the action—or 'relation'—through which people attempt to perform 'good work' (Hesmondhalgh & Baker, 2011). This is both in the sense of creating things of value, but also in terms of working in ways that seem more socially just. And so, domestically orientated crafts can be seen today to represent a more ethical space of consumption for a more ecologically minded consumer, and yet there is clearly a need to attend to the particular memorial investments this involves.

Engaging through the lens of the past, especially 'the aura of the analogue' or the handmade, has become a means of creating a sense of 'the "authentic" in a seemingly "inauthentic" world' (Luckman, 2015, p. 68). It also provides, as Luckman's research shows, a means of creating a 'material' relation against the backdrop of the 'immaterial' preponderances of the online world. Craft and the analogue today signify personal connection and social presence, and yet the capacity to recognise and engage in the conceptual use of the past is dependent upon the ability to understand the reifying processes of contemporary art and the capacity to see 'art' in the everyday, ordinary, and banal. Sociological concepts such as Pierre Bourdieu's 'cultural capital' (1986) again become appropriate in helping to bring into relief the significance of newer modes of cultural consumption. However, within online spaces, we are witnessing the inverse situation; the functional and utilitarian aspects of a past medium acquire cultural status where once they were previously devalued or ignored. This can be seen especially within new areas of visual expertise that today initiate certain kinds of identification with 'the amateur', as I now turn to consider.

Photography and the amateur

Photography criticism has recently described a form of 'mass amateurisation' (Rubinstein & Sluis, 2008, p. 11) within the field, and within this, the potential of 'the networked image' to secure a form of 'mediated' (Villi, 2015, p. 3) social presence. The 'newness' of digital photography and its potential to articulate ordinary and everyday interests has clearly become a popular theme, but, while the critical literature recognises the limits of the technologically determinist discourse predominating in public life, it has generally failed to consider how social presence today involves recourse to texturalities of the analogue world. As I wish to suggest, the presence of the analogue within the digital field is often used to signify a more feminine and playful mode of creative self-expression. Retro visual forms, such as the lo-fi production of toy cameras (Bates, 2011), are prevalent across social media. This includes the square-frame and sepia-toned productions of photo-sharing tools such as Instagram, which provide evidence of the various ways in which the 'social' turn in photography is indebted to the past and involves a distinctly memorial lens.

Historically, attachment to the 'amateur' is understood as an attempt to construct an 'artistic ego ideal' (Roberts, 2008, p. 22) in the face of institutional and commercial professionalisation. However, the internalising of the 'amateur' can also be considered to represent a wider feminising of practice by performing the relational care for 'the other' often associated with the act of mothering. Manifestos relating to the snapshot aesthetic during the early 1970s, for instance, describe the photographer as needing to adopt the vision of the figure of the mother who, acting out of love, gazes adoringly at her children as she lifts the camera to capture the memory (Jay, 1999[1971]). Clearly, this is heavily connected with the commercial discourse of Kodak and the use of emotion and nostalgia to sell photography. And yet, the artistic intention during this period was to represent the most culturally derided area of photographic production as the source of inspiration for a new practice.

Elsewhere, I have written of the way that amateur forms, especially the family snapshot, have been deployed within conceptual art practice (Cross, 2015). I have also discussed the importance of the snapshot aesthetic within the construction of a field of 'citizen journalism' (Cross, 2016). As I have shown, the curation of amateur forms by professionals within the wider cultural industries implies a relation of care whereby snapshots come to represent 'objects of salvage' (Cross, 2015, p. 44). As the snapshot aesthetic infiltrates digital platforms, photography today signifies a form of maternal–feminine relatedness. Thus the process of remediating the amateur/professional relation through the snapshot aesthetic implies a turn away from traditionally masculine elitist discourses of technical and aesthetic mastery. The establishment of such emotional relatedness extends right through the wider cultural framings of photographic practice, including newer forms of training and self-help forms of knowledge now on offer to the consumer of technological devices. Moreover, these newer outlets of gaining (non-)expert insights reveal exactly the complex and paradoxical arrangements of new forms of contemporary labour and work, and their play upon emotionality. They further bring into relief the process described by Taylor (2015), in which the creative worker, now a feminised figure, does not necessarily compete within professionalised art worlds but rather works in order to carry out 'an almost therapeutic, personal creative project' (2015, pp. 182).

'Social photography' as sm(art) work

Past forms of photography education and training just prior to the digital turn effectively served to inhibit traces of the feminine domestic sphere (Cross, 2014, p. 78) and, thus, set apart the experience of the snapshooter from more technologically advanced forms of camera use. This was, however, at a time when the 'mystique of the professional' was in the process of becoming replaced by a 'mystique of the everyday' within certain areas of art practice, which were beginning to spill out across the popular cultural field. In light of this, the emergence of a new field of amateur photography training is perhaps surprising given previous links with a now outmoded tradition of visual discipline, but it is precisely through the connection of new technologies to the critical practices of the artistic avant-garde that we are now beginning to see the reformulation of expert forms of knowledge orientated around so-called smart devices.

Texts that now orientate towards consumers of camera phones offer an advanced form of knowledge that is based upon the critical discourses of art practice. The specific kind of publication to which I am referring is that represented by such titles as *The Art of iPhoneography: A Guide to Mobile Creativity* (Calabrese Roberts, 2012), *The New Street Photographer's Manifesto* (Nagar, 2012), *Social Photography: Make All your Photos One in a Billion* (Bowker, 2014), *The Citizen Journalist's Photography Handbook: Shooting the World As It Happens* (Miller, 2014), and the more recent *The Joy of iPhotography: Smart Pictures from your Smart Phone* (Hollingsworth, 2016), whose author describes regaining his 'love' of photography after packing up his SLR and instead using his iPhone to create images.

All of these titles are produced by Ilex Press, an independent book publisher set up in the UK in 2000 with the aim of publishing its own brand of literature for creatives. In 2014, they were taken over by Octopus Publishing Group, but prior to this had established links in North America, with some of the titles being reprinted by Focal Press, a well-known photography education publisher, and by O'Reilly Media, which is known for its policy-focused work on new technologies. While the evolution of networks within this field of publishing is itself interesting, for the purposes of my argument I wish to focus on the particular way texts published by this group reframe photography practice as socially orientated and underpinned by the wider ethos of working for 'love' and 'passion', as is so often reported within recent research relating to new forms of gendered labour (e.g., Gill, 2007; Gill & Pratt, 2008; McRobbie, 1998; Taylor, 2010).

Each of the Ilex titles mentioned here is unique in its approach, but together they represent a growing field of practice that positions the expert as a pioneering creative or activist positioned precariously within the labour market. The biographies of the individual authors often include a narrative of departure from more professionalised domains. This is suggestive of the currency of the amateur lens, and it is by making a distinction between one's commercial work and the new forms of practice using a smart phone that the expert gains a new currency. The authors of new how-to texts offer readers advice about monetising their work within the new landscape of social media use. This is reflective of a discourse of media democratisation, which sees the distinction between the amateur and professional eroded as a consequence of 'complete mobility, ubiquity, and connection' (Gómez Cruz & Meyer, 2012, p. 217). Newer texts offer an insight into the inner workings of mobile technologies and ways that they can be creatively utilised, but they also position the newly defined expert as an essentially precarious labourer, and as one who is dependent upon the individualising self-representational strategies of the neoliberal economy. Amateur/users of cameras must now not only be skilled in the use of technology; they must also be able to understand how it can be operationalised in the service of economic gain and the acquisition of other forms of social and cultural capital. From this, it can also be seen that the field of amateur practice, perhaps once performed out of genuine interest in the art of photography, is now governed by a kind of futurist policy, with leisure interests as a potential source of employment (Leadbeater & Miller, 2004).

The amateur serves as a key figure driving forward societal change, working for 'love' rather than personal financial gain. One the one hand, this involves an investment in the idealism of the self-made entrepreneur, usually male. On the other, it configures a new space of creative exploration that is governed by 'other-orientatedness' and desire for social justice, which takes on distinctly feminine expressions. For instance, within the aforementioned how-to texts, the biography and story of the expert are important, but many also curate the work of previously unrecognised amateurs. Authors rewrite the history of photography according to the new socially orientated visual aesthetics. This is especially evident in the text by Carlos Miller (2014), who focuses upon the historical emergence of citizen production, from the shooting of JFK and the case of Rodney King to anonymous and unknown individuals in political uprising, such as seen during the so-called 'Arab Spring'. The advice offered in his text, which covers subjects such as ethical and legal issues that may be faced by the citizen reporter, represents a whole new dimension of photographic training, which extends beyond the usual technical and aesthetic advice. While there is some discussion of receiving payment, the primary focus is labouring in service to 'justice', with an underlying highly aggressive masculine vigilantism. This is a kind of photographic practice that intends to speak back to power, with Miller monitoring the actions of public institutions such as the police through his website Photography is Not a Crime (PINAC).

In contrast to this essentially remediated version of visual documentary 'truth', other authors within the field represent a more loosely framed counter-cultural perspective that is representative of recent investments in the feminine frame. Daniela Bowker's *Social Photography* (2014), for instance, seeks to introduce readers to the etiquette of photo sharing and the potential uses of social media tools, including deciphering the language of @symbols and #hashtags, and yet the use of the smart phone is also positioned largely as a kind of by-product of a renewed interest within the everyday field of vision. This extends beyond older forms of social documentary; the new social frame of photography relates more directly to the representation of the domestic setting. This is apparent in terms of both content and form, and is often represented through the square-frame format of photographic production, which today signifies creativity and craft. The acknowledgement that it is now 'hip to be square' (Bowker, 2014, p. 60) suggests a relationship to fashion and a heightened awareness of the distinct value of the domestic setting and its lens of visual reproduction, but it also implies the adoption of a more critical perspective.

Creative self-reflection and feminine relation

In Stephanie Calabrese Roberts' (2012) text *The Art of iPhoneography* in particular, we see a more overtly therapeutic exploration of the capacity of the camera phone to document social life. This is evident in the way that she encourages the reader to enter into a kind of autobiographical self-reflection, which involves not only visually documenting one's life but also regularly returning to look at personal archives of images and exploring feelings about them. Although not directly stated, this represents a kind of 'memory work' that is in certain respects akin to earlier feminist interventions such those found in the work of Jo Spence (1986), Valerie Walkerdine (1991) and Annette Kuhn (1991 and 2002). These involve the interrogation of ideological and cultural meanings of the family album, but Calabrese Roberts' model of self-exploration appears a little less radical, especially considering the contemporary investment in maternal–feminine practices now apparent within the wider cultural field.

The author promotes a method that encourages engagement with the messier aspects of domestic and familial life, and through this reaches beyond the simple nostalgia and sentimentality that is otherwise inferred by the retro-analogue photographic lens. It is precisely by focusing upon the messiness of life and the emotionality of photography, however, that Calabrese Roberts' text forms part of the wider therapeutic culture underscoring contemporary media practice. Her version of photography expertise reaches beyond the more sanitised performances of the maternal–feminine relation often performed within the post-feminist frame. It also extends the opportunity to engage with a new 'visual vocabulary' (2012, p. 100) situated within the field of personal experience, but it is yet uncertain what can really be achieved by adopting this mode of practice.

Calabrese Roberts' engagement through the domestic space seems more strategic than passive. The idea of 'shoot how you feel' (2012, p. 78) connects photographic practice to emotional experience, and she argues that by doing so it is possible to 'see shifts in your perspective' over time. This poses a challenge to previously held discourses of geometric form and instead orientates the reader to the notion of 'the self' as a constant ever-changing strategy. The reader is aware of the socially constructed nature of her (or his) vision and orientating towards a 'creative' identity necessitates a form of therapeutic reflection. By herself attempting to establish a practice that is premised upon intuitive feminine connections, which is also evident through her involvement in the Shutter Sisters network (and their book *Expressive Photography: Shutter Sisters' Guide to Shooting from the Heart*: Clark et al., 2010), Calabrese Roberts makes us aware of the problems associated with constructing a distinctly feminine creative practice. This demonstrates how an exclusive zone of communication 'written for women, by women' is in the process of being staged, but there is a potential that this simply coheres the marginality of women through the celebration of domestic familial interests aside from any other. The hyper-emotionality of the new creative field that her work stands to represent also potentially undermines any real therapeutic potential for self-reflection it initiates. Furthermore, it is by aligning with a rather vague visual framing of 'love' (as an image, rather than experience) that such texts undermine the potential of the relatedness that forms the basis of maternal–feminine experience. Such texts celebrate the maternal sphere as the ground upon which a more emotionally driven kind of practice should naturally and inevitably unfold, and replay the earlier artistic appropriations of the snapshot form previously discussed here. They are also reflective of the compounded form of 'love-work' that more widely underpins new discourses of labour proliferating across the social field, especially those that proclaim to represent feminine interests. What is yet unclear is whether such kinds of cultural identification can really solidify the growth of women-centred forms of labour. Such texts certainly do not relate directly to all women's experience.

Concluding remarks

Generally speaking, it is by beginning to look more deeply at the emergence of such forms of photographic expertise that we can begin to respond to the representational strategies that both enable and inhibit women, and others historically marginalised from work, to think of themselves as labourers whose creative work is deserving of recognition. As my reflection on some key examples of how-to literature has begun to show, the social media settings connected with photographic self-representation and expression offer a specific site for the evolution of a socially grounded aesthetic renewal, which is feminised in certain ways. The process I have described involves a complex dynamics of gender. It also requires engagement with a specific form of relational practice that foregrounds both the capacity to understand more recent cultural artistic languages premised upon the ability to recognise art in the ordinary and banal, and an ability to adopt the other-centredness that this new creative frame of reference demands.

Working through the concept of 'immaterial' labour and the critiques relating to it, however, it has been my intention to also show how the amateur–feminine has become the source material of contemporary articulations—the content, form, and textural underpinning to the establishment of new forms of labour, which are not inevitably equitable. Added to this, we have seen how past modalities of cultural production today provide the grounds for working through previous forms of professional knowledge. By reflecting more critically upon this, however, we can begin to unravel the contemporary fascination with the domestic field and the investments within the maternal–feminine that this appears to necessitate, and which now provide the framework for the emergence of a new form of photographic expertise.

References

Adkins, L. (2008). From retroactivation to futurity: The end of the sexual contract. *NORA—Nordic Journal of Feminist and Gender Research, 16*(3), 182–201.
Banks, M. (2007). *The politics of cultural work*. Basingstoke: Palgrave Macmillan.
Bates, M. (2011). *Plastic cameras: Toying with creativity*. Abingdon: Focal Press.
Berlant, L. (2011). *Cruel optimism*. Durham: Duke University Press.
Bourdieu, P. (1986). *Distinction: A social critique of the judgment of taste* (R. Nice, Trans.). London: Routledge.
Bowker, D. (2014). *Social photography: Make all your smartphone photos one in a billion*. Lewes: Ilex.
Bramall, R. (2013). *The cultural politics of austerity: Past and present in austere times*. Basingstoke: Palgrave Macmillan.
Calabrese Roberts, S. (2012). *The art of iPhonography: A guide to mobile creativity* (2nd ed.). Lewes: Ilex.
Clark, T., Scher, A., Inglis, K., Sarah-Ji, M., Wilson, I. N., et al. (2010). *Expressive photography: The shutter sisters' guide to shooting from the heart*. Abingdon: Focal Press.
Conor, B., Gill, R., & Taylor, S. (2015). Gender and creative labour. *The Sociological Review, 63*(1), 1–22.
Cross, K. (2014). Training the eye of the photographer: The education of the amateur. *Visual Studies, 29*(1), 68–79.
Cross, K. (2015). The lost of found photography. *Photographies, 8*(1), 43–62.
Cross, K. (2016). Memory, guardianship and the witnessing amateur in the emergence of citizen journalism. In M. Baker & B. Blaagaard (Eds.), *Citizen media and public spaces: Diverse expressions of citizenship and dissent* (pp. 225–238). Abingdon: Routledge.
Ekinsmyth, C. (2011). Changing the boundaries of entrepreneurship: The spatialities and practices of UK 'mumpreneurs'. *Geoforum, 42*(1), 104–114.
Ekinsmyth, C. (2013a). Mothers' business, work/life and the politics of 'mumpreneurship'. *Gender, Place and Culture, 21*(10), 1230–1248.

Ekinsmyth, C. (2013b). Managing the business of everyday life: The roles of space and place in 'mumpreneurship'. *International Journal of Entrepreneurial Behaviour and Research, 19*(5), 525–546.

Fantone, L. (2007). Precarious changes: Gender and generational politics in contemporary Italy. *Feminist Review, 87*(1), 5–20.

Friedan, B. ([1963]1971). *The feminine mystique*. London: Victor Gollancz.

Gill, R. (2007). *Technobohemians or the new Cybertariate? New media workers in Amsterdam after the web*. Amsterdam: Institute of Network Cultures.

Gill, R., & Pratt, A. (2008). In the social factory? Immaterial labour, precariousness and cultural work. *Theory Culture & Society, 25*(7–8), 1–30.

Gómez Cruz, E., & Meyer, T. E. (2012). Creation and control in the photographic process: iPhones and the emerging fifth moment of photography. *Photographies, 5*(2), 203–221.

Hardt, M., & Virno, P. (Eds.). (1996). *Radical thought in Italy: A potential politics*. Minneapolis: University of Minnesota Press.

Hesmondhalgh, D., & Baker, S. (2011). *Creative labour: Media work in three cultural industries*. London: Routledge.

Hollingsworth, J. (2016). *The joy of iPhotography: Smart pictures from your smart phone*. London: Ilex Press.

Jay, B. (1999[1971]). In praise of the snapshot. In D. Brittain (Ed.), *Creative camera: Thirty years of writing* (pp. 44–45). Manchester: Manchester University Press.

Kuhn, A. (1991). Remembrance. In J. Spence & P. Holland (Eds.), *Family snaps: The meanings of domestic photography* (pp. 17–25). London: Virago.

Kuhn, A. (2002). *Family secrets: Acts of memory and Imagination* (new ed.). London and New York: Verso.

Lazzarato, M. (1996). Immaterial labour. In P. Virno & M. Hardt (Eds.), *Radical thought in Italy: A potential politics* (pp. 133–147). Minneapolis: University of Minnesota Press.

Leadbeater, C., & Miller, P. (2004). *The pro-am revolution: How enthusiasts are changing our economy and society*. London: Demos. Retrieved April 21, 2017 from https://www.demos.co.uk/files/proamrevolutionfinal.pdf

Littler, J. (2013). The rise of the 'yummy mummy': Popular conservatism and the neoliberal maternal in contemporary British culture. *Communication, Culture and Critique, 6*(2), 227–243.

Luckman, S. (2015). *Craft and the creative economy*. Basingstoke: Palgrave Macmillan.

McRobbie, A. (1998). *British fashion design: Rag trade or image industry?* London: Routledge.

McRobbie, A. (2007). Top girls: Young women and the post-feminist sexual contract. *Cultural Studies, 21*(4–5), 718–737.
McRobbie, A. (2010). Reflections on feminism, immaterial labour and the post-Fordist regime. *New Formations, 70*, 60–76.
McRobbie, A. (2013). Feminism, the family and the new 'mediated' maternalism. *New Formations, 80*, 119–137.
Miller, C. (2014). *The citizen journalist's photography handbook: Shooting the world as it happens*. Lewes: Ilex.
Nagar, T. (2012). *The new street photographer's manifesto*. Lewes: Ilex.
Roberts, J. (2008). The amateur's retort. In R. Rugoff (Ed.), *Amateurs* (pp. 15–24). San Francisco: CCA Wattis Institute of Contemporary Art.
Rubinstein, D., & Suis, K. (2008). A life more photographic: Mapping the networked image. *Photographies, 1*(1), 9–28.
Skeggs, B. (1997). *Formations of class and gender: Becoming respectable*. London: Sage.
Spence, J. (1986). *Putting myself in the pictures: A political personal and photographic autobiography*. London: Camden Press.
Taylor, S. (2010). Negotiating oppositions and uncertainties: Gendered conflicts in creative identity work. *Feminism & Psychology, 21*(3), 354–371.
Taylor, S. (2015). A new mystique? Working for yourself in the neoliberal economy. *Sociological Review, 61*(S1), 174–187.
Taylor, S., & Littleton, K. (2012). *Contemporary identities of creativity and creative work*. Farnham: Ashgate.
Terranova, T. (2000). Free labor: Producing culture for the digital economy. *Social Text, 18*(2 63), 33–58.
Villi, M. (2015). 'Hey, I'm here right now': Camera phone photographs and mediated presence. *Photographies, 8*(1), 3–22.
Walkerdine, V. (1991). Behind the painted smile. In J. Spence & P. Holland (Eds.), *Family snaps: The meaning of domestic photography* (pp. 35–45). London: Virago.
Wilson, J. A., & Chivers Yochim, E. (2015). Mothering through precarity: Becoming mamapreneurial. *Cultural Studies, 29*(5–6), 669–686.

Karen Cross is a Senior Lecturer at the Department of Media, Culture and Language, University of Roehampton, London, UK. Her recent research focuses mainly on the topic of photography and social media, including the emotional, psychological, and memorial dynamics of new forms of digital labour that constitute the social relational field of new media.

Creative Labour, Before and After 'Going Freelance': Contextual Factors and Coalition-Building Practices

Frederick Harry Pitts

Introduction

The work that takes place in design and other creative industries possesses many of the characteristics of what thinkers in the Italian postoperaist tradition call 'immaterial labour' (Lazzarato, 1996). For these thinkers (e.g. Hardt & Negri, 2004: 107–109), immaterial labour is the 'new normal' of contemporary work insofar as it holds a 'hegemonic'—and not necessarily numerical—dominance within capitalist production akin to the position of factory labour at the time Marx was writing his *Capital* (1990). Postoperaists suggest that the spontaneous, autonomous and ephemeral creativity of this labour causes a crisis in the capacity of capitalism to measure work and the value it creates, inspiring a revolutionary vision of a postcapitalist or postwork future incipient within the present.

F.H. Pitts (✉)
Department of Management, School of Economics, Finance & Management, University of Bristol, Bristol, UK

This immaterial labour is exemplified by creative labour in the creative industries and also creativity as more broadly valorised in the 'gig' or 'sharing' economies. By illustrating the trends and tendencies ascribed to immaterial labour, work in the creative industries epitomises employment transformations on which the future is said to hinge. In a study of creative workers presented here, I will specifically look at freelancing—an increasingly common form of work (ILO, 2015)—in order to critically reflect on and contest some of these claims made about immaterial labour. In particular, I will focus on freelancers working in graphic design, branding, and advertising.

The kind of work that takes place in design, branding and advertising is specifically celebrated as an archetypal example of immaterial labour (Fumagalli, 2011, cf. Pitts, 2015a). It manipulates symbols and attaches meaning to goods and services in pursuit of commodity exchange. Due to its reliance upon ephemeral and unquantifiable qualities, such as creativity, communication and cognition, theorists of immaterial production including Hardt and Negri (2001) have suggested that this kind of labour and the value that it creates are essentially immeasurable and pose the possibility of capitalism's collapse and overthrow (see Pitts, 2016a for a critique). In its association with this immaterial character, creative labour is cast as self-organised and self-valorising, and productive beyond the capacity of capital to capture it.

This chapter will contest this ascription of immanent self-organisation and self-valorisation by situating freelance creative work within a situation of struggle in which institutional factors influence the movement from formal to freelance employment and, by degrees, constrain and control the creativity of those involved. Examination of these contextual factors highlights a criticism that I have made elsewhere of the postoperaist approach to immaterial labour (Pitts, 2016b). This is that thinkers in this tradition extrapolate from microscopic changes in how we work to wider changes in capitalism as a whole. I argue that this takes a myopic stance with reference to labour, seeing it entirely apart from its imbrication in wider social relations and social forms that both precondition the labour process and ultimately arbitrate its results in the sphere of exchange. Market-mediated factors bear as much determination over the form of work as the purportedly immanent desires of workers themselves—and around this tensions and conflicts circulate, the practical responses to which I explore later in the chapter.

Theoretical foundations

This chapter comes at an interesting time when the celebration of labour's spontaneous productiveness and the unencumbered 'creativity of desire' we find in Hardt and Negri dovetails with some of the same ideas through which capital understands itself in popular discourse around the creative economy. We see a fresh uptake of the same ideas in the present day, with a number of bestselling books using a similar perspective to sell radical ideas in rational forms to policymakers around the post-work potential of the 'gig' or 'sharing' economies and the move to a supposed postcapitalist society, the beginnings of which co-exist within the shell of the present (e.g. Mason, 2015, cf. Pitts, 2015b). By examining the claims made in the contested literature of postoperaismo and its forerunner, operaismo, about changes in labour and the forms of class composition and conflict they imply, we can illuminate the assumptions that undergird a growing uptake of these ideas in the spheres of politics, policymaking and popular debate (Dinerstein, Taylor, & Pitts, 2016).

The postoperaist approach of Hardt and Negri, among others, differentiates itself from the early operaismo of its adherents by seeing liberation arising not from an antagonistic relationship with labour but through that labour itself. By seeing labour under capitalism sowing the seeds of its own liberation, every development in capitalism is met with an unremitting positivity (see Pitts, 2016b). Operaismo, however, is more circumspect, its theoretical influence having long passed over, continuities outweighed by discontinuities, into postoperaismo. An operaist analysis of changes in labour relevant to this piece still circulates, however, and has recently been applied to freelancers by one of the founding fathers of the movement, Sergio Bologna (2007; Bologna & Banfi, 2011). It is this application we will draw upon here. This work lay untranslated into English at the time of writing, with the publication of a monograph forthcoming (Bologna, 2017). As such, the English translation cannot be fully taken account of in this chapter, which relies instead on the translated passages given in Marco Boffo's excellent introduction to the works in *Historical Materialism* journal (2014). Bologna gives a brief account, in English, of the origins of the work in a recent chapter, but little substantial detail (2013).

As Boffo (2014: 428) outlines, in his most recent work, Bologna, a flagbearer for the more antagonistic politics of operaismo, 'debunks the proclamations of a new organisation of capitalism [...] characterised by greater freedom and autonomy for workers' found in the work of Negri and other postoperaists. He does so though a focus on 'second-generation autonomous work' by which it is meant self-employed and freelance labour falling under a specific set of juridical relationships (Boffo, 2014: 429). The revolutionary 'novelty' attached to supposedly new ways of working by theorists like Negri, Bologna's analysis suggests, ignores the specific nature of the 'constraints and opportunities faced by the second-generation autonomous work-force in the processes of self-protection, representation of its own interests, and coalition-building' (Boffo, 2014: 430, cf. Pitts, 2016a). The posing of a 'social worker' engaged in 'immaterial labour' as the key social subject of contemporary capitalism elides how the forms of struggle engaged in by workers still come up against the same factors and forms of action as the earlier 'mass worker', to which, Bologna suggests, the always-already liberated 'immaterial labourer' is posed as an alternative only to conveniently hide from the difficulties associated with traditional modes of mobilisation in a new economy (Boffo, 2014: 428).

The contemporary economy witnesses the institution of contractual flexibility partly owing to an attempt to 'eradicate' the 'conditions for coalition-building' among workers. But, for Bologna, this flexibility is also itself 'deliberately pursued by workers to safeguard autonomy and independence, and to reconcile working life with care-activities' (Boffo, 2014: 432). This autonomy and independence has, Bologna suggests, led researchers to 'neglect' how coalitions between freelancers are and can be built (Bologna, quoted in Boffo, 2014: 434). Freelancers, treated as independent firms in themselves, enter not into typical contracts of employment but commercial contracts of service provision for a fee and not a wage. With this relationship comes an absence of all the normal benefits and entitlements, such as sick pay and pensions, that attend a formal contract of employment. Thus, the bases for labour organisation and coalition-buildings are radically different from those experienced by the Fordist worker, for instance. However, for Bologna, analyses of immaterial labour neglect the material and contractual forms into which contemporary workers enter, and the possible grounds for organisation and antagonism they establish (Boffo, 2014: 434). Indeed, we might attribute this to a pervasive optimism that sees the transformations in labour themselves, and the modes of capitalist development they determine, completing the work of human liberation immanently, expressing struggle as a matter of course rather than an external force fighting for it. Here, we explore the potential and actual dimensions of this struggle as it applies to creative labourers in their transitions into and out of freelance working lifestyles, in resistance to rather than compliance with the capitalist determination of their creative work.

In considering struggle, I assume a theoretical position informed by John Holloway's conceptualisation of creativity as 'human doing' denied in the abstract forms of value to which it is subject in capitalist society (2002, 2010; see also Tischler, 2005). Rather than something realised in the present, as both postoperaist accounts and mainstream celebrations like that of Richard Florida (2002) suggest, creativity is seen as something potential but denied, and therefore subject to struggle. This is waged on the part of employers, to control and cajole it to the ends of profit and valorisation, which entails stifling it within reasonable limits, to the point of what Nitzan and Bichler call 'sabotage' (2009).[1] But it is also waged on the part of employees to secure the conditions for the pleasurable and fulfilling exertion of their creative desire even within the rubric of the wage relationship. By following Hesmondhalgh and Baker (2008, 2011) in characterising the work that takes place in the creative industries as 'creative labour', we can highlight the imbrication of creative activity in the context of capitalist valorisation and accumulation, in which we situate it in the first part of the case study below. Looking at it as creative labour allows access to the conflict and struggle that ensues around exploitation and working conditions in the creative industries (Gill & Pratt, 2008; Ross, 2008). Applying this to freelancing, we can see the search for independent working lifestyles as itself a form of struggle to secure the basis for unalienated creativity, and therefore freelance work as what Nicole Cohen (2012) calls a 'site of struggle' more generally, including at the level of the 'coalition-building' considered in the closing parts of the case study that follows.

The research project

My analysis draws upon data collected over the course of 33 semi-structured interviews with people working in graphic design, branding and advertising agencies in the UK and the Netherlands. Twenty-one of these interviews were with formal employees. Twelve of these interviews are with freelancers. Kuipers (2014) describes interviewing as the 'obvious method for studying cultural intermediaries'. It offers an 'open-ended approach and richer data' than, say, a survey. Furthermore, it allows informants to 'give their own account of their lives and their activities', from which researchers can gauge feelings, meanings and evaluations of life and work. But, moreover, it applies specifically to workers in the creative industries in that the method draws upon 'conversation[s] in which meanings and values are discussed, dissected and co-produced'. My approach sought to provoke the participant into actively engaging with those occasions on which their expectations and self-understandings of their vocation were confounded and upended by workplace practices of measurement, valuation and control, and the alternatives they desired and accessed by means of 'going freelance' and creating new forms of collective activity as independent workers.

Competition and decomposition

A number of contextual factors underlie the movement from formal employment to freelance working arrangements among the creatives interviewing in this study. In turn, the movement itself participates in these processes. The research took place at a time where, as one participant put it, 'the industry has expanded massively' (Interview with designer conducted February 2014). But with this expansion comes added pressures.

Amid intensified competition, there is some evidence of declining fee income in the design sector. Moor and Julier (2009) quote figures which show a long-term decrease in fee income, despite a steady level of designers and design firms over the same period. These figures suggest that, while design firms are becoming more productive due to greater efficiency, quicker turnaround and technological advances, the benefit of this increasing productivity is being passed on to clients rather than felt directly by the companies themselves. As the clients seek to claw what they can from the process, agencies lose out. There was general consensus that, post-recession, clients were more constrained in what they could spend, but expected the same level of service, so that agencies 'end up trying to deliver the same quality of work as people have been doing for the last twenty years', but, owing to the client having less cash to spend, trying to match this standard 'in a much shorter time', said one designer. Companies were merely trying to 'keep up appearances' in any way they could, without the monetary means to do so (Interview with designer conducted February 2014).

As budgetary constraints take hold, agencies swim in a client pool where the room to compete is reducing. This intensifies competition within the creative sector, dovetailing with a handful of other trends in its development. Participants testified to a general fragmentation in the creative industries. Big agencies break down into smaller ones. Employees break away to go independent, either as freelancers or in small enterprises with others. Other employees face redundancy, only to be hired back as freelancers by the same company that sacked them—an upmarket version of full-time staff being moved onto zero-hours contracts. There is a growing specialisation of creative tasks, facilitated by the ability to search for freelancers offering specific creative skills online. Specialisation has accelerated due to the informationalisation of recruitment via the Internet. There are sites 'for freelancers to find work, and for clients to put projects up' (Interview with freelance designer conducted May 2014). This allows further specialisation in the sector, as clients 'can search a massive pool of freelancers and […] find someone who can specialise in what they need' rather than recruit an agency for full-spectrum service. An expansion of the freelance sector expresses the breakdown in company size, as fixed staff decrease in favour of a constantly circulating satellite workforce that service the constellation of small firms in the sector. As a result, there are 'not many' big agencies left (Interview with freelance designer conducted July 2014). They are getting 'smaller and 'smaller'.

The proliferation of agencies, studios and freelancers that occurs by virtue of this fragmentation creates an added burden of competition in the sector, specifically for those medium-sized firms who find themselves squeezed between the big shareholder-owned corporates and one-man-bands working with loose networks of freelancers attracting work through the web with few other overheads. The same participant explained this dynamic thus:

> there's a lot of squabbling over the scraps at the very bottom, so you've got one or two man studios doing the odd bits because you know their overheads are low, they're able to hit some of these clients and also they're winning some quite good ones because they'll go to the biggest studios, who've got massive overheads, and they're like 'we're eighty pounds an hour', well, the guy down there can do it for twenty pounds an hour, and the guy down there's still making a profit because he's just in his bedroom, um, so it gets difficult […].

The added competitiveness produced by this tendency towards fragmentation in the sector induced agencies to sell themselves short seeking work, by pitching lower than a job will cost in order to secure projects from potential clients, or overdelivering on an agreed budget at a loss to keep a client for future work. As we shall see, this is a crucial influence in creating the kind of negative working conditions creatives seek to escape in 'going freelance'.

The imperative to overdeliver is fuelled by the rate of unsuccessful pitches, which is high for a variety of reasons. In a constrained economic climate where competition between firms for scarce business is intense, clients are cagey about the budget they are working with. As a designer at Company 1 told me, agencies will 'work up a scheme' for work totalling £20,000, only to find the company has half that to spend (Interview with designer conducted January 2014). But, moreover, in a competitive sector, there is a finite amount of work to go around, and the entry of lower-cost design solutions through the Internet-driven 'gig economy' has made it easier for established agencies to be undercut. In an economic climate where companies across the board are seeking to cut costs, potential clients will use the pitch as a chance to gather ideas from more skilled and expensive firms only to redistribute the insights their pitches contain to lower-cost agencies able to implement the concepts already delivered for free (Interview with Managing Director conducted November 2014). This dovetails, then, with tendencies towards fragmentation and competition, as upstart studios steal work from under the noses of big design firms. Freelancers, and their ability to take scraps of work from bigger studios, are central to this. Ironically, the pressure this puts upon agencies actually motivates employees to seek freelance work as an alternative, as the constraints and pressures at the pitching end make work less pleasurable.

As one designer at Company 4 told me, 'I've seen friends in this industry really be put under pressure for pitches when they have 48 hours to turn around a really ridiculously amazing pitch and they need the work and other agencies are fighting them because they need the work and the budget becomes narrower' (Interview with designer conducted July 2014). The pressures at this end of the process then impinge adversely on the creative labour performed once the plan and price are set in place post-pitch. A creative director at Company 2 explained how, when the company did 'overdeliver for the client in order to get more work out of them in the future', the intensity of work and the extent of working hours would increase, as the agency tried to do as much as they could within the remit of an insufficient budget (Interview with Creative Director conducted March 2014). Interestingly, this situation arises partly because of fragmentation that itself owes to freelancers breaking away from agencies precisely because of these conditions, a contradictory and destructive self-fulfilling prophecy concealed underneath the surface appearance of a mere change in contractual status governed by a legal framework geared towards the sublation of open antagonism. What is in fact the active struggle for unalienated creative activity appears as—in the form of a real appearance—a shift in the legal relationship between equal parties.

The search for freedom

What all this shows is that freelancers participate in a decomposition of the design sector, and take advantage of it to break away, usually tiring of formal employment at agencies and seeking a greater degree of independence and specialisation. Wearying of being asked to subordinate their creative impulses to organisational demands, they escape in order to commit themselves to a specific aspect of their work that they particularly enjoy. In the process, they often sell their services back to the same company that they broke away from, for better pay and a more desirable job specification. The range of tasks they perform narrows, and they are hired on the basis of this specialised knowledge. Meanwhile, the other parts of the more comprehensive array of tasks they completed formerly will be, in theory, picked up by other freelancers making the same move. One participant, for instance, expressed this situation well when he recounted how he first decided to work full-time as a freelancer. Agencies were not recruiting the strategic specialism he offered. It was too specific, and not worth the outlay on a permanent post. As a result, he resolved that he could pick up work on this specific, smaller basis by going freelance and servicing the needs of many creative agencies rather than seeking formal employment with one such agency (Interview with freelance strategist conducted June 2014). Another drew the distinction between his younger self, who 'want[ed] to do everything', and his present self, focused on a narrow specialism. 'For the other things', he said, they can 'ask another freelancer' (Interview with freelance designer conducted June 2014).

The search for freedom here presents itself as a form of resistance against the stultifying effects wrought upon creativity by the quantitative rule of the workplace—even though, as we have seen, and as I show elsewhere (Pitts, 2016c), workers quite often end up subsumed under it once more. The specialisation and fragmentation of the sector sparked by the exodus of formal employees as freelancers has implications for how they organise to secure better conditions for the exertion of the creative activity they have prioritised in going freelance in the first place. By placing freelancers in competition with one another for a series of commercial contracts in a context of market constraints, the building of practical and political solidarity becomes an uphill task.

Competition among freelancers has accelerated due to the informationalisation of recruitment via the Internet. For one participant, the Internet provides a means of extending the search for jobs beyond one's immediate locale (Interview with freelance designer conducted May 2014). There are sites 'for freelancers to find work, and for clients to put projects up'. This allows further specialisation of freelance work, as clients 'can search a massive pool of freelancers and [...] find someone who can specialise in what they need'. This specialisation fragments not only the freelance sector but the experience of work among the freelancer community. The variety of different client relationships, working patterns and contractual arrangements introduces considerable internal differentiation and fragmentation with the freelance workforce. Even the career trajectory of one freelancer will feature multiple forms and experiences of work. This fragmentation is exemplified in the different self-understandings of the freelancers in this study. Some freelancers see themselves as a firm or small business. Others collaborate with fellow freelancers in small, temporary teams that constitute mini-businesses in themselves. Many freelancers in the study see themselves as entrepreneurs, with a creative identity forged in many side-projects, all contributing towards an outwardly sellable self. This variation, forged from fragmentation of the freelance workforce through specialisation and competition, makes organising for alternatives very difficult. But, as we see, a growing 'guild' mentality mediates the individual within a loose and shifting network of collectivities.

Coping strategies

A greater degree of competition between freelancers, dovetailing with a wider fragmentation and specialisation of design and design work, makes collective relations much harder. One participant had seen members of his 'network' walk away with 'his' clients after pushing work their way (Interview with freelance designer conducted June 2014). This occurred twice, he said. This exemplifies the level of competition among freelancers for the jobs available. Although most freelancers did not struggle to get work, there is a hierarchy, both of kinds of work in terms of quality and price, and of the freelancers themselves and the type of jobs they can access. The participant in particular felt the pressure from fellow freelancers who could work for €60 an hour rather than the €100 that he asks. But he considers the latter the value of his work. His conundrum is that, if he drops down to €60 to compete, the next time he works for the client, that will be the going rate. He sells himself on the basis that he costs €100 an hour because what he does is worth €100 an hour. The influx of younger, more eager rookie freelancers into the market exerts this kind of downward pressure on rates, in what becomes, in effect, a race to the bottom that freelancers rely on their profile and prestige to resist. Another participant was moving away from freelance work for this reason. There is a 'bunch of young people willing to do it for less money', and this means 'you can only go so far' (Interview with freelance Creative Director conducted July 2014).

This competitive scenario suggests that the creative will bends itself to money. The freelancer, after all, subsists on a commercial contract rather than a formal contract of employment (Boutang, 2011: 142, 153). This makes open competition a feature of a free market rather than of the employment relationship. In the latter, solidarity is possible. The monopolisation of overtime by one worker in a factory runs up against the need for collective strength against management. But, among freelancers, this collective sensibility runs up against their status as service providers competing in the open market. This subordinates their creative identity to money. Their creative identity expresses itself through a market relation that inhibits their ability to relate to fellow freelancers. Successful attempts to group together via networks, co-working spaces, or professional guilds are achieved in spite of this economic basis.

Networks, professional bodies and co-working spaces constitute coping strategies to deal with the isolation and atomisation of freelance existence. One participant explained that he enjoyed the balance of doing a few days with a client, as it broke up the solitude of working alone and gave 'the benefit of a full-time job' insofar as it felt as if he had 'mates there' (Interview with freelance designer conducted May 2014). For another, getting a freelance stint at an agency was 'like coming home' (Interview with freelance designer conducted June 2014). However, more often than not, this sociality manifests differently than desired. It is common for freelancers to feel like an eternal 'new guy', going from one job to the next without ever really fitting in. One must connect with the temporary peer group encountered with each job. As the latter participant suggests, it is necessary to build rapport so as to secure future work. But this pressure to connect conflicts with the temporariness of the situation, and the more banal feeling that one does not really want to make friends with every person one sits next to. Put simply, freelancers are forced to be social in ways not of their choosing—a state of affairs familiar to any worker, ultimately. The social rhythm established more autonomously in, say, a co-working space or networking drinks is different to the social rhythm demanded of them in client workplaces. It beats to a different drum.

Alongside the Internet as a tool for connecting with clients, networking is used as a means by which potential jobs are passed around peer groups of freelancers and employees from creative agencies. A cycle of events such as 'network drinks' situate these networks in a face-to-face setting, but one's 'network' is also a more distant, virtual relationship. Participants talk about their 'network' as a vital resource that can be drawn upon and accessed for opportunities and support. It is even spoken of as something that others would be keen to access, but which remains sealed to those involved. In this way it exemplifies something like a guild mentality operating within the freelance community.

This guild mentality expresses itself best in the range of professional groupings the freelancers involved in the study belong to. One is a web platform that brings together freelancers in the Netherlands to promote themselves to potential clients. It is conceived as a collective through which freelancers work together in order to advance themselves as individuals. Similarly, professional associations have sprung up for the different specialisms of the creative professions: strategists, account planners, branding consultants and designers. These offer an opportunity to network and gain advice on pricing, legal matters and copyright issues. One participant chose a professional body not so much for its direct relevancy to their own professional identity, but based on the kinds of job role it represented for other people. It provided an opportunity to meet account planners who would then allocate work for the agencies at which they are employed (Interview with freelance strategist conducted June 2014). 'Networking' with planners can be a lucrative time investment for freelancers.

If they play their cards right, the freelancer will be top of the planner's contact list when the agency is short of staff or they need a last-minute push to meet a deadline.

Here, the brave new world of social media and information and communications technology (ICT) connectivity is no substitute for old-fashioned face-to-face interaction. This demonstrates why freelancers seek out more physical, rather than virtual, means for connecting with one another. One such method is the establishment of co-working spaces with other freelancers. For one participant, co-working spaces 'catalyse [...] creativity' by bringing creatives together (Interview with freelance strategist conducted June 2014). Collectivising is often for professional, guild-style reasons, but here it is in service to creativity itself—as a force nurtured away from, and in the gaps between, the chaotic conditions of the commercial relationship of individual creative freelancers with their client businesses. It operates to a different rhythm. At the co-working spaces freelancers fall into more traditional rhythms. They tend to have lunch together. This differs from agencies, the co-working space providing a structure more attuned to sociality and collectiveness.

Co-working spaces, according to one participant, allow freelancers to concentrate on the creative aspects of their work (Interview with freelance designer conducted June 2014). Their co-workers comment on work, collaborate with one another, encourage the pursuit of creative impulse, and sit and discuss work openly and freely over lunch. This is seen by this participant as being a productivity-raising measure. It relates to a conception of productiveness that differs from the one that structures the experience of working to the rhythms of agency or company workplaces. Rather than 'freelance factories', then, where independent creatives assemble to self-discipline themselves into the productive rhythms of business, they point towards a different possibility. Agencies have 'big offices' where 'everyone is on the hour', and there is no other motivation than 'the money that they need'. Co-working spaces, for the latter participant, differ radically. The motivation—temporarily—becomes creative production rather than fidelity to the hours system. And, instead of a 'freelance factory' where individuality and sociality are stifled under the forces of hierarchy and organisation, freelancers in co-working spaces are both 'equal and independent', as one designer put it (Interview with freelance designer conducted July 2014). Thus, the pursuit of creativity is attached to a wider political goal, of what, as we shall see, Bologna correctly identifies as self-determination and egalitarianism.

Conclusion

We should see this search for an alternative in light of the inability for creatives to truly escape the confines of the workplace in their transition to freelance work. The infrastructure of information and communication technologies (ICTs) both renders freelance creatives mobile and subjects them to new forms of measurement and control that mandate their subsumption within the regimes and routines of the workplace, even if at arm's length. This generates antagonisms around which freelancers can organise on the basis of a second aspect, also related to ICTs. This is that the dispersed connectivity and mobility of freelance work enabled by ICTs facilitates the formation of what Bologna calls new 'dynamics of sociality' (quoted in Boffo, 2014: 436). In this study, the formation of professional networks for finding and sharing work, and the migration of freelancers to shared 'co-working spaces' as an alternative to agency and client workplaces, are the key manifestations of these dynamics. Interestingly, each of these aspects challenges the simplistic characterisation of technology as the determining influence. As we shall see, the first is conditional on the composition of social relations in the workplace, and the contextual economic imperatives placed upon these relations by wider factors of profit, valorisation and accumulation. And, in the second, the role of technology is secondary to the formation of new social relations that stress the tangible and face-to-face, contrary to the radically communicative connectivity that techno-utopians like Mason (2015) ascribe to new revolutionary subjects such as the 'networked individual'.

The new forms of being together and belonging generated by freelancers in the case study cannot recapture the conditions on which workers' movements of the past mobilised, which operated around coalitions Bologna characterises as 'within the workplace, among people carrying out the same tasks' with 'the same working hours' and 'salaries' (Bologna, quoted in Boffo, 2014: 436). These movements organised publicly, with 'meetings tied to a physical place' (Boffo, 2014: 437).

Those circumstances are not immediately available to freelancers. And, Bologna suggests, they exhibit different motivations, towards individualism and entrepreneurship, that defy the desires and aspirations of workers in the past. While this can often result in a simplistic attachment to 'professionalism' as the locus of political mobilisation, Bologna, writing with Banfi, suggests that other models for activity are in emergence. Whereas traditional trade unionism mediates the individual through frameworks of representation, Bologna and Banfi argue that second-generation autonomous workers 'distrust delegation mechanisms and institutional negotiation structures' and hold out little hope for the attainment of collective benefits like welfare provision (Boffo, 2014: 437–438). Thus, they seek alternative ways to reconcile the individual in the collective. They place their trust instead in coalitions 'advancing demands directly related to one's professional activity', in a manner akin, Boffo suggests, to 'medieval guilds', and coalitions that shore up their 'social status' in the form of 'mutual help'. These coalitions seek, on the one hand, some sense of 'organisational belonging' around the guild mentality, and, on the other, a guard against 'the uncertainty of compensation' attendant on freelance work. Thus, the two factors Bologna and Banfi (quoted in Boffo, 2014: 438) class as 'sense of sociality and perception of risk' are central to the nascent forms of coalition-building among freelancers.

The Internet, Bologna and Banfi suggest (quoted in Boffo, 2014: 438), is an instrument of 'struggle in the social demand of a new space of encounter'. As my research suggests, professional networks for job sharing depend on the Internet and, as Bologna notes, act as 'shock-absorbers' to 'tame risk' associated with intermittent work. The Internet strengthens the 'weak ties' that bind the spatial and temporal existences of freelancers on an individual basis (Boffo, 2014: 439). But, the evidence I present here suggests, the coalitions established by freelancers do not reduce to ICTs, and in fact work in spite of this to generate other ways of being and acting together in order to recreate some of the foundations of past pre-Fordist modes of worker mobilisation oriented around craft and guild mentalities. The Internet does not afford the 'physicality' of past coalitions, and this must somehow be reconstructed by freelancers. As such, 'relations of proximity' are reinvented as 'an inescapable instrument of coalition' (Bologna and Banfi, quoted in Boffo, 2014: 439). Bologna and Banfi identify co-working spaces as central to this rediscovery of practical and physical proximity. But they do not simply reconstruct the forms of sociality associated with labour's past. Indeed, as Bologna and Banfi contend, the use of the Internet to bring freelancers together in coalitions of independent workers co-exists with, and gives rise to, 'a need of sociality entirely different' from that to which waged labour has traditionally been taken to relate.

Rather than the establishment of a collective worker capable of generating the utopian 'general intellect' Negri and his fellow travellers conceptually derive from Marx's Fragment on Machines (1973: 704–706, cf. Pitts, 2016b), what this opens out upon are a series of humbler aims associated with the realisation of a stifled creativity: 'physical contact, human relations, and less individualistic instruments and practices to confront the workings of the market' (Boffo, 2014: 439–440). What is at stake here is creativity itself, a quantity repressed and denied in the forms of economic objectivity to which it is subject in the course of its valorisation in labour. The immanent and liberatory creativity attributed to creative labour by accounts influenced by theories of immaterial labour suggests that it is something already realised, and elides the struggle that must be waged for it. Bologna's operaist account, therefore, offers a vital counterweight to postoperaist imaginings of the changing world of work that are gaining increasing currency in the delineation of radical policy responses to the future of capitalism.

Theorisations of the specificity of creative labour under the banner of immaterial labour are a mistaken attempt to get to grips with the dualness of creative activity under capitalism, as something that exists but only does so in the mode of being denied, and struggles to be realised in society where livelihoods are determined by their relationship with capital by means of the wage. If Bologna's 'second-generation autonomous workers' really do constitute the 'best candidates for' the creation of a 'society on new and more humane bases' (Bologna, quoted in Boffo, 2014: 433), exemplified in their 'egalitarianism' and drive for 'self-determination' in search of a greater capacity to pursue their creative desire, this must be fought for. What the analysis presented here suggests is that this status is by no means given, as wishful thinkers would have us believe. Liberation is not inherent in the form of creative labour, freelance or otherwise. Rather, it must be struggled for, and the forms assumed by this struggle are, at present, a work in progress (see Bologna, 2013, and for examples from the UK, Conaty, Bird, & Ross, 2016).

Most of all, it tells us that the 'new normal' of work under capitalism is not inherent or immanent, but fought over and up for grabs. Changes in labour are not sufficient in and of themselves to suggest changes in capitalism as a whole, but exist in tension with factors and imperatives that take hold of working life from outside in the market and elsewhere. Creative labour, operating at the intersection of commodity production and exchange, is well-placed to address the antagonistic compulsions and relationships that constitute the contradictions of contemporary work. Freelance creatives, starting from scratch to craft a new infrastructure of twenty-first century struggle, possess the exciting capacity to leverage their pivotal position in the circulation of commodities to effect a real shift in the 'new normal' of working life. Blowing dust off old analytical and political tools may well be vital for doing so.

Acknowledgements This chapter reports findings of research conducted under two separate grants. The first is as part of PhD research funded by the Economic and Social Research Council [grant number ES/J500015X/1], the thesis resulting from which is drawn upon at various points over the course of this chapter. The second is a three-month Short-Term Scientific Mission funded by EU COST Action IS1202: The Dynamics of Virtual Work. My thanks to the COST Action, especially Ursula Huws, for this support. The STSM took place at Erasmus University Rotterdam, and facilitated my contribution to the research consortium 'Bonding E-Rhythms'. I would like to thank my academic host at Erasmus, Marli Huijer, for her time and support in helping me complete the research. Thanks are also due to the Bath Alumni Fund for the additional funding they provided to support my time in the Netherlands.

Note

1. See Pitts (2016c) for an empirical case study.

References

Boffo, M. (2014). From post- to neo-: Whither operaismo beyond Hardt and Negri? *Historical Materialism, 22*(3–4), 425–528.

Bologna, S. (2007). *Ceti medi senza futuro? Scritti, appunti sul lavoro e altro.* Rome: DeriveApprodi.

Bologna, S. (2013). Workerism: An inside view. From the mass-worker to self-employed labour. In M. van der Linden & K. H. Roth (Eds.), *Beyond Marx: Theorising the global labour relations of the twenty-first century* (pp. 121–143). Leiden: Brill.

Bologna, S. (2017). *Independent work in a postfordist society.* Milan: Mimesis International.

Bologna, S., & Banfi, D. (2011). *Vita da freelance. I lavoratori della conoscenza e il loro future.* Milan: Feltrinelli.

Boutang, Y. M. (2011). *Cognitive capitalism* (trans. E. Emery). Cambridge: Polity Press.

Cohen, N. S. (2012). Cultural work as a site of struggle: Freelancers and exploitation. *tripleC: Communication, Capitalism & Critique, 10*(2), 141–155.

Conaty, P., Bird, A., & Ross, P. (2016). *Not alone: Trade union and co-operative solutions for self-employed workers.* London: Cooperatives UK.

Dinerstein, A., Taylor, G., & Pitts, F. H. (2016). A post-work economy of robots and machines is a bad utopia for the left. *The Conversation*, 23rd May. Retrieved October 29, 2016, from https://theconversation.com/a-post-work-economy-of-robots-and-machines-is-a-bad-utopia-for-the-left-59134

Florida, R. (2002). *The rise of the creative class.* New York: Basic Books.

Fumagalli, A. (2011). Valorization and financialization in cognitive biocapitalism. *Investment Management and Financial Innovation, 8*(1), 88–103.

Gill, R., & Pratt, A. (2008). In the social factory? Immaterial labour, precariousness and cultural work. *Theory, Culture and Society, 25*(7–8), 1–30.

Hardt, M., & Negri, A. (2001). *Empire.* Cambridge, MA: Harvard University Press.

Hardt, M., & Negri, A. (2004). *Multitude.* London: Penguin.

Hesmondhalgh, D., & Baker, S. (2008). Creative work and emotional labour in the television industry. *Theory, Culture and Society, 25*(7–8), 97–118.

Hesmondhalgh, D., & Baker, S. (2011). *Creative labour: Media work in three cultural industries.* London: Routledge.

Holloway, J. (2002). *Change the world without taking power.* London: Pluto Press.

Holloway, J. (2010). *Crack capitalism*. London: Pluto Press.
ILO. (2015). *World employment and social outlook 2015: The changing nature of jobs*. Geneva: International Labour Organization.
Kuipers, G. (2014). Ethnographic research and cultural intermediaries. In J. Smith Maguire & J. Matthews (Eds.), *The cultural intermediaries reader* (pp. 52–63). London: SAGE.
Lazzarato, M. (1996). Immaterial labor. In P. Virno & M. Hardt (Eds.), *Radical thought in Italy* (pp. 133–150). Minneapolis: University of Minnesota Press.
Marx, K. (1973). *Grundrisse*. London: Penguin.
Marx, K. (1990). *Capital*. London: Penguin.
Mason, P. (2015). *Postcapitalism: A guide to our future*. London: Allen Lane.
Moor, L., & Julier, G. (2009). Introduction: Design and creativity. In *Design and creativity: Policy, management and practice* (pp. 1–22). Oxford: Berg.
Nitzan, J., & Bichler, S. (2009). *Capital as power: A study of order and creorder*. New York: Routledge.
Pitts, F. H. (2015a). Creative industries, value theory and Michael Heinrich's new reading of Marx. *tripleC: Communication, Capitalism and Critique, 13*(1), 192–222.
Pitts, F. H. (2015b). Review of Paul Mason, Postcapitalism. *Marx and philosophy review of books*. 4th September. Retrieved September 13, 2015, from http://marxandphilosophy.org.uk/reviewofbooks/reviews/2015/2008
Pitts, F. H. (2016a). A crisis of measurability? Critiquing postoperaismo on labour, value and the basic income. *Capital and Class* [online]. Retrieved October 29, 2016, from http://cnc.sagepub.com/content/early/2016/09/21/0309816816665579.full.pdf+html
Pitts, F. H. (2016b). Beyond the fragment: The postoperaist reception of Marx's fragment on machines and its relevance today. *School of Sociology, Politics and International Studies Working Paper Series*, 2016-02. University of Bristol. Retrieved October 29, 2016, from http://www.bristol.ac.uk/media-library/sites/spais/documents/Working%20Paper%2002_16_FHP.pdf
Pitts, F. H. (2016c). Creativity and power in freelance creative work. In K. Randle & J. Webster (Eds.), *Virtual workers and the global labour market* (pp. 139–159). Basingstoke: Palgrave.
Ross, A. (2008). The new geography of work: Power to the precarious? *Theory, Culture and Society, 25*(7–8), 31–49.
Tischler, S. (2005). Time of reification and time of insubordination. Some notes. In W. Bonefeld & K. Psychopedis (Eds.), *Human dignity: Social autonomy and the critique of capitalism* (pp. 131–143). Aldershot: Ashgate.

Frederick Harry Pitts is Lecturer in Management in the School of Economics, Finance and Management at the University of Bristol. He holds a PhD in Global Political Economy from the Department of Social and Policy Sciences at the University of Bath. A monograph, *Critiquing Capitalism Today: New Ways to Read Marx*, is forthcoming with Palgrave late 2017.

Searching, Sorting, and Managing Glut: Media Software Inscription Strategies for 'Being Creative'

Frédérik Lesage

Introduction: Inscribing creative figures

Critical scholarship in studies of cultural production claims that creativity has been used to redefine cultural work by displacing and masking its previous associations with critical political traditions (Garnham, 2005). For Angela McRobbie (2016), the shift from cultural work to creative work represents a shift towards a more individual economic activity. She describes contemporary politics of creative work as encouraging young people to shed any aspiration to job security or social welfare. Creative work drives young and old to internalise risk and uncertainty as middle class values. Capitalist forms of labour organisation have absorbed artistic critiques of early- to mid-twentieth-century European avant gardes by elevating the artistic career as the template for success in a networked information economy (Boltanski & Chiapello, 2005). The romantic ideal of the free-spirited artist has become a subject for everyone to aspire to and has been used as a model for a new order for cultural work based on short-term projects

---

F. Lesage (✉)
School of Communication, Simon Fraser University, Burnaby, BC, Canada

between enterprising networked individuals. Education and media institutions incite people to 'be creative' through what McRobbie (2016) calls the 'creativity dispositif': 'The creativity dispositif comprises various instruments, guides, manuals, devices, toolkits, mentoring schemes, reports, TV programmes and other forms of entertainment' (pp. 10–11).

The ubiquity of such instruments as part of everyday life renders the creativity dispositif and the imaginary it sustains as a key part of the new normal in cultural, creative, and media work. Media institutions foster narratives of creative visionaries who 'make it' in fields of cultural practice because of their individual passion and talent. Pedagogical institutions blur the boundaries between capitalist and artistic labour. And while business schools have adopted the art school's idea of the artistic spirit, the entrepreneur has become the model art school student (McRobbie, 2016, p. 59). The parallel between both pedagogies is that they encourage students to eschew traditional categories, embrace uncertainty, and model their careers on the 'unpredictable pathway':

> The personal pathways, individualized on the basis of possession of an original portfolio of skills, have an accumulative momentum, which in turn allows us to analyse how short-term, or project-based 'creative' careers develop. (pp. 70–71)

If education and media are instrumental in sustaining imaginaries of the creative as an ideal subject and of creativity as an ideal objective, then the tools of creativity are certainly key objects of the creativity dispositif. The artistic imaginary has always been entangled with its paraphernalia and its spaces for practising culture: the studio, the theatre hall, the gallery, instruments of creation and dissemination, and appreciation.

One of the dimensions that McRobbie (2016) leaves underdeveloped in her critical analysis of the creativity dispositif is how digital tools are integral to its development and reproduction, particularly to sustaining a creative subjectivity. In this chapter, I would like to extend the conceptual construct of the creativity dispositif to an analysis of how it mediates and is mediated by digital technologies, specifically media software; that is, software for creating, editing, and sharing media content and the institutions for designing, marketing, and consuming the software (see Manovich, 2013, p. 24). In particular, I will introduce the concept of 'glut' as a software inscription strategy and then develop a case study of media software that exemplifies the qualities of glut. I will examine three ways in which this strategy is operationalised for the widely used software Adobe Photoshop: its design, its commodification as part of upgrade culture, and its instruction through a just-in-time learning platform. Through this case study, I hope to show how technologies like media software are essential to the creativity dispositif and how they enable and constrain what it means to 'be creative' today.

Glut as dis-ordered order

The instruments of the creativity dispositif shape and are shaped by digital infrastructures that support and sustain political, economic, and cultural flows. We live in a technological society (Barry, 2001) that promotes a conception of innovation that conflates invention and technological change in ways that are inextricably tied to the deployment of creativity discourse:

> Innovation, in turn, is embedded within a broader cultural imaginary that posits a world that is always lagging, always in need of being brought up to date through the intercessions of those trained to shape it: a world, in sum, in need of design. (Suchman, 2011, pp. 4–5)

I do not want to argue that the creativity dispositif is ensconced in or the product of digital technologies. Rather, in this chapter, I will explore how media software has been a crucial means by which cultural production is designed to 'be creative'. Even the most seemingly innocuous tool for cultural production reflects, through its design, beliefs and prejudices stemming from cultural, political, and economic values. If creativity is one such value, then it is likely designed into the tools used to make culture.

I will use the concept of scripts as developed in science and technology studies (STS) (Akrich & Latour, 1992; Suchman, 2007, pp. 187–205) to examine to what extent, and in what ways, creativity is part of media software. This approach means conceiving of technological designs like software as something that different social actors 'inscribe' with traits and qualities, beliefs, and values (e.g., see Born, 1997; Knochel, 2016).

Designers and engineers give meaningful form to the technologies in ways that can be 'read' as instruments (Ihde, 1998, p. 150). Sociotechnical inscriptions, much like texts, generate figures or 'figurations' for action. In this sense, designers and marketers not only create affordances for users when designing media software, but they also generate a material and semiotic model of who acts with/through these affordances. Scholarly research in STS as well as in media studies working with (or in reaction to) this conception of design has convincingly shown that technological scripts do not determine how technologies are read. People who use technologies can develop de- or re-inscriptions that challenge the designer's original intended reading. Therefore, by analysing technological inscriptions and their figurations, and how both are read or reinterpreted, the researcher is able to examine the power dynamics contingent between different social and technological actors involved in mediation.

Inscribing a creative figuration cannot simply trick people into thinking they are being creative. It must enable some form of cultural work that is deemed creative through its design *and* its use. Media software must in some way embody qualities that are consistent with social and technical imaginaries of creativity. Designers of digital technologies draw from creative and technical imaginaries to ensure that software enables the expression of, for example, spontaneity and skill, choice and invention. In this chapter, I will focus on one inscription strategy (or what some in STS would call 'programme') for creativity: *glut*. This strategy entails designing software for cultural production that figure creativity along McRobbie's 'unpredictable pathway': enabling and constraining cultural work as an individual, unpredictable, yet economically grounded activity.

Vannevar Bush's influential 1945 article 'As we may think' in the *Atlantic Monthly* of July 1945 set the tone for the mid-twentieth century's postwar concern with the incredible potential of information and communication technologies.

> There is a growing mountain of research. But there is increased evidence that we are being bogged down today as specialization extends. The investigator is staggered by the findings and conclusions of thousands of other workers—conclusions which he cannot find time to grasp, much less to remember, as they appear.

Bush's solution to tackling this mountain of research was the Memex, 'a sort of mechanised private file and library'. Bush's vision is credited as the inspiration for future digital innovations including the personal computer, the graphical user interface, and the Internet (Barnes, 2000, pp. 355–357). The ironic twist to Bush's vision is that instead of becoming the solution to information surplus, digital technologies inspired by the Memex are now blamed as the primary source of this surplus. Alvin Toffler's 1970 bestselling book *Future shock* popularised this connection as 'information overload'. He predicted that the affordances of digital technology would make it so easy to replicate and disseminate so much information that it would exceed decision-makers' capacity to absorb it and thereby impede their ability to make decisions. The concern for the technological effect of this glut of information has been a recurring theme ever since. David Shenk's 1997 book *Data smog: surviving the information glut*, for example, examines its psychological cost and its link to profit motives. Some have reinterpreted this same infoglut as a necessary evolution of human culture (Wright, 2007), whereas others have attempted to prescribe techniques for dealing with its effects. Kristin Luker (2010), for example, warns aspiring academic researchers that the only way to survive the 'world of info-glut' is to remember the adage 'work smarter, not harder' (p. 93). To critical communication scholar Mark Andrejevic (2013), however, infoglut is tied to capitalist and reactionary interests, who use it to cast 'an equal regard on all objects of data collection' (p. 160), thereby privileging comprehensiveness over simplicity and clarity. He refers to glut as a strategy used by those in power, to dominate by disseminating uncertainty under the semblance of facticity—an attempt to spur the demise of the kind of 'symbolic efficiency' necessary for critical engagement with the world.

Concern for information glut is therefore deeply rooted in digital culture. Infoglut implies an undifferentiated data mass that encapsulates both valuable information and 'infojunk' (Koski, 2001, p. 484). The distinguishing feature of glut is not its quantity per se; there is no magic amount of information that tips it over from comprehensible into glut. Rather, its key feature is that digital data's mass *dis*-order undermines our ability to make it intelligible, to find its stable meaning or worth.

Lev Manovich argues that the way in which the dis-order of digital data undercuts our ability to create narratives is not an accidental outcome of digital media but one of the essential characteristics. If, he claims, 'the world appears to us as an endless and unstructured collection of images, texts, and other data records, it is only appropriate that we will be moved to model it as a database' (Manovich, 1999, p. 81). Using de Certeau's (1984) complementary concepts of strategy and tactic, Manovich argues that digital media, particularly social media platforms like YouTube, have adapted tensions between narrative and database as a design strategy. Social media platform designers strategically organise software in ways that will allow its users to use tactics to customise and change the platform; tactics become a design strategy.

Both Manovich's conception of the digital database and some of the elements of Andrejevic's work on infoglut can be usefully incorporated into a conception of glut as a software inscription strategy. If strategies for designing software are exercised by those in power to impose a proper order, then tactically using the adaptability and open-endedness of software affordances entails working within the proper order for which the design is intended. This re-territorialisation of tactical agency into a set of inscriptions has important implications for power relations. If tactics such as individual customisation are part of the strategic architecture of software, then they are no longer a form of resistance or de-inscription but arguably are part and parcel of a disciplinary technology closer to Andrejevic's conception of infoglut. Glut, when applied to software design, entails a strategy that figures an individual actor who searches, sorts, and manages a dis-ordered order in the (potentially futile) hopes of finding meaning and value. In other words, it generates a disciplinary figure that, upon first reading, seems anathema to a creative figure. However, in the next two sections, I will show how the creativity dispositif is reproduced through glut in the Adobe Photoshop software tool.

Adobe Photoshop's command glut

During the late 1980s and early 1990s, as personal computers and digital imaging software became more popular, cultural practitioners were apprehensive about the changing role of the digital image and also about how to *figure digital image creation*: how to ensure that humans are the ones making 'judgments and choices' (Mitchell, 1992, p. 76). During this same period, new commercial, consumer-oriented software tools began to emerge as the future de facto standards of digital imaging workflows. Since then, these same software tools have become essential for 'daily production of typography, symbols, images, and information systems' (Lupton, 2007, p. 149). Few of these tools are as ubiquitous today as Adobe Photoshop. It has been a mainstay of digital image production workflows in numerous fields of cultural production for more than 25 years.

Photoshop is digital image editing software that packages together thousands of individual commands nested in tool bars and dropdown menus. Its designers originally intended Photoshop 'to be a very powerful and easy-to-use tool for everyone from naïve users to the top of the high end' (John Knoll in Poole, 1991, p. 146; see also Lesage, 2016, p. 224). The number of commands it affords has grown extensively since it was first licensed by Adobe in 1990. It was relatively easy to increase the complexity and sophistication of the software over the years because of the continuing decrease in hardware costs for storing and running digital information, the software's object-oriented architecture, and because it was profitable for Adobe to sell new versions of the software as individual and institutional licences. However, as I argued above, glut as a software inscription strategy is not about increasing quantity so much as it is about creating a 'dis-ordered order'. My goal here is not to ascertain the reason for Photoshop's commercial success but to show how glut is used as an inscription strategy to design the application in ways that figure creativity. If, as argued above, creativity is modelled in part on the 'unpredictable pathway', then glut is a powerful strategy for (dis)ordering cultural production into 'being creative' with Photoshop.

As a starting point for my analysis, I draw from Manovich's (2013, p. 125) attempt to develop a typology for systematically analysing its features and commands. Manovich's formal analysis of its commands focuses on one subset of digital imaging effects, called 'filters'. One of the formal differentiations he initially uses to devise his typology is based on whether individual filters are a simulation of an older medium or whether each represents a new medium itself (p. 129). But Manovich soon abandons this distinction because it does not capture the different meanings of fabrication. Unlike Photoshop filters, older media provide clues about how they work: 'the possibilities of each tool and material were driven by what was meaningful to a particular human sense. A paintbrush could create brushstrokes that had colour, thickness, and shape—properties directly speaking to human vision and touch' (p. 133).

For Manovich, the phenomenological points of reference of earlier media are no longer available in individual Photoshop commands unless they are each encoded with information about their effects. Building on Manovich's work, I would argue that we must extend our analysis from individual commands to how multiple commands combine to enable and constrain creative figurations. To illustrate how this might work, I will examine a different aspect of Photoshop's design and use: colour correction and management.

As mentioned, Photoshop was designed to afford as broad a range of commands for altering digital images as possible. One of Photoshop's key features is therefore that it includes commands that are appropriate for different groups of cultural practitioners: photographers, graphic designers, web designers, prepress specialists, 3D designers, 2D animators, and so on. This is not to claim that Photoshop is superior to other media software for any or all of these disciplines, but that its extensive suite of discrete commands are relevant for some or all of these disciplines. An example of how this wider range of different commands works for various practitioners is how Photoshop affords 'colour correction and management'.

When creating a new document on Photoshop, the software offers the creator a number of choices to determine some key aspects of the document's size and format, including a dropdown menu to determine its 'colour mode'. The creator can choose between modes such as bitmap colour, greyscale, RGB colour, CMYK colour, and lab colour, as well as additional 'advanced' options related to the document's colour settings (the exact number of options will vary, depending on what profiles have been downloaded to the computer in use). Once the document is open, the application affords many different commands for altering the image's colour mode or altering specific aspects of the image's hue, contrast, brightness, and so on—also known as colour correction—in different dropdown menus, toolbars, and windows. These various commands are available to all users without the contextual phenomenological cues discussed by Manovich above. A casual Photoshop user is unlikely to consider most, if not all, of these commands, and is free to simply accept the application's generic 'pre-sets' when creating and editing an image. It is entirely possible to create and share images with Photoshop in ways that leave colour correction and management up to the software. However, specific settings and commands will have implications for specific workflows such as photography, web design, and prepress or video colour correction. For example, a graphic designer may want to ensure that an image's colours will be printed in a particular way with a specific printer, or a web designer may want to ensure that an image is displayed in a particular way on a screen by a web browser.

The ability to identify and properly apply commands related to colour correction and management has become one of the indices of a creator's skill and professionalism with Photoshop. In 23 in-depth interviews conducted with Photoshop users between 2012 and 2014 (see Lesage, 2015), half of the respondents referred to the proper management and/or correction of colour as important markers of an individual's talent and/or expertise, and its absence as a sure sign of unprofessionalism. However, Photoshop affords the opportunity to achieve similar (if not identical) types of colour effects through very different combinations of commands. For example:

> [41:50] … a lot of people use Photoshop and they might know 'levels' [a set of commands for colour correction]. A lot of people use auto-levels and they don't really know how to read a histogram [that accompanies the levels commands]. That's another thing, to be comfortable to read a histogram and know what those peaks of colours mean and to understand where you're clipping it is gonna affect your lights and your shadows. [Steve, photographer working in Vancouver, interviewed in June 2012]

In this case, the photographer being interviewed distinguishes and prioritises a particular feature (histograms for visualising colour intensity) that is included as part of a set of commands for colour correction (levels). But when asked to elaborate in the same interview on how he would teach these techniques to others:

> [44:11] It doesn't mean that it's the right way or the only way. It's the way that works for me but there's 18 different ways to end up with the same results and you need to know what's gonna work best for you. [Steve]

Steve relates a typical account from many of the interviews: that each individual should find their own pathway through the glut of Photoshop commands (Lesage, 2015, p. 103). By providing access to sets of commands with few cues for how to order them through practice, Photoshop figures creativity as individually searching, sorting, and managing large swaths of extraneous commands. A common statement in the Photoshop literature and among those I interviewed is that people only use a certain 'percentage' (10%, 25%) of the commands available. I use the term 'Photoshop ratio' to refer to the vast difference between the total number of commands available in Photoshop and the number of commands an individual actually uses or knows (Lesage, 2015, p. 100). An individual's ability to define and apply his or her own Photoshop ratio stands as a sign of creativity and experience.

Matthew Fuller (2003, p. 143) suggests that one can glean the 'forces and drives' that shape how software is designed by studying how deeply some commands and features are nested within toolbars and menus: 'To many users it is likely that [an] option should be so far down a choice tree that it drops off completely'. Glut turns this depth into a disciplinary technology, placing onus on the individual to sort through and separate the frivolous and unrelated from the valuable. What emerges in this analysis of Adobe Photoshop's design is a creative figuration based on searching, sorting, and managing commands; the pathway through its command glut simultaneously enables and constrains the exercise of human judgement and choices while aligning itself with the individualised 'unpredictable path' espoused by the creativity dispositif.

In the example above, meaning is not only undermined at the level of individual commands, but the individualised dis-ordered path through combinations of commands also undermines the ability to generate collective meaning through shared practice: Steve's way works for him, but he does not believe his approach is necessarily of value to anyone else. But a complete picture of how Photoshop's command glut is inscribed as part of the creativity dispositif requires more than attention to the application's design and use. Steve's approach to using Photoshop is not determined by its design. One of the ways that this dis-ordered entanglement is reinforced is through Photoshop's marketisation as a consumer product. There have been 13 major versions of Photoshop between 1990 and 2013, not including spinoffs and minor upgrades. This 'versioning' approach is consistent with a broader 'upgrade culture' (Dovey & Kennedy, 2006, pp. 52–53), in which cultural production and consumption are subjected to the perpetual threat of technological obsolescence. The constant churn increases the likelihood that the order of commands that one is familiar with has changed and so compels the practitioner to try to keep up with the pace of change as both a consumer and a creative practitioner. As each new version arrives on the market, individuals are faced with questions of if and how to re-engage the same process of searching and sorting to re-learn the application. Adobe's shift in 2013 to a software-as-a-service model (called the Creative Cloud) refined its alignment with upgrade culture even further by providing updates directly through an online subscription service. I have now established two ways in which a dis-ordered order is created with Photoshop: its technical design and its marketisation as a consumer product. A third way in which glut is used to entangle software and cultural practitioners through the creativity dispositif requires that we return to McRobbie's concern with pedagogy.

Lynda.com as just-in-time learning platform

One of the emerging trends in pedagogical technology is 'just-in-time' education (Selingo, 2014): the possibility of learning a specific skill when it is called for without having to commit the time or money required by more traditional forms of education. These digital platforms promise to give their clients personal access to a limitless selection of up-to-date information about countless subjects in a format that fits their schedules. Just-in-time can be characterised as a trend that subscribes to a discourse of self-service—empowering students and giving them greater control over their education through digital infrastructure. This discourse has increasingly gained currency within institutions of higher learning (Pollock, 2003). Just-in-time learning platforms are able to mimic and replicate the individualisation and self-responsibilisation required of the creativity dispositif as defined by McRobbie (2016).

Pedagogy seems like the perfect way to bring meaningful order to Photoshop's command glut. Before the development of proper documentation and its own certification programme, Adobe provided little in terms of instructional documentation to accompany early versions of the software (McClelland, 1993, p. 1). Thousands of third-party product reviews, promotional materials, software demonstration videos, and training manuals have been published to fill that void and continue to supplement the newer Adobe material. With so many different and competing sources of training, it is difficult to clearly distinguish what constitutes formal from informal learning. Learning Photoshop represents a particularly complex entanglement between the creativity dispositif and the technological society. At this same intersection are other emerging for-profit media and technology firms that present transformative technologies as the solution to an under-resourced public education sector that finds it difficult to develop curriculum for Photoshop (Sefton-Green, 1999, p. 142). Education institutions are undeniably also dealing with the challenges presented by upgrade culture.

One just-in-time learning platform for Photoshop is Lynda.com, one of the longest-running providers of just-in-time learning materials for cultural practitioners. Established in 1995, it found initial success in providing web-design training material such as classroom training, books, and instructional videos by mail, before turning to digital platforms for the delivery of its training services. By 2013, Lynda could claim two million members and more than US $100 million in revenue the previous year, while adding 400 new courses per year (Roush, 2013). LinkedIn acquired the platform in 2015 for US $1.5 billion (LinkedIn, 2015). In 2002, it started selling subscription services to all of its videos online. Through its design, Lynda mediates Photoshop's glut as part of the figuration of creativity. However, as will be made clear in the following analysis, how it re-inscribes Photoshop as something to be learned does not necessarily mitigate the glut's dis-ordered order but instead reproduces upgrade culture and the personal pathway through Photoshop commands. To show this, I will provide a basic overview of the platform's architecture, followed by a more detailed examination of its section dedicated to learning Photoshop.

Lynda's online platform is conceived as a data repository for instructional videos. By creating an account with the platform, each client is offered the opportunity to tailor a custom learning programme out of the repository. At the time of writing, it offered 226 categories of courses listed on its main subject webpage (Lynda.com, 2014b), ranging from '2D Drawing' to 'Writing', from 'Business Intelligence' to 'Creativity'. Within these categories are listed a total of nearly 20,000 different courses, with each course containing its own series of individual video clips of various length ranging from approximately 1 minute to more than 10 minutes. Lynda refers to its entire repository of videos as an 'online training library'. This database structure is one of the ways in which Lynda.com replicates the just-in-time self-service discourse. As Lynda Weinman, one of Lynda's founders, explains, 'It's not about what grade you're in, it's not about certification, [...] It's really about needing knowledge and having a resource that will give you that knowledge exactly the way you need it, wherever, whenever, on any device.' (Quoted in Roush, 2013)

Lynda's own course, 'How to use Lynda.com', (2014a) explains how the platform was designed to be used, including demonstrations of how to individually search and sort through the videos. The instructor takes the viewer through a search on the platform with advice such as:

> [1:11] 'So, currently I have 59 results for CSS, and if I switch over to Videos in the filtered by section, now we have over 1600 results for videos. That's a pretty large list. So, you can further narrow down the list of videos by selecting the filter terms under these headings on the left, of Skill Level, Subject, Software, Version, Company, Author, and more options for closed captioning.'

The student is encouraged to filter the ever-expanding repository of videos through category lists, using additional keywords according to personal interests and desires. The platform also provides numerous tools to help track and monitor progress. There exists a growing body of scholarly literature, particularly around YouTube and similar types of video data repositories (see Gehl, 2009 for an excellent example) that develop the idea of curating as a practice for working with these platforms. But the term 'curating' may be problematic in Lynda's case, because it suggests a level of personal control over the data. The videos are labelled within an ordered set of categories but in a way that provides little in terms of re-editing or collective sharing of remixes. Lynda's designers likely have determined an underpinning order for the library, but this order is not revealed to the client, affording instead a categorical order that is contingent on the individual's personal learning path.

Photoshop is not one of the 226 subject categories, but a sub-topic. Although a detailed examination of how Lynda classifies Photoshop is beyond the scope of this chapter, it is instructive to consider how some of the basic elements of the Lynda site mediate it as an object of learning. The main header for Lynda's Photoshop Tutorials and Courses page invites the learner to:

> Watch our expert-taught Photoshop tutorials and learn image editing, retouching, and color correcting for all skill levels. Find out how to use Photoshop shapes and layers, how to retouch photos, and more. (Lynda.com, 2016)

The Photoshop topic is subdivided into: 'Photoshop Version', 'Subject', 'Author', and 'Photoshop Skill Level'. These subcategories connect to other categories beyond Photoshop—for example, it connects to subject categories like graphic design, web design, and photography. From 1 September 2015 to 6 September 2016, the material labelled Photoshop grew from 415 Photoshop courses (made up of a total of 20,809 videos by 70 different authors) to 458 courses (with 22,299 videos by 74 authors). Estimating that the average length of time for each video is 5 minutes, this archive grew from approximately 1734 hours of Photoshop-related material to 1858 hours. Some videos were taken down and others updated during this period, but the total amount continued to climb steadily. Just as with Photoshop commands, it is highly unlikely that all of these videos are relevant to any one individual. Lynda is designed to be too much information, requiring the user to search, sort, and manage according to personal preferences. It represents a classificatory order based on glut through which the learner is invited to advance and develop an 'unpredictable pathway'.

In line with Photoshop's numerous features and continuous upgrades, Lynda's video instructions are continuously edited and updated. Instead of prescribing a limited and clearly defined curriculum, Lynda meets glut with glut. It offers an abundance of video instructions that can be navigated as a personalised self-serve learning path and thereby inscribes a figure of the Photoshop student searching, sorting, and managing glut.

Conclusion: Beyond searching, sorting, and managing to 'be creative'

Any understanding of the new normal for contemporary cultural work, I have argued, requires attending to the ways in which the creativity dispositif is inextricably intertwined with the imaginaries and inscriptions of the technological society. This analysis of Photoshop may lead the reader to think that I am arguing that people who use Photoshop are doomed learners—a group of exhausted, pathological digital foragers forced to try to keep up with its perpetually growing trove of commands. This is not the case. What I set out to analyse here is how media software like Photoshop is designed, sold, and taught using the inscription strategy of glut and how this strategy is the product of the unpredictable pathways prescribed by the creativity dispositif. Although the inscription strategies for ordered dis-order described here do represent a powerful means through which the creativity dispositif is reproduced, it in no way prevents alternatives and tactics of resistance. Although the case study described in this chapter presents Lynda as a platform that perpetuates glut, other media platforms have provided opportunities for creating meaningful exchanges and debate about creative practice with Photoshop (Lesage, 2016). The pursuit of a vigorous critique of what it means to be creative today is only possible if we identify and nurture techno-social arrangements that help us resist and replace inscription strategies such as glut.

References

Akrich, M., & Latour, B. (1992). A summary of a convenient vocabulary for the semiotics of human and nonhuman assemblies. In W. E. Bijker & J. Law (Eds.), *Shaping technology/building society: Studies in sociotechnical change* (pp. 259–264). Cambridge, MA: MIT Press.

Andrejevic, M. (2013). *Infoglut: How too much information is changing the way we think and know*. New York: Routledge.

Barnes, S. B. (2000). Bridging the differences between social theory and technological invention in human-computer interface design. *New Media & Society, 2*(3), 353–372.

Barry, A. (2001). *Political machines: Governing a technological society*. London: Athlone Press.

Boltanski, L., & Chiapello, E. (2005). *The new spirit of capitalism* (G. Elliott, Trans.). London: Verso.

Born, G. (1997). Computer software as a medium: Textuality, orality and sociality in an artificial intelligence research culture. In M. Banks & H. Morphy (Eds.), *Rethinking visual anthropology* (pp. 139–169). New Haven: Yale University Press.

Bush, V. (1945, July). As we may think. *The Atlantic, 176*(1), 101–108. Retrieved November 24, 2016, from http://www.theatlantic.com/magazine/archive/1945/07/as-we-may-think/303881/

De Certeau, M. (1984). *The practice of everyday life* (S. Rendall, Trans.). Berkeley: University of California Press.

Dovey, J., & Kennedy, H. W. (2006). *Game cultures: Computer games as new media*. Maidenhead: Open University Press.

Fuller, M. (2003). *Behind the blip: Essays on the culture of software*. Brooklyn: Autonomedia.

Garnham, N. (2005). From cultural to creative industries: An analysis of the implications of the 'creative industries' approach to arts and media policy making in the United Kingdom. *International Journal of Cultural Policy, 11*(1), 15–29.

Gehl, R. (2009). YouTube as archive: Who will curate this digital Wunderkammer? *International Journal of Cultural Studies, 12*(1), 43–60.

Ihde, D. (1998). *Expanding hermeneutics: Visualism in science*. Evanston, IL: Northwestern University Press.

Knochel, A. D. (2016). Photoshop teaches with(out) you: Actant agencies and non-human pedagogy. *Visual Arts Research, 42*(1), 71–87.

Koski, J. T. (2001). Reflections on information glut and other issues in knowledge productivity. *Futures, 33*(6), 483–495.

Lesage, F. (2015). Middlebroware. *Fibreculture Journal, 25*, 89–114.

Lesage, F. (2016). Reviewing Photoshop: Mediating cultural subjectivities for application software. *Convergence, 22*(2), 215–229.

LinkedIn. (2015, 9 April). LinkedIn to acquire lynda.com. Retrieved November 2, 2016, from https://press.linkedin.com/site-resources/news-releases/2015/linkedin-to-acquire-lyndacom

Luker, K. (2010). *Salsa dancing into the social sciences: Research in an age of infoglut*. Cambridge, MA: London: Harvard University Press.

Lupton, E. (2007). Learning to love software: A bridge between theory and practice. *Artifact, 1*(3), 149–158.

Lynda.com. (2014a). Finding content with the search feature, 4m58s. Updated 7/5/2014, Released 2/21/2011.

Lynda.com. (2014b). All subjects. Accessed at the time of writing. https://www.lynda.com/subject/all

Lynda.com. (2016). Photoshop—Online courses, classes, training, tutorials on Lynda. Retrieved November 5, 2016, from https://www.lynda.com/Photoshop-tutorials/279-0.html

Manovich, L. (1999). Database as symbolic form: Convergence. *International Journal of Research into New Media Technologies, 5*(2), 80–99.

Manovich, L. (2013). *Software takes command*. New York: Bloomsbury Academic.

McClelland, D. (1993). *Macworld Photoshop 2.5 bible*. San Mateo, CA: IDG Books.

McRobbie, A. (2016). *Be creative: Making a living in the new culture industries*. Malden, MA: Polity Press.

Mitchell, W. J. (1992). *The reconfigured eye: Visual truth in the post-photographic era*. Cambridge, MA: MIT Press.

Pollock, N. (2003). The 'self-service' student: Building enterprise-wide systems into universities 1. *Prometheus, 21*(1), 101–119.

Poole, L. (1991). Pictures perfected. *Macworld, 8*(1), 144–151.

Roush, W. (2013, March 28). Knowledge when you need it: Lynda.com and the rise of online education. Retrieved November 5, 2016, from http://www.xconomy.com/national/2013/03/28/knowledge-when-you-need-it-lynda-com-and-the-rise-of-online-education/

Sefton-Green, J. (1999). From hardware to software: The resource problem? In J. Sefton-Green (Ed.), *Young people, creativity and new technologies: The challenge of digital arts* (pp. 138–154). London: Routledge.

Selingo, J. (2014, 21 April). The new lifelong learners. *Slate*. Retrieved December 1, 2014, from http://www.slate.com/articles/technology/future_tense/2014/04/just_in_time_education_is_a_technological_reality_economic_necessity.html

Shenk, D. (1997). *Data smog: Surviving the information glut*. San Francisco, CA: HarperEdge.

Suchman, L. (2007). *Human-machine reconfigurations: Plans and situated actions* (2nd ed.). Cambridge: Cambridge University Press.

Suchman, L. (2011). Anthropological relocations and the limits of design. *Annual Review of Anthropology, 40*(1), 1–18.
Toffler, A. (1970). *Future shock*. New York: Random House.
Wright, A. (2007). *Glut: Mastering information through the ages*. Washington, DC: Joseph Henry Press.

Frédérik Lesage is an Assistant Professor in the School of Communication at Simon Fraser University. His current research interests deal with the vernacular and middlebrow in digital media cultures. His most recent work applies mediation theory to an investigation of how consumer-driven creative digital tools like Photoshop and iOS software development kits are designed and used.

Part II

Digital Working Lives

Negotiating the Intimate and the Professional in Mom Blogging

Katariina Mäkinen

Mom bloggers[1] are mothers who write online blogs about their everyday lives and, in doing so, create interactive collectivities. Contemporary mom blogging is thus a digital practice of 'networked life writing' (Friedman, 2013, p. 9) that concentrates on the intimate and the personal and allows for a sense of congruency and community. While blogging is simply a hobby for many, the commercialisation of the lifestyle blogosphere means that blogging has also become increasingly monetised and can be recognised as a form of micro-entrepreneurship and freelance work. Blogging, then, has become a field of work in which the telling of intimate lives and personal narratives in the 'publicised private' sphere of the Internet is an indispensable part of becoming successful, and in which forms of peer support and building a community are also ways of creating networks of sociality centred around products that can be delivered to companies and advertisers (Taylor, 2016). In this way, mom blogging combines the intimate with the professional in a way that challenges the assumed boundaries between paid work and leisure as well as between paid work and mothering.

K. Mäkinen (✉)
Gender Studies, University of Tampere, Tampere, Finland

© The Author(s) 2018
S. Taylor, S. Luckman (eds.), *The New Normal of Working Lives*, Dynamics of Virtual Work, DOI 10.1007/978-3-319-66038-7_7

In the Finnish language blogosphere, the emergence of mom blogging at a large scale around the turn of the decade coincided with the launch and development of commercial product-placement services targeted at bloggers and owned by big media houses. These services provide easy-access platforms and communities for bloggers concentrating on issues of lifestyle and parenting. Bloggers, most of whom are women, provide content for the platforms. Some of them have an agreement with the commercial service and receive a small monthly compensation for updating their blog. Most professional or semi-professional bloggers, however, gain money through the (more or less) frequent cooperation with business companies. Many have also established their own sites independently of the large commercial services, as this independence is often more profitable for the more popular bloggers. Recently, the emergence of blogging agencies has also provided bloggers with the option to sign up with an agency who acts as a go-between between the bloggers and commercial companies.[2] Although the work of blogging can be profitable and the most successful lifestyle bloggers earn well, the contracts and agreements are often temporary and there are no fixed pay rates, so every deal must be negotiated, either by the blogger herself or by an agency. Income from blogging is thus constantly dependent on varying cooperation opportunities and negotiating power, which in turn is dependent on the popularity of the blog. For the mom bloggers, blogging is often tied to family life, not only in terms of the content of the blog but also in a very concrete sense, as many of them work at home and their work tends to be organised according to the rhythms of everyday family life: blogs are updated when children are sleeping.

Mom blogging in Finland has emerged at a moment in which the mothers of small children, in mainstream political rhetoric, are expected to participate in the labour market, but they are also in a precarious or weak position to do so (Julkunen, 2010, pp. 127–128); the tendencies towards neofamilism (Jallinoja, 2006) and intensive parenting (Faircloth, 2014) put pressure on women to take care of small children at home. Although 'temporary at-home mothering' (staying at home while children are small) has been a prevalent feature of the Finnish women's employment model since the 1990s (Julkunen, 2010, pp. 127–128), the recent introduction of strict austerity measures in Finland has led, for instance, to the dismantling of the universal right to public childcare (Salmi & Lammi-Taskula, 2015) and also to welfare cuts targeted at public childcare services. This development serves to intensify the tension between the call to participate in paid employment, the possibilities of doing so, and the incentives to stay at home. The emergence of freelance writing in the blogosphere can thus be seen to reflect a situation that has become the new normal for mothers of small children: negotiating between these contradicting ideals and demands in the practices of their everyday life, and 'making do' by combining different kinds of precarious part-time jobs and forms of micro-entrepreneurship with varying childcare arrangements.

Most of the successful mom bloggers are highly educated and they often have prior professional experience in journalism, communications, or marketing. Some are on maternity leave or home care allowance[3] and take care of their children at home while working on their blog. Others combine part-time public or private day care with part-time or full-time freelancer work, and some are working full-time in paid employment or as entrepreneurs. Sometimes a blogger's partner is at home with the children. Some bloggers have permanent jobs they can return to after taking childcare leave, whereas others are on childcare leave because there either is no job to which they can return, or they do not want to continue in that job and are looking for other options. Some have already made blogging a part of their 'entrepreneurial lifestyle', in which *lifestyle* and *work* have become inseparable. Indeed, a recurring theme both in the mom blogosphere and in the interviews I have conducted with bloggers is a need to find alternatives to 'life organised by paid employment' through different arrangements of micro-entrepreneurship or freelancer work. This search for alternatives is motivated by the hope that these arrangements will provide a chance to live a more fulfilling life, both professionally and personally (Rokkonen, 2015). Similar to other forms of women's digital micro-entrepreneurship (Luckman, 2015), mom blogging can thus be seen to happen at a crossroads, where the concrete realities of precarity and austerity that make digital micro-entrepreneurship or freelancing a viable option for many (highly educated) women, come together with the aspirations and hopes of escaping paid employment and living an alternative way of life.

It is my intention here to begin to unwrap the 'new normals' of this alternative life as it is made possible through practices of blogging. I will do so by thinking through the characteristics of blogging as work: what it demands from the bloggers and what kind of occupational identities it brings into being. The analysis builds on both interviews with Finnish mom bloggers[4] and the insight I have gained from following the Finnish 'mom blogosphere' closely for several years. In what follows, I will trace some of the complexities and contradictions that mom bloggers encounter in this emerging field of work, and the ways in which they negotiate these complexities as they construct their lives and occupational identities around and through the practices of blogging.

Being professional

Most of the bloggers that I interviewed spend several hours a day writing blog posts, responding to comments, managing the discussion in the comments section, and doing other blog-related work, such as Google optimisation, or photo editing, or negotiating commercial campaigns. Writing a blog post usually takes a couple of hours, and the editing and optimising of posts is also time-consuming. Many of the bloggers answer comments throughout the day, often via their mobile phone. Many have Instagram and Snapchat accounts that they update regularly, sometimes several times a day. Some of the interviewees describe being unable to 'block' thoughts related to blogging, and so their 'editorial mind' constantly surveils the everyday happenings and notices which ones would make great posts. Blogging, then, is not something that is done only in that specific two-hour time slot when children are sleeping; rather, it is something that does demand undisturbed attention for a certain while, but also, as is typical for women's home working (Luckman, 2015; Taylor, 2015), leaks into the everyday and demands almost-constant digital presence as well as continual reflecting and planning.

The bloggers usually have a 'post calendar' or plan made weeks ahead with sketches and ideas of possible blog posts, which makes it easier to do a post if there is little time. Blogging, then, is not necessarily—though it can be—spontaneous or tied to accounts of day-to-day life in the way a journal or an online diary would be. The possibilities for timing posts on the publishing platforms means that posts are not always published straight after they are written. A week's worth of blog posts might be written in one day and then timed to be published in the following days or at the most optimal moment for a certain post. The bloggers whom I interviewed had expectations for themselves about how often they should publish a post (e.g., six or seven times a week), and when travelling they might also time posts to appear, so as not to 'abandon' the blog for a long time. This temporality, which is very much scheduled and consciously managed, means that the bloggers are keenly aware of the need to keep producing content and not to wait for inspiration, as well as of the need to stay online and alert in between publishing posts. Blogging thus implies that 'networked life writing' needs to follow a strict, time-bound production schedule. It is also clear that the life that is written about is not 'separate' from practices of blogging, but that these practices become an unremarkable part of everyday life, a form of work that is also life. Everyday happenings are turned into blog posts, and blog posts are written and managed as part of the everyday. The blog, then, can be simultaneously a place for support and self-expression and 'a room of one's own', and a tiring, everyday duty that also needs to be done when it doesn't feel great.

> […][5] it's my most loved, my most wonderful of all jobs, it's my own place that I have created myself, and I can do what I, I can do everything my own way. But then, still sometimes it just feels like work, you have to write them, probably my background as a journalist helps there, if I think of today for example, today I will write at night when the children have gone to sleep. I might be really tired, and I would rather do something else. I have that kind of feeling, the nights have not been so good lately. But then I sit down by the computer and I know what I will write about because of course I have my plan for posts, for a week ahead, weeks ahead, there's room for adjustment of course but I have a tentative plan. And then you sit down and you write.

The bloggers, then, are often managing their writing in a highly organised way. They think of their blogs not only in terms of self-expression or creativity but also in terms of publishing schedules and site views.[6]

This is telling of professionalised blogging, which is oriented towards calculable 'output' that can be used to manage the work flow, but also exchanged for money through commercial cooperation. Digital media technologies allow for the gathering of exact data for different aspects of blogging, such as the number of unique visitors, site views, and shares in social media in any given time. Although the networks of sociality created in blogging can be seen as examples of how the digital economy privileges affective relationships and produces processes rather than finished products (Banet-Weiser, 2012, pp. 71–72), it is important to recognise that these processes, rather than being beyond measure or non-quantifiable, are actually organised and exchanged in a numerical form. The bloggers and blogging sites or agencies offer to commercial agents very precise calculable and comparable information of who has viewed a certain campaign post or clicked a certain link, and when. All of the bloggers I interviewed could instantly give me a statistic that represents the popularity of their blog.

Being ordinary

The idea of mom blogging as a form of community and peer support as well as a form of 'life writing' implies that the bloggers need to appear as 'one of us' and not as someone speaking from a high ground or someone who appears inauthentic. The bloggers, then, cannot be professionals in a way that would make them distinct from their readers. Indeed, some of the bloggers that I interviewed explicitly describe themselves or their blogs as 'ordinary' compared with other, 'glossy' lifestyle blogs. Whereas clearly the commercially inclined mom blogs with their displays of design clothes and eco-friendly lifestyles can be viewed as a form of middle-class femininity (cf. Taylor, 2016), for the bloggers themselves and for their readers this femininity can be characterised as ordinariness. The value of the blog and the 'personal brands' that the bloggers are building is based on being ordinary, as in being somebody the readers of the blogs can relate to. This kind of ordinariness, even if shaped by the relatively affluent lifestyles of highly educated women, nevertheless, also serves to challenge certain traditional or hegemonic ideals of femininity, motherhood, and home making that might be fortified in other types of lifestyle blogs or other media targeted at women:

> It's authentic and ordinary. Often, many of my readers have told me that they love it that I am so ordinary, [they tell me that] even if you do really cool stuff, which I don't think I even do, I live a really ordinary everyday macaroni casserole life, still, that you are not like that, like really fancy, well really I am not, I don't have time to do make up, I would rather use that half an hour writing a book, life is about choices and I love that I can show these choices through my blog.

Some of the bloggers have managed to combine ordinariness and authenticity with being a professional writer. They write very openly in their blogs about how blogging as a form of work makes it possible for them to live the kind of life they are living. Many are also quite open about the commercial relationships that they have and aim to make the logic of these forms of cooperation clear for the readers. This openness in relation to which content is commercial and what exactly 'commercial' means is a topic of constant discussion in blogs and occasionally also in other media.[7] Furthermore, the general increase of commercial content in the blogosphere has prompted negative reactions from the readers of the blogs, and in response the bloggers often strive to make the point that the commercial aspects of blogging are necessary for them to be able to keep blogging as much as they do. The message is that blogging is time-consuming and, in order to be able to devote so much time to it, it is necessary to gain something from it financially. These recurring issues around commercial content contribute to the ways in which 'blogging for living' is not disguised but more or less openly discussed in the blogs.

On some occasions, the peer support that usually revolves around mothering is extended as the bloggers also become inspirational examples of a certain lifestyle in which parenting is combined with micro-entrepreneurship. One could even claim that entrepreneurship as a life-style or as an identity has become a part of the 'personal brands' of several mom bloggers. This is evident, for instance, in the case of two mom bloggers, Satu Rämö and Hanne Valtari (2017), who have together written a book in Finnish, called *Doing a dream job*. The book is, according to the promotion material, 'an inspiring peer support guide for all those who want to love their work' in which the bloggers give readers advice on how to find alternatives to paid employment and transform their passions into a form of entrepreneurship or freelance work. In this sense, the blogs can be seen as a place in which the 'alternative life' outside day-to-day paid employment is not only made possible but also negotiated, normalised, and championed—even idealised. The atmosphere of the mom blogs, however, and in contrast to, for instance, the digital craft economy discussed by Luckman (2015), also seems to provide a space for admitting to have failed, not only in terms of personal life and parenting, but also entrepreneurship. Thus, some of the bloggers, although not many, have written also about their failures or disappointments in micro-entrepreneurship, and about the mental and emotional cost of working at night and taking care of children during the day.

On display, however, are not only aspects of peer support but also tensions relating to the need to stay ordinary and relatable. One of the bloggers I interviewed described how she does not foreground her professional experience in the blog because she is still living on a home care allowance and the blog needs to be from the perspective of an at-home mother. Of beginning her blog, she said, 'I could have asked one of my advertising agency friends to design me [a banner] but it wasn't what I wanted, what I wanted was for it to be ordinary'. Although she was rather ambitious from the beginning and wanted the blog to become popular, she figured that what would make her blog and her 'personal brand' succeed was not professional design but rather what appears to be the opposite, being ordinary. In this sense, even if mom blogging as a form of 'mumpreneurship'[8] (Ekinsmyth, 2011, 2014) combines mothering and entrepreneurship and blurs the division between everyday mothering and being a professional, the division is not completely dissolved but continues to 'haunt' the blogging professionals as they negotiate their occupational identities and personal brands.

Ordinariness, I suggest, defines the mom blogs in two ways. Firstly, ordinariness is made of stories of everyday 'macaroni casserole' life—a life that is not 'glossy' or 'fancy' and in which the house is not always clean and the children are not always happy. This is what several researchers have recognised as the radical potential of mom blogging, such everyday accounts serve to challenge and rebel against hegemonic ideals of motherhood and femininity (Lopez, 2009; Petersen, 2015). Secondly, ordinariness is out-of-focus photographs and not-so-fancy site designs, and also, I would suggest, posting photos of yourself in which you do not look your best. In this way, ordinariness is related to not taking yourself too seriously and not caring about appearances. What is important, however, is that even if the aesthetics of the blogs are sometimes 'played down' and the writer's take on herself and her mothering is ironic, the writing, for instance, using vivid language and telling capturing stories, is never played down. Instead, it is what the bloggers take pride in and cherish. It is then almost as if the surface of the blog can be non-professional and ordinary if the heart, or the writing, is professional and extraordinary.

Many of the bloggers, however, noted in the interviews that the aesthetics and especially the photographs published in blogs have gained a much heavier meaning in recent years, following the professionalisation and monetisation of the blogosphere. It, thus, seems that there may be a current shift in emphasis away from out-of-focus photos and capturing accounts of ordinary mothers, towards a more polished and professional look and feel. The professionalisation of blogging, then, means that the tension between ordinariness and 'glossy' professionalism intensifies.

Being close

There is, of course, variety in the proximity of blogs to authentic or 'ordinary' life writing, and it is not something that all the bloggers would even aim for—though it is quite clear, as one of the interviewees noted, that the readers would always like to hear more about the most personal, intimate things. To capture readers, the blogger thus needs to create a sense of closeness and intimacy with them (Lopez, 2009, p. 734; Morrison, 2014). The blog, as another interviewee says, is based on a 'personal relation' between the blogger and her readers: 'It is that certain person there who writes the blog about whom people are interested in'. The mom blog as a genre thus demands that the entrepreneur is personally involved and prepared to publicly share some intimate or self-revelatory details of one's life, that one is willing to be 'that certain person there'. In the context of monetised and professionalised blogging, this display of subjectivity in the blogs is an intrinsic part of work, as it is through the sharing of intimate details and through revealing the self that networks of sociality are built and maintained. In this sense, professionalised blogging can be characterised as implying practices of self-branding; the marketisation of the self through strategies of emotional engagement and authenticity (Banet-Weiser, 2012, pp. 71–72). Indeed, the bloggers that I interviewed occasionally refer to building or maintaining their 'personal brands'.

The subjectivity that is displayed in a blog and the closeness or intimacy that is created with the readers might rely on assumed authenticity, but they are, of course, not simply 'authentic', if that is taken to mean access to an 'essence' or 'truth' of the subject (Smith & Watson, 2013, p. 75). Rather, they are a complex combination of authenticity and performance, at the same time both real and not-real:

> Our family, is a real family, and what you see in the blog is a real family but then again, in the blog, it's somehow a blog family. How could I say this? The stories that I choose to tell, they tell about these blog characters, who live in that blog, even if they are real persons and our life and they are very truthful and consistent with us, the real persons. But still, I think that in the blog there are … caricatures of us. […] The characters are somehow, selected. A little bit like […] in reality television, you build a person, by choosing material, a person who is that person but isn't, so it's like that, in our blog.

Many of the bloggers that I interviewed described themselves as people who were open or upfront about their lives before they started blogging, and thus they felt that blogging was not such a big step towards 'public display of subjectivity' from what they had already been doing, for instance in Facebook, even if the audience was now much bigger. But for them it was also clear, as described in the quote above, that a blog self or a blog family are a consciously selected version of a life that is much richer and more complex than what is shown in the blog. In this sense, the display of subjectivity in mom blogging could be characterised as the production of staged or calculated authenticity (Pooley, 2011, cited in Smith & Watson, 2013, p. 75).

Mom blogging is a genre in which community is a built-in feature (Petersen, 2015). Blogs invite their readers to feel close to the bloggers and to relate to their lives in many ways. The combination of a sense of community and intimacy with staged authenticity can be hard to grasp for the readers. This becomes visible in the comments that the bloggers sometimes receive in which the readers make far-reaching assumptions of their family life based on what they have told in the blog. There are, for example, discussions in which the blogger tries to make explicit that she has not told everything in the blog and that writing is a practice of choosing and some aspects of life are always left outside the blogosphere. The readers, though, are often nevertheless 'playing by the rules' of assumed intimacy and authenticity, and thus they can hang on to something that was said in the blog and hold the blogger responsible for it. The invitation to closeness and the related complexities of ordinariness and authenticity might thus prompt the readers to be suspicious (Smith & Watson, 2013, p. 75) and to monitor the consistency of the self that is displayed or narrated in the blog:

> People think they know you inside out. They often talk about, I get these absurd messages sometimes, 'Hey six years ago you wrote that you hate yellow, so how come you now have a yellow shirt, did you lie to us back then?'

An important part of blogging, then, is the management of the comment section as a way of maintaining a good, close relationship with the blog's readers. Most of the bloggers I interviewed celebrated comments from readers as one of the most rewarding aspects of blogging, because of the direct feedback they got for their writing, and many also felt that the comments provide genuine support and exchange of thought, for instance, in terms of parenting. Many of them, however, also talked about how time-consuming certain kinds of comments can be. Blogs often attract not only a supportive community but also malicious comments and remarks, mostly from anonymous readers. The blog can thus be 'one's own place', a room of one's own, but it is not necessarily a safe space. Rather, it is an interface through which maliciousness, too, can leak into the intimate sphere (cf. Jokinen, 2009).

The attitude of the bloggers towards negative comments varies. One of the interviewees said that she just 'fetches the popcorn' when the bad comments start coming in, and feels happy that she gets more site views and so the statistics of her blog look better. More comments and more site views mean better monetising opportunities, which is, of course, also an important aspect in any comment section management. Several bloggers, however, talked about how crushing the bad comments can feel, especially if they concern the blogger as a mother, or her children. The bloggers who mentioned this aspect of blogging in the interviews also described some coping strategies, such as not responding to comments straight away but giving oneself time to calm down, or moderating the readers' comments before they are published.

The bloggers also described how, despite how bad they might feel, they nevertheless need to 'take care of the situation' in the comment section in a thoughtful and calm manner. They feel they should keep their own emotions in check and not, for example, answer mean comments in a mean way, but rather, try to restore the 'good spirit' in the blog. In managing both their own as well as the readers' emotional reactions, they are thus performing emotional labour, as theorised by Arlie Hochschild (1983).[9] In this way, blogging as a form of work bears a resemblance to many other forms of women's work, in which emotional management and 'taking care of situations' is an intrinsic but seldom acknowledged part of the work. I would suggest, however, that in the case of mom blogs, this emotional labour has a particular weight to it, as the comments that need to be managed also 'hit close' (or 'below the belt' as one of the bloggers put it), as they relate directly to the personality and family life of the blogger. In this case, then, emotional labour needs to be performed and professionalism maintained in a context of self-revelation, assumed intimacy, and closeness.

Being a mother

The bloggers are constantly reflecting on what they reveal in the blog, particularly about their children. Although the ethics of blogging about children have been discussed both academically (Rogers & Green, 2015) as well as in the blogosphere, it is the practical, day-to-day decisions that the bloggers need to make that demand their attention, rather than general ethical ruminations. There might be clear boundaries around, for instance, posting photographs of children ('the kind of photos I will never put to my blog'), but most often the boundaries are a question of 'gut feeling' that might also change as the blog grows or the blogger becomes more experienced. A photo that once seemed suitable, or a story that once felt like it should be in the blog, can now feel like it reveals too much. Mostly, the bloggers that I interviewed pondered on how to write about and photograph children, and they rarely had any definitive answers. Writing about being a mother implies that the children are somehow present in the text, as one of the interviewees noted:

> But ok for instance if we say that I had a really hard first year with the baby, well of course everyone knows then, ok, why that was, so in a way I have to, I sometimes think really hard about how somehow, people do not maybe realise how you kind of try to hide it when it is in a way really clear, about whom you are talking about when you say the first year was really hard, but [...] I do not have photos of them and somehow trying to talk in a way that 'a kid' or somehow make it into a general category of something, of course everyone realises [that you are talking about your own children].

Rather than have any clear principles, the interviewees then came across with the feeling that there cannot be perfect solutions, and thus the constant boundary work as well as occasional bad conscience or at least a fleeting moment of doubt seem just to be an inevitable part of the work of blogging. Furthermore, the decisions that are made about children's appearance in the blog are not only about blogging but also about parenting, and thus the occupational identity of a blogger becomes inextricably intertwined with that of mother, and the boundary work that is done bears a sense of responsibility and guilt that is tied directly to mothering.

Alternative lives?

In this chapter, I have sketched a tentative map of the complexities and contradictions that are an intrinsic part of practices of mom blogging and of bloggers' occupational identities. The characteristics of work outlined above, such as the importance of emotional labour and public displays of subjectivity, as well as the ambivalence around professionalism, can also be recognised in other feminised occupations, but I suggest that mom blogging as an emerging form of work marks the *intensification* of such characteristics. Furthermore, as an emerging form of work, not only do aspects of intimate life (e.g., practices of mothering and relationship building) merge with the work of blogging, thus rendering the boundaries of work and life porous or even dissolved into each other (Jokinen, 2009; Jokinen, Venäläinen, & Vähämäki, 2015), but also, these aspects of life are rendered highly organised and calculable, and monetised. In professional blogging, negotiating such complexities becomes an everyday part of living, working, and parenting. The 'new normal' that emerges here is thus one in which the monetisation of everyday life, the construction of public displays of subjectivity, and the ways in which parenting is made into work are not remarkable happenings or notable exceptions. Rather, they are just part of life that has come to organise itself around and through newly emerged practices of micro-entrepreneurship and the 'old normal' of women being primary carers for and of young children.

The alternative lives that emerge in this new normal are discussed, also by the bloggers themselves, as resonating with the ideals of 'downshifting' or escaping the demands of a hectic and precarious working life (Rokkonen, 2015). Arrangements of digital micro-entrepreneurship can often provide a more autonomous or meaningful alternative to lives organised by paid employment, especially if that paid employment is precarious, and this is precisely the experience of some of the bloggers I interviewed. It does seem, however, if one looks at the complexities that I have outlined, that these alternative lives are not 'shifted down' in any unambiguous sense. Instead, one might characterise them as *intensive lives*—full of negotiation, emotional as well as practical management, and boundary work, together with everyday moments of exhaustion, failures, rewards, and joy.

Notes

1. These blogs are usually called 'mommy blogs', but it is a contested concept (Friedman 2013, pp. 9–10; Rogers & Green 2015, p. 34). I think 'mom blogs' best captures the common characteristics of the blogs that I am researching. Many of the bloggers themselves also embrace the terms

mom or mommy ('mamma' in Finnish), often with some irony. This, however, does not mean that the blogs would be solely concerned with mothering and family issues, but rather that the bloggers themselves are claiming and reflecting on the identity of 'mother' as a more or less significant part of their blogging. Many of the blogs' names bear some reference to either mothers or babies.
2. These agencies take care of the practical aspects of making marketing agreements with commercial companies while allowing the bloggers independence in deciding which companies to work with, but they of course also charge a certain percentage for their work (e.g., 50%). Moreover, the agencies also indirectly affect the ways in which the bloggers perceive themselves and others. For example, one of the bloggers I interviewed described how the agency's practices of openly sharing statistical information reflecting the popularity of the blog means that she could not help comparing her site's statistics to those of other mom blogs. For her, the agency's practices have led to a heightened sense of being in a 'popularity' competition with others.
3. Finnish law has provided home care allowance for the care of children under three years of age since 1985. In 2013, the proportion of children aged nine to 24 months taken care of at home and supported by the home care allowance was 49% (Salmi & Lammi-Taskula 2015). Home care allowance, though also available for men, has for its whole existence been used almost entirely by women, especially women in precarious labour-market positions (Anttonen 2003; Salmi & Lammi-Taskula 2015). Subsidised at-home mothering (and also at-home grand-mothering) until the child is three years old differentiates Finland from other European countries (Anttonen 2003). It is, however, important to note that home care allowance is not tied to the mother's labour-market position, and thus it is possible to combine part-time or freelance work with receiving home care subsidy.
4. I conducted these eight interviews in 2015 and 2016 as a part of a still ongoing research project. They were semi-structured and each lasted approximately an hour. The interviewees were bloggers who themselves viewed blogging as work and who had received some monetary compensation for their blog. The quotations from interviews were translated from Finnish to English by me.
5. Transcription style: … indicates words have been omitted in a sentence, often just the repetition or a word or two; […] indicates a sentence or an aside has been omitted; [words in brackets] are inserted to clarify meaning.

6. In some of the interviews, the bloggers noted that they were not really doing as well as they could—for instance, they could be posting more often or putting more hours towards the blog if they just had the time. This feeling of inadequacy was nothing dramatic, but rather, an everyday experience (Purokuru & Paakkari 2015), accepted as part of the job. Although I cannot here reflect properly on this, it is worth mentioning as an everyday, unnoticeable part of the type of professionalism in which success is measured by numbers, as it is in blogging.
7. Recently a complaint was made to the Council of Ethics in Advertising concerning a marketing campaign involving several lifestyle and mom blogs in Finland.
8. Like 'mommy blogging', 'mumpreneur' is a contested concept (Ekinsmyth 2014). In discussing the politics of using this concept, Carol Ekinsmyth highlights the need to investigate 'mumpreneurship' in terms of the meanings that individuals attach to their identities as well as to their everyday lived experience, which I find critical also in relation to mom bloggers.
9. Hochschild (1983) uses the term 'emotional labour' to refer to emotion management that has exchange value. In the case of blogging, it could be said that emotional labour has both use value and exchange value, as it is aimed to maintain a supportive and good community *but* in the context of monetisation and micro-entrepreneurship.

References

Anttonen, A. (2003). Lastenhoidon kaksi maailmaa. In H. Forsberg & R. Nätkin (Eds.), *Perhe murroksessa: kriittisen perhetutkimuksen jäljillä* (pp. 159–185). Helsinki: Gaudeamus.

Banet-Weiser, S. (2012). *Authentic™: The politics of ambivalence in a brand culture*. New York: New York University Press.

Ekinsmyth, C. (2011). Challenging the boundaries of entrepreneurship: The spatialities and practices of UK 'mumpreneurs'. *Geoforum, 42*, 104–114.

Ekinsmyth, C. (2014). Mothers' business, work/life and the politics of 'mumpreneurship'. *Gender, Place and Culture, 21*(10), 1230–1248.

Faircloth, C. (2014). Intensive parenting and the expansion of parenting. In E. Lee, J. Bristow, C. Faircloth, & J. Macvarish (Eds.), *Parenting culture studies* (pp. 25–50). Basingstoke: Palgrave Macmillan.

Friedman, M. (2013). *Mommyblogs and the changing face of motherhood*. Toronto: University of Toronto Press.

Hochschild, A. (1983). *The managed heart*. Berkeley, CA: University of California Press.
Jallinoja, R. (2006). *Perheen vastaisku: familistista käännettä jäljittämässä*. Helsinki: Gaudeamus.
Jokinen, E. (2009). Home, work and affects in the fourth shift. In H. Johansson & K. Saarikangas (Eds.), *Homes in transformation: Dwelling, moving, belonging* (pp. 358–375). Helsinki: SKS.
Jokinen, E., Venäläinen, J., & Vähämäki, J. (2015). Johdatus prekaarien affektien tutkimukseen. In E. Jokinen & J. Venäläinen (Eds.), *Prekarisaatio ja affekti* (pp. 7–30). Nykykulttuurin tutkimuskeskuksen julkaisuja 118. Jyväskylä: Nykykulttuuri.
Julkunen, R. (2010). *Sukupuolen järjestykset ja tasa-arvon paradoksit*. Tampere: Vastapaino.
Lopez, L. K. (2009). The radical act of 'mommy blogging': Redefining motherhood through the blogosphere. *New Media Society, 11*(5), 729–747.
Luckman, S. (2015). *Craft and the creative economy*. Basingstoke: Palgrave Macmillan.
Morrison, A. (2014). Compositional strategies of conflict management in personal mommy blogs. *Feminist Media Studies, 14*(2), 286–300.
Petersen, E. J. (2015). Mommy bloggers as rebels and community builders: A generic description. Communicating motherhood/mothers communicating in popular culture and social media. *Journal of the Motherhood Initiative for Research and Community Involvement, 6*(1), 9–30.
Purokuru, P., & Paakkari, A. (2015). Riittämättömyys. In E. Jokinen & J. Venäläinen (Eds.). *Prekarisaatio ja affekti* (pp. 153–169). Nykykulttuurin tutkimuskeskuksen julkaisuja 118. Jyväskylä: Nykykulttuuri.
Rämö, S., & Valtari, H. (2017). *Unelmahommissa: tee itsellesi työ siitä mistä pidät*. Helsinki: WSOY.
Rogers, J. M., & Green, F. J. (2015). Mommy blogging and deliberative dialogical ethics: Being in the ethical moment. Communicating motherhood/mothers communicating in popular culture and social media. *Journal of the Motherhood Initiative for Research and Community Involvement, 6*(1), 31–49.
Rokkonen, L. A. (2015). Moratorio. In E. Jokinen & J. Venäläinen (Eds.), *Prekarisaatio ja affekti* (pp. 113–133). Nykykulttuurin tutkimuskeskuksen julkaisuja 118. Jyväskylä: Nykykulttuuri.
Salmi, M., & Lammi-Taskula, J. (2015). Finland country note. In P. Moss (Ed.), *International review of leave policies and research 2015*. International Network on Leave Policies & Research. Retrieved June 24, 2017, from http://www.leavenetwork.org/lp_and_r_reports

Smith, S., & Watson, J. (2013). Virtually me: A toolbox about online self-presentation. In A. Poletti & J. Rak (Eds.), *Identity technologies: Constructing the self online* (pp. 70–95). Wisconsin: The University of Wisconsin Press.

Taylor, S. (2015). A new mystique? Working for yourself in neoliberal economy. In B. Conor, G. Rosalind, & S. Taylor (Eds.), *Gender and creative labour, Sociological review monograph series* (Vol. 63 S1, pp. 174–187). Hoboken: NJ: Wiley.

Taylor, J. (2016). Laptops and playpens: 'Mommy bloggers' and visions of household work. In L. Adkins & M. Dever (Eds.), *The post-Fordist sexual contract: Working and living in contingency* (pp. 109–128). Basingstoke: Palgrave Macmillan.

Katariina Mäkinen is a Post-doctoral Researcher in gender studies at the University of Tampere, Finland. Her PhD research on work-related coaching traced the intersections of individualisation and gender in the context of late capitalism, and her current work on blogging continues the inquiry into changing forms of gendered work. Other research interests include anti-immigration activism from the perspectives of neoliberal citizenship regimes and relations of class.

Vlogging Careers: Everyday Expertise, Collaboration and Authenticity

Daniel Ashton and Karen Patel

Introduction

The rise in 'entrepreneurial vlogging' has attracted widespread attention in the global media, with articles emerging about the superstar vloggers who are earning a lot of money for pursuing their professed passions. The phenomenon of vlogging is positioned as something that 'anyone' can do, with YouTube appearing to offer the opportunity to combine freedom of creative expression with the possibility of making a living. The idea that anyone can vlog and make a career out of it is pervasive, yet only a few manage to do so.

For those who are successful, there follows hostility from some critics (Bish, 2014) and stories of failure. Some of the most popular vloggers attract a great deal of criticism for attention-seeking when seemingly doing little more than sitting in front of the camera and talking. Critique

---

D. Ashton (✉)
Winchester School of Art, University of Southampton, Winchester, UK

K. Patel
School of Media, Birmingham City University, Birmingham, UK

© The Author(s) 2018
S. Taylor, S. Luckman (eds.), *The New Normal of Working Lives*, Dynamics of Virtual Work, DOI 10.1007/978-3-319-66038-7_8

that focuses on the celebrity, however, tends to obscure the additional labour that is involved alongside the creation of video content. The effort in designing, creating and sharing that goes into these videos is little acknowledged. These complementary activities and the specialist subject knowledge that is often in evidence highlight the expertise required by vloggers. To examine vlogging's status as part of the 'new normal' of cultural work, we show how signalling expertise is a key aspect of vloggers' online self-presentation as they build their cultural work career.

This chapter is organised into two main parts. In part one, we reference a range of media sources to examine the increasing public visibility of vlogging as a cultural work career. Of particular note is the curiosity around vlogging as a commercially viable undertaking and the how-to guidance materials that have emerged to steer would-be YouTube entrepreneurs onto a successful path. The notion of career paths is particularly relevant to our discussion of the 'new normal' and the ways in which vlogging can be understood both as a stepping stone towards established careers in media, journalism, fashion and so on, and as a distinctive occupation in its own right. In bringing together a mixture of 'how-to' materials and more general journalistic coverage, we consider how 'starting up' and 'sustaining' oneself as a vlogger are explored. Having considered some of the broader stories of the successes and failures of vlogging and questions of career-building, part two examines the importance of expertise for vlogging careers.

In part two, we specifically focus on how expertise is signalled by four prominent vloggers from around the world: UK, Ireland and Korea. The vloggers were involved in gaming, fashion, make-up and comedy. These areas were chosen because they require a degree of knowledge and skill on behalf of the vlogger, and we wanted to analyse how such forms of expertise were presented. We analysed the social media presence of each vlogger to address how signalling-expertise strategies may be tailored to suit multiple platforms and multiple audiences. Our discussion for this chapter focuses on two themes from our analysis. The first is the ways in which associations with other vloggers formed an important part of how they signalled their expertise and helped to attract more fans. The second is the ways in which expertise is signalled in the staging of authentic vlogging identities and locations. Beyond the more obvious work involved in creating and uploading a video, our analysis highlights the extensive range of other activities and undertakings that help to signal expertise as vloggers negotiate their 'career'.

Part one: Constructing careers?

In examining media coverage of entrepreneurship, Taylor (2015) notes the wide range of representations and suggests that journalistic reporting and editing is one of the ways in which understandings of entrepreneurship are constructed. Likewise, we are interested in the ways in which vlogging as a potential career is afforded visibility through how-to guides and journalistic accounts of vloggers. When it comes to career opportunities and pathways, how-to guides proliferate in various forms and styles. As Ashton and Conor (2016) have explored, how-to guides provide resources through which sources of information, often industry 'professionals' and 'experts', establish themselves as authorities in guiding aspirants in the ways of a particular role or sector. This chapter builds on previous cultural work research looking at screenwriting (Conor, 2014) and film and television production (Ashton, 2014) to explore how-to guidance for aspiring YouTubers. In relation to the new normal, exploring public accounts of vlogging can help to investigate the ways in which vlogging is woven into established career occupations and careers, and the ways in which it is positioned as a 'job' in its own right.

How to understand vlogging as a career

Creative Skillset (n.d.), a UK organisation that works with industry to 'develop skills and talent, from classroom to boardroom', created an entry for vlogging in its job role directory that gives the 'lowdown' for the role:

Communicating an idea, thought or story to a wide online audience
Regularly posting content for new and existing subscribers and followers
Generating revenue either by working for a company, utilising advert space, or by product placement

The creation of a job role for vlogging shows the growth in significance and visibility of vlogging. The job role overview also provides guidance on how vlogging can be both a stepping-stone career and a standalone career. In relation to the former, the Creative Skillset job role overview notes how many vloggers 'expand elsewhere', including into social media positions, based on the associated skills, and TV and radio presenting, based on personality and performance (see also Singh Chawla's 2014 conversation with vlogger Alfie Deyes).

Referring to vlogging as a career in its own right, Creative Skillset (n.d.) notes how vloggers operating as freelancers can make careers through a number of activities, including establishing relationships with brands and advertising. The growth in freelance cultural work careers has been well documented across academic scholarship (Hesmondhalgh & Baker, 2011), policy reviews (Oakley, 2009) and industry reports (Tambling, 2015). Of specific relevance for vlogging is recent research that has focused on the emergence of entrepreneurship in relation to digital media platforms, such as Burgess and Green's (2009) research on YouTube and Luckman's (2015) research on Etsy, the online design craft marketplace. Vlogging has been associated primarily with celebratory discourses around freedom, following a passion as a dream job, and being your own boss (Solon, 2016). In turn, issues around maintaining a secure and sustainable income that have been examined in relation to freelance cultural work more widely (Hesmondhalgh & Baker, 2011; Oakley, 2009) also feature in some discussions of vlogging (Dunn, 2015). With some vloggers, however, it is more appropriate to see an overlap between freelance vlogging and vloggers working in more established media occupations. Rather than offering a linear path from one into the other, these activities can mutually reinforce each other. This overall approach also helps for better identifying and understanding the entrepreneurial ethos and activities that existing studies of YouTube have examined (Burgess & Green, 2009).

The entrepreneurial ethos is explicitly addressed in the Creative Skillset 'lowdown' when it brings together the communication and posting of ideas with generating revenue. The YouTube Creator Academy (n.d.), a place to 'learn tips from savvy creators as they showcase their secrets and best practices', also brings together courses and videos on production practices and content creation with advice on growing an audience and making money. Alongside the official YouTube offering that includes courses, lessons and quizzes, there are similarly themed videos from YouTubers. Another useful way to identify major areas of interest and entrepreneurial guidance for career vlogging comes with *YouTube channels for dummies* (Ciampa & Moore, 2015), part of the well-known series of instructional books. This book is structured around the following themes: getting started, making videos, growing audiences and serious business. These themes are also picked up in a further source of guidance we reviewed—the Vlog Nation website. Specifically, this website uses the menu headings: 'Starting a vlog', 'How to vlog', 'Get more views' and 'Earn money'. These guidance themes provide instructive ways to organise a closer analysis of how vlogging is understood and constructed as a cultural work career.

Starting up as a vlogger

Unsurprisingly, on YouTube itself, there are many videos on vlogging and how to start and develop a channel. Honor's *How to make your first YouTube video* is one of many similarly titled and themed videos (at the time of writing in November 2016, a search within YouTube for 'how to vlog' returns 42,300,000 results). In this video, there is the often stated and widely circulated view that personal interests and passion are essential: 'When you make a YouTube channel it shouldn't be about how many subscribers you can get or how popular you can get. It's about doing something you love because you love it.' This approach resonates with that set out within the YouTube (n.d.) Creator Academy videos, which emphasise passion and building relationships with audiences before any consideration of monetisation. With vlogging, the passionate investment and love of creating and sharing content on a particular topic is often held to be the starting point above and beyond making money (Postigo, 2016). The 'do what you love' mantra is in clear evidence in the advice to those setting up as YouTube vloggers. As Tokumitsu (cited in Lam, 2015) notes as part of the critique associated with her book, *Do what you love and other lies about success and happiness*, there is a 'pantheon of super successful blissful workers who are held up as these cultural ideals, and there is this kind of lifestyle peddling that goes along with it, the imagery of which is saturating our visual landscape more than ever.' To this visual landscape, we could add the stories of the vloggers who 'own the world of YouTube' (Samuelson, 2014) are 'changing the face of youth culture' (Singh Chawla, 2014), and are vlogging their way 'to a million pounds' (Solon, 2016). The lifestyles associated with prominent vloggers do not fit a particular formula, and there can be significant differences across, for example, fashion and videogaming. Nevertheless, passion remains a recurring theme in how-to guidance materials.

A common approach with how-to materials is to help encourage and facilitate by stressing accessibility and providing suggestions that would lower barriers to participation. As our analysis in part two reveals, however, there are significant further levels of expertise in operation as vlogging is pursued as a career. While it is important to show passion, as suggested in how-to materials, the expertise to construct a public performance and profile is a different matter.

A further aspect of guidance concerns the set-up costs and the resource implications of vlogging. The most celebratory accounts of YouTube and participatory cultures emphasise democratisation and the equal availability of opportunities for creating content. Vlogging connects with wider accounts of participation and creativity, in which the tools and technologies are readily available for many to pursue their own creative and political agendas (Shirky, 2008). However, as Burgess (2012) notes in examining the YouTube Creator Hub, the larger host for the YouTube Creator Academy, the range of tips and suggestions are orientated towards professionalising content. Burgess (2012, p. 55) goes on to suggest that 'this initiative can be seen as an attempt on behalf of YouTube to reduce the ratio of non-monetisable to monetisable amateur content.'

Similarly, other commentators, such as Jenkins and Carpentier (2013), have addressed tensions around participatory promises and potentials. While the sentiment that vlogging is available to all was clearly evident, the analysis we undertook also connected with these cautionary accounts of challenges to access and participation. For example, Dennis (2015) provides a list of required equipment, noting that 'DSLR cameras and lenses can cost upwards of $800, and then you need lighting equipment, tripods, and microphones', and summarising by reflecting, 'it takes quite a lot of dedication for these vloggers to do what they do.' Having reviewed their start-up costs, Lennard (2015) adds that, 'unlike most jobs, working on YouTube is something you have to pay to do for a long time before anybody will pay you back.' Again, there are some strong parallels with extant research examining cultural work, in which essential risks and choices in cultivating employment opportunities operate at the individual level (Gill, 2010). The examination of expertise in part two critically addresses the requirements and pressures of vlogging. The comments on set-up costs also lead to a similar set of concerns around the viability of maintaining a sustainable YouTube channel.

Sustaining vlogging practices

The how-to materials we reviewed focused mainly on the low-level requirements for getting going as a vlogger. There is, however, a range of further considerations in growing and sustaining a vlogging profile. The how-to materials produced by YouTube and Vlog Nation emphasis that a vlogger's growth is associated with building audiences and the consistent creation of new materials. For videogame commentator Destructnatr (2015), sustainability and growth are the major considerations driving his decision to post an eye-catching video to save viewers from making a mistake of setting up a YouTube channel. With a provocatively titled twist on the how-to genre, *Why you shouldn't start a YouTube channel*, Destructnatr laments the saturation of the field and the near impossible task of standing out in a way that can generate significant subscriptions. As highlighted by Marwick's (2016) discussion of YouTuber creator Amanda Sings, there are different strategies and scales for connecting with audiences and the kinds of how-to materials we reviewed might be an irrelevance for some (successful) vloggers. Nevertheless, by highlighting oversupply, Destructnatr's approach marks an interesting contrast to that of Honor (2014) and others, who suggest that passion and personally purposeful content will be enough. Destructnatr attributes his success to timely membership of a specific videogaming clan, and makes the claim that, from 2015, YouTube has reached a scale where the challenges for starting a new channel and generating significant subscriptions, presumably in relation to videogaming, are too great. Destructnatr also signals the effort required in creating videos.

These comments are echoed by those from other commentators, which highlight the relentless production schedule and constant pressure on creating content. In reflecting on her channel, *Just between us*, Dunn (2015) outlines the commitments involved: 'when we're not producing and starring in a comedy sketch and advice show, we're writing the episodes, dealing with business contracts and deals, and running our company Gallison, LLC.' Similar accounts come in Harvey's (2013) interview with vloggers, in which Anna Gardner (*Vivianna does makeup*) recounts a 7 a.m.–6 p.m. working day. Harvey outlines how vlogger Lily Pebbles 'spends her days tweeting, recording vlogs, writing blogs, researching beauty products, chatting with followers and negotiating contracts'. From these accounts, we can see that the viability of a successful YouTube channel is closely connected with understanding and expertise that extends well beyond making the video. As our later analysis through the signalling-expertise framework shows, the cultivation and maintenance of a social media profile is intricately enmeshed with creating content on YouTube.

For other commentators, the issue of survival and sustainability loom much larger than questions of 'where next?' While it is the high-profile vloggers that might attract attention, an important part of understanding vlogging, and cultural work more generally, is to ask questions of feasibility and sustainability. This is something Heritage (2017) takes aim at in his satirical career guide, noting the salary for starters as 'nothing', the salary for experienced as 'almost nothing', and for highly experienced as 'hundreds of thousands of pounds a month'. For this final salary range, Heritage adds: 'note: you will never reach this stage.' For Dunn (2015), this issue of income and sustainability is most pressing for 'moderately successful YouTubers' and 'mid-level web personalities', where 'the disconnect between internet fame and financial security is hard to comprehend for both creators and fans.' Specifically, Dunn identifies a tension in which 'many famous social media stars are too visible to have "real" jobs, but too broke not to.' Again, there are strong parallels with extant research on cultural work and multiple job-holding (Ashton, 2015; Throsby & Zednik, 2011). Earlier, we argued that vloggers' entrepreneurial approach is evident in how vloggers can overlap YouTube vlogging with TV presenting and more established media roles (Singh Chawla, 2014). To this, we should add that vlogging portfolio working and multiple-job-holding extend into *other* forms of employment, such as retail and service industry work (see Dunn, 2015, for example). Alongside the coverage that focuses on the novelty of 'bedroom millionaires' and (micro)celebrity heroes for teenagers, there is pointed discussion of bloggers' working routines, conditions and challenges (see Duffy, 2015; Duffy & Hund, 2015; Graefer, 2016). The 'always on' nature of vlogging, the raft of skills demands and the need to develop expertise in a range of areas also highlight the strong parallels with ways of working common to established forms of cultural work.

The how-to guidance and journalistic coverage position vlogging as a viable career that anyone can do, provided they have passion for their subject and are able to put that across on camera. Such coverage suggests low barriers to entry and the potential for widening participation in cultural production, yet it obscures the need for expensive equipment, the time required to invest in creating and promoting videos, and thus the various forms of expertise required beyond talking in front of the camera. This can include using social media for promotion and self-branding, and the technical skills to operate camera equipment and editing software. In our consideration of vlogging as part of a 'new normal' of cultural work, these practices require further critical attention.

Part two: Expertise, self-branding and micro-celebrity

In their exploration of cultural production and participation in digital environments, Cruz and Thornham (2015, p. 315) argue that discourses around expertise and the digital 'seem to conflate ideas of participation with literacy, content with engagement, novelty with innovation and ubiquity with meaning'. The authors take issue with discourses of participation in the social media age as equating to expertise—in other words, anyone who is able to participate in cultural production online can be perceived as an expert. The signalling-expertise analysis we use in this research demonstrates how vlogging requires much more than the passion and knowledge of the subject that is suggested in the how-to guidance. The expertise involved goes far beyond mere participation. Additional and varied skills are required in creating the content, tailoring it for promotion on social media, and using social media to foster relationships with audiences and potential collaborators. These practices are crucial for building an online following and gaining visibility as a vlogger.

What is expertise? It is a term often used and yet taken for granted in accounts of cultural work (Patel, 2017), and defining expertise itself is an area of contention. However, we will approach it by drawing out commonalities across definitions. One common feature is the possession of knowledge and/or skill in a specialist area (see Prince, 2010; Schudson, 2006), and the second is recognition and endorsement of that knowledge or skill from others of a higher status within the same sector or industry (Cruz & Thornham, 2015; Prince, 2010; Turner, 2001). Bassett, Fotopoulou, and Howland (2015, p. 28) provide a useful definition that acknowledges both knowledge and skill, and social context. They suggest that:

> building expertise in a particular area demands particular kinds of cognitive activity and work. However, this process is also always contextualised within social contexts, which not only tend to define what constitutes the cut-off level … but that also temper or condition how expertise is acquired.

This definition informs our own understanding of expertise as the possession of specialised knowledge and skill that is recognised by others as legitimate, and mobilised, accumulated and signalled within a particular social context (Patel, 2016).

The relationship between expertise and cultural careers is explored by Candace Jones (2002), who proposes that the project-based nature of work in the cultural industries means that signalling expertise is important because projects need to be matched to the right people. The process of signalling by the cultural worker conveys information to others about their competencies, skills, relevant relationships, individual context and prior projects. Jones devised a signalling-expertise framework to characterise expertise signals, and we use an adapted version of this framework (Patel, 2017) as a methodological tool. According to Jones (2002, p. 223), the final product is the most important form of expertise signal, and 'the market niche in which one gains experience then showcases specific skill sets and shapes one's opportunity structure. Thus, initial experiences constrict or open up opportunities for work in different niches.'

The signalling-expertise framework can provide a nuanced analysis of social media performance which considers not only how expertise is signalled but cross-platform strategies, and the individual context behind online signals. Social media platforms are central to the work of the vloggers in this research, not only for distributing their work but for self-presentation and interacting with others, particularly fellow vloggers and fans. The popularity of social media has led to a growing body of research into self-presentation and much of this centres on ideas of self-branding and micro-celebrity (see Duffy & Hund, 2015; Gandini, 2015; Hearn, 2008; Jerslev, 2016; Khamis, Ang, & Welling, 2016; Marwick, 2013; Senft, 2008). The two ideas are interlinked; self-branding is 'the strategic creation of identity to be promoted and sold to others' (Marwick, 2013, p. 166) and micro-celebrity is associated with 'the presentation of oneself as a celebrity regardless of who is paying attention' (Marwick, 2013, p. 114).

Micro-celebrity is not only about promoting one's own image, it also involves what Jerslev (2016, p. 5238) describes as 'permanent updating', where social media celebrities, particularly vloggers, are expected to continuously upload 'performances of a private self; it is about access, immediacy and instantaneity'. As well as posting and updating, there is also an expectation that the micro-celebrity will interact with followers. In reflecting on the cultivation of micro-celebrity, Senft (2013, p. 349) suggests that the curating and circulating of pictures, videos and status updates 'in a professional venue would be a concerted audience-segmentation strategy'. As we show through the following analysis, vloggers' interactions with audiences operate in a natural and everyday conversational manner while forming part of a carefully considered communication strategy. Nancy Baym (2015, p. 16) examines relationships with audiences in terms of relational labour—'regular, ongoing communication with audiences over time to build social relationships that foster paid work'—and argues that this relational labour is an important part of cultural work. As well as creating their videos, vloggers must also maintain the rest of their social media presence, taking into account different platform strategies (Marwick, 2015; van Dijck, 2013) and their 'imagined audience' (Marwick & Boyd, 2011), which may differ across platforms. The adapted version of the signalling-expertise framework we use can help us understand these cross-platform strategies and how they relate to vloggers' expertise signals online. The framework consists of three elements: institutional context (the context of the user, the user's background and career trajectory), signalling content (the style of social media text and images, exhibiting the requisite skills and career-relevant connections on social media) and signalling strategies (using affordances such as retweets to enhance status, type of relationships pursued on social media and strategic approaches to impression management on social media).

The framework was used to analyse samples of social media posts by four prominent vloggers: UK-based fashion commentator Tanya Burr, UK-based comedian Danisnotonfire, Korean-based beauty reviewer Lia Yoo and Ireland-based game reviewer Jacksepticeye. Each element of the signalling-expertise framework was considered for the post sampled, which included one of their YouTube videos and samples from one or two of the social media accounts that they used most frequently (most often Twitter). The common themes emerging from both the exploration of materials about vlogging and the signalling-expertise analysis of vloggers' social media posts reveal a set of tensions at the heart of this new normal of cultural work. In the following sections, we focus on the ways in which associations with other vloggers formed an important part of how vloggers signalled their expertise by facilitating greater recognition, and the ways in which expertise is signalled in the staging of authentic vlogging identities and locations.

Collaborations, associations and networks

From our analysis of four vloggers, the relational aspects of signalling-expertise were prominent. In an area dominated by micro-celebrity and individualistic 'attention-seeking', we found that associations and networks can form an important part of how vloggers signal expertise. One way that this appeared was that all of the vloggers teamed up with other vloggers in some way for their videos. For example, Tanya Burr, a fashion commentator, created a video with arguably the UK's most famous vlogger, Zoella, generating a positive reaction from fans of both, as demonstrated in this retweet by Tanya:

Tanya Burr Retweeted

> Maddy 22 Aug 2016
> @TanyaBurr @Zoella Tanya and Zoe's videos together always make me so happy. Please do more soon. #TanElla

The partnership even has its own hashtag, '#TanElla', adopted by fans. At the time of writing, Tanya has around 3.5 million YouTube subscribers. Zoella has over 11 million subscribers of her channel and is, in comparison, hugely successful. By creating a video with Zoella and promoting it on Twitter, Tanya can try and attract more views and potential subscribers from existing fans of Zoella, and vice versa. The two vloggers comment on similar topics and are seemingly in competition with each other, but instead they collaborate so they can benefit from each other's following through a joint performance of expertise in the areas of fashion and beauty.

Some scholars argue that social media platforms are structured to encourage self-promotion and micro-celebrity practices that focus on the individual (Marwick, 2013; Williamson, 2016). While we do not disagree with this, our research indicated that the platforms can also facilitate or present examples of collaboration for the benefit of all parties involved. Grünewald, Haupt, and Bernardo (2014) argue that YouTube is the site for a 'post-industrial media economy' that 'involves cooperation of YouTubers, cultural references between YouTubers, parodies and other types of cultural intertextuality that they call "cross-promotion"'. This, they argue, is backed up by social bonds, friendships and networks that are crucial for the careers of vloggers. This was in evidence among all of vloggers in our research. For example, comedy vlogger Danisnotonfire often creates videos with his collaborator, Phil, who he also tours with. Beauty reviewer Lia Yoo also features other vloggers in her videos, and Jacksepticeye appears to have remix videos made for him by a fan/friend.

Interaction with fans and audiences was also evident from the signalling-expertise analysis. Sometimes vloggers would reply to comments directly on Instagram, as Lia Yoo often did. Most replied to Tweets from fans, too, either directly or by quoting the Tweet first and replying, as in this Tweet by Tanya Burr:

Tanya Burr @TanyaBurr 22 Aug 2016
Yay! Tweet me photos of what you bake—I'd love to see! #TanyaBakes

> Leah
> Went out and brought @TanyaBurr's #TanyaBakes today so excited to see what things I can make this week!

Tanya is cultivating her relationship with her fans by showing that she reads their Tweets and takes the time to reply to them, and the practice of quoting the Tweet rather than replying directly means it appears on Tanya's own Twitter profile and not in the 'replies' column, which is separate. In the particular example above, Tanya is also encouraging further interaction from her fans by asking them to Tweet photos of what they bake from her book. This direct engagement with fans contributes to a sense of authenticity, in that Tanya appears approachable and willing to interact with her audience. Marwick (2015) argues that audience interaction is key for micro-celebrities, as a means for them to position themselves as 'authentic' in opposition to mainstream celebrities or, in the case of fashion vloggers, luxury brands. Behind these interactions is a great deal of relational labour (Baym, 2015), where the cultivation of relationships and audience interaction online are key to the vloggers' success. As Baym (2015, p. 16) states, 'the shift to media that enable continuous interaction, higher expectations of engagement, and greater importance of such connections in shaping economic fortunes calls for new skills and expertise in fostering connections and managing boundaries'. Our signalling-expertise analysis shows that expertise in fostering connections extends to audiences and to other vloggers.

Deuze and Lewis (2013, p. 169) argue that 'as individuals in the workforce increasingly either choose to or are forced to build their own support structures, they must do so within the context of a peer group and some kind of organization.' Though vlogs may appear to be the work of individuals, many of the more prominent vloggers rely on collaborations and networks in order to sustain their success. As Mayer and Horner (2016, p. 246) suggest, 'the act of making/crafting a product ... catalyzes connections and helps to build affinity groups'. For vloggers, these networks include their audiences, who must be replied to, acknowledged and publicly appreciated. Our analysis demonstrates how important relationships and collaborations are for vloggers signalling their expertise. These relationships and collaborations also contribute to a sense of authenticity that vloggers establish with audiences. Reflecting on a survey conducted for *Variety* magazine, celebrity brand strategist Jeetendr Sehdev addresses how 'teens enjoy an intimate and authentic experience with YouTube celebrities' and refers to 'unvarnished individualism' (see Ault, 2014). Part of this is the 'real-world' relationships that vloggers show off with fellow vloggers. As the following section addresses, these relationships and collaborations form part of the context by which vloggers signal their expertise. An equally important aspect is the presentation of authenticity in a strategy for signalling expertise that allows vloggers to appear accessible to their audiences.

Staging authenticity

In her reflections on vlogging, Dunn (2015) addresses 'the huge amount of emotional labor inherent in being an online personality'. Part of this involves the strategic deployment of authenticity. Dunn goes on to add: 'Authenticity is valued, but in small doses: YouTubers are allowed to have struggled in the past tense, because overcoming makes us brave and relatable. But we can't be struggling now or we're labelled "whiners"'. The success of vloggers in establishing rapport with followers and building a subscription base can be in large measure attributed to authenticity (Ault, 2014).

The authenticity of bedroom spaces (which are the common setting for vlogs) as the locus for everyday forms of sociality and intimacy with audiences is nuanced and sometimes contradicted by the presence of camera equipment. As the analysis of how-to materials and media coverage alluded to and our signalling-expertise analysis shows more explicitly, vloggers often employ sophisticated production equipment to create their videos. For example, videogame commentator Jacksepticeye appears to use large headphones and microphone to record his commentary. Danisnotonfire's videos are situated in his bedroom, yet there is sophistication in the editing of the video and, in particular, the re-staging of the events and incidents that happen to him (which is important for the comic element of his videos).

These findings resonate with Burgess and Green's (2009, p. 24) suggestion that 'productive play, media consumption, and cultural performance have always been part of the repertoire of these semi-private spaces of cultural participation'. With vloggers, the bedroom is not just a low-cost, convenient site for making videos. It is a specific space for cultural production and performance. The importance of the visibility of the home is a key element in Susan Luckman's (2015) research on women's micro-entrepreneurial homeworking. Focusing on Etsy, Luckman examines how the home both operates as workplace and features in the online public presence of craft producers. Luckman (2015, p. 148) argues that 'the public performance of the craft producer's personal identity as part and parcel of the consumer value of their products … has become an essential part of the home-based maker's online marketing identity'. Our signalling-expertise analysis highlights that the bedroom/home operates for many vloggers as a domestic on-screen set and as a place of work.

There can, however, be significant tensions between the staged authenticity that is presented on camera and on social media, compared to everyday working realities. As the account from Dunn reveals, authenticity is welcomed in relation to ordinary lives, but a detailed account of the production contexts and a fuller picture of working and vlogging lives is not entertained. Dunn addresses this as follows: 'a picture of me out to brunch in Los Feliz will get more likes than a video of me searching for quarters in my car'. Here, Dunn reflects on her expertise in choosing what to communicate and share to her audience. Similarly, through her analysis of UK YouTuber Zoella, Jerslev (2016) suggests that playing down expertise in their subject area is another way for vloggers to perform authenticity. She identifies that, in her vlogs, Zoella gives off a sense of spontaneity by appearing to forget brand names and stumbling over her words. Jerslev identifies this as a way for Zoella to attach authenticity to situations where brand names are usually repeated. Though she is playing down her expertise in brand names, Zoella demonstrates an awareness of her audience and what they will relate to. Such a strategy is also exercised by Tanya Burr in our analysis, who avoids mentioning brand names herself, but instead acknowledges them in the YouTube video description.

The presentation of authenticity is an expertise signalling strategy designed to appeal to audiences and thus increase online exposure, as highlighted by Dunn (2015) and Jerslev (2016). The expertise is in the strategy—vloggers must consciously choose, edit and then create their content with their audience in mind. Milly Williamson (2016, p. 153) argues that the 'technology of freedom' offered by social media and the Internet is in fact a 'technology of self-promotion and celebrity', where celebrity culture has contributed to the construction of hierarchy in the cultural industries. Creating content and managing social media channels take time and effort for vloggers, and as Williamson argues, although social media platforms are positioned as offering everyone the chance to express themselves and connect with others, the promise and the reality are deeply contradictory. The signalling-expertise analysis reveals that the vloggers in our research are currently relatively successful at what they do. However, what they do not talk about are the struggles they have gone through. One vlogger who did is Zoella, who posted a video of herself breaking down in tears, explaining how her rise to fame and the pressures of what she does has become too much for her (Jerslev, 2016). Zoella's status as the UK's most famous vlogger means that, while she opens herself up to further scrutiny through her admission of vulnerability, she is also performing authenticity and gaining sympathy and support from her audience; something which appears to be spontaneous can be understood as part of a signalling strategy. The examples we have presented in this chapter show how for vloggers, signalling expertise is much more than the communication of knowledge or deployment of skill; it requires an ability to engage others (the audience) by staging a relatable authenticity. Sometimes, that authenticity is based in the very real struggles vloggers face.

Conclusion

This chapter has examined vlogging as a form of new normal in cultural work, using the analytical lens of expertise. For vloggers, the demands can be constant. The process of creating their videos, maintaining social media profiles and multiple job-holding are aspects of vlogging production that are obscured by the how-to guidance, which often positions vlogging as a viable career with low barriers to entry, with passion the main requirement for participation. Such guides promote an entrepreneurial ethos and while they allude to the diversity of skills and level of time and economic investment required, the full extent and challenges of expertise are only touched upon.

Our analysis reveals the multiple processes that occur around a seemingly 'polished' final video, particularly vloggers' strategies to engage their audience by interacting with fans and collaborators, and the skills required to stage a relatable authenticity. We argue that vloggers possess a certain amount of expertise in their area, which is crucial to their success. Focusing only on the videos and performance, as Bish (2014) does in lamenting vloggers' poor training in the art form of entertainment, overlooks the extensive and diverse skills and demands associated with vlogging, which are glossed over in associated career guidance.

In addition, there remain concerns around access to the right equipment and having the money and connections to 'make it' as a vlogger, which, for most, will not become a reality. The critical perspectives of vloggers such as Dunn (2015) and Lennard (2015) open up revealing comparisons with debates on cultural work more widely, as Lennard (2015) suggests in commenting that 'no-one should be fooled by the idea that YouTube is somehow different to the more traditional media industries'. Highlighting cultural work continuities invites a line of comparison around wider production cultures and industry contexts. For example, a number of the vloggers in our study were managed by agencies. Connecting with existing research on what Burgess (2012) describes as 'new commercial cultural intermediaries' (see also Lobato, 2016), future research could explore the role such agents have in vloggers' online performances, in particular, the reinforcement of conventional vlogging tropes such as the narrative conventions in videos and the common setting of the home or bedroom.

References

Ashton, D. (2014). Making media workers: Contesting film and television industry career pathways. *Television and New Media, 16*(3), 275–294.

Ashton, D. (2015). Creative work careers: Pathways and portfolios for the creative economy. *Journal of Education and Work, 28*(4), 388–406.

Ashton, D., & Conor, B. (2016). Screenwriting, higher education and digital ecologies of expertise. *New Writing, 13*(1), 98–108.

Ault, S. (2014, August 5). Survey: YouTube stars more popular than mainstream celebs among U.S. teens. *Variety*. Retrieved November 4, 2016, from http://variety.com/2014/digital/news/survey-youtube-stars-more-popular-than-mainstream-celebs-among-u-s-teens-1201275245/

Bassett, C., Fotopoulou, A., & Howland, K. (2015). Expertise: A report and a manifesto. *Convergence: The International Journal of Research into New Media Technologies, 21*(3), 328–342.

Baym, N. K. (2015). Connect with your audience! The relational labor of connection. *Communication Review, 18*(1), 14–22.

Bish, J. (2014, September 4). Vain and inane: The rise of Britain's dickhead vloggers. *Vice*. Retrieved November 4, 2016, from http://www.vice.com/en_uk/read/vloggers-are-the-death-of-entertainment-194

Burgess, J. (2012). YouTube and the formalisation of amateur media. In D. Hunter, R. Lobato, M. Richardson, & J. Thomas (Eds.), *Amateur media: Social, cultural and legal perspectives* (pp. 53–58). Abingdon: Routledge.

Burgess, J., & Green, J. (2009). The entrepreneurial vlogger: Participatory culture beyond the professional-amateur divide. In P. Snickars & P. Vonderau (Eds.), *The YouTube reader* (pp. 89–107). Stockholm: National Library of Sweden.

Ciampa, R., & Moore, T. (2015). *YouTube channels for dummies*. Hoboken: John Wiley and Sons.

Conor, B. (2014). Gurus and Oscar winners: How-to screenwriting manuals in the new cultural economy. *Television and New Media, 15*(2), 121–138.

Creative Skillset. (n.d.). Blogger/vlogger. Retrieved November 4, 2016, from http://creativeskillset.org/job_roles/4244_bloggervlogger

Cruz, E. G., & Thornham, H. (2015). 'Raw talent in the making': Imaginary journeys, authorship and the discourses of expertise. *Convergence: The International Journal of Research into New Media Technologies, 21*(3), 314–327.

Dennis, R. J. (2015, March 24). Life as a vlogger: What's it like? We asked 10 YouTubers. *MakeUseOf*. Retrieved November 4, 2016, from http://www.makeuseof.com/tag/life-youtube-vlogger-whats-like/

Destructnatr. (2015, January 31). Why you shouldn't start a YouTube channel (AW double DNA bomb) [vlog]. Retrieved November 4, 2016, from https://www.youtube.com/watch?v=GS9uEQXItLA

Deuze, M., & Lewis, N. (2013). Professional identity and media work. In M. Banks, R. Gill, & S. Taylor (Eds.), *Theorizing cultural work: Labour, continuity and change in the cultural and creative industries* (pp. 161–174). Abingdon: Routledge.

Duffy, B. E. (2015, March 18). The gendered politics of digital brand labor. *Antenna*. Retrieved November 4, 2016, from http://blog.commarts.wisc.edu/2015/03/18/the-gendered-politics-of-digital-brand-labor/

Duffy, B. E., & Hund, E. (2015). 'Having it all' on social media: Entrepreneurial femininity and self-branding among fashion bloggers. *Social Media + Society, July–December*, 1–11. https://doi.org/10.1177/2056305115604337

Dunn, G. (2015, December 14). Get rich or die vlogging: The sad economics of internet fame. *Fusion*. Retrieved November 4, 2016, from http://fusion.net/story/244545/famous-and-broke-on-youtube-instagram-social-media/

Gandini, A. (2015). The rise of coworking spaces: A literature review. *Ephemera, 15*(1), 193–205.

Gill, R. (2010). 'Life is a pitch': Managing the self in new media work. In M. Deuze (Ed.), *Managing media work* (pp. 249–262). London: Sage.

Graefer, A. (2016). The work of humour in affective capitalism: A case study of celebrity gossip blogs. *Ephemera: Theory and Politics in Organization, 16*(4), 143–162.

Grünewald, L., Haupt, J., & Bernardo, F. (2014, July 14). Media-intermediation and careers on YouTube: How musicians get empowered in post-industrial media-economies. *Muke*. Retrieved November 4, 2016, from http://muke-blog.org/media-intermediation-careers-on-youtube-2665

Harvey, D. (2013, November 13). Meet the vloggers: Self employed and 'worth a fortune'. *BBC Newsbeat*. Retrieved November 4, 2016, from http://www.bbc.co.uk/newsbeat/article/24726895/meet-the-vloggers-self-employed-and-worth-a-fortune

Hearn, A. (2008). 'Meat, Mask, Burden': Probing the contours of the branded 'self'. *Journal of Consumer Culture, 8*(2), 197–217.

Heritage, S. (2017, May 22). How to be a vlogger: A guide for wannabe YouTubers. *The Guardian*. Retrieved May 25, 2017, from https://www.theguardian.com/technology/shortcuts/2017/may/22/how-to-be-a-vlogger-a-guide-for-wannabe-youtubers

Hesmondhalgh, D., & Baker, S. (2011). *Creative labour: Media work in three cultural industries*. Abingdon: Routledge.

Honor. (2014, January). How to make your first Youtube video. Retrieved June 13, 2017, from https://www.youtube.com/watch?v=zUJ1l-n0UOc

Jenkins, H., & Carpentier, N. (2013). Theorizing participatory intensities: A conversation about participation and politics. *Convergence, 19*(3), 265–286.

Jerslev, A. (2016). In the time of the microcelebrity: Celebrification and the YouTuber Zoella. *International Journal of Communication, 10*, 5233–5251.

Jones, C. (2002). Signaling expertise: How signals shape careers in creative industries. In M. Peiperl, M. Bernard, & A. Anand (Eds.), *Career creativity: Explorations in the remaking of work* (pp. 209–228). Oxford: Oxford University Press.

Khamis, S., Ang, L., & Welling, R. (2016). Self-branding, 'micro-celebrity' and the rise of social media influencers. *Celebrity Studies*, 1–18. https://doi.org/10.1080/19392397.2016.1218292

Lam, B. (2015, August 7). Why 'do what you love' is pernicious advice. *The Atlantic*. Retrieved November 4, 2016, from http://www.theatlantic.com/business/archive/2015/08/do-what-you-love-work-myth-culture/399599/

Lennard, O. (2015, January 30). How to really be a YouTube star: Be white and wealthy. *The Independent*. Retrieved November 4, 2016, from http://www.independent.co.uk/voices/comment/how-to-really-be-a-youtube-star-be-white-and-wealthy-10013760.html

Lobato, R. (2016). The cultural logic of digital intermediaries: YouTube multi-channel networks. *Convergence, 22*(4), 348–360.

Luckman, S. (2015). Women's micro-entrepreneurial homeworking: A 'magical solution' to the work–life relationship? *Australian Feminist Studies, 30*(84), 146–160.

Marwick, A. E. (2013). *Status update: Celebrity, publicity, and branding in the social media age*. Haven: Yale University Press.

Marwick, A. (2015). Instafame: Luxury selfies in the attention economy. *Public Culture, 27*(1), 137–160.

Marwick, A. E. (2016). You may know me from YouTube: (Micro-) celebrity in social media. In P. D. Marshall & S. Redmond (Eds.), *A companion to celebrity* (pp. 333–350). Chichester: John Wiley & Sons.

Marwick, A. E., & Boyd, D. (2011). I tweet honestly, I tweet passionately: Twitter users, context collapse, and the imagined audience. *New Media & Society, 13*(1), 114–133.

Mayer, V., & Horner, J. (2016). Student media labor in the digital age: MediaNOLA in the classroom and the university. In R. Maxwell (Ed.), *The Routledge companion to labor and media* (pp. 242–251). Abingdon: Routledge.

Oakley, K. (2009). *'Art works'—Cultural labour markets: A literature review*. London: Creativity, Culture and Education.

Patel, K. (2016). Cultural labour, social media and expertise, the experiences of female artists. Presented at *ECREA*, Prague, 12 November 2016. Retrieved November 4, 2016, from https://www.academia.edu/29829180/Cultural_labour_social_media_and_expertise_the_experiences_of_female_artists._Presented_at_ECREA_Prague_12_Nov_2016

Patel, K. (2017). Expertise and collaboration: Cultural workers' performance on social media. In J. Graham & A. Gandini (Eds.), *Collaborative production in the creative industries* (pp. 157–176). London: University of Westminster Press.

Postigo, H. (2016). The socio-technical architecture of digital labour: Converting play into YouTube money. *New Media & Society, 18*(2), 332–349.

Prince, R. (2010). 'Fleshing out' expertise: The making of creative industries experts in the United Kingdom. *Geoforum, 41*(6), 875–884.

Samuelson, K. (2014, December 26). 25 vloggers under 25 who are owning the world of YouTube. *Huffington Post*. Retrieved November 4, 2016, from http://www.huffingtonpost.co.uk/2014/12/17/25-vloggers-under-25-who-are-owning-the-world-of-youtube_n_6340280.html

Schudson, M. (2006). The trouble with experts—And why democracies need them. *Theory and Society, 35*(5–6), 491–506.

Senft, T. (2008). *Camgirls: Celebrity and community in the age of social networks*. New York: Peter Lang.

Senft, T. M. (2013). Microcelebrity and the branded self. In J. Hartley, J. Burgess, & A. Bruns (Eds.), *A companion to new media dynamics* (pp. 346–354). Malden: Wiley-Blackwell.

Shirky, C. (2008). *Here comes everybody*. London: Allen Lane.

Singh Chawla, D. (2014, September 28). The young vloggers and their fans who are changing the face of youth culture. *The Guardian*, 28 September. Retrieved November 4, 2016, from https://www.theguardian.com/technology/2014/sep/28/vloggers-changing-future-advertising

Solon, O. (2016, March 15). How to vlog your way to a million pounds. *Glamour*. Retrieved November 4, 2016, from http://www.glamourmagazine.co.uk/article/how-to-be-a-youtube-millionaire

Tambling, P. (2015, March 20). Freelancing and the future of creative jobs. *Creative and Cultural Skills*, Building a Creative Nation blog. Retrieved November 4, 2016, from https://ccskills.org.uk/supporters/blog/freelancing-and-the-future-of-creative-jobs

Taylor, S. (2015). A new mystique? Working for yourself in the neoliberal economy. *The Sociological Review, 63*(S1), 174–187.

Throsby, D., & Zednik, A. (2011). Multiple job-holding and artistic careers: Some empirical evidence. *Cultural Trends, 20*(1), 9–24.

Turner, S. (2001). What is the problem with experts? *Social Studies of Science, 31*(1), 123–149.

van Dijck, J. (2013). 'You have one identity': Performing the self on Facebook and LinkedIn. *Media, Culture & Society, 35*(2), 199–215.

Vlog Nation. (n.d.). Retrieved November 4, 2016, from http://www.vlognation.com/

Williamson, M. (2016). *Celebrity: Capitalism and the making of fame.* Cambridge: Polity.

YouTube Creator Academy. (n.d.). Retrieved November 4, 2016, from https://www.youtube.com/user/creatoracademy

Daniel Ashton is a Lecturer and an MA Programme Leader in the Winchester School of Art at the University of Southampton. His research focuses on different ways of organising cultural work, including the intersections between professional and amateur media making.

Karen Patel is a Postgraduate Researcher in the School of Media at Birmingham City University. Her PhD focuses on the politics of expertise in cultural work, particularly how cultural workers signal expertise on social media, gendered dynamics of expertise and the role of signalling expertise in cultural labour.

From Presence to Multipresence: Mobile Knowledge Workers' Densified Hours

Johanna Koroma and Matti Vartiainen

Introduction

A pivotal property and capability of mobile information and communication technology (mICT) is to enable mobile, multilocational work. 'Virtual communication' refers to the social use of mICT, which enables its users to be continually available in cross-boundary work. It is typically practised in multinational companies and other networks in which workers operate and collaborate across organisational and cultural boundaries, time zones, and geographical locations. It is part of the 'new normal' of work in such fields. While working across different boundaries, mobile workers are 'multipresent', using mICT to be concurrently present and related in changing physical, virtual, and social spaces.

In this chapter, we focus on why and how knowledge workers increasingly use mICT to communicate and collaborate with other individuals while working in different locations and social situations, as well as the

---

J. Koroma (✉) • M. Vartiainen
Department of Industrial Engineering and Management, Aalto University
School of Science, Aalto University, Finland

factors that drive this behaviour. Based on our data from interviewing 25 mobile knowledge workers, we propose a novel concept of 'multipresence' that arises from a ubiquitous connectivity in different places. We also describe how it is experienced as benefits and costs that influence an individual's productivity and work–life balance. We claim that this type of work has become a normal work approach; however, it remains new from the research point of view.

Theoretical background

Effects of mICT usage on work practices

Our multi-disciplinary approach is based on work and organisational psychology, as well as communication and organisation studies since the 1990s (e.g., Allen & Shoard, 2005; Gibson & Gibbs, 2006; Herbsleb & Mockus, 2003; Herbsleb, Mockus, Finholt, & Grinter, 2000; Hinds & Bailey, 2003; Ruppel, Gong, & Tworoger, 2013). Researchers of these disciplines have deep-dived into the development of digital technologies and their potential to fulfil the needs of global collaboration by enabling cross-boundary communication while also increasing the intensity and fragmentation of work. In particular, emails have been widely adopted, used, and studied as a technological medium in a worldwide business community (e.g., Barley, Meyerson, & Grodal, 2011; Bellotti, Cuchenaut, Howard, & Smith, 2003; Bellotti, Cuchenaut, Howard, Smith, & Grinter, 2005; Mazmanian, Orlikowski, & Yates, 2005; Middleton & Cukier, 2006; Renaud, Ramsay, & Hair, 2006; Thomas et al., 2006). In mobile multilocational work, practical actions as suggested by sociomaterial theory (Orlikowski, 2000, 2007, 2009) arise as an interplay of face-to-face and virtual social interactions in the physical and digital contexts. According to Sproull and Kiesler (1991a), the effects of communication technologies in a networked organisation have two levels of potential consequences. The first-level technical efficiency effects are predictable and planned, whereas the second-level social effects are unpredictable and difficult to control. The first-level ubiquitous communication possibilities appear to increase the efficiency of collaboration, whereas the second-level social effects may change employee behaviour in a way that has unexpected or unwanted consequences on collaborations (Sproull & Kiesler, 1991b), as well as the work–life balance of individual employees (Hill, Hawkins, Ferris, & Weitzman, 2001; Middleton & Cukier, 2006; Murray & Rostis, 2007).

Working from multiple locations

The pressure to be available 24/7 and communicate if possible have strengthened with the increased use of smart mobile technologies (Mazmanian, Orlikowski, & Yates, 2013; Perlow, 2012; Ruppel et al., 2013). Virtual online (synchronous) and delayed (asynchronous) communications are necessary in distributed organisations when mobile knowledge workers increasingly collaborate with their contacts (e.g., Cousins & Robey, 2005; Gareis, Lilischkis, & Mentrup, 2006; Hyrkkänen & Vartiainen, 2005) and coordinate their work with colleagues (Bellotti et al., 2003, 2005). During their daily and weekly work, mobile workers move from one place to another and work from several locations other than their main workplace and home (Koroma, Hyrkkänen, & Vartiainen, 2014). In addition to meeting individuals face-to-face in these locations, they expect those individuals, and are expected in turn by their colleagues and customers, to be socially available because of virtual connectivity (Barley et al., 2011; Mazmanian et al., 2005, 2013). One of our study participants, a male global business human relations manager, summarised how his work-related communication practices had entered other life domains and filled most of his days:

> Sometimes, I use the whole train journey for phone calls; at airports, I usually read my emails and make phone calls to Finland. Then, while driving [from the airport] home, I also talk on the phone and ... This is how my life is right now.

From social presence to multipresence

Researchers have been interested in social presence from the telecommunication perspective for decades (e.g., Rice, 1993; Short, Williams, & Christie, 1976). In this discussion, social presence has included both face-to-face and technologically mediated interactions (Steinfield, 1986) even though this comprehensive definition is rather ambiguous in mediated communication. Social presence requires the multisensory experience of another human being (Biocca, 1997; Ijsselsteijn & Riva, 2003); therefore, it has been defined as the 'sense of being with others' (Biocca, Harms, & Burgoon, 2004, p. 456). Biocca and co-authors (2004) introduced the concept of 'mediated social presence' a decade ago to capture the unique features of interactions mediated by telecommunication technology (e.g., virtual presence). The concept is clearly needed, as mICT provides broader possibilities for virtual presence than ever before. In addition, virtual presence may be both synchronous and asynchronous.

Social presence may also be analysed from the 'absence' viewpoint. Presence and absence are at two ends of a continuum, both socially and virtually (Biocca et al., 2004). Traditionally, social absence occurs when an individual is disengaged and withdrawn from social activities that occur in the same physical space (Kahn, 1990). In addition, an individual may be virtually absent. 'Mediated social absence' signifies the unavailability and non-attendance of an individual in activities that occur in a virtual workspace (Sivunen, 2015; Sivunen & Nordbäck, 2015).

Research on dual presence highlights the significance of social presence in both physical and virtual spheres. Jackson (2002, p. 8) introduced the concept of 'dual presence' not only to explain how workers choose a gender-related strategy to combine their work and domestic duties but also to characterise the social interaction as a general phenomenon 'of being physically present in one domain of experience while virtually present in the other domain via ICT' (Golden, 2009, p. 4). Jackson (2002) and Golden (2009) conceptualised dual presence by enlarging social presence to handle both face-to-face presence in a physical location and virtual presence in a work domain. Rather than separating different tasks and performing them successively, which has previously been considered typical work behaviour, a worker now attempts to perform the tasks simultaneously, thereby benefitting from dual presence. This has been a characteristic behaviour for accomplishing more in the same amount of time (Barley et al., 2011; Golden, 2009), not only while working at home (Daly, 1996) but also at any work place. Smaller, lighter, and more accessible technologies enable synchronous and asynchronous communication almost anywhere using several media, which can result in complex situations. Therefore, we argue that the phenomenon of presence is more diverse than allowed by the dual-presence approach. Our analysis indicates that workers are present in not only two but often multiple spaces (physical, virtual, and social), using several technologies concurrently or successively when changing their physical locations; thus, they are multipresent.

Research on mobile workers (e.g., Koroma et al., 2014) indicates that mICT usage results in both benefits and costs. It increases flexibility and feelings of autonomy (Barley et al., 2011; Hill et al., 2001); however, ubiquitous access to mICT resulting in simultaneous communicative incidents initiates various challenges, such as interruptions in workflow and disruptions in worker concentration (Bellotti et al., 2005; Gonzalez & Mark, 2004; Jackson, Dawson, & Wilson, 1999, 2001, 2003; Manger, Wiklund, & Eikeland, 2003; Mark, Gonzalez, & Harris, 2005; Thomas et al., 2006). Neurophysiological research supports these findings by indicating that it is possible to successfully combine a cognitive activity with a physical activity but not with another cognitive activity (e.g., Jackson, 2008; Just, Keller, & Cynkar, 2008). In many cases, work occurs after official working hours (Fenner & Renn, 2004, 2010). The material properties of asynchronous technologies make it possible to send messages at any time of the day or night, seemingly without disturbing a recipient, as the messages are stored until they are handled. This often results in experiences of stress and extended working hours, because messages pile-up when a receiver is busy performing other tasks (Barley et al., 2011). The need to be almost constantly available adds an extra, often stressful, demand to mobile work.

Data and methods

Research design and data collection

We are interested in answering the following questions:

1. What are the specific causes of multipresence and what are the circumstances that lead to a multipresence strategy?
2. How does the use of mICT enable multipresence events across multiple locations?
3. What types of benefits and costs are attached to these events?

We collected data from individual and focus group interviews, which also included new interviewees. In addition, individual diary records were kept for five workdays. The participants were selected from four companies in the telecommunications, oil, and banking industries, which operated globally or across Northern Europe. The company headquarters were in Helsinki or Espoo, Finland. Prior to data collection, we contacted the company human resources (HR) representatives to obtain additional information about the company and the intensity of the employees' mobility. The company HR department informed its employees of the study, and 25 voluntary candidates (12 women and 13 men, aged 27–63 years) individually contacted the researchers. They were all Finnish-speaking, experienced, white-collar mobile workers occupying different positions, including executive and middle managers, project managers, and experts who worked in partly distributed teams and whose co-located subgroups were located across multiple sites. Three participants worked with teammates who were dispersed in Finland, 12 collaborated with partners in other Nordic countries (Denmark, Sweden, and/or Norway), three worked with partners elsewhere in Europe (Belgium, Germany, Italy, the Netherlands, Switzerland, or the UK), and the remaining seven had global collaborators (Canada, China, India, Singapore, or the USA). Performing their work required or had recently required them to travel regularly, work from a range of different locations, and use ICT extensively across different boundaries.

The data collection proceeded in three phases. First, the voluntary participants contacted the researchers. We explained the data collection protocol and gave them instructions on how to complete a diary for one work week prior to the interview. The participants used electronic Outlook calendars that were partially completed with their pre-booked meetings to make diary completion as simple and easy as possible, particularly when on the move. They colour-coded the calendar items according to the level of mental stress experienced: high strain was marked red, moderate strain was marked yellow, and no strain was marked green. Several participants also wrote detailed notes in the appointment fields of their calendars. Each participant completed a diary record for five full working days, if possible, days that involved business travel.

We printed the electronic diaries and used them as a basis for the individual interview, both to facilitate the informant's recollection and as a separate source of data. We conducted and recorded the semi-structured interviews in a meeting room at the informant's office building. They lasted between 60 and 90 minutes. The aim of an interview was to enrich the diary-based description of the workday. We created the interview themes deductively using the existing literature on mobile work. We asked specific questions of all participants and subsequently allowed them to discuss other significant issues. The key themes explored in the interviews were as follows:

- The use of physical work environments;
- The use of different mobile technologies in different locations and while travelling;
- The experiences of these situations and control of work, and work–life balance.

First, we asked generally about the substance of the participants' work. Next, we discussed their calendars in detail, asking questions such as follows:

1. What happened during the meeting you marked in red [high strain]?
2. Who were you working with?
3. What type of technologies did you use?

We conducted three pilot interviews in one of the companies to ensure the congruence of the interview protocol. All participants were interviewed in their native language, in this case Finnish. Face-to-face interviews fostered an openness to discuss subjective views. After the interview, the participants delivered the printed calendar for more detailed analysis. Only two participants were not able to provide their calendar because of technical problems. Finally, we held two focus group meetings including both our participants and their team members to present our preliminary results and request feedback from them. Initially, we were interested in the specific types of multipresence events the employees experienced and how they perceived them, rather than the prevalence of these experiences. However, using the focus group interviews, we were able to confirm the commonness and, particularly, the familiarity of the experiences among a larger group of mobile workers.

Data analysis

The research undertaken and analysis presented are indicative and explorative rather than generally representative. The method of analysis used was inductive. The interviews were fully transcribed, listened to, and read several times. We coded the transcribed interviews using Atlas.ti® software (Scientific Software Development GmbH, Berlin, Germany) for qualitative data analysis, conducted the coding process independently, and resolved occasional differences through discussion. Coding was an iterative process: we added new codes as we progressed and subsequently recoded previous transcripts to incorporate the new codes. We constantly went back and forth to refine the codes. The intent was to remain at a proximal level of analysis to provide a better vision of obtaining valid and practical knowledge of the different situations during the workweek.

We used event system theory (Morgeson, Mitchell, & Liu, 2015) as the framework to identify events in the data. Event system theory is based on the principle that the controlled information-processing events bounded in space and time are separate from the responses to them, but form individual experiences. According to Morgeson and co-authors (2015), these responses or circumstances are perceptible. Individuals notice particularly novel, disruptive, and critical events that have an effect on their behaviour or, more widely, on an organisation. We followed Morgeson and colleagues in our analysis by defining events initially as being part of the environment or context that is external to the perceiver. Second, they are bounded in space and time (i.e., discrete) such that they have an identifiable temporal beginning and end and evolve in a specific setting. Third, they constitute observable actions or circumstances.

We began our analysis by identifying communication events to understand the usage of mICT in different locations. This provided the answer to our second research question: *How does the use of mICT enable multipresence events across multiple locations?* At first, we used only the codes for specific technologies in use and different physical places where the events occurred; however, we determined that it was necessary to add other codes to include social and virtual interactions as well, because of the embeddedness of the activities. We started to recognise a pattern: interviewees would repeatedly describe themselves in situations communicating with one or many, or of being contacted by someone through communication media when they were busy doing something else in a physical place. Our participants described situations that appeared as multipresence events. We subsequently began to recognise the causes and circumstances that led to this behaviour. This provided the answer to our first research question: *What are the specific causes of multipresence and what are the circumstances that lead to a multipresence strategy?* To answer the third research question, *What types of benefits and costs are attached to these events?*, we identified the benefits and costs that were observed in these events. In some cases, the participants described benefitting from these situations; however, they also described challenges or hindrances to communication and collaboration, which we categorised as costs.

We identified 341 communication events that developed in specific work-related settings and had a detectable and consecutive beginning and end. We obtained very rich data. The participants explained being accompanied by other individuals (family members, colleagues, supervisors, or unknown individuals) in 239 events. Our participants used asynchronous technology in 188 events and synchronous technology in 224 events. In 77 events, different technologies were used in the same event. The events varied from short to rather long and had different effects on individuals and groups. An example of a short event is as follows: 'The flight was late, and I stood in a queue to the gate. Then, I called my team members and boss. We discussed a few minutes'. A long event might be working one or more hours on accumulated emails on a kitchen table at home in the evening, when other family members are watching TV and eventually going to bed. We edited some quotations to improve readability; however, we carefully avoided altering the speaker's intent.

Findings

Continuous availability and access lead to multipresence

Our first research question investigated the specific causes and circumstances that led mobile workers to use a multipresence strategy. As communication technology allowed online and mobile phone access, as well as availability to other individuals physically present (such as family members), our participants developed two main approaches to handling these situations. They would either attempt to divide their attention simultaneously between two social situations (face-to-face and virtual) or postpone virtual communication and handle it later when they had time, privacy, and a peaceful environment. If they were participating in something that required their full attention and was difficult to interrupt, they typically postponed the virtual communication, which very often led to longer, sometimes very long working hours, typically at home or in a hotel room. This approach often resulted in a lack of sufficient recovery time and quality of work/communication. It appeared that it was mostly asynchronous technology, particularly email, which was causing the need to decide between these two strategies. A young male company lobbyist, who was working two to three weeks every month in Brussels and spending his workdays and evenings meeting with politicians, activists, and other contacts, described a commonly felt pressure to react to incoming messages, which made him continue to work late in the evening in his hotel room:

> These business trips are full of back-to-back meetings, and I have noticed that I have no time to read emails until late in the evening after arriving at my hotel room. Then, I have a hundred emails waiting in my inbox.

Although this was a commonly used strategy, we were more interested in events in which the participants attempted to divide their attention between two or more activities that required a simultaneous social and virtual presence. In addition, we aimed to understand the causes of these multipresence events and the circumstances that led to them.

Email overload

One reason participants selected a multipresence strategy was the volume of emails that required their constant attention because of a collectively developed habit to use email as a main medium of communication. Email was mentioned in 177 events. A male sourcing manager of a large telecommunication company indicated that some individuals used mainly email to communicate:

> These people work 'through email'. If you reply, you can be sure that you will receive exponentially more emails.

Constant availability expectations

Collaborators were not aware of each other's physical and social contexts; however, they had begun to interpret those contexts; although their contacts were not constantly online, they would regularly read their emails. This generated a spiralling use of mostly asynchronous technologies to communicate with contacts as soon as they are available; an approach that resulted in an increasing number of emails that required attention, as well as a pressure to be available as much as possible during or after office hours. A male HR manager who travelled between company sites explained this:

> Everybody is trying to be online to get things done. If you cannot be available when you are travelling, the messages are definitely piling.

In many cases, the participants were not able to control the time or number of meetings they were expected to attend, which resulted in a limited time to handle incoming messages and perform other tasks. In addition, when booking the meeting time from invitees' calendars, a meeting inviter regularly selects the media in advance. Many participants felt that they did not have control over their workday schedule. As a male lobbyist explained:

> People very often book meetings from each other's calendars; as a result, you don't really have control over your own calendar as other people can see all your appointments and have access to make reservations ...

Substantial time was spent in meetings. A female talent development manager of a large corporation attempted to book time from her own calendar for the tasks that required concentration. She explained how difficult it was to control the calendar:

> Even my assistant may book a meeting to the only available spot in my calendar, which is my lunch time, even though I have specifically ordered her not to do so.

Expectations that they should participate in at least some of the meetings organised by their team in the main workplace, despite the geographical and temporal boundaries created by the time-zone differences while travelling, resulted in multipresence events. For example, although geographical and time-zone boundaries existed for all collaborating partners, diverse environments and technologies made boundaries more visible to some collaborating partners, particularly those who were participating from a business trip, than to others.

Uncertainty

Asynchronous rather than synchronous media were used intensively for urgent messages. Many participants felt they needed to monitor incoming emails because of the anxiety of not knowing if the content was urgent and required their immediate action. A young female HR specialist explained this concern:

> Previously, before I started to get emails to my phone, it was sometimes difficult to know what type of 'bombs' were waiting there if I could not access my email from vendor premises or a hotel. However, it is now easy. I can monitor what is going on and send a short reply or make a phone call if needed.

In some cases, the combination of a large number of emails and not knowing the contents resulted in an almost compulsory habit of checking messages. For many participants, the solution was to read and reply to emails in every possible situation. A male business HR manager described this response:

> I have to use every available moment to handle my emails because I am getting them all the time and I have no way of knowing whether there is important information in them.

Controlling

The participants attempted to keep themselves updated by monitoring the flow of messages, which provided a feeling of being in control of their work. A male vice-president of production described his strategy to be aware and in control of global activities:

> Carrying a smart device 24/7 with me, I am very aware that even if I haven't activated push email, I only need to push one button to access everything. This awareness is a source of stress. I am always online. I never know what will appear in my email; so, I am reading it quite frequently during evenings and on weekends. It feels good to know that everything appears to be ok.

The participants explained that they individually decided how and when to use mICT to cope with the volume of emails according to the situation, their availability, and the uncertainty of the incoming message contents. They also decided how to control their work and work–life boundary; no participant indicated that she or he had discussed how to resolve these situations with their manager. A female talent manager explained that she decided to use a multipresence strategy for work–life balance:

> I would rather take the calls from my car while driving than from home after office hours.

Multipresence occurs in multiple places

The second research question investigated how the use of mICT enables multipresence events across multiple locations. The participants described five basic types of physical places they used for working: the main workplace, home, moving places (i.e., different means of transportation), secondary (e.g., customer premises and employer's other office) and 'third places' (e.g., airports, cafés, and hotels). 'Third places' are the central settings of informal public life and places to meet outside of the work environment (Oldenburg, 1989). mICT enables these places to be used for work purposes in different situations (e.g., Breure & Van Meel, 2003; Brown & O'Hara, 2003; Forlano, 2008; Perry, O'Hara, Sellen, Brown, & Harper, 2001). The circumstances in the physical environments influenced both social and virtual interactions. The participants identified the restrictions and possibilities of these places. In addition, the use of mICT did not tie them to working in one place; therefore, it was possible to change environments and use a chosen media when moving from place to place.

Main workplace

Most communication events ($N = 114$) occurred in the main workplace, typically in meeting rooms and open office premises, surrounded by local colleagues. The main workplace was used to meet other individuals unofficially in an open office area and officially in face-to-face meetings. The most frequent event was the use of synchronous and asynchronous technologies in an open office environment, surrounded by many colleagues doing the same. The other common event was to be present in online or face-to-face meetings while also using technology, often email, for virtual presence. Asynchronous technology was often used during the meetings inconspicuously and without disturbing other members. A female HR manager was typical of many participants. She described how she did this:

> I was in a live meeting for an hour and a half in our [open] office. I naturally wrote emails during the meeting because we did not use video cameras.

Synchronous technology was used on short breaks between meetings. The participants appeared to feel obligated to be available as much as possible during normal office hours in their main workplace, more than in any other location, despite their other assignments.

Home

Many communication events occurred at home ($N = 104$). The participants worked at home occasionally or regularly, typically once a week. For many participants, teleworking from home required extra arrangements and affected their choice of communications media for several reasons. For example, their children under school age were taken care of at home or by a spouse who arrived home from a night shift and attempted to sleep, or their retired spouse was at home. Nevertheless, very often, they worked before and after office hours while other family members were present. A female head of sourcing explained how she began her mornings:

A typical situation or almost my habit is that first thing in the morning, I try to react without a delay to the emails that I have received from the USA during the night and determine whether I will need to be the first one rushing out the door to the office or if I can take it easy and send the kids to the school first making sure they have their bus tickets in their pockets….

Late-evening virtual meetings from home when other family members were also present were relatively common and essential for global collaborations because of time-zone differences. In some cases, being available at late hours required making special arrangements, because the home role was not visible to the collaborating partner. A male business HR manager explained that his availability depended on the situation:

> How I handle the incoming phone calls after working hours depends entirely on the situation and who is calling. For example, if my manager calls in the middle of a family dinner, what else can I do but take the call.

Moving places

Events in moving places (N = 51) occurred in aeroplanes, taxis, trains, and cars. There was a constant need to use time efficiently and be available, despite the means of transportation. In aeroplanes, work and communication were asynchronous because of a lack of network access, whereas synchronous communication events, such as phone calls, were typically executed in cars, both while driving and as a passenger in a taxi. A female talent development manager who regularly used all travel times to make phone calls explained how situations changed when moving from home to the office while also attending a conference call:

> I attended a conference call [while driving]. It lasted longer than I expected. After I arrived at work, I ended up sitting in my car in the company parking garage to continue the call. Then I walked to our office and walked around the floor, still talking on the phone.

The need to remain in contact occasionally led to attempting to work in undeniably quite demanding and unsuitable conditions such as dangerous physical environments. A female chief director of HR managers noted:

> Although my drive to the office is very short and I don't have time to work in my car, I admit that I occasionally read emails at a traffic light and decide to make a short phone call or take a call.

Often the pressure to use every available situation for working appeared to be strong, even though it is illegal in Finland, as in many other countries, to use a hand-held device (i.e., not mounted and voice-activated) for phone calls or reading and writing emails or text messages while driving. The participants indicated that they scheduled conference and other phone calls for their travel time in a private car or a taxi because they felt it was the only available time and was a sufficiently private place to have a discussion. Even travelling time to a vacation home with family was used for urgent or important phone calls. Colleagues and subordinates learned that some individuals were easier to reach while they were commuting at a specific time of the workday, and changed their behaviour accordingly, as a female HR specialist explained:

> In the mornings when I am driving to work, it is early afternoon in Singapore, and they have just returned from lunch. They have learned that it is easier to reach me at that time by phone while I am sitting in a car.

Some participants emphasised that their organisations expected them while travelling to handle the same tasks they would perform when in the office.

Secondary places

The smallest number of communication events ($N = 22$) occurred in secondary places. The participants found it challenging to be available for virtual communication and to identify a place and time to read emails while working in secondary places, such as a customer's premises, the employer's other office, or a manufacturing site. They described mainly using the short breaks in their busy meeting schedule to make phone calls or handle emails. An experienced female project manager explained how she attempted to incorporate necessary work tasks in her day:

We were required to take laptops to the training. I felt pressure to use every possible situation to read my emails and received a couple of urgent phone calls as well. Therefore, I needed to use the breaks to listen to my voice mails and make phone calls. In practice, I could not concentrate on what was taught.

In general, the participants were fully occupied while working in secondary places; however, at the same time, they were aware of messages piling up and used every possible opportunity to check that there were no urgent messages in their inbox or voice mail.

Third places

We identified many events in third places ($N = 53$). The participants used mostly asynchronous technologies because they were typically communicating after regular office hours across time zones or surrounded by unknown individuals and concerned about privacy issues. The medium was chosen according to not only the task but also the local situation. A female talent manager described how she chose a communication media while travelling:

[At the airport] The technology I use depends on how much time I have available. It takes more time to use a laptop, so I often use my mobile phone for quick tasks.

In some cases, our participants communicated using their phone from very unusual places, such as a shopping mall or a playground, when babysitting their children.

Multipresence results in benefits and costs

Our third research question investigated the benefits and costs related to multipresence events. To address this question, we assessed events in which the participants described benefitting from these situations or perceiving inconveniences as individual costs. Many participants indicated how devices enabled them to use their time more efficiently, but also resulted in pressure to use the devices in every possible situation during their work and leisure time.

Benefits

mICT provided our participants with resources that they would otherwise not have had. The participants clearly felt that technology was a resource for them and they benefitted from using it, even though they needed actively to adjust their work practices, and to plan and control specific situations as they arose. They described having more possibilities, opportunities, and flexibility.

Efficient use of time. The most important benefit was an opportunity to use 'unproductive' time efficiently between different work activities or when moving between places, such as the time between meetings, following a schedule change, or sitting in a taxi or cafe. Typically, the social component in these physical places was weak and did not require their complete attention. The participants described circumstances in which they were surrounded by strangers or when their social role differed from their ordinary work role but was not very demanding, such as role of a passenger, customer, or visitor. A talent manager who travelled in all Nordic countries and regularly used a taxi as her transportation to and from airports described how she used such time:

> I could say that I have teleconferences regularly while I am in a taxi. I know in advance the time slot, and I can schedule a teleconference or make other phone calls and use that time efficiently.

The flexibility to check messages in different times and places was described as saving substantial time in responding to demanding situations and preventing subsequent problems. A male production designer, who had previously worked in a position that included regular evening phone calls, explained:

> I would rather deal with a problem in five minutes at home by phone than attempt to fix it for several hours the next day or week.

Mobility enabler. The ability to work from different locations using mICT was considered essential for mobile workers and was therefore perceived positively. A young male lobbyist said that the opportunity to use portable technologies was fundamental to his work:

> I think that the possibility to make phone calls and read emails on my phone while, for example, waiting in a lobby for a postponed meeting to begin makes my work truly mobile.

Flexibility enabler. The flexibility to use multiple technologies and devices instead of relying on only one technology or device that may not operate sufficiently in all situations was described positively. In addition, the participants were able to arrange virtual meetings in two separate situations, namely, when a face-to-face meeting was not feasible and to reduce the amount of work-related travel.

Costs

In addition to benefits, the participants also identified several costs of communication events, particularly difficulty concentrating, productivity losses, disturbances in their work–life balance, and stress. They were typically unable to plan and control these situations, which they described as externally initiated.

Concentration difficulties. Our participants attempted to cope by being physically present in a meeting while using asynchronous media that did not interfere with the meeting to manage their other tasks. Therefore, they were unable to follow the meeting and ended up not concentrating well on any task. A male sourcing manager summed up the impression of many study participants:

> If I look at my colleagues in meetings, most of them are not really present but handle their emails instead. ... Afterwards, they don't have any idea what issues were dealt with in the meeting.

The same sourcing manager also indicated that restlessness and frequent interruptions in open office areas resulted in concentration difficulties.

> We have [in this company] reduced travelling and instead increased the number of teleconferences to a witless amount without developing ground rules on how to behave. Some individuals participate in teleconferences from their desks and 'yell' into their phone. There may be three teleconferences going on simultaneously in a small open office area, and there is this hullabaloo going on.

Productivity losses. The participants said that they regularly interrupted their work because they needed to pay attention to what is going on around them when surrounded by colleagues because some of the information could be useful. A male HR manager who routinely received several messages and calls on the top of a dense daily meeting schedule described how this affected his productivity:

> … my phone keeps ringing and emails are appearing in my inbox, and I haven't really done anything that requires concentration for at least six months … and I should …

Challenges in work–life balance. The connectivity and 24/7 availability had several consequences for the participants' family lives and work–life balance. Many participants (both male and female) had difficulties managing their work–life balance. A female chief director of HR managers confessed that she had given up trying to keep up, for example, with family dinners:

> I have nagged my husband about being online 24 hours a day. Now I have understood that life has changed, and everybody is doing it, including myself. Families used to eat dinner together at 5 p.m., but we are not even at home at that time. Fortunately, my mother said that not even she could do it anymore in these circumstances.

Stress. Many participants described how an email overload, easy access to the network, and portable devices made it sometimes difficult to resist checking emails. They felt that they needed to know 'what is going on' and be 'on top of things' even though they were aware that this habit resulted in disruptions to work, difficulties in managing their work–life balance, and therefore, a stressful experience. A male vice-president of production explained that regularly accessing his email often led to unwanted consequences:

> I know that it does cause me stress to be constantly online because I never know what I will find in my inbox. I quite often check my emails in the evenings and during weekends because it keeps me peaceful to know that nothing serious is happening and everything appears to be ok. However, if I realise a message that will make me worry about what is going on and read it more carefully, then I am in the loop of stressful thoughts and my leisure time is sacrificed.

Most participants indicated that they experienced stress because of the pressure to be available for synchronous contacts or to monitor asynchronous messages despite their busy work schedule and after-office hours.

Discussion and conclusions

Mobile ICT has enabled knowledge workers to work and collaborate flexibly in almost any place, thereby creating an increasingly common mobile and multilocational lifestyle. However, this development has brought expectations from employers, collaborators, and the mobile workers themselves that they will make themselves available at all times, regardless of the local context. To meet the communication and collaboration demands, mobile workers often use a multipresence strategy. Consequently, mobile workers use it because they feel that they *have* to or are *expected* to be present in multiple spaces to perform successfully on their job or they *try to manage* their working hours and work–life balance. These situations occur during work or leisure time when an individual is also occupied with other activities that demand attention and concentration. Thus, they are creating and maintaining a cycle of responsiveness (Perlow, 2012) that reinforces their need to be available. Our findings are in line with previous research on how sociomaterial distinctions between different technologies shape behaviour and create not only new possibilities but also new work demands (e.g., Barley et al., 2011). This new normal behavioural change has an effect on the entire organisation or network of workers, as well as on the workers' private lives.

Our study contributes to the presence literature by introducing technology-enabled multipresence as a novel concept to define workers' preference to be simultaneously present in physical, virtual, and social spaces while working across boundaries in multiple locations and on the move. States of presence arise from different combinations of physical, virtual, and social spaces ranging from absence to presence, both socially and virtually. Communication and collaboration events are divided into four types of event categories depending on the type of space and the method of communication used, as indicated in Fig. 1. The events take place in different and changing circumstances, and are influenced by the technology in use, the local context, and situational demands. The multipresent event occurs when an individual works virtually by using simultaneously different synchronous and asynchronous technologies in a physical place that is also occupied by other people. mICT does not bind a user to one physical place but instead it is possible to maintain virtual presence and availability while changing physical and social environments. Multipresence enlarges the concept of dual presence by including simultaneous synchronic and asynchronic communication using different technologies in changing locations.

Mobile knowledge workers are more exposed to multipresence events than stationary workers are because they are on the move and mICT is often the only available communication channel through which they can reach colleagues or other collaborators. They cannot select absence as a permanent strategy because of their collaboration and coordination demands. They are likely to be virtually available and present, which results in both benefits and costs. As they work from different locations,

From social presence to multipresence

Space				
Physical place	Yes	Yes	Yes in one place	Yes in changing places
Social/face-to-face	Yes	No	Yes	Yes
Mediated/virtual	No	Asynchronously and/or synchronously with other(s)	Asynchronously or synchronously with other(s)	Asynchronously and synchronously with other(s)
Presence	Social	Virtual	Dual	Multi-

Fig. 1 Different types of communication and collaboration events in mobile multi-locational work

they typically need to decide on their own how to balance the benefits and costs. They may choose to perform their online tasks simultaneously with other activities, solving work-related problems 'just-in-time', or they may choose to postpone online communication. If they do not make themselves available, messages will accumulate and they will need to handle them after office hours. However, if they respond to the interruption, they will not be able to concentrate sufficiently on either communication, resulting in productivity loss.

Our study is not without limitations. Since we did not include observations of the participants' daily work but relied on retrospective interviews and calendar entries, it remains unclear how the actual communication events occurred. It may be difficult for the participants to recall all events and separate the different technologies used in one event. Therefore, we suppose that there were even more and more complex communication events than our findings suggest. It is also unlikely that the participants would have described or marked their calendars for events that did not occur. Our data were obtained only from Finnish participants. Cultural and organisational differences in the norms and preferences for using specific types of technologies are likely have an effect on worker behaviour, even in global companies.

Our results emphasise the responsibilities of an organisation, a team, and a manager to support individual employees to manage work-related communication and work–life boundaries. When using current technologies and beginning to utilise new technologies, both employers and mobile multilocational employees must consider and agree on the following:

1. How to use varied and new technologies to create and maintain the required continual, open dialogue in teams and organisations, while maintaining mobile workers' productivity;
2. Better work practices for use in varied communication and collaboration events in the knowledge workflow to ensure sufficient recovery time, work–life balance, and well-being at work;
3. These decisions cannot be relegated to an individual employee. Instead, laws and societal policies, and organisational strategies and guidelines should guide and control common work practices. Advising individual employees to learn new skills and competences so that they can process information faster, and that they must also prioritise their tasks, manage their time, or remove distractions that disrupt their work, does not solve the problem. In the interests of efficiency and well-being, individuals who work together must have a common understanding about how and when to withdraw from multipresence and safeguard their ability to concentrate at work, and about how to achieve recovery time both off- and on-the-job.

The occurrence of multipresence events in work will continue to increase because of mobile lifestyles, the availability of new physical premises in which to work (e.g., cafés and hubs with good Internet access), developing technologies such as augmented reality (e.g., optical head-mounted displays and other wearable technologies), and new ways to communicate, such as company social media. The current practices of mobile email and online meetings are in transition; technologies will change and progress rapidly. We do not think that our findings are device-specific; rather, they are more dependent on the properties of the technologies used; for example, the synchronicity or asynchronicity of communication, and the social effects. Additional research is required to understand technology-mediated collaboration and the consequences for worker productivity, work–life balance, and well-being. We anticipate that the construct of multipresence provides a conceptual tool for scrutinising and investigating presence in a work environment of rapidly digitalising communication.

References

Allen, D. K., & Shoard, M. (2005). Spreading the load: Mobile information and communications technologies and their effect on information overload. *Information Research, 10*(2). Retrieved July 2014, from http://www.informationr.net/ir/10-2/paper227.html

Barley, S. R., Meyerson, D. E., & Grodal, S. (2011). E-mail as a source and symbol of stress. *Organization Science, 22*(4), 887–906.

Bellotti, V., Cuchenaut, N., Howard, M., & Smith, I. (2003). Taking email to task: The design and evaluation of a task management centered email tool. In *CHI '03 Proceedings of the SIGCHI Conference on Human Factors in Computing Systems* (pp. 345–352). New York: ACM.

Bellotti, V., Cuchenaut, N., Howard, M., Smith, I., & Grinter, R. E. (2005). Quality versus Quantity: E-mail-centric task management and its relation with overload. *Human–Computer Interaction, 20*(1), 89–138.

Biocca, F. (1997). The cyborg's dilemma: Progressive embodiment in virtual environments. *Journal of Computer-Mediated Communication, 3*(2). https://doi.org/10.1111/j.1083-6101.1997.tb00070.x

Biocca, F., Harms, C., & Burgoon, J. K. (2004). Toward a more robust theory and measure of social presence: Review and suggested criteria. *Presence, 12*(5), 456–480.

Breure, A., & Van Meel, J. (2003). Airport offices: Facilitating nomadic workers. *Facilities, 21*(7/8), 175–179.

Brown, B., & O'Hara, K. (2003). Place as a practical concern of mobile workers. *Environment and Planning A, 35*(9), 1565–1587.

Cousins, K. C., & Robey, D. (2005). Human agency in a wireless world: Patterns of technology use in nomadic computing environments. *Information and Organization, 15*(2), 151–180.

Daly, K. J. (1996). *Families & time: Keeping pace in a hurried culture*. Thousand Oaks, CA: Sage.

Fenner, G. H., & Renn, R. W. (2004). Technology-assisted supplemental work: Construct definition and a research framework. *Human Resource Management, 43*(2 & 3), 179–200.

Fenner, G. H., & Renn, R. W. (2010). Technology-assisted supplemental work and work-to-family conflict: The role of instrumentality beliefs, organizational expectations and time management. *Human Relations, 63*(1), 63–82.

Forlano, L. (2008). Working on the move. The social and digital ecologies of mobile workplaces. In D. Hislop (Ed.), *Mobility and technology in the workplace* (pp. 28–42). London: Routledge.

Gareis, K., Lilischkis, S., & Mentrup, A. (2006). Mapping the mobile e workforce in Europe. In J. H. E. Andriessen & M. Vartiainen (Eds.), *Mobile virtual work. A new paradigm?* (pp. 45–69). Heidelberg: Springer.

Gibson, C. B., & Gibbs, J. L. (2006). Unpacking the concept of virtuality: The effects of geographic dispersion, electronic dependence, dynamic structure, and national diversity on team innovation. *Administrative Science Quarterly, 51*(3), 451–495.

Golden, A. G. (2009). A technologically gendered paradox of efficiency. Caring more about work while working in more care. In S. Kleinman (Ed.), *The culture of efficiency. Technology in everyday life* (pp. 339–354). New York: Peter Lang.

Gonzalez, V. M., & Mark, G. (2004). 'Constant, constant multitasking craziness': Managing multiple working spheres. In *CHI '03 Proceedings of the SIGCHI Conference on Human Factors in Computing Systems* (pp. 113–120). New York: ACM.

Herbsleb, J. D., & Mockus, A. (2003). Formulation and preliminary test of an empirical theory of coordination in software engineering. In *ESEF/FSE'03* (pp. 138–147). New York: ACM.

Herbsleb, J. D., Mockus, A., Finholt, T. A., & Grinter, R. E. (2000). Distance, dependencies, and delay in global collaboration. In *Proceedings of the ACM Conference of Computer-Supported Cooperative Work (CSCW) 2000* (pp. 319–328). New York: ACM.

Hill, E. J., Hawkins, A. J., Ferris, M., & Weitzman, M. (2001). Finding an extra day a week: The positive influence of perceived job flexibility on work and family life balance. *Family Relations, 50*(1), 49–58.

Hinds, P. J., & Bailey, D. E. (2003). Out of sight, out of sync: Understanding conflict on distributed teams. *Organization Science, 14*(6), 615–632.

Hyrkkänen, U., & Vartiainen, M. (2005). *Mobiili työ ja hyvinvointi [Mobile work and wellbeing]* (Vol. 293). Helsinki: Ministry of Economic Affairs and Employment.

Ijsselsteijn, W. A., & Riva, G. (2003). Being there: The experience of presence in mediated environments. In G. Riva, F. Davide, & W. A. Ijsselsteijn (Eds.), *Being there: Concepts, effects and measurement of user presence in synthetic environments* (pp. 4–15). Amsterdam, The Netherlands: IOS Press.

Jackson, M. (2002). *What's happening to home? Balancing work, life, and refuge in the information age*. Notre Dame: Sorin Books.

Jackson, M. (2008). *Distracted: The erosion of attention and the coming dark age*. Amherst, NY: Prometheus Books.

Jackson, T. W., Dawson, R., & Wilson, D. (1999). Improving the communications process: The costs and effectiveness of email compared with traditional media. In C. Hawkins, E. Georgiadou, L. Perivolaropoulos, M. Ross, & G. Staples (Eds.), *Fourth International Conference on Software Process Improvement Research, Education and Training. British Computer Society, INSPIRE'99* (pp. 167–178). Crete: British Computer Society.

Jackson, T. W., Dawson, R., & Wilson, D. (2001). The cost of email interruption. *Journal of Systems Information Technology, 5*(1), 81–92.

Jackson, T. W., Dawson, R., & Wilson, D. (2003). Reducing the effect of email interruptions on employees. *International Journal of Information Management, 23*(1), 55–65.

Just, M. A., Keller, T. A., & Cynkar, J. (2008). A decrease in brain activation associated with driving when listening to someone speak. *Brain Research, 1205*, 70–80. https://doi.org/10.1016/j.brainres.2007.12.075

Kahn, W. A. (1990). Psychological conditions of personal engagement and disengagement at work. *Academy of Management Journal, 33*(4), 692–724.

Koroma, J., Hyrkkänen, U., & Vartiainen, M. (2014). Looking for people, places and connections: Hindrances when working in multiple locations—A review. *New Technology, Work and Employment, 29*(2), 139–159.

Manger, T., Wiklund, R. A., & Eikeland, O. J. (2003). Speed communication and solving social problems. *Communications, 28*(3), 323–337.

Mark, G., Gonzalez, V. M., & Harris, G. (2005). No task left behind? Examining the nature of fragmented work. In *Proceedings of ACM CHI 2005* (pp. 321–330). Portland, OR: ACM Press.

Mazmanian, M. A., Orlikowski, W. J., & Yates, J. (2005). Crackberries: The social implications of ubiquitous wireless email services. In C. Soerensen, Y. Yoo, K. Lyytinen, & J. I. DeGross (Eds.), *Designing ubiquitous information environments: Socio-technical issues and challenges, IFIP—The International Federation for Information Processing* (Vol. 185, pp. 337–343). Boston, MA: Springer.

Mazmanian, M. A., Orlikowski, W. J., & Yates, J. (2013). The autonomy paradox: The implications of mobile email devices for knowledge professionals. *Organization Science, 24*(5), 1337–1357. https://doi.org/10.1287/orsc.1120.0806

Middleton, C. A., & Cukier, W. (2006). Is mobile email functional or dysfunctional? Two perspective on mobile email usage. *European Journal of Information Systems, 15*(3), 252–260.

Morgeson, F. P., Mitchell, T. R., & Liu, D. (2015). Event system theory: An event-oriented approach to the organizational sciences. *Academy of Management Review, 40*(4), 515–537.

Murray, W. C., & Rostis, A. (2007). Who's running the machine? A theoretical exploration of work, stress and burnout of technologically tethered workers. *Journal of Individual Employment Rights, 12*(3), 249–228.

Oldenburg, R. (1989). The character of third places. In R. Oldenburg (Ed.), *The great good place* (pp. 20–42). New York: Marlowe.

Orlikowski, W. J. (2000). Using technology and constituting structures: A practice lens for studying technology in organizations. *Organization Science, 11*(4), 404–428.

Orlikowski, W. J. (2007). Sociomaterial practices: Exploring technology at work. *Organization Studies, 28*(9), 1435–1448.

Orlikowski, W. J. (2009). The sociomateriality of organizational life: Considering technology in management research. *Cambridge Journal of Economics, 1*(17). https://doi.org/10.1093/cje/bep058

Perlow, L. A. (2012). *Sleeping with your smart phone: How to break the 24/7 habit and change the way you work.* Boston, MA: Harvard Business Review Press.

Perry, M., O'Hara, K., Sellen, A., Brown, B., & Harper, R. (2001). Dealing with mobility: Understanding access anytime, anywhere. *ACM Transactions on Computer-Human Interaction, 8*(4), 323–347.

Renaud, K., Ramsay, J., & Hair, M. (2006). 'You've got mail!' … Shall I deal with it now? Electronic mail from the recipient's perspective. *International Journal of Human-Computer Interaction, 21*(3), 313–332.

Rice, R. E. (1993). Media appropriateness: Using social presence theory to compare traditional and new organizational media. *Human Communication Research, 19*(4), 451–484.

Ruppel, C. P., Gong, B., & Tworoger, L. C. (2013). Using communication choices as boundary-management strategy: How choices of communication media affect the work–life balance of teleworkers in a global virtual team. *Journal of Business and Technical Communication, 27*(4), 436–471. https://doi.org/10.1177/1050651913490941

Short, J. A., Williams, E., & Christie, B. (1976). *The social psychology of telecommunications.* London: Wiley.

Sivunen, A. (2015). Presence and absence in global virtual team meetings: Physical, virtual and social dimensions. In J. Webster & K. Randle (Eds.), *Virtual workers and the global labour market* (pp. 199–217). London: Palgrave Macmillan.

Sivunen, A., & Nordbäck, E. (2015). Social presence as a multi-dimensional group construct in 3D virtual environments. *Journal of Computer-Mediated Communication, 20*(1), 19–36. https://doi.org/10.1111/jcc4.12090

Sproull, L., & Kiesler, S. (1991a). A two-level perspective on technology. In L. Sproull & S. Kiesler (Eds.), *Connections: New ways of working in networked organization* (pp. 1–18). Cambridge, MA: MIT Press.

Sproull, L., & Kiesler, S. (1991b). Beyond efficiency. In L. Sproull & S. Kiesler (Eds.), *Connections: New ways of working in networked organization* (pp. 19–36). Cambridge, MA: MIT Press.

Steinfield, C. W. (1986). Computer mediated communication in an organizational setting: Explaining task-related and socio economic uses. In M. L. McLaughlin (Ed.), *Communication yearbook 9* (pp. 777–804). Newbury Park, CA: Sage.

Thomas, G. F., King, C. L., Baroni, B., Cook, L., Keitelman, M., Miller, S., et al. (2006). Conceptualizing e-mail overload. *Journal of Business and Technical Communication, 20*(3), 252–287.

Johanna Koroma is a doctoral candidate in the Virtual and Mobile Work Research Unit (http://www.vmwork.net/), Department of Industrial Engineering and Management, Aalto University School of Science. She is a senior expert in the Finnish Institute of Occupational Health. Her research interests focus on designing new ways of working in distributed settings and on developing digital services for occupational health and well-being at work.

Matti Vartiainen is Professor of Work and Organisational Psychology in the Department of Industrial Engineering and Management, Aalto University School of Science. He is a mentoring professor in the Virtual and Mobile Work Research and Work Psychology and Leadership Units (http://tuta.aalto.fi/en/about/bit/). With his research teams, he is studying organisational innovations, digital work, leadership and well-being in new ways of working, mobile and multilocational distributed teams and organisations, reward systems, knowledge and competence building, and e-learning systems.

Affectual Demands and the Creative Worker: Experiencing Selves and Emotions in the Creative Organisation

Iva Josefsson

Self-expression is arguably at the core of creative practices and creative work. As creative work is focused on the production of aesthetic products largely through autonomous and self-regulated work practices, individuals and selves are called upon more directly in its production. For example, it has long been observed that creative workers express a strong sense of attachment to their work that is unrivalled in other forms of work (Hesmondhalgh & Baker, 2011; Thompson, Parker, & Cox, 2016). Creative work, therefore, is particularly relevant for understanding new work norms that demand an intimacy in the experiences of self and work (Gregg, 2011). Similarly, creative work settings are viewed as sites that are increasingly reliant on 'mobilising the subjectivity of labour' (Thompson et al., 2016) in order to capture qualities of the individual that benefit the production of creative work. Management attempts this by capturing the desires of the workers, including those for self-realisation, thereby aligning

---

I. Josefsson (✉)
University of Bath, Bath, UK

Lund University, Lund, Sweden

the interests of the worker with the interests of capital. Work is no longer seen as a constraint on the individual's freedom to 'fulfil his or her potential through strivings for autonomy, creativity and responsibility', but rather as 'an essential element in the path of self-realization' (Miller & Rose, 1990, p. 27). Such attempts reflect a kind of 'soft capitalism' approach to work that tries to incorporate intimate 'life' experiences of the worker directly in and through work in the hopes of securing worker commitment and replacing more coercive forms of control, which are often resisted more actively (Boltanski & Chiapello, 2005; Heelas, 2002; Thrift, 2005).

And yet, an individual's attempts to capture life and intimacy in his or her work have a largely affective component; that is, they call on emotional experiences of 'love' and 'fulfilment' in what can be considered a new form of affective labour (Gregg, 2011). Such demands inspire the collapsing of boundaries between self and work. This collapsing of boundaries and workers' emotion work in attempting to navigate them is particularly salient within an organisational setting, where individuals are guided by dominant organisational discourses and practices. This chapter attempts to make sense of the 'new normal' experiences of living and working with the self in the creative organisation by exploring the emotion talk of creative workers within an organisation that develops video games.

Creative work, self, and affect

Much has been already said about the rise of the 'new creative class', about the rise of creative labour, cultural work, and cultural and creative industries and their economic significance (cf. Howkins, 2013; Menger, 2014). While little agreement is reached about how to label this new frontier of work, creative work and creative workers are 'in the cockpit of attention, front and centre of the latest rollouts of neoliberal programs' (Ross, 2008, p. 32). Addressing creative work as defined by the activities and work that stems from the symbol-making of immaterial production casts a very wide net and almost captures the activity of individuals in many, if not almost all occupations. Instead, like Hesmondhalgh and

Baker (2011), I include here in my definition of 'creative worker' those working in organisations where the primary activity is to produce aesthetic products.

Empirical research on creative workers and their conditions have focused on various conditions of their work, including autonomy, specialisation, and social engagement (Lingo & Tepper, 2013; Thompson et al., 2016), identity (Alvesson, 1994; Taylor, 2010; Taylor & Littleton, 2013), as well as establishing definitions of 'good' and 'bad' creative work (Hesmondhalgh & Baker, 2008, 2011). Despite the contemporary interest in the creative worker, most recent studies continue to call for more empirical research in the area, as it appears that a superabundance of individuals are answering the call to creativity (Caves, 2000). As Banks (2007, p. 4) states, 'we still know very little about the working lives of this new army of dot-commers, music-makers, fashionistas, net gurus, brand-builders, cool-hunters and image-entrepreneurs'. Of the studies published since Banks' observation, we know that creative work is primarily described as flexible, insecure, highly mobile, poorly paid, and with a 'mixture of anxiety and attachment to creative endeavours and aesthetics' (Thompson et al., 2016, p. 3). The most frequently discussed aspect of creative work seems to be uncertainty (cf. Menger, 2014), or the political and precarious nature of work where stable forms of work are absent and boundaries are porous (Gill & Pratt, 2008; Ross, 2008; Thompson et al., 2016).

The majority of in-depth empirical studies on creative workers have therefore explored creative workers working in precarious positions within organisations (for example, as on short-term contracts, Hesmondhalgh & Baker, 2008, 2011), either as aspirants (McRobbie, 1998; Taylor & Littleton, 2013) or as self-employed (Taylor, 2015). The demands and experiences of work in a creative organisation under stable employment may imply rather different structural and socio-psychological dynamics. In these settings, workers become hardened subjects of organisational discourses and structures that offer resources for creative work but also regulate behaviours and norms as well as experiences. Studying the dynamics of creative work in the setting of a creative organisation can further develop our understanding of creative work and workplace relations of the creative worker. Critical literature examining workplace relations in organisations argues for the unequal power relations between employer and employee or between management and worker. To this end, studies have been quick to criticise management approaches that attempt to incorporate aspects of the individual as part of the means of production by aligning organisational interests with individual interests (Andersen & Born, 2008; Bojesen & Muhr, 2008; Du Gay, 1996; Hanlon, 2017; Heelas, 2002). These theorists address the capturing of desires for self-realisation but also the capturing of affect as part of the demanded intimacy of the new normal of contemporary work (Gregg, 2011).

Not only are experiences of self and work regulated by these new approaches within organisations, but so is the workers' capacity and demand for emotional expression, as witnessed in the emotion talk of workers. This type of emotion work is clearly exhibited in other in-depth studies of creative workers (cf. Hesmondhalgh & Baker, 2011; Taylor & Littleton, 2013). The regulation of selves in organisational environments has already been studied empirically through the lenses of identity (Boussebaa & Brown, 2017; Brown, Kornberger, Clegg, & Carter, 2010), organisational culture (Casey, 1995; Kunda, 1992), the dialectics of control and resistance (Fleming & Sturdy, 2010), and even emotional labour (Hochschild, 1983), to name just a few key dimensions. However, the creative organisation as a context for exploring relations of selves and work offers a new frontier for exploring these dimensions further.

These existing studies present detailed accounts of organisational activities but also of individuals' reactions to them. In most accounts, there has been a great deal of ambivalence in the experience of, and attempts at, self-regulation at work, with many coping by distancing the self from work through cynicism (Fleming & Sturdy, 2010; Kunda, 1992) or questioning the authenticity of self-performances (Hochschild, 1983). These studies also show how workers who attempt to capture their selves in their work are able to articulate and reflexively redraw the boundaries between themselves and their work through their talk, which is a form of resistance and coping. In this chapter, I show how such activity becomes rather challenging for creative workers, how the individual's relationship to his or her work becomes difficult to uncouple in the shadows of the affectual demands of working in creative fields. The complication of selves and these affectual demands on individuals implies the potential value of exploring the emotion talk of creative workers in creative organisations to offer new insights about the experiences and challenges of work and life in the contemporary creative organisation.

The case of Octant Studio

The empirical material that forms the basis for this chapter formed a part of a larger research project exploring the relationships between creativity and identity in a creative workplace. The study's aim was to explore and unpack the experiences of creatives working in a creative organisation and relate them to the broader organisational qualities. The nature of this research project was qualitative–interpretive, gathering largely observational and interview material at a Swedish video game development company over a seven-month period. The materials collected over this period comprise 41 semi-structured interviews with organisation members and field notes from observations at meetings and everyday interactions. Interviews were conducted on site at the organisation in various private meeting rooms. They were audio-recorded and later transcribed. All 41 interviews were conducted in English and lasted between 40 and 100 minutes, with the average interview lasting approximately 60 minutes. All names, including the organisation's name, are pseudonyms, to respect the promised confidentiality of the interviewees. During the interview sessions, the talk focused on (1) the individuals' backgrounds and life stories, (2) the relationship between the self and creativity, (3) creativity issues they experienced, and (4) creativity and the organisation. The interviews were conducted mainly with workers directly engaged in various forms of creative work, for example, game and concept artistry, music and sound design, level design, and game production. Nearly all interviewees identified themselves and their work as being highly creative, with creativity being particularly meaningful to their self-understandings. Observations in meetings and everyday interactions corroborated the narratives of these creative selves. For example, the observation of a team-building exercise involving one of the design teams and run by Human Resources, encouraged team members to reflect on results from psychometric testing they had done in order to 'make sense of who you are' and to 'get to know yourself' for the purposes of 'working better in the team'. This reflected how the organisation was rather instrumental in fostering selves as a part of the work. Such observations contextualised the talk and texts of the creatives and offered insights into the organisational dynamics of creative work. These observed organisational dynamics further contextualised the emotion talk of interviewees, or the 'speakable emotions', as discursive constructions (Coupland, Brown, Daniels, & Humphreys, 2008) and allowed a deeper understanding of the social constructions of emotions in the context of contemporary creative work within a creative organisation.

Octant Studio (Octant), a major video game development studio in Sweden, began in 1999 as a start-up company producing small, easy-to-market games. Their attention to detail and production of high-quality games slowly began to garner the attention of the global market, and the studio was swiftly purchased in 2008 by a well-known global video game producer. Following the purchase, the studio became one of the key developers of a major game franchise and, in 2014 (when the fieldwork began), was in the last stages of developing the blockbuster (triple A) game that would launch the franchise. For the purposes of developing the blockbuster game, the studio was undergoing a period of significant growth, growing the employee base as much as 20% within one year. The structure of the organisation went through several changes during the growth period, with many promotions of individuals to team 'leads' and changes to the production management team. The game itself had also seen a number of changes to its initial design, with people taking some 'big hits' and even walking off the project, which some felt had 'cut features to the bone' and consequently things were 'going in all and any directions'. These changes, coupled with impending deadline pressures, were expressed as 'difficult' and 'horrible'. With this challenging and insecure working environment, as well as the growing organisational demands on individuals, the studio was an appropriate site for exploring the 'new normals' for selves and emotions that may be called upon and experienced in contemporary creative work settings.

The collapsed self

The interviewees were asked about their general ideas around their work and their relationship to it—if they struggled with it, how they experienced it, and how it made them feel to do creative work. Similar to the findings of other studies of creative work (Hesmondhalgh & Baker, 2011; Taylor & Littleton, 2013; Thompson et al., 2016), many of the interviewees expressed a strong and personal relationship between themselves and their work:

> I think for me … this might be very personal but … I really like the feeling of using my creativity to deliver a something that is unique to me, 'this is a piece of me right there' […][1] I find that very interesting and fun and engaging. (Felix, Sound Engineer)

> But when I bring something to the table that [colleagues] can't do … that isn't based on expertise … that isn't based on how long I've worked here … that's based on *me*. And that's the difference between being good at something and having learnt something. (Aidan, Level Designer)

> I guess it's also a matter of not being too afraid of putting yourself out there. Because I guess being creative is a bit intimate in that sense … it's very much you, you're putting *yourself* out there … like it's part of my personality and I'm expressing myself when it comes to music or art or something. (James, Games Artist)

> I want them to understand how good I am […] Like when we show stuff to the world … like that is directed by me or written by me or … or the whole creative package *is* me on a plate … it's me … everything that you see here is … it's me … that's me. (Ryan, Game Designer)

In their accounts, Felix, Aidan, James, and Ryan expressed a very entangled relationship between themselves and their work. They experience their work as not only representative but actually constitutive of who they are—'I'm expressing myself'—so that through their work they have the opportunities to work on and construct desirable selves. As Ryan states, he wants others and the world to 'understand how good' he is and it is through his work that he has the chance to be recognised as the 'good' creative worker he desires to be. This relationship between self and work, therefore, has a deeper meaning for individuals. For Felix, delivering a piece of himself is a source of interest, fun, and engagement and brings joy to his experience of work. Aidan is able to prove himself relative to his peers by delivering something that is a part of him. For James, expressing himself through his work is a part of how he understands himself, which is a very personal and intimate experience for him.

Such accounts do not represent a simple and superficial attachment to the individual's work but are constitutive of much more complex and complicated entanglements of selves with work. These entanglements blur or even collapse boundaries between self and work. Individuals describe their work as a 'part of' themselves and their self-understandings, as well as an essential part of how they derive meaning from their work. The collapsing of these boundaries is particularly interesting in the Octant context, where such collapsed self-understandings are actively encouraged through the organisation's practices. For example, at Octant, 'loving your work' is considered an ideal, and having love and passion for one's work is disciplined through the discourses of the 'ideal worker'. We see this as Tim, a senior producer on the game, describes what he considers important when recruiting new organisational members:

> I mean it's important to us that they are so in love with what they do that [...] most of the guys [in the job interview] we ask them 'what do you do in your spare time?' and if the answer isn't 'oh I love games, I play games ... I wrote this mini game for the Apple ... for the Apple iOS' ... if they say 'no' to that then we kinda go—'Okay so you don't play games in your spare time? You don't programme in your spare time? You're not interested in art outside of work? Okay well maybe we're not the employer for you.' (Tim, Producer)

This disciplining of an intimate relationship with one's work is evident in the accounts of other senior managers, some of whom clearly articulated to me that passion and care for one's work is 'super important' for individuals to exhibit at Octant. In the following account, James describes how such views are part of the culture at Octant, where people working here have a 'passion' for the kinds of games that are produced there:

> I guess it has to do again with like the scope of the project they have here and the size of the company like it's very hard-core in that sense. In some other companies you might get a bit more of a varied ... like they [workers] are all from different backgrounds and it's kind of weird how they all ended up there ... but here it's just the profile the company has and the type of games they're developing. So you're not just going to end up here by

accident, you kind of have to actively be interested in these types of games and have a passion for working with them. (James, Games Artist)

In line with these demands, many workers did express strong feelings of love for their work:

I think it's something I *need*. I think you learn that there are some things that give you joy. Like some people have joy by doing bank stuff, for other people it's running or just climbing things. For me this is something that makes me very happy. It's one of the things I love the most. (Janet, Level Designer)

I love it but I work really really hard. Harder than I should actually … which is really interesting. There's a lot I constantly think about cause I do probably do the most hours […] Oh I live for this. I live for … the rest of … I mean I have a lot of joy in my life—in fact my life outside of work is wonderful. I have a great life but the reason I do everything in my life is to do this well. (Charlie, Team Lead)

I felt like 'oh my god I created this, I wrote this story' and it was a really good feeling in my stomach and I always felt like that. Being creative is, when it goes well, it's almost like a drug. You get some kind of dopamine … whatever the good chemical is in your body … it's a really fantastic feeling. (Daniel, Programmer)

From these accounts, we see that the close relationship between self and work can be a source of meaningfulness and many positive emotions for individuals carrying out creative work. Workers experience emotions such as love, happiness, fulfilment, even a 'rush' from doing creative work. In this way, encouraging affectual and intimate relations between workers and their work may be beneficial to individuals' sense of selves and their well-being. In further exploring the emotion talk of creative workers at Octant, it became evident that just as experiences of positive emotions were intensified by the relationship to one's work, darker and more challenging emotions were also expressed and dealt with in response to the new norms that demand affections for one's work and that ultimately collapse the boundaries between selves and work.

The emotional self

Although this strong coupling of selves to work may be a reason for workers to have powerful, positive emotional experiences of work, it became clear in the workers' talk that this coupling also resulted in a variety of other less positive emotional experiences, including pain, resentment, frustration, anger, disengagement, fears, and insecurities:

> With this project that I was talking about that I was immensely proud of it was eventually scrapped so that was quite painful to be honest. It can be very very very painful because I was very proud of the work we had done and I was a very happy with the work itself ... and I had put a lot of myself into it and then it took a while to readjust. And for a while I was quite bitter that I had to work on a project that I thought was less creatively satisfying. (Conrad, Game Designer)

> The most frustrating aspect of this is if you're working on a prototype project and for some reason it doesn't get approved [...] This was your baby that you were working on [...] First of all you feel very frustrated because you spent a lot of time working on it [...] so cutting out one of the things you might get a little bit angry because you wasted your time working on it. (Anthony, Producer)

> See that's why it hurts so much if somebody cuts [something] off ... or if they criticise it. So you need to be both brave and a bit hard but still when it's creative work you need to be very sensitive and give a part of yourself—so I think that's why it's so difficult. If you put yourself into it and it doesn't go well it's really hard not to take it a bit personal. So it really hurts. And after if this happens I think after a while you get very distant and you say 'ok I will not put myself in this at all'. (Linnea, HR)

> I still get very upset and passionate. Like I would feel very strong about something and I would be protecting it like it's my baby and I could be upset to the core of me because *it is* the core of me and then I would regret being so upset afterwards [...] so I need to take all the good with the bad ... like everything is a part of me. (Ryan, Game Designer)

In the emotion talk above, workers expressed a variety of emotions, most of which resulted from the intimate and personal relationships they had developed with their work. Expressing such darker and more challenging emotions uncovered the insecurities the individuals experienced. In the case of Ryan, who earlier in our interview states that he is 'super dependent on a pat on the shoulder' and getting recognition from his work, the strength of his relationship to his work made him so dependent on getting constant affirmation of his desired self from others that he felt a need to deliver something that would produce this affirmation every week. Not receiving this desired recognition had serious outcomes for him, and could affect his life quite dramatically:

Iva: And how do feel if you don't get that recognition?
Ryan: I feel bad. But sometimes all I need is … I need a boss that recognises that … that sees me … and I need something … someone I can trust and I can understand is always there for me …
Iva: And if you were working at a place where you felt you didn't have that …?
Ryan: I would quit … I wouldn't work there … I couldn't because it would affect my life too much. I would feel too bad.

This instability and insecurity meant that many struggled to cope with the emotional experiences they felt as a result of their relationship to their work:

Different contexts that I find I struggle in … one is like I said I deliver my creativity to somebody else and they do something with my creativity. If that person doesn't take care of the work that I provide them then it becomes difficult to hand your baby over to them which was a problem with a few people earlier in the project […] I would like to get recognition for the job I've done among the people I'm doing it for. So that's one thing … if I don't trust the person that I'm supposed to deliver [my work] to that affects me. (David, Programmer)

David's relationship to his work leads to an issue of mistrust as he struggles to deliver his work to others. For Ryan, this becomes something more detrimental to his well-being, as it transpires into 'mental issues'.

> I don't know. I don't know how to deal with … I've tried so many things. The thing is now we're not talking about creativity like 'drawing a picture' we're talking about my mental fucking issues. (Ryan, Game Designer)

In previous studies of work, where selves and affect are co-opted into contemporary work and organisational settings, we are able to see a variety of responses that enable individuals to resist such organisational initiatives by distancing themselves or redrawing and carefully demarcating the lines between selves and work, or between selves and organisations (Casey, 1995; Hochschild, 1983; Kunda, 1992). The collapsing of the self into work increases both the positive and negative emotional experiences and presents challenges for workers trying to cope with them. The new normal demands creative workers entangle their selves and affect in experiences and conceptions of work at Octant give us a glimpse into the sometimes rewarding and often challenging emotions elicited as a response to such affectual demands and new norms in organisations and contemporary working life.

Discussion

In making sense of these experiences of work, we first turn to understanding why these affectual demands may be made in the context of creative work. Creative work is largely dependent on constructing novel and imaginative ideas—many of which are not necessarily derived from following strict processes, but rather are an outcome of individuals' cognition or subjectivity. Creative products then, rely on unique configurations of subjectivities that can be considered a 'consummate expression of individual selfhood' (Negus & Pickering, 2004, p. 4). Creative organisations may seek to capture this selfhood in work for dual interests. First, creative products may be better off if the incorporation of selves in work delivers particularly novel or valuable work. Second, promoting affectual relationships with employees' work not only aligns with their desires for meaning in work but also inspires commitment to their work (working 'really really hard' because you love your work), which negates the necessity for harsher controls of workers as workers become largely self-disciplining in line with organisational goals (Alvesson & Willmott, 2002). This can be interpreted as another source for the enchantment of work, in addition to ideologies and other work practices that lead to positive work affect (Endrissat, Islam, & Noppeney, 2015). As such, the language of love and intimacy with one's work is a source of positive experiences that capture the desires of an 'aspiring professional class that seeks ultimate fulfilment and passion in creative work' (Gregg, 2011, p. 170). These positive experiences of working with the self at work also explain some of the mysteries around tensions between the self-actualisation and self-exploitation of creative workers (Taylor, 2010), where workers engage themselves in insecure employment, long working hours (Hesmondhalgh & Baker, 2011), precarious working environments, and a general blurring between life and work (Fleming, 2014).

Admittedly, disciplining the self through discourses of love and passion for one's work may not result in altogether bad outcomes for individuals. For many, this personal relationship was experienced as a source of meaning, joy, fulfilment, and happiness. Positive experiences of collapsing the self into work is a way of both instilling engagement and self-realisation while drawing personal meaning from the work. At a time when meaningfulness of work is of scholarly interest (Bailey & Madden, 2017), it may be possible to argue that we see the experience of meaningfulness more commonly in creative work than in other work settings. However, it is also possible to explore the darker and more challenging experiences and outcomes of the collapsing of self and work. These come in the form of the emotion work that individuals carry out. Experiences of work can become painful and frustrating, while also leading to struggles and 'mental issues' that have a powerful impact on the quality of their experiences, not only of their work but also of their lives and their well-being, especially given the tight coupling of the individual's self-understanding with their work.

The collapsing of the self into work, therefore, may teeter into an area where there is little room to construct boundaries around selves outside of work, making self-understandings dangerously dependent on work and work outcomes. For this reason, we need to do more to understand affectual relations in contemporary experiences of work as well as the norms that govern such activity. As Wetherell (2015) argues, affect involves 'many complicated flows across bodies, subjectivities, relations, histories and contexts', which entangle and intertwine to produce affective moments. In the context of the creative organisation, it is therefore important to understand these affective articulations in the emotion talk of individuals as situated within the sociocultural, as well as governed by organisational demands on these individuals. Simultaneously exploring creative work from an organisational and individual level allows us to make sense of some of these complex relations and structures that shape the norms of contemporary work and life. Creative organisations and other sites for creative work may make emotion work particularly salient (Hesmondhalgh & Baker, 2011), but more could be done to explore these affectual relations and their implications across different contemporary work contexts.

In exploring the experiences of work of creative workers at Octant, we can observe how contemporary creative work demands an intimacy where selves become inextricably entwined with work. This demand for intimacy is a new form of affective labour where workers' experiences and affect are constantly regulated (Gregg, 2011). Such attempts may be beneficial to organisations that turn to new 'soft' forms of controlling workers, and in the case of creative work, employing affect may benefit the creative product. From the case of Octant, we see how subjectivities such as love and passion for one's work are articulated in the discourses of senior members of the organisation and how such discourses are replicated in the talk of many individuals, so that it essentially operates to collapse boundaries in the relationship between selves and work. Although such activity may prove rewarding for those who derive personal meaning from their close relationship with their work, in others it inspires intense emotion work, which may ultimately have a significant impact not only on their work but also on their lives. Understanding the organisational context is particularly illuminating in understanding the intricate challenges faced by creative workers who work in contemporary creative organisations.

Note

1. Transcription style: … indicates a pause in speech prior to the next utterance; […] indicates a sentence or more has been omitted; [words in brackets] are inserted to clarify meaning.

References

Alvesson, M. (1994). Talking in organizations: Managing identity and impressions in an advertising agency. *Organization Studies, 15*(4), 535–563.

Alvesson, M., & Willmott, H. (2002). Identity regulation as organizational control: Producing the appropriate individual. *Journal of Management Studies, 39*(5), 621–644.

Andersen, N. Å., & Born, A. W. (2008). The employee in the sign of love. *Culture and Organization, 14*(4), 325–343.

Bailey, C., & Madden, A. (2017). Time reclaimed: Temporality and the experience of meaningful work. *Work, Employment and Society, 31*(1), 3–18.

Banks, M. (2007). *The politics of cultural work*. Basingstoke: Palgrave Macmillan.

Bojesen, A., & Muhr, S. L. (2008). In the name of love: Let's remember desire. *Ephemera, 8*(1), 79–93.

Boltanski, L., & Chiapello, E. (2005). *The new spirit of capitalism*. London: Verso.

Boussebaa, M., & Brown, A. D. (2017). Englishization, identity regulation and imperialism. *Organization Studies, 38*(1), 7–29.

Brown, A. D., Kornberger, M., Clegg, S. R., & Carter, C. (2010). 'Invisible walls' and 'silent hierarchies': A case study of power relations in an architecture firm. *Human Relations, 63*(4), 525–549.

Casey, C. (1995). *Work, self and society: After industrialism*. New York: Routledge.

Caves, R. E. (2000). *Creative industries: Contracts between art and commerce*. Cambridge: Harvard University Press.

Coupland, C., Brown, A. D., Daniels, K., & Humphreys, M. (2008). Saying it with feeling: Analysing speakable emotions. *Human Relations, 61*(3), 327–353.

Du Gay, P. (1996). *Consumption and identity at work*. London: SAGE Publications Ltd.

Endrissat, N., Islam, G., & Noppeney, C. (2015). Enchanting work: New spirits of service work in an organic supermarket. *Organization Studies, 36*(11), 1555–1576.

Fleming, P. (2014). *Resisting work: The corporatization of life and its discontents*. Philadelphia: Temple University Press.

Fleming, P., & Sturdy, A. (2010). 'Being yourself' in the electronic sweatshop: New forms of normative control. *Human Relations, 64*(2), 177–200.

Gill, R., & Pratt, A. (2008). In the social factory? Immaterial labour, precariousness and cultural work. *Theory, Culture & Society, 25*(7–8), 1–30.

Gregg, M. (2011). *Work's intimacy*. Cambridge: Polity Press.
Hanlon, G. (2017). Digging deeper towards capricious management: 'Personal traits become part of the means of production'. *Human Relations, 70*(2), 168–184.
Heelas, P. (2002). Work ethics, soft capitalism and the 'turn to life'. In P. D. Gay & M. Pryke (Eds.), *Cultural economy*. London: SAGE Publications Ltd.
Hesmondhalgh, D., & Baker, S. (2008). Creative work and emotional labour in the television industry. *Theory, Culture & Society, 25*(7–8), 97–118.
Hesmondhalgh, D., & Baker, S. (2011). *Creative labour: Media work in three cultural industries*. New York: Routledge.
Hochschild, A. R. (1983). *The managed heart: Commercialization of human feeling*. Berkeley: University of California Press.
Howkins, J. (2013). *The creative economy: How people make money from ideas* (2nd ed.). London: Penguin Books.
Kunda, G. (1992). *Engineering culture: Control and commitment in high tech corporation*. Philadelphia: Temple University Press.
Lingo, E. L., & Tepper, S. J. (2013). Looking back, looking forward: Arts-based careers and creative work. *Work and Occupations, 40*(4), 337–363.
McRobbie, A. (1998). *British fashion design: Rag trade or image industry*. London: Routledge.
Menger, P. M. (2014). *The economics of creativity*. Cambridge: Harvard University Press.
Miller, P., & Rose, N. (1990). Governing economic life. *Economy and Society, 19*(1), 1–31.
Negus, K., & Pickering, M. J. (2004). *Creativity, communication and cultural value*. London: SAGE Publications Ltd.
Ross, A. (2008). The new geography of work: Power to the precarious? *Theory, Culture & Society, 25*(7–8), 31–49.
Taylor, S. (2010). Negotiating oppositions and uncertainties: Gendered conflicts in creative identity work. *Feminism & Psychology, 21*(3), 354–371.
Taylor, S. (2015). A new mystique? Working for yourself in the neoliberal economy. *The Sociological Review, 63*(1), 174–187.
Taylor, S., & Littleton, K. (2013). *Contemporary identities of creativity and creative work*. Surrey: Ashgate Publishing Ltd.
Thompson, P., Parker, R., & Cox, S. (2016). Interrogating creative theory and creative work: Inside the games studio. *Sociology, 50*(2), 316–332.
Thrift, N. (2005). *Knowing capitalism*. London: SAGE Publications Ltd.
Wetherell, M. (2015). *Trends in the turn to affect: A social psychological critique. Body and Society, 21*(2), 139–166.

Iva Josefsson is a doctoral researcher at the University of Bath and a visiting researcher at Lund University. Her work addresses issues of organising and identity in contemporary organisations and work—with a particular focus on creative work and creative organisation.

Coworking(s) in the Plural: Coworking Spaces and New Ways of Managing

Silvia Ivaldi, Ivana Pais, and Giuseppe Scaratti

A brief overview of coworking

In recent decades, globalisation and technological changes have coincided with and enabled important transformations in the labour market. These transformations have given rise to new forms of production/consumption, including the so-called collaborative economy (Benkler, 2006; Benkler & Nissenbaum, 2006; Botsman & Rogers, 2010; Schor, 2016) and new forms of collaborative organisation (Adler, 2005; Engeström, 2009; Adler & Heckscher, 2006; Nardi, 2007). These emphasise the combined dimensions of labour and are based on simultaneous, multidirectional, and reciprocal work, as opposed to forms that take place in organisations with an established division of labour, demarcated communities, and formal and informal sets of rules. Coworking has been emerging in the current social and organisational scenario as one of the relevant manifestations of such unfolding transformations. The first coworking space appeared in 2005 in San Francisco. At that time, the

S. Ivaldi (✉) • I. Pais • G. Scaratti
Università Cattolica del Sacro Cuore, Milano, Italy

initiators emphasised the collaborative potential of coworking in promoting social changes in the labour market and values related to accessibility, openness, sustainability, community, and collaboration (Capdevila, 2015; Gandini, 2015; Rus & Orel, 2015). The coworking space is described in the literature as a new type of workplace where different kinds of professionals (Gandini, 2015; Kojo & Nenonen, 2016)—heterogeneous by occupation and sector of work, organisational status, and affiliation (Parrino, 2013)—work alongside each other in the same place (Kojo & Nenonen, 2016; Spinuzzi, 2012). The number of coworking spaces has grown all over the world: from 75 in 2007 to 310 in 2009, 1130 in 2011, 3400 in 2013, and 7800 in 2015, with more than half a million members worldwide (Deskmag, 2016).

Coworking today is widely diffused and attracts the interest of both professionals and the academic world. Coworking has been studied in different countries, continents, and milieus from different disciplinary perspectives: psychology (Gerdenitsch, Scheel, Andorfer, & Korunka, 2016), sociology (Gandini, 2015), economic planning (Avdikos & Kalogeresis, 2017), urban informatics (Bilandzic, 2016), management (Butcher, 2013, 2016; Capdevila, 2015; Leclercq-Vandelannoitte & Isaac, 2016), design (Parrino, 2013), real estate (Green, 2014), urban studies (Groot, 2013), and engineering (Kojo & Nenonen, 2016; Liimatainen, 2015). The potential of coworking has been identified in terms of the facilitation of social processes (Parrino, 2013; Rus & Orel, 2015; Spinuzzi, 2012), innovation, and entrepreneurship (Capdevila, 2014, 2015), as well as the promotion of social change (Merkel, 2015). Similarly, coworking spaces are described in the academic literature as new forms of organisations based on the values of collaboration, openness, community, accessibility, and sustainability (Capdevila, 2015; Merkel, 2015; Spinuzzi, 2012), which freelancers and knowledge workers access with the purpose of fostering networking practices and social interactions (Capdevila, 2015; Parrino, 2013). However, there is still no shared interpretation of coworking, which seems to be difficult to grasp as a coherent phenomenon (Spinuzzi, 2012). Coworking has now reached a certain degree of maturity, and it becomes important to critically analyse it by understanding the phenomenon as a new normal: as a way of working, organising, and managing that increasingly influences wider organisations and emergent economic structures. In this framework, we analyse the plural characteristics of coworking as a new form of organisation, and we identify the connected different managerial practices that articulate the various coworking spaces identified. Thus, our work contributes to the literature of coworking by identifying the specific and differential qualities of different coworking spaces. At the same time, the chapter will enrich the discussion around coworking space management by shedding light on the tensions and challenges that trace the evolution of the ways of managing these new kinds of organisations.

Theoretical framework: Discourses on managers

An analysis of coworking and the role that the coworking manager plays can be addressed from two perspectives: the changes in the current organisational configurations and the development of conceptions of management. Many authors in the field of organisational studies (e.g., Engeström, 2009) highlight the gradual evolution and transformation of production modes and related organisational contexts, whereas conceptions of management are increasingly characterised by blurred and interconnected borders around activities that require increased communication, interaction, and reciprocity within simultaneous operational and multidirectional processes: Nardi (2007) speaks about placeless organisations, Blunden (2009) about project collaboration, and Mintzberg (2009) about the prospect of reshaping companies in communities. We can summarise this trend by recalling the contributions of Adler and Heckscher (2006) and Adler, Kwon, and Heckscher (2008), who underlined the emergence of a new model of 'collaborative community' within which knowledge workers focus on fluid, mutually understanding, and trust-oriented collaborative activity. We can also identify the ways of thinking and constructs underlying the profession of a manager. In particular, Ann Cunliffe (2014) distinguishes four phases that have historically characterised the management and organisational phenomena connected to the profession: the traditional interpretation of management; the affirmation of the school of human relations; the creation of the managerial ideology; and the development of a critical approach to management. The field of critical management studies highlights the problematic nature of professional identity and the management function based on two assumptions: that managerial activity implies an identity work, and that this is performative.

The outcome of these phases, which do not appear to be linear and contain wide margins of overlap and the co-existence of different management models, relates to a more complex configuration of the role and profile of the manager and enriches the well-established definition of a manager as a member of an organisation that makes sure that things are done by other people (Cunliffe, 2014). Contemporary discourses around management have shifted from the focus on the application of standardised procedures, to a more complex profile of the manager embedded in constant social interaction, relations, and processes. Cunliffe in her work (2014) describes different profiles of the manager that derive from an analysis of the historical phases of management and their connected theories. The first and most traditional is the manager as a *rational agent*, the one who owns a sufficient level of technical knowledge to use functional tools to standardise processes and streamline operations, ensuring adequate forms of management control, planning, budgeting, and coordination. The manager as an *actor*, is called on to manage what Goffman (1978) defined a role of frontstage and backstage within an organisation that, as a theatrical performance, requires the wearing of 'masks' and dress. The challenge in this case is maintaining a balance between authenticity, the need to adapt to different contexts, and the needs of the situation: playing their part without losing face (impression management), especially in contexts requiring emotional work (Hochschild, 1983). The manager can also be a *storyteller*, required to create meanings through stories and through what Weick has described as sense-making (Weick, 1995). The manager shapes her/his reality through stories and meanings, interacting with others. Furthermore, the manager as *discursive subjectivity* is also embedded in language systems and talked discourses of the organisation that involve values, culture, and institutional structures. The manager is influenced by different meanings that derive from the organisations in which he operates. At the same time the manager generates shared collective identity using languages, genres, rhetoric, and knowledge that convey values and institutional criteria; and these are at the basis of different forms of performing and operating (Foucault, 1978). Storytelling and discursive subjectivities, drawing on post-structuralist perspective, shed light on the tension by which the manager creates sense around stories in which he can identify and recognise himself (or not). Finally Cunliffe, by strongly criticising the rational way of considering the manager, introduces the profile of the manager as a *relational and reflexive practitioner*, who is able to reflect on his own actions, and is engaged together with others in the construction of organisational realities. Managers are the authors of contexts, questioning habits, rules in use, and routines in order to open up new and unprecedented solutions when the organisational activities encounter challenges and problems.

Inside this framework, a complex and articulated profile of the manager emerges. It fits well with the challenges that the coworking phenomenon conveys. Adopting a critical stance, we can question in which sense the coworking managers are operating effectively as managers, the challenges that they face, and how they face them. Most of the authors (Capdevila, 2014, 2015; Merkel, 2015; Parrino, 2013) in the literature see the main challenge for coworking managers as promoting relationships and sharing knowledge, as well as creating a sense of community in order to support a positive working environment, professionalism, and entrepreneurial opportunities. Inside this framework, managerial practices associated with the coworking phenomenon are related to the strategies adopted both to maintain the physical structure of the spaces, and to promote and facilitate interactions among coworkers inside the space and between coworkers and other organisations outside. More specifically, some authors identify co-location as a sufficient enabler of self-managed, autonomous communities, where natural relationships emerge in bottom-up ways (Merkel, 2015; Parrino, 2013). Other researchers underline the facilitation of internal interactions and relationships between coworkers and with organisations external to the space as the main objective of the coworking spaces and the most important task of coworking managers (Gerdenitsch et al., 2016; Parrino, 2013). These contributions highlight that the simple co-location of professionals who work inside the same working environment and are focused on different working tasks and objectives is not in and of itself sufficient to promote interactions, and consequently, collaboration (Spinuzzi, 2012), innovation (Capdevila, 2014), and community (Rus & Orel, 2015). Therefore, they underline the importance of a manager role based on the 'facilitation' of social interactions. Merkel (2015), for example, identifies two different profiles of the coworking manager: the 'service provider', who concentrates on work aspects and on the promotion of a good and positive working environment by providing attendant services; and the 'visionary', who focuses more on the promotion and enhancement of communication and collaboration among the coworkers inside the space. There are various strategies that the coworking managers can adopt to accomplish this. As Capdevila (2014) shows in his work on coworking and local innovation, those strategies refer to how physical spaces are used (location, distribution of material assets, size, etc.), projects (where coworkers and also other external organisations can work collaboratively), and events (focused on work, but also social events that can be intended for internal coworkers or opened to the public).

All these contributions start from the consideration that coworking spaces are oriented mostly to the promotion of social interactions. They demonstrate that managerial strategies that are focused on this aspect bring advantages at different levels, including increasing workers' performance, activation of new businesses, and the creation of new professional opportunities. In fact, the coworking spaces are described as possessing distinctive features compared with traditional organisations. The literature suggests that coworking spaces should be interpreted as places that freelancers and independent workers access with the purpose of fostering networking practices and social interaction (Capdevila, 2015). Coworking provides a solution to 'professional isolation' (Spinuzzi, 2012); and sharing a common space provides community to those who otherwise would not enjoy relational support while working from home. Among other benefits (e.g., flexibility, being able to mingle and work with like-minded individuals, better work–life balance, and greater job or career satisfaction), community and a sense of belonging have also been found to be critical in stimulating business development (Spinuzzi, 2012). From our perspective and through the research that we present here, we problematise this perspective and shed light on how the managers of the coworking spaces experience both traditional and new ways of management. We will argue that different types of coworking spaces are, in fact, characterised by the co-presence, even if in different forms, of the four profiles of the manager presented by Cunliffe (2014).

Methodological approach

The research underpinning this chapter was conducted in Italy, starting in 2013 and concluding at the beginning of 2016. It was made possible thanks to a collaboration with the Cowo, the biggest network of coworking spaces in Italy. Founded in 2008, today it includes more than 120 spaces in 73 cities in Italy. The research was conducted in two main stages. First, we conducted a qualitative exploration from narrative interviews with 63 founders of individual coworking spaces. The thematic analysis of the data collected within the interviews permitted us to shed light on how the coworking founders interpret and construct the structure, and orient the social dynamics inside their coworking spaces. We identified a typology of coworking composed of four different types of coworking spaces that present different objectives, rules, strategies, roles, and divisions of labour. The typology was validated in a public presentation organised by the founder of the Cowo Network in May 2015, where the results were presented and discussed in three focus groups with coworking managers and coworkers. Second, to further test the research hypothesis, we conducted ethnographic observations of four coworking spaces, one for each type of space, three of which were external to the Cowo Network. The ethnographic observations enabled us to analyse in greater depth the four types identified in the first stage of the study and to observe 'in the field' the managerial practices that characterise each type.

Coworking as the new normal: A typology of coworking spaces

The data collected in the interviews regarded particularly: the role and the motivations of the managers in opening a coworking space, the objectives and aims of the coworking space, and the types of processes and relationships that the manager promotes and orients inside the space. This analysis shed light on the varied nature of coworking. In particular it resulted in the identification of four different types of coworking spaces: *infrastructure*, *relational*, *network*, and *welfare* coworking. The typology was identified using a grounded theory approach (Strauss & Corbin, 1997).

Infrastructure coworking space

The first type of coworking space is what we define as infrastructure coworking. Here, the manager, through the coworking space, provides independent professionals a physical workplace at a competitive price. The manager considers the coworking space a place where independent professionals can find all they need ('as in a real office') to perform their work. The manager of the space considers the role of coworking manager to be supplementary, indeed often marginal, to their prevalent professional activity:

> […][1] In 2009, I bought a very large apartment, too big for my needs. An apartment with many rooms, which was definitely just a waste for me, considering that I was only at the beginning of my professional career. The idea of providing the rooms, that were unused, for other people and professionals stems from there. This is also because I know how hard it is to find a working place at decent a price for those who are at the beginning of their activities […]. (V., Freelance, Male)

As a whole, the coworking manager tends to consider her/himself the owner of the space, the proprietor of the physical assets, who makes available to other professionals all the basic tools they need to accomplish their daily work (e.g., desks, Wi-Fi connection, computers, printers, and fax machines). In this sense, the role of manager is to maintain the economic sustainability of the space, mostly by guaranteeing continuous demand and also by renting the spaces. On the other hand, the role also involves regulating the cohabitation of the space by various professionals inside a single working environment through basic rules about opening and closing times, the ownership of keys, and respect of privacy:

> […] Our main goal is to have the positions occupied and to try renting them all […]. (S., Freelance, Female)

> [...] We have no particular rule, only that of good manners such as not speaking too loudly when talking on the phone [...]. (F., Entrepreneur, Male)

> [...] I am the one who has the keys, sometimes people leave the space later and I give them a copy of the keys. But basically it's me who opens and closes [...]. (L. Entrepreneur, Female)

In this model, the coworking manager sees social interactions as beneficial to the working environment and climate, and conducive to the creation of business opportunities. However, no responsibility is taken for creating connections between people inside and outside the space: social relations are seen as not having to be guided or promoted; they arise naturally from the physical proximity of the professionals who share the space:

> [...] for sure, a positive aspect is also the social dimension, like the possibility of making friends [...] this occurs because obviously everybody [is] in the same place, thus comparisons and exchanges of ideas regarding the work are inevitable [...]. (A., Entrepreneur, Male)

Infrastructure coworking spaces are usually small places, owned by small/medium business entrepreneurs who dedicate part of their private office to coworking.

Relational coworking space

In the relational coworking space, the main objective is the promotion of knowledge sharing among coworkers. From the perspective of the managers, the space provides coworkers with the opportunity to interact and learn from each other. However, these interactions are not simply a natural consequence of physical proximity—they need to be facilitated:

> [...] my idea was to create a space where sharing can be easily organised. In a sense, my idea was to create events where it was possible for coworkers to exchange information as part of their work, but not only that [...] I wanted a place where people could create synergies in a simple way [...]. (G., Freelance, Male)

In this sense, the coworking manager assumes the role of facilitating social interactions. The manager feels responsible for the organisation of events and activities, as well as the circulation of information and knowledge among coworkers:

> [...] I believe that the creation of relationships and networks within the space is not something that happens by itself. I think it's a specific task of those who manage the space to organise different events that allow everyone to get to know each other [...]. (M., Entrepreneur, Male)

> [...] I consider myself a facilitator of the space. I only handle the matching: bringing people together and making them work together [...]. (M., Freelance, Male)

Relational coworking, as in infrastructure coworking, is peculiar to small spaces owned by entrepreneurs who also work as 'community managers'. They manage the space by promoting knowledge sharing and encouraging coworkers to establish social relations.

Network coworking

Network coworking spaces are oriented to the promotion of professional connections between coworkers and other subjects outside the space (professionals, organisations, and firms). To this aim, the managers apply selection criteria for identifying talented professionals and small businesses that work in the same sector (e.g., design, architecture, and digital innovation):

> [...] we give people the space, the community and the network to create and develop their work within a specific professional field. [...] We also help companies and organisations develop their talents in the field of the digital [...]. (C., Community manager, Female)

The managers work with an eye on the external world through the creation of partnerships with the local system of organisations/institutions, the promotion of connections for businesses opportunities, and the enhancement of reputation both for professionals/organisations (users and stakeholders of the space) and for the space itself. Within the coworking space, the managers are interested in promoting social interactions among coworkers, believing that such interactions will form the basis for constructing useful professional connections and partnerships:

> [...] We want to make it clear that in this place we can trigger a process of change [...] we are responsible for everything from the management of the functioning of the space, to the organisation of the events, to the construction of internal community [...]. (A., Entrepreneur, Male)

To enable this aim, the managers pay special attention to the design and disposition of the space in order to reflect the nature and spirit of the specific field of work. Explicit rules regulate the use of the space, while implicit rules cover relationships with coworkers and ways that coworkers should approach work in order to innovate and develop their business. Network coworking is associated with large coworking spaces with a more complex internal structure in the sense that the space is managed by a group of operators with different roles (e.g., events/project manager, community manager, and marketing manager).

Welfare coworking

In welfare coworking spaces, the fourth type of coworking space that we identified, the managers design the coworking structure in response to social/cultural issues that affect society (e.g., women and work, environmental sustainability, and unemployment). In these cases, the managerial practices are mostly directed towards promoting and diffusing specific values among coworkers and involving them in the creation and implementation of social projects:

> [...] the change that we want to bring is a cultural change. Often, we talk about the digital divide. Instead, we believe that there is really a cultural divide. Here, we live in an area where people work in a black market. And our goal is just to generate new forms of economy and new jobs [...]. (R., Freelance, Male)

The coworking manager is focused mostly on the promotion of a specific ethical culture among coworkers, the creation of conditions for collaboration among them, and the fostering of partnerships with other organisations/institutions connected to the social/cultural issue on which they are working. The manager sees the space as an opportunity to gather people around a specific problem and organise their efforts to solve the issue at stake. The manager is a facilitator in the identification of individual paths for the coworkers in the space, and is responsible for the activation of projects:

> […] the not-for-profit association manages the coworking space through its members: the governing board, and the president […], our coworkers are usually members of the association, and some of them actively participate in the implementation of our projects […]. (G., Freelance, Male)

Welfare coworking spaces are usually small/medium spaces and part of not-for-profit organisations or social enterprises. They have an internal organisation similar to that of network coworking spaces, with operators in different roles (in particular, the community manager and project manager).

The plural discourses of the coworking manager

The research presented so far, in Stage 1 of the study, has enabled us to achieve another result. In fact thanks to the identification of the typology composed of four different types of coworking spaces through the voice of the coworking managers, it has been possible to operate some distinctions of the profiles of the managers according to the organisational configuration of the space they construct and operate in. The analysis about the managers can be not limited only to the identification of their roles, but also needs to consider how they construct and make discourses and create sense around their profile of coworking manager (Cunliffe, 2014). These results have been enriched through another qualitative study. In Stage 2 therefore, we tested the typology in the field through ethnographic observations of four coworking spaces. Each of the observed spaces was selected because it fits with one of the four types of coworking space identified through the interviews. All four of the selected case studies were situated in Milan. The choice to limit the ethnographic research to Milan was guided by the fact that Milan was the first city in Italy to adopt coworking and has the longest tradition of coworking in Italy. Furthermore, different public and private institutions in Milan are currently investing in the development of coworking, meaning that it has a competitive and growing market. The four case studies were:

- *Infrastructure coworking space*: a small coworking space (100 m^2), part of a pre-existing office, and located in a central area of the city close to two main train stations.
- *Relational coworking space*: a small space (90 m^2) that is also part of an office, located in an industrial area, and also a member of a franchise network of coworking spaces.
- *Network coworking space*: a large space (500 m^2), part of a European franchise network in an industrial area.
- *Welfare coworking*: a small space (100 m^2) connected to a not-for-profit association.

Using the interpretative keys offered by Cunliffe (2014) to examine the ethnographic observations, it is possible to trace the discourses that describe how the coworking spaces are characterised by the co-presence of the different profiles of managers previously described (i.e., *Rational agent*, *Actor*, *Storyteller*, *Discursive subjectivity*, and *Relational and reflexive practitioner*).

Manager as actor

Using the actor discourse, the Goffmanian category of frontstage and backstage is particularly useful for the analysis of coworking, starting from two main analytical frameworks: the analysis of the sociomaterial dimensions of space and the role played by the manager as a broker (Burt, 2005). In the *infrastructure* coworking space under investigation, the manager is a professional who carries out her own activity and is only marginally responsible for the management of space and the relationships among coworkers. The manager in fact pursues her own work inside the coworking space. The 'backstage' of the manager is therefore represented by the office where she carries out this professional activity, enclosed and separate from the coworkers' work space. The material boundaries thus mark the symbolic spaces between the two roles of the founder of the space (her professional activity and as coworking manager), and between manager and coworkers. In Burt's terms, the manager plays a liaison role, brokering a relation between two parties, but not part of either. However, the manager's role in this model remains physically circumscribed and separate to that of the main workspace; separating her out from other workers.

This is quite different to the physical relationship in the *relational* coworking space, where there are no physical boundaries between coworkers and founders; the founders work at and occupy the same desks as the coworkers. However, there appears to be a symbolic barrier between the coworkers and the founders. They operate mainly as *coordinators* (in Burt's terms) of actors within the same group as itself, remaining inside the organisational boundaries and focusing on the transfer of information and knowledge between coworkers:

> [...] when I had problems with X, for reasons I don't want to explain now, but matters linked to work and to how we both behaved at work, I went to Y (community manager), to ask her for advice on what I should do. She was a reference point for me [...]. (A., Employee, Female)

Meanwhile, in the *network* coworking space, the managers operate from the frontstage. Here, they are positioned physically and symbolically at the boundary of the coworking space to control the input and output flows, or the flows between the coworking and outside spaces, while maintaining a strong attention to internal dynamics as they emerge from a conversation with a coworker. In Burt's terms, they operate as *representative* (bringing issues/requests that come from the organisations outside the space) and as *gatekeeper* (transferring outside the inputs that rise from coworkers inside the space):

[…] our role is to connect, so what's nice is getting to know people well; this is important to us. So, maybe, I'll give you an example: when a new coworker arrives, initially you should say, 'Okay, this person here is a printer and he likes tennis'; F. over there likes tennis, so I tell him, or, 'Ah OK, he's a freelance', so that startup might be interested in him […]. (C., Employee, Female)

Finally, in the *welfare* coworking space, the coworking managers usually work and stay in the same space as the coworkers, and take part to some of the same services (e.g., cobaby, training, and programmes) but acting in a different role. The manager has a *brokerage role* and acts as what we have defined as a *consultant*, that, in Burt's terms, does not refer to the role of providing expert advice but to a network position, as the manager is brokering a relation between two members of the same group. In this case, the backstage is conveyed by a distinction between the management of the functioning of the coworking space and the services provided, and the management of the not for profit association for the promotion and implementation of social projects. Thus, the managers shift between these two positions (in the coworking space and in the association) and their role mostly consist in supporting the internal community (coworkers) and the external one (people who take part in the social projects, services, and activities without being coworkers and supporters, like institutions and organisations involved in the realisation of the projects) and create links between the two communities.

Manager as storyteller

The ethnographic analysis shows that the storyteller perspective is clearer in spaces that are more open to the outside (*network* and *welfare* coworking spaces). Rhetoric is an element that strengthens the values shared by the community and enables passing on this knowledge in building networks and agreements with third parties. The need to aggregate external stakeholders around shared dimensions requires building a story/narrative that helps a process of building shared meaning. There is ample evidence of such narratives, including the interviews revealing, for example, the symbolic centrality of the mottos on the walls. In the network space where we conducted the ethnographic analysis, there are sentences on the walls like: 'Share ur life with others/u will have a joyful life'; 'Small opportunities are often the beginning of large businesses'; 'Behind every successful business, there's someone who made a courageous decision', and so on. It is worth highlighting that from the coworker's perception the slogans are not only functional to 'building a brand' in the relationship with the outside world but they constitute real elements of organisational culture:

> [...] the writing on the wall reinforces the sense of belonging, not only within the community but also professionally, they enrich you. I often read the same sentences, I like reading them, it gives you a sense of belonging and of potential, it is something that enriches me [...]. (R., Entrepreneur, Male)

The storytelling discourse is also at the centre of the *welfare* space. The idea for this particular coworking model was born from the personal experience of one of the founders, who experienced discrimination after becoming a mother in the company she worked for:

> [...] If option A is a career, and option B is being a mother and dedicating oneself to a family, I think there should be an option C that permits workers to choose another way [...]. (R., Entrepreneur, Female)

Today, the space proposes various projects and activities related to the support of women at work. On the front door is a sign inscribed with the question: 'Is this a home or an office?' emphasising the opportunity to integrate and balance these two aspects of life. Similarly, inside the space, on the walls are other sentences underscoring the possibility of finding alternative ways of life that do not necessarily already exist: 'Logic will get you from A to B. Imagination will get you everywhere'. The activity of coworking and the association that supports it are also largely oriented towards building a different narrative of woman's work, for example, by promoting the idea of 'motherhood as a master', an opportunity for mothers to acquire skills in the world of work.

Manager as discursive subjectivity

Another aspect that emerged from the analysis of the coworking spaces is related to the way in which the managers regulate their identity as managers trough inter-subjective discourses and negotiations with coworkers and other operators. External forces generate different contradictions in the various organisational configurations. For example, in the *infrastructure* space, the manager declared an initial intention to accommodate professionals who perform complementary activities so as to promote cooperation between them and exercise a role closer to that of the network space manager. Instead, she had set this project aside in favour of the profitability of the space:

> [...] For me, it would be ideal to open to people who work in the same field as me, so to architects or people like that. That would be ideal for me, that's what my vision would be. However, I can only achieve that if I direct the search for coworkers and the advertising in certain fields. In this way, I'd reduce the number of potential coworkers. But if I leave entry free ... even people who don't belong might ask to come here, so it would be easier for me to occupy the desks, because I need to, in order to support the space economically [...]. (L., Entrepreneur, Female)

A contradiction in the regulation of the identity as manager also emerges in the *welfare* space, dictated by the simultaneous presence of the coworking space and the association through which the projects are managed. When the space first opened, most of the investments were dedicated to coworking. The space in fact was expected to be the most important source of income. However, over the years, the most consistent part of the income has been derived from the projects. The manager had to redirect resources according to their activities and functions to strengthen the external community rather than internal one:

> [...] At the beginning, the idea was that the start-up should prevail, we wanted to be a commercial business. Then, we realised that we had social projects that were not commercial, so we established a non-profit association beside the startup. Then we realised that the sustainability of our organisation came from the projects of the association [...]. (R., Freelance, Male)

Manager as relational and reflexive practitioner

The manager's relational and reflexive identity work emerges from relationships with significant persons in all the analysed spaces. For example, in the *relational* coworking space that we observed, the manager had initially decided to dedicate his offices to coworking because most of the desks and rooms were not being used, and he saw coworking as an opportunity to utilise the resources at his disposal:

> [...] OK, we no longer needed the cutting table, the bureaus full of layouts and cardboard to stick the storyboards on, but we didn't feel we wanted to forgo the space. It was as though we felt the importance of the resource, but were looking for a new way of making the most of it [...]. (M., Entrepreneur, Male)

Starting from this idea that he describes as 'individualistic and opportunistic', and after having worked side by side with other coworkers, he discovered the importance of both professional and informal relationships in making everyday work more pleasant and effective. Today, he declares that the main objective that he wants to achieve with the space is to promote 'a shared use of spaces, for professionals who are interested in broadening their knowledge and relationships'.

Conclusion

In this chapter, we wanted to contribute to the debate on the deployment of coworking through two main inputs: the identification of different organisational configurations of coworking spaces and the identification of different discourses and interpretations of the managerial activities. In our work, we consider coworking spaces a new normal in the sense that they seem to introduce new ordinary ways of working and managing, characterised by principles of collaboration, openness, community, accessibility, and sustainability. We critically analyse coworking and identify a typology of spaces that shed light on different delineations and interpretations of coworking as a new normal. In infrastructure coworking, the coworking managers are focused mostly on the economic sustainability of the space and seem to be managers more of the space than of people. They create boundaries between themselves and coworkers by working in a backstage area. In relational coworking, however, the coworking managers interpret managerial practices as concentrated on the coordination of coworkers inside the organisational boundaries; they are focused on the transfer of information and knowledge between and among coworkers. Finally, in network coworking and welfare coworking, the managers are more oriented towards creating a community of people with shared values and promoting connections between the people inside the coworking space and the organisations/subjects outside. Here, the profile of the manager as a storyteller becomes fundamental in articulating and reinforcing the values shared by the community and passing on this knowledge in building networks and agreements to third parties.

These results present some useful inputs for understanding coworking as a new normal work practice. However, in order to explore the phenomenon further, it is important to underline some limitations of our study. Firstly, the way in which time has influenced the emergence of different types of coworking spaces as well as different profiles of managers, may reasonably be questioned. The typology of the coworking spaces was built from something of a snapshot of the spaces analysed, with little concern for their history. It would be interesting to integrate an evolutionary perspective into the typology to highlight the movement of the spaces between the various organisational models and related forms of management. Secondly, the analysis focused on individual spaces. It would be interesting to analyse the spaces comparatively and across organisational networks to test, for example, hypotheses of organisational isomorphism between coworking spaces belonging to networks. Similarly, the typology we propose is not related to the analysis of the environmental conditions of the spaces, that means the territorial context, and the connected social and economic characteristics, in which the space is positioned (e.g., creative cities). It will be interesting to test, on the one hand, the hypothesis that coworking arises mainly in contexts rich in local collective competition and, on the other hand, that the presence of the space can stimulate the creation of new collective goods. But apart from these limitations, it remains valuable to stress the results of this initial study that offer interesting insights for further exploration of coworking as a new normal. The identification of a typology of coworking spaces facilitates the understanding of the evolution of organisations as neither linear, nor uniform, nor even singular in nature. Instead, it is characterised by the co-presence of diverse forms of management and thus organisational focus, by which the principles of collaboration, communities, openness, accessibility, and sustainability are interpreted in different ways, producing different potential outcomes and, indeed, spaces.

Note

1. Transcription style: … indicates words have been omitted in a sentence, often just the repetition or a word or two; […] indicates a sentence or more has been omitted; [words in brackets] are inserted to clarify meaning.

References

Adler, P. S. (2005). The evolving object of software development. *Organization, 12*(3), 401–435.

Adler, P. S., & Heckscher, C. (2006). Towards collaborative community. In C. Heckscher & P. S. Adler (Eds.), *The firm as a collaborative community: Reconstructing trust in the knowledge economy* (pp. 11–105). Oxford: Oxford University Press.

Adler, P. S., Kwon, S., & Heckscher, C. (2008). Professional work: The emergence of collaborative community. *Organization Science, 19*(2), 359–376.

Avdikos, V., & Kalogeresis, A. (2017). Socio-economic profile and working conditions of freelancers in co-working spaces and work collectives: Evidence from the design sector in Greece. *Area Journal, 49*(1), 35–42.

Benkler, Y. (2006). *The wealth of networks. How social production transforms market and freedom*. New Haven & London: Yale University Press.

Benkler, Y., & Nissenbaum, H. (2006). Commons-based peer production and virtue. *The Journal of Political Philosophy, 14*(4), 394–419.

Bilandzic, M. (2016). Connected learning in the library as a product of hacking, making, social diversity and messiness. *Interactive Learning Environments, 24*(1), 158–177.

Blunden, A. (2009). An interdisciplinary concept of activity: Outlines. *Critical Practice Studies, 11*(1), 1–26.

Botsman, R., & Rogers, R. (2010). *What's mine is yours: The rise of collaborative consumption*. New York: Harper Collins.

Burt, R. S. (2005). *Brokerage and closure: An introduction to social capital*. New York: Oxford University Press.

Butcher, T. (2013). Coworking: Locating community at work. In M. Grimmer (Ed.), *Proceedings of the 27th Annual Australia New Zealand Academy of Management (ANZAM) Conference, New Zealand, 4–6 December 2013* (pp. 1–13). Sydney: Macquarie University Graduate School of Management.

Butcher, T. (2016). Co-working communities: Sustainability citizenship at work. In R. Horne, J. Fien, B. Beza, & A. Nelson (Eds.), *Sustainability citizenship in cities: Theory and practice* (pp. 93–103). London: Routledge.

Capdevila, I. (2014). Different inter-organizational collaboration approaches in coworking spaces in Barcelona. *Social Science Research Network*. SSRN 2502816.

Capdevila, I. (2015). Co-working spaces and the localised dynamics of innovation in Barcelona. *International Journal of Innovation Management, 19*(3). https://doi.org/10.1142/S1363919615400046

Cunliffe, A. L. (2014). *A very short, fairly interesting and reasonably cheap book about management*. London: Sage.

Deskmag. (2016). *Coworking statistics: All publishings of the global coworking survey*. Retrieved March 2017, from http://www.deskmag.com/en/coworking-statistics-all-results-of-the-global-coworking-survey-research-studies-948

Engeström, Y. (2009). The future of activity theory: A rough draft. In A. Sannino, H. Daniels, & K. Gutierrez (Eds.), *Learning and expanding with activity theory* (pp. 303–328). New York: Cambridge University Press.

Foucault, M. (1978). *Discipline & punish: The birth of the prison*. New York: Pantheon Books.

Gandini, A. (2015). The rise of coworking spaces: A literature review. *Ephemera Theory Politics in Organization, 15*(1), 193–205.

Gerdenitsch, C., Scheel, T. E., Andorfer, J., & Korunka, C. (2016). Coworking spaces: A source for social support for independent professionals. *Frontiers in Psychology, 7*. https://doi.org/10.3389/fpsyg.2016.00581

Goffman, E. (1978). *The presentation of self in everyday life*. Harmondsworth: Penguin Books.

Green, R. (2014). Collaborate or compete: How do landlords respond to the rise in coworking? *Cornell Real Estate Review, 12*(9), 52–59.

Groot, J. (2013). *Coworking and networking*. MSc Thesis, Universiteit van Amsterdam. Retrieved from http://scriptiesonline.uba.uva.nl/document/518051

Hochschild, A. (1983). *The managed heart*. Berkeley: University of California Press.

Kojo, I., & Nenonen, S. (2016). Typologies for co-working spaces in Finland what and how? *Facilities, 35*(5/6), 302–313.

Leclercq-Vandelannoitte, A., & Isaac, H. (2016). The new office: How coworking changes the work concept. *Journal of Business Strategy, 37*(6), 3–9.

Liimatainen, K. (2015). *Supporting inter-organizational collaboration in coworking clusters: The role of place, community and coordination*. Master's Thesis, School of Science, Aalto University. Retrieved from https://aaltodoc.aalto.fi/bitstream/handle/123456789/16774/master_Liimatainen_Karoliina_2015.pdf?sequence=1

Merkel, J. (2015). Coworking in the city. *Ephemera Theory & Politics in Organization, 15*, 121–139.

Mintzberg, H. (2009). Rebuilding companies as communities. *Harvard Business Review, 87*(7/8), 140–143.

Nardi, B. A. (2007). Placeless organizations: Collaborating for transformation. *Mind Culture and Society, 14*(1/2), 5–22.

Parrino, L. (2013). Coworking: Assessing the role of proximity in knowledge exchange. *Knowledge Management Research & Practice, 13*(3), 261–271.

Rus, A., & Orel, M. (2015). Coworking, a community of work. *Teorija in Praksa, 52*(6), 1017–1038.

Schön, D. (1983). *The reflective practitioner. How professionals think in action*. New York: Basic Books.

Schor, J. (2016). Debating the sharing economy. *Journal of Self-Governance and Management Economics, 4*(3), 7–22.

Spinuzzi, C. (2012). Working alone together coworking as emergent collaborative activity. *Journal of Business and Technical Communication, 26*(4), 399–441.

Strauss, A., & Corbin, J. M. (1997). *Grounded theory in practice*. London: Sage.

Weick, K. E. (1995). *Sensemaking in organizations*. London: Sage.

Silvia Ivaldi is a PhD student at the Faculty of Sociology, Università Cattolica, Milano. Her PhD is on the topic of coworking. Her research interests are in new forms of work and organisations, and social impact evaluation.

Ivana Pais is Associate Professor of Economic Sociology at the Università Cattolica, Milano. Her research focuses on the sharing economy and digital labour.

Giuseppe Scaratti is Full Professor of Work and Organizational Psychology at the Faculty of Economics, Università Cattolica, Milano. He is the Director of Trailab, a research centre that is oriented to implement projects related to the issues of the collaborative economy. His research interests focus on the changes of work and organisations.

Part III

Transitions and Transformations

'Investment in Me': Uncertain Futures and Debt in the Intern Economy

Kori Allan

Introduction

Post-recession, the intern has become a prominent figure in both the Canadian and international media. The insecure nature of the labour market and the blurring of the distinction between paid and unpaid work are at the centre of the interns' recent visibility. Internships have garnered attention because the promise that low or no wage work experience leads to secure, paid work has been fractured, particularly for youth, whose unemployment rate was double the national rate at 14% (Goar, 2013) and even higher in Toronto at 17.6% in 2013 (Bedard, 2014). In Ontario, the Ministry of Labour's recent internship inspection blitzes revealed rampant employee misclassification. In addition to addressing such misclassifications, activists lobbied for the extension of health and safety laws in the wake of three interns' deaths, which exposed gaps in legal protections and the precarity of young interns. The activists' criticism of 'exploitive' unpaid internships in Canada is part of an 'intergenerational

K. Allan (✉)
York University, Toronto, ON, Canada

© The Author(s) 2018
S. Taylor, S. Luckman (eds.), *The New Normal of Working Lives*,
Dynamics of Virtual Work, DOI 10.1007/978-3-319-66038-7_12

inequality' discourse that argues younger generations are worse off than previous ones. A local television programme on youth un(der)employment neatly encapsulates this perspective through its title: *Dude, where's my future?* (TVO). This discourse reproduces nostalgia for the security of Fordism through desires for a linear path to future prosperity (Muehlebach & Shoshan, 2012). It is the flipside of the breathless promotion of flexibility and the entrepreneurial potential of unpaid exposure and experience in the neo-liberalised post-industrial economy.

Under post-Fordist workfare states, unpaid work, historically feminised, is now central to unemployment, not just for interns but also for welfare recipients, who are required to volunteer or work for free in exchange for social assistance. This unpaid work experience does not garner as much attention as that of the intern because it is not caught up in middle-class anxieties about class reproduction through certain futures (see also Lee, 2015). Interns are also generally viewed as deserving remuneration because they are perceived of as engaged in work and not requiring activation by punitive workfare measures. While un(der)paid work experience as a form of improving one's employability and work-readiness is an endemic feature of the current labour market, what we tend to call an internship is thus inherently classed.

In line with such classed politics, scholarship has taken a temporal turn (Bear, 2016). Arguing that temporality is an under-examined yet important aspect of free labour debates, Kuehn and Corrigan (2013) propose that their concept of 'hope labour' can help explain interns' unpaid work as an investment in their future. This chapter further unpacks the temporality of internships, and its relationship to inequality, by examining intern experiences in the creative industries in Toronto, Canada. Rather than critiquing how interns replace employees, my research participants tended to characterise internships as problematic because they did not provide equality of opportunity; that is, equal opportunity to invest in one's future because of classed inequities, since only the relatively wealthy can afford unpaid internships. I argue that the 'speculative work' and 'speculative time' (Adkins, 2017) of interns' investments exacerbate inequalities perpetuated by the individualisation and (re)privatisation of social reproduction under neoliberal post-Fordism. I further argue that the internship is one example of 'indebted free labour' (Allon, 2015) that proliferates in the current economy as a result of the financialisation of social reproduction.

More specifically, I examine how interns generally value internships that offer meaningful work experience, as a future-oriented investment in one's stock value (Feher, 2009). This promissory value facilitated enthusiastic self-exploitation despite low or no wages. The payoff of these investments was nevertheless problematised. While anticipation and expectation often initially underlie young people's investments in internships, interns soon recognise the radical uncertainty of the future and the centrality of luck in the current labour market. While my research participants prioritise work that is fulfilling and accept insecurity as an endemic feature of the 'new normal', they still desire security, indicative of earlier standard employment norms. They strive to obtain fulfilling, yet relatively secure work, by accruing as much potential value as possible through internships. Interns' hope labour, however, is characterised by 'speculative time' (Adkins, 2017), as their assets' value cannot be measured along a linear path, but rather is constantly being re-evaluated and recalibrated. Finally, I examine how the privatisation of social reproduction and employability intensifies reliance not only on family resources, but also on debt. Hope labour reproduces classed privilege, not through the ability to plan a future, but by enabling one to increase one's assets. While the value of one's assets is speculative, indebted hope labour nevertheless subsidises and creates surplus value for employers.

Internships in the media industries

The growth of non-standard or precarious work (Vosko, 2006) has exacerbated job insecurity among cultural and media workers, who increasingly work as freelancers on even shorter contracts that are only days or weeks long (Conor, Gill, & Taylor, 2015, p. 9). Just as the number of good jobs is decreasing, there is a 'growing 'reservoir of labour' of junior workers' (Hesmondhalgh & Baker, 2011, p. 114) in print media industries, which can be attributed to several factors, including job cuts and an increase in the number of university graduates. According to one professor I interviewed, the problem is that 'while the number of journalism jobs is decreasing, the overall number of journalism students is not in decline'. In recent years, there has also been an explosion of academic internship programmes in Canada; that is, universities and colleges offering internships for credit.

Activists have recently focused on challenging internships through a series of lawsuits, prompting governments to clarify legal ambiguities. According to the Ontario Ministry of Labour it is illegal to offer an unpaid internship unless the training benefits the individual trainee, rather than the trainer. The intern also cannot displace an employee. One exception is work performed for an intern programme approved by a college or university (De Peuter, 2014; Webb, 2015). Media conglomerates subsequently terminated unpaid internship programmes or introduced pay as interns filed lawsuits for wage theft. In Toronto, for example, Bell cancelled its unpaid internship programme in the face of Patel v. Bell Mobility Inc. (Webb, 2015). As one activist noted at an intern event, several local companies (e.g., the Walrus, Rogers Media) paid their interns after political pressure was applied. They could thus afford to pay their interns and had merely chosen not to. When controversy over illegal internships erupted, many other programmes shifted to accepting academic interns. For instance, the magazine *Toronto Life* paid its interns a stipend when the intern programme was introduced in 1993, until 2009, when internships became unpaid. In 2014, the magazine's internship positions were closed and reintroduced as part of an academic programme (Salamon, 2015, p. 444). Although academic internships are governed to some degree through university programmes and thus offer a more valuable learning experience, interns essentially pay to intern through their tuition fees. Universities thus contribute to and are complicit with the growth of precarious labour (Discenna, 2016, p. 449).

The research discussed in this chapter is part of a larger project on un- and under-paid work placements in Toronto, Canada. This chapter is based on this larger corpus of data, but focuses on 12 in-depth interviews with interns and intern supervisors in the publishing and journalism industries. I also conducted participant observation at numerous events for interns hosted by activists, academics, and unions. In the discussion that follows, I refer to participants using pseudonyms.

'Investment in me': The future of hope labour in the intern economy

Kuehn and Corrigan (2013) state: 'Hope labor is an important logic—perhaps *the* guiding logic—behind the academic internship' (p. 20). They define 'hope labour' as 'un- or under-compensated work carried out in the present, often for experience or exposure, in the hope that future employment opportunities may follow' (p. 10). Thus, they explain that hope labourers work for non-financial rewards or for deferred compensation (e.g., higher wages in later contexts) (p. 12). In line with human capital theory, students and recent graduates certainly viewed internships as a valuable and future-oriented investment in their 'skills, professional networks, and personal brands' (Corrigan, 2015, p. 336; see also Perlin, 2012; Hope & Figiel, 2015). For example, one journalist told me that he accepted 'any opportunity where I [could] intern or get experience' because it contributed to his 'portfolio'. Internships also act as a signal for employers by indexing desirable attributes: it is a form of self-branding, regardless of the skills acquired (Perlin, 2012, p. 130).

Although some scholars (Kuehn & Corrigan, 2013, p. 12; Rodino-Colocino & Beberick, 2015, p. 488) argue that interns do not consider their labour to be exploited, I show how the 'shadow of exploitation' (Chillas, Marks, & Galloway, 2015, p. 2) is evident for the majority of my interviewees, particularly since they work in journalism or the publishing industry, where recent coverage of interns has been prolific. My research participants reproduced discourses of both employability *and* labour rights. Although they valued internships as investments in their careers, they nevertheless acknowledged that employers often exploit interns, using them as a source of free or cheap labour. They did not define exploitation in the Marxist sense, as creating surplus value through coercive and alienating relations. Rather, they equated it largely with free labour; first, because internships constitute an uncertain investment, and second, because they reproduce class inequities. The former lead to highly differential payoffs, whereas the latter result in unequal access to experience and exposure. Neither of these critiques necessarily problematised for them the investment logic of internships nor the creation of surplus value from their labour, which contributed, in part, to *unthinking work*, that is, 'viewing internships as almost-but-not-quite labour' (Rodino-Colocino & Beberick, 2015, p. 488). Rather, they problematised the privatisation of social reproduction and, in particular, how the reproduction of labour relies on unpaid familial resources. Internships thus presuppose and naturalise intergenerational dependence (McDowell, 2016).

Although the majority of my research participants valued internships, as I noted above, 'exploitation' was on the tips of everyone's tongues. At one union-organised intern event, the moderator asked, 'What is the role of the school in offering meaningful, not exploitive internships?' All of the respondents, university professors and employers, noted that they are 'not supposed to do dry cleaning or get coffee' or 'photocopy'. Rather, as the following example illustrates, interns and administrators overwhelmingly valued their internships as learning experiences. Emily worked 60 hours a week as an intern in the publishing industry to get 'access to more of an investment in me because for three months the thousand-dollar cheque was not compensating me, the learning was'. She said of another intern, 'we really pitied [her] because all she did was ... courier books all day long ... it was grunt work, putting in her time'. Interns wanted to do meaningful work, rather than administrative grunt work, as an 'investment' in their human capital or, as Emily put it, as an 'investment in me'. The ideology that internships were learning experiences thus naturalised internships, to some extent, as not quite work, for interns felt 'compensated beyond wages' (Rodino-Colocino & Beberick, 2015, p. 492). Indeed, the majority of interns and university supervisors felt that if students had graduated, an internship was 'exploitive free labour': it loses its status as a learning experience.

Even if internships involved grunt work, they were nevertheless mandatory in publishing and journalism. Emily noted, 'In general, to be hired in the publishing industry you need to have done at least one internship [...]'[1] All the Canadian [publishing] houses have these programs ... so it's kind of required'. Here, the entry-level position is the internship. Even if internships merely entailed 'putting in time' doing grunt work (Shade & Jacobson, 2015, p. 190), they were thus pursued as a 'product of coercion' (Corrigan, 2015, p. 344). Although interns' enthusiasm for meaningful internships as learning experiences generally masked coercive mechanisms

(Cohen, 2012; Corrigan, 2015; Duffy, 2016), the spectre of the 'bad internships' exposed such coercive potential. Emily, for instance, argued that internships should be paid 'for that 25% of the time it's just sweat … buying a man's labour off of him' and 'some days they don't want to come in … and they still show up'. If interns did not feel alienated from their labour because it was work they deemed meaningful as an investment in the self, they were less likely to view it as exploitive. It was the pure 'grunt work', like 'fetching coffee', that was alienating and coercive, for it did not contribute to their self-appreciation (Feher, 2009): it was 'just labour'. Emily also suggested, however, that since interns do not have full control over their schedules, all of their work was not completely free and should thus be compensated.

On the other hand, a few interns felt they should be paid because their work had as much value as an employee's, for their stories often made it 'on air' or were published. These interns, like labour rights activists, aimed to reinstate clear divisions between work and life, and between labour and love, as the intern embodies the increasing production of surplus value outside waged employment in the 'free economy'. The interns' free labour was part of and contributed to the devaluation of labour and intergenerational inequality in an economy that increasingly profits from 'free stuff' (Allon, 2015). For instance, unskilled workers are often asked to undergo unpaid training or a trial day prior to being potentially hired, just as skilled workers in creative industries often perform 'spec work' or free labour for exposure.

My interviewees did not all agree that interns replaced employees; it depended on the size of the organisation and the degree to which it was unionised. However, most felt as Andrea did, that 'internships provide a very convenient source of cheap labour for struggling papers and television stations'. Jessica, who supervises interns at her current workplace, told me: 'Ideally there is always one intern to eliminate the need to have a person on staff'. Even if they did not replace employees, interviewees all agreed that internships are 'a way to source talent'. They are, as Jessica noted, 'like an audition: you need to prove yourself'. The internship as an audition encouraged self-exploitation. At an intern event, for example, one employer noted, 'students are hungry, they understand the real world is not 9–5. They volunteer to work longer hours'. Andrea, who worked more than 40 hours a week as an intern, learned 'about being adaptable' and that 'you need to over-perform all the time'. Internships thus encourage over-working and being amenable. As Matthew told me, 'there was an expectation that if you want to do well at this ... if you want to use this person as a future reference say yes to everything ... that's drilled into you'. Employers thereby can source talent relatively risk-free and withhold benefits and a better wage until the value of a prospective employee is clear (Perlin, 2012, p. 131).

Some people felt that any payment, even if it was just a modest honorarium, made an internship escape the stigmatised 'exploitation' of unpaid positions. While some internship programmes are paid, they all nevertheless provide cheap, temporary labour or risk-free hiring processes for companies and thus contribute to the precariatisation of labour. Even paid interns, for instance, provided cheap vacation relief at several for-profit organisations. The less interns are paid, however, the more potential surplus value an employer can capture. Whereas the expansion of value extraction into new spaces outside of work, such as the freelancer's home (Cohen, 2012), is often invisible, the visibility of the intern's unpaid work in for-profit organisations exposes the expansion of free labour. Furthermore, academic internships subsidise employers' labour costs, 'capitalize[ing] on students' willingness to pay to work' (De Peuter, Cohen, & Brophy, 2015, p. 332). While my interviewees largely did not characterise internships as problematic if they created surplus value or even illegally replaced employees, they recognised that meritocratic neoliberal discourses of investment obfuscate both the uncertainty of hope labour and structural power asymmetries (cf. Kuehn & Corrigan, 2013, p. 18). Determining an internship's potentially lucrative or exploitative nature was complicated temporally for interns themselves, as the future benefits of internships are neither linear nor predictable. Rather, internships are truly spec work, as I outline below.

Hope and hustle in the luck economy

While interns often value their intern experiences as providing not income but assets, the competition and volatility of the market problematises the view that such assets would pay off in the future. Adelaide, who interned at a publisher, said: 'I internalised the idea that if you … just work like a dog as an intern there's a gold ring waiting for you at the end and there isn't. [...] It's not a direct line from internship to job, and you still have to do all of that *hustling*'. Parlaying your intern experience into a job required hustle, a key word that came up often in interviews. An entrepreneurial mantra, it reproduces a version of neoliberal personhood that entails doing whatever it takes to be successful, to sell oneself as a business, in a volatile market (see also Gershon, 2011). For example, Matthew, who described getting his job through 'pure hustle' and being flexible, told me: 'it is all uncertain, but you kinda just try any avenue that you can and hope a door will open. That is all we can really do because there is no certainty'.

Even the 'success stories' did not attribute their current employment to merely hard work or hustle, although both were essential. Rather, their investments' payoffs were contingent upon luck, another key word in my intern interviews. Adelaide told me,

> You can't pick and choose in a job market like this [...] Lots of people … are not anywhere as *lucky* as I have been on the job market and I credit that to *luck*. I know how hard I work, but I know how hard other people work.

When I asked Emily who benefits more from interns' work, the employer or intern, she argued,

> The organisation would get more value out of the labour of the interns … because interns individually get quite a bit … but I was *lucky* enough to get a job where that value I received could be activated … but for every one of me there are nine who end up leaving the industry … not able to use [their experience] to create value for themselves …. There aren't that many jobs.

Successful interns were often in digital, the one growing area in the field of journalism. But even they did not describe their career choice as a calculated decision. Jessica, for example, told me she fell into web journalism accidentally. When she was at the paper, she was the only intern there and the first to work on the web, which was still new. After completing a second internship and a string of contract positions, her old intern boss emailed her and offered her a contract that eventually parlayed into a full-time permanent job to launch a new app. She recalls, 'When you are on contract, it seems never-ending' and they 'rarely hire [...] so it was totally a relief'. Many interviewees, like Jessica, spoke of working in a series of contract jobs, holding out for the good, meaningful, more secure job as long as they could. Interns recognised, however, that even if they were doing everything right, it was still necessary to be at the right place at the right time, especially given the simultaneous increase in the number of interns and decrease in the number of permanent jobs. Andrea, for example, spoke of how the newspaper she works for outsourced the job she used to do. Her friend works at one of the companies they outsource to and makes $40,000 a year, whereas the 'lifers' she replaced were making '$100,000/year with 6 weeks of vacation'. The competition of the labour market predicted failure for the majority.

In my interviews, those who had interned years before recognised that their investments were always a gamble. Luck, as a keyword, connotes a particular structure of feeling in 'millennial or casino capitalism' (Comaroff & Comaroff, 2000) or 'a jackpot economy' (Ross, 2009, p. 10). My intern interviewees did not quite buy into their ability to be rational entrepreneurs; rather, their entrepreneurial hustle required favourable market conditions, which were beyond predictability. As Adelaide noted, 'Nobody can plan their time properly: you can't plan time and especially under the conditions that we're living in. You can do all the things right, all the strategic and tactical planning and still end up just on the verge of not surviving'. The notion of a knowable, linear time that can be planned for, that can be used to make rational calculations, is non-existent for these young people. In a sense, they experience a crisis of agency (Bear, 2016): 'We lack agency, so we hope' (Kuehn & Corrigan, 2013, p. 17).

The temporality of internships is not linear: outcomes require not just hustle, but hope, because of the randomness and luck of one's networks and experiences. In the financialised neoliberal economy, Feher (2009) outlines how the invested self is concerned less with acquiring money and more with enhancing credit or assets (see also Allan, 2016; Hope & Figiel, 2015). Interns aim to accumulate assets or stock value that they hope to leverage in the future. Their investments are filled with potentiality, but not certainty. One's relationship to one's human capital is speculative (Feher, 2009). Hope labour is thus thoroughly speculative, as its investments are not characterised by predictable delayed returns. For an internship, 'the time of profit lies in the non-chronological and indeterminate movements of speculative time' (Adkins, 2017, p. 12). Thus far, I have shown that, largely, internships are not viewed as exploitive if they provide a learning experience that pays off in the future. The speculative value of future investments, however, problematises such temporal expectations. As I will show in the following section, interns also problematised internships because they reproduced classed inequities.

The financialisation of social reproduction

Interviewees focused on the asymmetries of opportunities to invest, while still emphasising the need for experience. Who could bear the risks of continuing to invest in one's employability is understood as a classed phenomenon contingent upon access to material resources. I further argue that what interns' experiences reveal is that we need to understand how people buy 'time' to make more investments, not just via family resources, but also debt, which creates surplus value for lenders.

The majority of my interviewees reported being aware of how internships reproduce the privilege of those from higher social classes, which other researchers have also tracked (Chillas et al., 2015; De Peuter, 2014; Perlin, 2012). One student, whose grandmother paid her tuition, completed an unpaid internship over the summer in Washington, DC. She confessed: 'it was an experience that other people wouldn't be able to do [...] I recognise that unpaid internships entrench those inequalities'. Conversely, Zayneb, who did two internships in Toronto while living with her parents and on the Ontario Student Assistance Program (OSAP), told me she could not pursue her dream internship with Al Jazeera English for two months, as she calculated it would have cost her close to $10,000. Although financial resources certainly limited opportunities for international high-profile internships, access to student loans through enrolment in post-secondary education enabled people to intern even if they were not wealthy. And whereas many of my informants had familial support, the majority paid for their education and the privilege to intern through debt.

Post-secondary school still constitutes a valuable investment, despite declining returns, because there is an earning gap between high school and college graduates (Perlin, 2012, p. 129). I thus argue that being a university student affords privilege in the form of access to more debt through student loans. Debt enables one to invest in the self through access to academic internships, while others are excluded, relegated to volunteer in less prestigious unpaid positions (see Allan, 2016; Perlin, 2012). If one does not self-exploit, overwork or take risks through internships, one cannot even participate in the market. If one is privileged enough to buy time to invest in the self, via debt or familial supports, one can continue to self-appreciate.

Andrea, for example, noted that unpaid or low-paid honorarium-based internships are:

> … only acceptable if you're getting academic credit for it and if it's like a finite amount of time, because as soon as you start moving beyond four or six weeks you're starting to limit the type of people that can do that … who come from means … I could only do an internship where I was getting 50 dollars a week because I was living with my grandmother rent free […] That semester cost me $3000 in tuition and I'm working as well.

Like Andrea, many academic interns found it 'offensive' that they had to pay tuition for an intern credit, even though they felt supported by university staff. The support just 'wasn't $3000 per student worth'. Jessica noted that unlike wealthier students, 'you may not be able to afford to work for free if you are working your way through school … I don't know if employers just expect that everyone can afford to work for free'. Jessica, who was raised by a single mom, paid for her education with OSAP and a line of credit that a family friend co-signed for her. She worked two, sometimes three, jobs including cleaning houses, to make ends meet. In her fourth year she used her student line of credit only for rent and it was just after her internship. She reported that she 'only went $1000 in debt because of an internship … but considering I was so far into debt it didn't really matter'. Jessica graduated owing more than $70,000. She strongly disagreed with unpaid internships because the uncertainty of the labour market renders unpaid internships 'too long to go without pay'.

Most of her colleagues and friends work contract-to-contract; she is an exception. She has one friend who gave up on journalism after a 'shitty internship'. Another is willing to take a communications or public relations job after freelancing for ages: 'He lives at home and his parents are well off, so I always wondered when he will get to that point … when he would stop waiting for his dream job to come'. But if he wants his own family he needs to move on. Privilege, here, is thus measured by how long the dream of meaningful and secure work can be kept alive, which depends on parental and/or other support. While my informants and the research focuses on parental support (e.g., Shade & Jacobson, 2015), my interviewees reveal that partners and other family members, like sisters, also offered support, often through sharing the cost of rent. Familial support, interwoven with debt, frequently enabled students to shoulder unpaid work, as the following example illustrates.

Although he went to high school in Trinidad and Tobago, Matthew was a Canadian citizen and thus eligible for OSAP. It made sense for him to study in Toronto, where his sister lived, because they could share costs by living together. Throughout his undergraduate degree he pursued both unpaid and paid internship opportunities, while also working at a call centre or in retail. Matthew described his internships as leading up to a prestigious paid internship after his studies were completed. He described the latter as not living up to his expectations, 'and most of all', he said, 'I didn't get a job after it, which was really disheartening and disappointing'. He felt that professors did not manage students' expectations, for schools, as a business, had to sell the idea 'that the $30,000 you're spending is going to be an investment that will pay off [through the internship component]'. His sister, with whom he was living, was leaving Toronto. He moved in with an uncle in the suburbs and told himself that 'you need to draw on every single contact you have in journalism and see if you get a job with them because you need to pay the bills: that was the number one thing'. He 'chased down' a news managing director, who later offered him a couple weeks of work in eastern Canada. He decided that he was not going to wait around for perhaps a day a week of work in Toronto and paid to fly himself out east. He said, 'I was unemployed for a month … I have no money … my student loans are going to be due in six months. I need to pay that off'. He ultimately does not believe it was his internship that got him a job, but rather his willingness to be flexible, cheap(er) casual labour—all part of his hustle: 'When I approached that manager in the hallway … his face lit up when I said I'm willing to do anything … casual work I'm willing to do that … That's what kind of sealed the deal'. Matthew's story reveals that his student loans and ability to share living costs with his sister enabled him to invest in his future career through both low and no wage internships throughout his undergraduate degree. Once his final internship was finished, he was not in a financial position to continue to invest in his future in Toronto, waiting around until an opportunity arose or for his luck to turn.

Because interns are perceived of as being young, 'the prevailing ageist assumption holds that it is more acceptable for a young person to work without a wage' (De Peuter et al., 2015, p. 331). Indeed, it is assumed that young people will have parental support. McDowell (2014, 2016) argues that young men in the UK who are unable to access decent waged work often rely on their mother's domestic labour and financial assistance to be 'work-ready'. This growing intergenerational dependence signals, for McDowell, a 'new intergenerational sexual contract' between mothers and sons. The presumed increasing dependence of young men (and women), an intergenerational bargain (McDowell, 2014, 2016), is also evident in the intern economy, which operates on the assumption that parents should and can finance their children's employability. Coping with job insecurity and the privatisation of employability (and social reproduction more broadly) has led to increased reliance on support from family and friends, as well as increased labour market participation and debt (cf. Bezanson, 2006).

The increasing costs of post-secondary education in Canada have also reduced its accessibility (Bezanson, 2006). Even indebted academic interns are more privileged than the 'non-interns' (Perlin, 2012) who cannot access university and such unpaid work. Nevertheless, through debt, employability and social reproduction are not only individualised and (re)privatised, but thoroughly financialised (Adkins & Dever, 2014; Roberts, 2013). The surplus value of debt via interest payments profits from the expansion of post-secondary programmes in the creative industries, which are interlocked with the intern economy (see De Peuter et al., 2015, p. 331). While initially enabling, debt, for Matthew at least, was also ultimately a mechanism for reproducing labour discipline (Roberts, 2013). It encouraged him to chase down potential employers professing his willingness to 'do anything' as flexible labour.

Discussion and conclusion

As the 'intergenerational inequality' discourse referred to at the beginning of the chapter highlights, upwardly mobile or middle-class university students and graduates face an uncertain future. What enables them to hold out for more secure and meaningful work, however, is the ability to make more investments that are un(der)compensated, to hedge more bets outside of waged employment. Bear (2016, p. 495) noted that:

> … ethnographies of middle- and lower-middleclass groups experiencing downward mobility in austerity reveal a profound (and politically problematic) crisis of agency. Their previous investment in a linear historicism and sense of the limitless possibilities of a national growth economy lead to a deep disorientation.

Young people who have known only uncertainty in the labour market do not necessarily experience a deep disorientation, but they do nonetheless feel a crisis of agency. This crisis of agency does not immobilise them—they still invest in the self—but it is expressed through the lack of ability to 'plan time'. Several interviewees, for instance, described the time of being contract-to-contract and unemployed as seemingly never-ending. Chronic precarity challenges the legitimacy of anticipation's promise of particular futures (Bear, 2016, pp. 494–495). Interns who anticipate that internships will lead directly to jobs are soon schooled by their labour market experience: they learn that success requires not just hustle, but luck. In the new normal, the privilege that hope labour reproduces is thus not of secure futures, but of the ability to make more investments, albeit speculative ones.

This chapter also shows how classed privilege cannot be measured by income alone; it must also be measured by access to debt (Adkins, 2015), which creates opportunities to invest, but only for as long as one can defer or renegotiate payment. The privatisation and financialisation of social reproduction thus creates new forms of risk and sources of profit. Universities, students, and recent graduates all subsidise labour while creating profits for lenders and employers. As my research reveals, however, even if interns do not question the need for experience and exposure, they increasingly problematise the classed inequities that the precariatisation of labour and the privatisation of social reproduction exacerbate. Thus, much promise lies in continuing to build intern activism around a classed politics that calls for resocialising the reproduction of labour rather than requiring one to hustle harder.

Acknowledgements This research was supported by funding from the Social Science and Humanities Research Council of Canada. The author would like to also thank this volume's editors and Jessica Taylor for helpful feedback on earlier drafts of this chapter.

Note

1. Transcription style: … indicates words have been omitted in a sentence; […] indicates a sentence or more has been omitted; [words in brackets] are inserted to clarify meaning.

References

Adkins, L. (2015). What are post-Fordist wages? Simmel, labour money and the problem of value. *South Atlantic Quarterly, 114*(2), 331–353.

Adkins, L. (2017). Speculative futures in the time of debt. *Sociological Review.* https://doi.org/10.1111/1467-954X.12442

Adkins, L., & Dever, M. (2014). Housework, wages and money: The category of the female principal breadwinner in financial capitalism. *Australian Feminist Studies, 29,* 50–66.

Allan, K. (2016). Self-appreciation and the value of employability: Integrating un(der)employed immigrants in post-Fordist Canada. In L. Adkins & M. Dever (Eds.), *The post-Fordist sexual contract: Working and living in contingency* (pp. 49–70). Basingstoke: Palgrave Macmillan.

Allon, F. (2015). Money, debt, and the business of 'free stuff'. *South Atlantic Quarterly, 114*(2), 283–305.

Bear, L. (2016). Time as technique. *Annual Review of Anthropology, 45*, 487–502.

Bedard, E. (2014, October 8). Vital signs reports pain a stark picture of youth unemployment across Canada. *Rabble.ca*. Retrieved from http://rabble.ca/news/2014/10/vital-signs-reports-paintstark-picture-youth-unemployment-across-canada

Bezanson, K. (2006). The neo-liberal state and social reproduction: Gender and household insecurity in the late 1990s. In K. Bezanson & M. Luxton (Eds.), *Social reproduction: Feminist political economy challenges neo-liberalism* (pp. 173–214). Montreal-Kingston: McGill-Queens University Press.

Chillas, S., Marks, A., & Galloway, L. (2015). Learning to labour: An evaluation of internships and employability in the ICT sector. *New Technology, Work and Employment, 30*(1), 1–15.

Cohen, N. S. (2012). Cultural work as a site of struggle: Freelancers and exploitation. *tripleC, 10*(2), 141–155.

Comaroff, J., & Comaroff, J. L. (2000). Millennial capitalism: First thoughts on a second coming. In special issue: Millennial capitalism and the culture of neoliberalism. *Public Culture, 12*(2), 291–343.

Conor, B., Gill, R., & Taylor, S. (2015). Part 1: Introduction. Gender and creative labour. *Sociological Review, 63*(S1), 1–22.

Corrigan, T. F. (2015). Media and cultural industries internships: A thematic review and digital labour parallels. *tripleC, 13*(2), 336–350.

De Peuter, G. (2014). Beyond the model worker: Surveying a creative precariat. *Culture Unbound, 6*, 263–284.

De Peuter, G., Cohen, N. S., & Brophy, E. (2015). Interrogating internships: Unpaid work, creative industries, and higher education. *tripleC, 13*(2), 329–335.

Discenna, T. A. (2016). The discourses of free labor: Career management, employability, and the unpaid intern. *Western Journal of Communication, 80*(4), 435–452.

Duffy, B. E. (2016). The romance of work: Gender and aspirational labour in the digital cultural industries. *International Journal of Cultural Studies, 19*(4), 441–457.

Feher, M. (2009). Self-appreciation; or, the aspirations of human capital. *Public Culture, 21*(1), 21–41.

Gershon, I. (2011). Neoliberal agency. *Current Anthropology, 52*(4), 537–555.

Goar, C. (2013, August 15). Canada's job numbers don't tell the real story. *Toronto Star*. Retrieved from http://www.thestar.com/opinion/commentary/2013/08/16/canadas_job_numbers_dont_tell_the_real_story_goar.html

Hesmondhalgh, D., & Baker, S. (2011). *Creative labour: Media work in three cultural industries*. London: Routledge.

Hope, S., & Figiel, J. (2015). Interning and investing: Rethinking unpaid work, social capital, and the "human capital regime". *tripleC, 13*(2), 361–374.

Kuehn, K., & Corrigan, T. F. (2013). Hope labor: The role of employment prospects in online social production. *The Political Economy of Communication, 1*(1), 9–25.

Lee, D. (2015). Internships, workfare, and the cultural industries: A British perspective. *tripleC, 13*(2), 459–470.

McDowell, L. (2014). The sexual contract, youth, masculinity and the uncertain promise of waged work in austerity Britain. *Australian Feminist Studies, 79*, 31–49.

McDowell, L. (2016). Youth, children and families in austere times: Change, politics and a new gender contract. *Area*. https://doi.org/10.1111/area.12255

Muehlebach, A., & Shoshan, N. (2012). Introduction. In special Issue: Post-Fordist affect. *Anthropological Quarterly, 85*(2), 317–343.

Perlin, R. (2012). *Intern nation: How to earn nothing and learn little in the brave new economy*. London: Verso.

Roberts, A. (2013). Financing social reproduction: The gendered relations of debt and mortgage finance in 21st century America. *New Political Economy, 18*(1), 21–42.

Rodino-Colocino, M., & Beberick, S. N. (2015). 'You kind of have to bite the bullet and do bitch work': How internships teach students to unthink exploitation in public relations. *tripleC, 13*(2), 486–500.

Ross, A. (2009). *Nice work if you can get it: Life and labour in precarious times*. New York: New York University Press.

Salamon, E. (2015). (De)valuing intern labour: Journalism internship pay rates and collective representation in Canada. *tripleC, 13*(2), 438–458.

Shade, L. R., & Jacobson, J. (2015). Hungry for the job: Gender, unpaid internships, and the creative industries. *The Sociological Review, 63*(S1), 188–205.

Vosko, L. (2006). Precarious employment: Towards an improved understanding of labour market insecurity. In L. Vosko (Ed.), *Precarious employment: Understanding labour market insecurity in Canada* (pp. 3–42). Montreal and Kingston: McGill-Queen's University Press.

Webb, W. (2015). Ontario interns fight back: Modes of resistance against unpaid internships. *tripleC, 13*(2), 579–586.

Kori Allan is a Postdoctoral Research Fellow at York University, Canada, where she is working on a project that examines how the transition to a low-carbon green economy affects workers in the auto-manufacturing sector. In addition to examining the changing nature of work in financialised post-industrial economies, her work also analyses the governance of the un- and under-employed in the context of neoliberal welfare-state restructuring. She also investigates how citizenship and relations of inequality are constructed through immigration policy and practice.

Letting Them Get Close: Entrepreneurial Work and the New Normal

Hanna-Mari Ikonen

In the context of contemporary capitalism, entrepreneurs are viewed as people who show initiative and innovativeness (Beck & Beck-Gernsheim, 2002; Miller & Rose, 2008; Thrift, 2005). This chapter takes a closer look at such individuals' lives through the study of a group of entrepreneurs who engage in entrepreneurial practices relevant to the contemporary work context, in which the self is heavily invested and all risk is individualised. The case studies are of lifestyle based and hosting businesses targeted at dog owners located in Finland and Sweden. The entrepreneurs are people who have left their previous paid work either partially or entirely, moved to rural locations, and started firms either offering accommodation and training premises for people travelling with dogs or coaching people in various dog-related sports. Hosts and guests of these organisations become close to each other, both emotionally and spatially. The business model also means that production, reproduction, and consumption blur together, either with or without prior agreement.

H.-M. Ikonen (✉)
University of Tampere, Tampere, Finland

© The Author(s) 2018
S. Taylor, S. Luckman (eds.), *The New Normal of Working Lives*, Dynamics of Virtual Work, DOI 10.1007/978-3-319-66038-7_13

The blurring is reinforced by the use of digital technologies—the firms are constantly available online for customers' potential and actual evaluations. This commercially oriented way of living is desirable in many respects, but may also result in stressors for the business owners. In this chapter, I analyse how these entrepreneurs manage—both emotionally and through practical, material solutions—a life in which work is ongoing. I also trace the reasons for their prevailing happiness and sense of optimism.

Today's labour markets and working life can be described, with good reason, as insecure, unstable, and risky. Taking and managing these risks individually has become an institutionalised requirement (Beck & Beck-Gernsheim, 2002). Lauren Berlant (2011) calls this constant insecure state of work (and, consequently, life) the 'new normal'. She argues that we maintain unachievable fantasies of a moral–intimate–economic state of being, often called 'the good life'. We base our actions and plans on promises of upward mobility, job security, equality, and long-lasting intimacy, despite evidence that liberal–capitalist societies can no longer be counted upon to provide opportunities for individuals to make their lives 'add up to something'. Adkins (2016) approaches post-Fordist capitalism as a context in which the worker or would-be worker is guaranteed nothing but hope. The actual means to realise these hopes, however, are possible only through externalisation, sub-contracting, and entrepreneurialism. She, among others (Ekinsmyth, 2014; Ikonen, 2014; Taylor, 2015), sees that the archetype of the entrepreneur has emerged as the ideal form of working. Women, too, are seen increasingly as potential or existing entrepreneurial subjects (Luckman, 2016). As far back as 1991, McDowell wrote about the emerging post-Fordist economy and the interconnected, gendered spheres of production and social reproduction it needed. She pointed out 'the manner in which the flexibilization of labour was impacting both sexes as irregular employment conditions were becoming much more widespread' (MacLeavy, Roberts, & Strauss, 2016, p. 2067).

Increasingly, for both genders in the new economy, a hostessing attitude is becoming a requirement—providing individualised service and giving every business move a personal touch. For women, hosting is like a continuation of their other behaviours and duties in life, and because host(ess)ing is seen as a 'natural' feminine virtue, it is not generally appreciated as work that should be rewarded (Veijola & Jokinen, 2008). In home-based hosting businesses, particularly businesses that offer a traditional rural lifestyle as their commodity, traditional gender roles tend to be at play (Brandth & Haugen, 2012, 2014). This is because the farm tourism business often aims to offer the experience of a 'genuine' rural lifestyle (Bell, 2006; Bunce, 2003; Short, 2006). Therefore, for business purposes, it is men more than women who are required to alter their somewhat 'natural' roles to incorporate aspects of caring into their traditional farming and wilderness activities (Brandth & Haugen, 2014). However, gendered divisions of work do not appear as often in less traditional lifestyle businesses, such as the rural businesses studied here.

Self-organised employment is increasingly taken for granted in the new normal of modern-day work, where people who have created their own work and are self-employed are frequently to be found. The rising prevalence of different kinds of contracted and outsourced workers, forced freelancers, and entrepreneurs, has recalibrated class relations in society (Adkins, 2016, p. 2). Even so, the capacity for and norms of self-management differ based on the privileges available to different kinds of people, provided by their social location (Berlant, 2011). Capital received by birth or acquired through education, work experience, and one's environment and culture may be vital in enabling individuals to adapt to and utilise the changing economic environment with optimism.

Optimism is a kind of negotiated sustenance that makes life bearable, even as it presents itself in an ambivalent, uneven and incoherent manner (Berlant, 2011). From the cases studied, it seems that optimism is linked with passion—if the entrepreneur has a passion for something and can also make a living from it, it results in a sense of optimism. Nowadays, both optimism and passion are affects that are preferably expressed in life as well as in the sphere of work. Being seriously committed helps in being flexible and innovative and leads an individual to express excessive attachment to work (Irving, 2016). Berlant's (2011) method was to examine how singular things become general and resonate across many spheres. Although in a very different context, I also attempt to show how my single cases are illustrations of a more general trend—that of a working life in which people seek alternative routes to make a living and live a decent life. While a feeling of insecurity is widespread among post-Fordist workers, the would-be entrepreneurs studied here have had the lust and enough resources to change their lives—not towards greater security, but towards a more optimistic and happy sense of uncertainty.

Home-based hosting and coaching as a lifestyle: Materials and settings

This article presents interviews and participatory observations of six case study businesses engaged in lifestyle entrepreneurship, motivated by personal desire. Together, the case studies include 12 people, as some work alone whereas others have one or more business partners. Half of the firms provide coaching for dog sports, and the other half provide premises for dog sports, including accommodation and training areas. The firms are located in rural areas in southwest Finland (four cases), eastern Finland (one case) and southern Sweden (one case). The entrepreneurs work either at home or in another emotionally significant place. The cases include couples with small or school-aged children, couples without children, and singles. Self-employment is the only way they can live their desired lifestyle, which also represents a shared attribute among this group, which is otherwise heterogeneous, differing greatly in terms of previous work experience, skills, and resources. More information about the case businesses is presented in Table 1.

In some cases, the entrepreneurs had previous enthusiasm for dog sports, which was the main motivator behind their change in lifestyle and employment, as they built this enthusiasm into their business idea. In other cases, switching to entrepreneurship was prompted primarily by wanting to 'do their own thing' and 'have it all'—work, family, hobby, and a life close to nature. Even in these cases, it was their love for their pet dogs and their associated activities that led to the idea for their niche business. Businesses that provide services such as coaching for dog sports on their own premises and providing one-of-a-kind experiences are typical manifestations of the new economy, in which specialised knowledge, ideally drawn from personal commitment, is transformed into a profit-making activity and communicated to potential customers largely via

Table 1 Basic information about the case businesses

Business	Entrepreneur(s) and family situation	Location	Previous work	Age of business	Other sources of income
Coaching 1	Woman, 30, married, one small child	Southwest Finland	Banking sector	A couple of years	Wage work, which will likely continue in the future
Coaching 2	Woman, 30+, in a relationship, collaborating with another firm run by a couple, 60+	Southern Sweden	Student of natural sciences & farmers	Approximately ten years	None
Coaching 3	Couple, 40+	Southwest Finland	Trade sector	A few years	Another firm
Accommodation 1	Couple, 30+, small children	Southwest Finland	Education & economics	A few years	None
Accommodation 2	Couple, 50+, teenage children	Eastern Finland	Medicine & engineering	A few years	Wage work, which will likely continue in the future
Accommodation 3	Woman, 30+, divorced, a school-aged child & Woman, 30+, in a relationship	Southwest Finland	Several, mainly the trade sector	A couple of years	Wage work, which they would prefer to discontinue in the future

digital technologies, particularly social media. The motivation of 'having it all' is typically seen in case of mothers who work from home (Ekinsmyth, 2011, 2013; Luckman, 2015), but is also characteristic of businesses started from hobbies and for lifestyle-related motives (Andersson Cederholm & Åkerström, 2016; Ateljevic & Doorne, 2000). The firms studied operate in the field of human–non-human interactions, which is increasingly drawing the interest and attention of academics (for a review, see Schuurman, 2014). Although firms involved in dog-related services are rather new entrepreneurial actors, their numbers are growing, as are the numbers of services in that specialty. A growing subculture includes people who are interested in dogs that are used for active dog sports (Gillespie, Leffler, & Lerner, 2002; Haraway, 2008; Ikonen & Pehkonen, 2017; Lund, 2014); the case study entrepreneurs examined in this chapter fill the rising demand for proper coaching and training premises for such activities.

Coaches train owners and their dogs in agility or sheep herding. These coaches usually operate from premises where they can dedicate themselves to their own dogs' training while paying for it by offering their customers superb training facilities. Some coaches also travel to other places to coach, including abroad—a growing trend among professional coaches. Entrepreneurs who operate as accommodation hosts may invite coaches and attract customers to participate in training seminars on dog sports conducted on their premises. Additionally, they also serve as places where people can meet other dog enthusiasts, who may, for example, have a dog of the same breed or who are travelling with their dogs and in need of a dog-friendly place to stay. Accommodation hosts also offer food and lodging to lone guests or visiting groups. For this study, I wished to analyse hosts who explicitly target people who travel with their dogs and have advertised this choice, rather than those who merely allow dogs on their premises. All the case studies were found through various dog-related Internet forums, Facebook groups and interpersonal conversations—platforms through which dog enthusiasts regularly communicate and seek appropriate meeting places.

As part of my study, I conducted interviews with the entrepreneurs that lasted from one to three hours; observed their practices before, during and after customer encounters; informally asked the guests about their experience; and scrutinised the premises. I also participated in the offered activities, for example, I had lunch with some of the other guests and interacted with them while they were training or relaxing, and I also spent time training my own dog while enjoying the bed and breakfast services.

Towards generating income through lifestyle

It is remarkable with how much emotion the interviewees spoke about their past working lives. They mentioned the problems of working life in general and of work places in particular. It was clear that apart from 'pull' motivations around lifestyle and hobbies, many 'push' reasons led them to change their lifestyles. The interviewees criticised modern work culture, specifically for its accelerated pace, insecurity, conflicting requirements and heavy workload. These themes recurred throughout the data, whether in the form of direct personal experience, observations of others' predicaments, or predictions of their own futures. In the interview excerpt below, some inn owners describe their journey from an unhappy work life to potentially sustainable happiness:

> *Interviewee 1 (I-1)*: You know, these days paid work, it's somehow so uncertain [...][1]
> *Interviewee 2 (I-2)*: Yes, it's just like that, and profit seeking. It's also hard in that I was responsible for achieving results. We had this pressure and hypercritical feeling that we had such few sales, that we should have more, more, more, all the time. It was quite tough mentally. Even though I had a good steady salary, it did not compensate for the fact that I spent all my working hours and my commute in the morning and evening just thinking about work, and so on.
> *I-2*: Yes, and even though you might be praised by the clients, it always felt that the only comment you got from the management was that you should do your work better, you should do even more, and this and that, endlessly. And then our clients tell us that we are the nicest, friendliest and most business-like [company in the field] in the whole Uusimaa region, but we never hear from our employer that we are actually doing our jobs well.

I-1: And the employer gives us tools, but they are not necessarily the best tools there are, so you have to juggle to get the best possible end result. So we decided that now that we have an enterprise, we get to use all the proper tools that it is possible to get. And they are exactly like we want them to be.

I-2: And we get to hear all the feedback, whether it is critical or good, and we can just react to it directly. (Accommodation 3)[2]

Regular wage work was another frequently mentioned issue, implying that they still consider it a societal norm from which they deviate. This is illustrated in the following interview excerpt of a male sheep herding coach in his 40s:

Both of my parents are medical doctors [...], so we [he and his wife] haven't really followed in their footsteps. Particularly me, I'm the real black sheep in the flock. All the others are well educated and have regular jobs—I'm a rascal who just works on something odd. [...] They know that it's better not to intrude; everybody makes their own choices. (Coaching 3)

Although the interviewees recognise that regular wage work is the general norm, they also see how today's wage work often leads to insecurity and inconveniences, large and small, which they do not wish to face in the future. Therefore, in line with the institutionalised individual responsibility for life management and happiness (cf. Beck & Beck-Gernsheim, 2002), they have made the choice to achieve self-fulfilment by doing meaningful work as lifestyle entrepreneurs.

Lifestyle entrepreneurship is an economic activity that is not conducted solely for making profits, but to a great degree also for altering the personal lifestyle of the would-be entrepreneur (Ateljevic & Doorne, 2000; Peters, Frehse, & Buhalis, 2009; Stone & Stubbs, 2007). For some politicians and economists, the term has a slightly bad reputation, because self-employment in such cases is seen only as a practical means to fund the new lifestyle, while ambitions to grow the business are often low (Peters et al., 2009). The desired lifestyle stems from the entrepreneur's own enjoyments, meaning that there is a fair degree of clarity about the desired direction in which they want their lives to change (Andersson Cederholm & Åkerström, 2016). This was corroborated by my interviewees, who stated that their motivation for entering self-employment was to enable their desired lifestyle. Almost everybody considered their business a source of fulfilment and a part of their new lifestyle itself (Stone & Stubbs, 2007). 'Because this is also my hobby, this is not horrid in any sense' (Coaching 1). A couple that manages an inn and did not plan to give up their wage work also said, 'This is more like a hobby, like recreation for us!' (Accommodation 2). The woman even referred to her part-time job as a medical practitioner as a 'hobby' and mentioned that rearing dogs and inn-keeping was a 'family hobby'. Class-based resources for self-accomplishment were evident (e.g., Berlant, 2011). However, some interviewees emphasised that they 'do not aim to practise charity' but work for an increase in turnover to be able to take time off (Accommodation 1). The same goes for the innkeepers who, despite not aiming to grow their business in order to employ anybody else, wish to succeed enough to be able to enjoy their lives, 'because we are both basically very hedonistic' (Accommodation 3).

Being enthusiastic about what one is doing is a good thing for business success. However, all the risks are left to the entrepreneur alone, including the risk of enthusiasm waning over time, for whatever reason. Because these entrepreneurs have changed not only their way of earning a living but also their overall lifestyles, the possible negative consequences can be considerable, impacting upon all aspects of their and their family's lives. My interviewees did not believe, however, that their lust might suddenly disappear and were generally optimistic about their future. They also had tentative alternative plans: 'I believe I can change my work duties a bit so that I don't need to give up working with dogs' (Coaching 2). In the case of some entrepreneurs, a sense of trust in destiny and an undefined sense of optimism could be detected: 'We live day by day [...] time will tell [...] our activities go in different directions as required' (Coaching 3).

Customer closeness in everyday work and life

By serving niche markets, these entrepreneurs represent ideal post-Fordist workers who use their skills in a creative way and utilise digital technologies such as social media, along with their own desires and values, personal, material, multisensory, and mindfulness approaches in their day-to-day interactions. Because the entrepreneurs I studied often share a passion for dogs with their customers, the boundary between work and hobby or between public and private is porous. It is exactly their high degree of involvement in their work with dogs and their mission to do 'their own thing' that draws them into a close relationship with their customers. Thus, like other home-based hosting firms, the work of these self-employed people is often equated with their own lives and their very selves. Therefore, it is clear that their work prompts them to forge personal relationships with their customers. To counter this, the entrepreneurs have developed several strategies to prevent their workload from becoming too heavy and the customers becoming too close to their private lives. One successful strategy they employ is taking short breaks from work, which allows their lifestyle-based work to remain rewarding.

In cases where the entrepreneurs have dependent children, this affects the way in which they perform their hosting work. Both entrepreneurship and parenthood involve and engender passion, love, and frequent unpredictable situations. In this way, production and reproduction essentially intertwine, unavoidably but also purposefully (also, Ekinsmyth, 2011, 2013; Luckman, 2015; Wilson & Yochim, 2015). Allowing the various spheres of their lives to blend together is voluntary but also necessary for their goal of living 'the good life'. Ideally, their customers understand and accept this in totality. A female interviewee who, with her husband, has started an inn that caters to both dog hobbyists as well as anyone wanting a countryside holiday, speaks about being a home-based hosting entrepreneur while being the mother of a toddler and a baby:

> Everything has to be kept in some kind of order; we can't have total chaos here. Never. So it means continuously cleaning something, and it's a bit stressful. But after the birth of our second child, I have started to think that if somebody suddenly struts in and we have cockhorses in the middle of the

hall that day, then the person just gets to see that, okay, people are living here. Of course, the cockhorses are not there if I know that we'll have customers that day. Then I tell the kids that they can't build a hut here now! (Accommodation 1)

In their lives, where work/family and public/private have totally intermingled both in time and in space, there are constant efforts to establish boundaries. In time, this becomes almost autonomous and requires less conscious consideration. These efforts are two-way—keeping work away from family meals on the one hand, and, as above, keeping children and obvious traces of their presence away from customer interactions on the other. The work is restricted from entering every sphere of their lives primarily because of the children, without whom the entrepreneurs would be more than willing to let the work dominate their lives around the clock. It is no wonder one entrepreneur said, 'The kids help balance all this well, [as otherwise] we would kill ourselves in only a few years by working too hard'. The threat of working too much and the need to find a balance is seen in their speech about the future as well:

When the kids grow up, they have expectations for the summer [...] and they have free time from school [...] Also, to develop this place, we need somebody else besides ourselves to be able to work here and manage it someday. Because if we keep this as a family firm, it means that we will never be able to be away from here. (Accommodation 1)

The situation does change with time. A couple who hosts a part-time training centre said that their teenage children hardly come out of their rooms some days, and therefore they are not disturbed by having visitors spending time in their home environments: 'They do have their peace here. They are like teens everywhere. In the evenings, I go in and ask whether they have been outside today. The answer is usually, "Umm"' (Accommodation 2).

In all, entrepreneurs who were parents clearly had many more aspects to balance than childless entrepreneurs, and all four interviewees who had children had different ways to balance customer closeness with their family lives. The strategies were situational, both in terms of day-to-day things like finding time to put their children to bed while serving customers at night, as well as from a long-term perspective, considering how things will be different when the kids start attending or finish school or move away from home. Although the entrepreneurs have had to work towards striking a balance between work and life because of their children, it is also wise to do so for their own well-being.

Managing interactions

In most cases the work is seasonal in nature, meaning that there are more visitors during summers and more private time and space in winter. Seasonality is an advantage, because quiet times of year provide time to recuperate and allow the entrepreneurs to maintain a balance between showcasing their domestic environments to visitors and enjoying the benefits of rural privacy (Goulding, 2009, p. 109). But it also means that high season is extra busy, which is also necessary, as that is when the entire year's revenue is earned.

Even though the firms are always open, at least on the Internet, they do thus have quiet times and days off, even on a daily and weekly basis. Often, the entrepreneurs are most busy during evenings and weekends, when many other more conventionally employed people are free, whereas weekdays allow for more private time. This makes the situation a bit complicated—the entrepreneurs get only very little time to spend with their friends and family to compensate for the large amount of their time spent interacting with and serving their customers. As one entrepreneur said, 'Our working hours are totally different from those who work so-called normal hours. I mean, we are always working on weekends, and we have some free time on weekdays' (Accommodation 1). However, this same couple also optimistically noted that as most of their friends are also busy, working parents of small children, they all appreciate the need to plan meetings and activities well in advance.

A potentially challenging part of customer interaction for these entrepreneurs is that they know many of their customers very well, owing to regular visits or their shared interests as dog hobbyists, which makes their relationship rather informal and may also set expectations of uninterrupted availability. However, the relationship is still commercial, and while personal friendships have room for occasional disagreements, this is not necessarily the case when the friend is also a customer. The literature suggests that although all visitors have to be treated kindly, real feelings of friendship should be avoided (Andersson Cederholm & Hultman, 2010; Cohen, 2010). This means that emotional displays need to be regulated for commercial purposes. The issue of regulating emotions to produce the right state of mind in customers is a core aspect of service work in general (Hochschild, 1983). In her first book on emotion management in service work, Hochschild (1983) aspired to separate personal emotions from the emotional labour practised in waged work. Such a separation was not so simple then, and is even less so nowadays. Particularly in the case of lifestyle entrepreneurship, it is not possible to separate the private self from the professional self, given that the rules of feelings and emotions (Hochschild, 1983, pp. 118–119) are much more complicated. It is clear from my observations and interviews that, in practice, maintaining a friendship with one's customers is not simple, because sharing one's personal lifestyle while providing coaching and training premises is in fact the part of their work that entrepreneurs and their customers love the most. Being personally close to customers is thus both a motivation for and a requirement of lifestyle entrepreneurship (Andersson Cederholm & Hultman, 2010).

Interestingly, I found very few instances mentioned in the interviews or occurring in my field observations of customers crossing any lines or claiming any favours based on their relationship (cf. Cohen, 2010). Thus, although the entrepreneurs and their customers blend the role of consumer and producer by doing favours for each other, this is a mutually beneficial arrangement (Andersson Cederholm & Åkerström, 2016). As one interviewee said, 'I have a friend who helps in taking care of the sheep and I give her training in exchange' (Coaching 1). With regular and familiar customers, value is co-created, which is increasingly common—'the new normal'—in the new economy. However, the question of money sometimes results in untoward situations. Occasionally, customers must be reminded about their invoice, and if a reminder does not help, many self-employed entrepreneurs tend to let it slide and simply try to learn from it for the next time. In the case of familiar visitors, it is easier to think along the lines of, 'It's only money, we'll let it be for now and be much clearer right from the beginning next time' (Coaching 2), instead of engaging in battles with customer-friends. Generally, learning how to act with different people is extremely important. It leads to material solutions such as installing automatic door closers if the customers do not remember to close the doors, pasting written rules on the walls, and sending instructions via e-mail in advance. These preparations lead to smooth and polite customer situations and thus help in sustaining the lifestyle that brings the entrepreneurs happiness.

Unlike the pessimistic view that people in the neoliberal economy are forced to capitalise on their individual capacities and mould their enterprising selves according to customer needs, my data shows that many entrepreneurs have the power to choose how they wish to sell themselves. That is partly due to their class position—they are educated and have prior work experience, or even hold a job on the side, which brings them a sense of optimism and trust in the future. Many of the entrepreneurs believe that they cannot change their personality to something that does not come to them 'naturally'. The entrepreneurs' 'evermore privatized paths to happiness' (Binkley, 2014, p. 23) do not include feigning enthusiasm. In sporadic day-to-day situations of course, preventing and producing emotions cannot be avoided, but the core idea of the enterprise cannot be based on false feelings. The innkeeper couple I referred to previously constantly brainstorm ways to develop their activities to acquire more customers beyond dog enthusiasts. They define what they are ready to sell in the following way:

> You can sell and develop only the kinds of things that you can convincingly be enthusiastic about. I mean, it is not convincing enthusiasm if you have to force yourself and you can't just say, 'Now I'm going to be enthusiastic!' If you aren't excited, you just aren't excited. (Accommodation 1)

Happiness can be a work ethic that paves the way towards individualised freedom (Wilson & Yochim, 2015) or an enterprise (Binkley, 2014), but only if one's deepest emotions are genuine. When the self is deeply and willingly invested in this way, feedback is taken very personally. 'But it is precisely because we work with our personalities. I don't believe that somebody working in a chain restaurant would give a damn' (Accommodation 1). It is a complicated business putting one's personality to work.

Conclusions: Working for happiness

Lifestyle-based entrepreneurship requires very different practices from those learnt from paid employment from the Fordist era. Today, living a dream life and creating value by blending the spheres of production, reproduction, and consumption is an all-encompassing work. Engaging in emotional labour has generally become common in the new service economy, and people are increasingly required to commoditise themselves when participating in this variegated labour market (for an evaluation, see Hochschild, 2013; Wolkowitz, 2006, pp. 76–81). It is not as straightforward as an employer requiring employees to present certain feelings at work, as these employees are free to have their own genuine feelings in their leisure time. In the late-capitalist economy, commercial and non-commercial emotions truly blend, and it is normal to market and utilise one's individual personality in both paid employment and entrepreneurship. This personal figure also has to be constantly maintained and reformulated, which is unquestionably hard work.

However, using one's personality as an asset also makes it possible to design one's work according to one's own values, needs, and aspirations. The 'do-it-yourself' approach (Luckman, 2015) is experienced optimistically as free choice to achieve 'the good life' (Berlant, 2011). Moreover, personalising the home environment can be satisfying. The possibility of choosing one's place of residence and working there is indeed in opposition to current global capitalist trends, according to which people move around freely and do not settle down in any single place (Boltanski & Chiapello, 2007). This kind of individualised work may provide feelings of self-fulfilment and freedom from restrictive, unsatisfactory wage work. Pursuing lifestyle-based entrepreneurship leads to some abandonment of the middle-class chasing of success and an upwards career trajectory, and instead committing to choices such as participatory parenthood.

Even so, seeing how hard both male and female entrepreneurs work, it is clear that they also develop the 'can do and must do better' ethos (McRobbie, 2015), not really questioning either masculine ideals or productive entrepreneurialism, which governments around the world encourage in order to make citizens less dependent on government support. Lifestyle entrepreneurs work to acquire happiness, which for them means leaving behind variously precarious or more secure paid employment. However, self-employment is definitely another precarious situation. In post-Fordist economies in general, self-employment may be becoming 'institutionalised as an individualised carrot to wave in front of the noses of exhausted, over-committed parents, and specifically mothers' (Luckman, 2015, p. 155). Seeking happiness by producing commercialised happiness for others enables entrepreneurs—whether they are parents or not—to actively construct and maintain the logic of neoliberal economic and affective structures and, therefore, accept a state of precariousness as the new normal of work life.

Notes

1. Transcription style: […] indicates words have been omitted in a sentence, often just the repetition or a word or two.
2. All the interviews, barring one that was conducted in English with a person whose mother tongue was Swedish, were conducted in Finnish. I have translated these interviews into English, attempting to maintain the tone and cadence of the original speech.

References

Adkins, L. (2016). Contingent labour and the rewriting of the sexual contract. In L. Adkins & M. Dever (Eds.), *The post-Fordist sexual contract: Working and living in contingency* (pp. 1–28). Basingstoke: Palgrave Macmillan.

Andersson Cederholm, E., & Åkerström, M. (2016). With a little help from my friends: Relational work in leisure–related enterprising. *The Sociological Review.* https://doi.org/10.1111/1467-954X.12377

Andersson Cederholm, E., & Hultman, J. (2010). The value of intimacy—Negotiating commercial relationships in lifestyle entrepreneurship. *Scandinavian Journal of Hospitality and Tourism, 10*(1), 16–32. https://doi.org/10.1080/15022250903442096

Ateljevic, I., & Doorne, S. (2000). 'Staying within the fence': Lifestyle entrepreneurship in tourism. *Journal of Sustainable Tourism, 8*(5), 378–392.

Beck, U., & Beck-Gernsheim, E. (2002). *Individualization: Institutionalized individualism and its social and political consequences.* London: Sage.

Bell, D. (2006). Variations on the rural idyll. In P. Cloke, T. Marsden, & P. H. Mooney (Eds.), *Handbook of rural studies* (pp. 149–161). London: Sage.

Berlant, L. (2011). *Cruel optimism*. Durham: Duke University Press.

Binkley, S. (2014). *Happiness as enterprise: An essay on neoliberal life*. Albany: Suny Press.

Boltanski, L., & Chiapello, E. (2007). *The new spirit of capitalism*. London: Verso.

Brandth, B., & Haugen, M. (2012). Farm tourism and dilemmas of commercial activity in the home. *Hospitality & Society, 2*(2), 179–196.

Brandth, B., & Haugen, M. (2014). Embodying the rural idyll in farm tourist hosting. *Scandinavian Journal of Hospitality and Tourism, 14*(2), 101–115.

Bunce, M. (2003). Reproducing rural idylls. In P. Cloke (Ed.), *Country visions* (pp. 14–30). Harlow: Pearson.

Cohen, R. L. (2010). When it pays to be friendly: Employment relationships and emotional labour in hairstyling. *Sociological Review, 58*(2), 197–218.

Ekinsmyth, C. (2011). Challenging the boundaries of entrepreneurship. The spatialities and practices of UK 'mumpreneurs'. *Geoforum, 42*(1), 104–114. https://doi.org/10.1016/j.geoforum.2010.10.005

Ekinsmyth, C. (2013). Managing the business of everyday life: The roles of space and place in 'mumpreneurship'. *International Journal of Entrepreneurial Behaviour and Research, 19*(5), 525–546. https://doi.org/10.1108/IJEBR-10-2011-0139

Ekinsmyth, C. (2014). Mothers' business, work/life and the politics of 'mumpreneurship'. *Gender, Place & Culture, 21*(10), 1230–1248. https://doi.org/10.1080/0966369X.2013.817975

Gillespie, D. L., Leffler, A., & Lerner, E. (2002). If it weren't for my hobby, I'd have a life: Dog sports, serious leisure, and boundary negotiations. *Leisure Studies, 21*(3–4), 285–304. https://doi.org/10.1080/0261436022000030632

Goulding, P. J. (2009). Time to trade? Perspectives of temporality in the commercial home enterprise. In P. A. Lynch, A. J. McIntosh, & H. Turker (Eds.), *Commercial homes in tourism. An international perspective* (pp. 102–114). London and New York: Routledge.

Haraway, D. (2008). *When species meet*. Minneapolis: University of Minnesota Press.

Hochschild, A. R. (1983). *The managed heart: Commercialization of human feeling*. Berkeley: University of California Press.

Hochschild, A. R. (2013). *So how's the family? And other essays*. Berkeley: University of California Press.

Ikonen, H.-M. (2014). Precarious work, entrepreneurial mindset and sense of place: Female strategies in insecure labour markets. In M. Johnson (Ed.), *Precariat: Labour, work and politics* (pp. 83–97). London: Routledge.

Ikonen, H.-M., & Pehkonen, S. (2017). 'I <3 my high-performance dog': Love for the sport in agility coach representations in social media. *Sport in Society*. https://doi.org/10.1080/17430437.2017.1310201

Irving, D. (2016). Future investments: Gender transition as a socio-economic event. In L. Adkins & M. Dever (Eds.), *The post-Fordist sexual contract: Working and living in contingency* (pp. 31–48). Basingstoke: Palgrave Macmillan.

Luckman, S. (2015). Women's micro-entrepreneurial homeworking. *Australian Feminist Studies, 30*(84), 146–160.

Luckman, S. (2016). Micro-enterprise as work-life 'magical solution'. In L. Adkins & M. Dever (Eds.), *The post-Fordist sexual contract: Working and living in contingency* (pp. 91–108). Basingstoke: Palgrave Macmillan.

Lund, G. (2014). Taking teamwork seriously: The sport of dog agility as an ethical model of cross-species companionship. In J. Gillett & M. Gilbert (Eds.), *Sport, animals, and society* (pp. 127–139). New York: Routledge.

MacLeavy, J., Roberts, S., & Strauss, K. (2016). Feminist inclusions in economic geography: What difference does difference make? *Environment and Planning A, 48*(10), 2067–2071.

McDowell, L. (1991). Life without father and Ford: The new gender order of post-Fordism. *Transactions of the Institute of British Geographers, 16*, 400–421.

McRobbie, A. (2015). Notes on the perfect. *Australian Feminist Studies, 30*(83), 3–20.

Miller, P., & Rose, M. (2008). *Governing the present: Administering economic, social and personal life*. Cambridge: Polity Press.

Peters, M., Frehse, J., & Buhalis, D. (2009). The importance of lifestyle entrepreneurship: A conceptual study of the tourism industry. *Pasos, 7*(2), 393–405.

Schuurman, N. (2014). Blogging situated emotions in human–horse relationships. *Emotion, Space and Society, 13*(4), 1–8.

Short, B. (2006). The idyllic rural. In P. Cloke, T. Marsden, & P. H. Mooney (Eds.), *Handbook of rural studies* (pp. 133–148). London: Sage.

Stone, I. A., & Stubbs, C. (2007). Enterprising expatriates: Lifestyle migration and entrepreneurship in rural Southern Europe. *Entrepreneurship and Regional Development, 19*(5), 433–450.

Taylor, S. (2015). A new mystique? Working for yourself in the neoliberal economy. *Sociological Review, 63*, 174–187.

Thrift, N. (2005). *Knowing capitalism*. London: Sage.
Veijola, S., & Jokinen, E. (2008). Towards a hostessing society? Mobile arrangements of gender and labour. *NORA, 16*(3), 166–181.
Wilson, J. A., & Yochim, C. E. (2015). Mothering through precarity. Becoming mamapreneurial. *Cultural Studies, 29*(5–6), 669–686.
Wolkowitz, C. (2006). *Bodies at work*. London: Sage.

Hanna-Mari Ikonen is a post-doctoral researcher at the University of Tampere, Finland. Her research interests include micro-entrepreneurship, self-employment, and female entrepreneurship in rural areas and in the landscape of precarious working life.

Self-Employment in Elderly Care: A Way to Self-Fulfilment or Self-Exploitation for Professionals?

Elin Vadelius

Introduction

The world of work is changing, with forms of employment outside the scope of the traditional employer–employee arrangement becoming more common. Work is increasingly self-organised, and self-employment is on the rise in advanced economies (International Labour Organization, 2015; OECD, 2016). This chapter will explore opportunities for self-employment in woman-dominated professions in the context of restructuring of the Swedish public sector and contracting out of publicly funded welfare services.

According to the *Global Entrepreneurship Monitor Report 2015/2016* (Kelley, Singer, & Herrington, 2016), levels of entrepreneurial activity increased in Sweden in 2015. This was due largely to an increase in business start-ups among women (Braunerhjelm, Holmquist, Larsson, Skoogberg, & Thulin, 2016). In Sweden, as in other advanced economies,

E. Vadelius (✉)
Department of Social and Psychological Studies, Karlstad University, Karlstad, Sweden

women's employment opportunities have been affected by labour market changes (see, e.g., International Labour Organization, 2015). During the past two decades, there have been welfare-state retrenchments, and the public sector, which used to be a large and stable employer of women, was downsized. According to Ahl and Tillmar (2015), '[w]hile in 1987, 55 percent of all employed women worked for the public sector, this figure decreased to 47 percent by 2013' (p. 9). Part of the explanation for the decrease in public sector employment can be found in the transformation of public utilities to private enterprises from the 1990s onward. The first changes concerned privatisation of publicly owned companies in industries such as railways and telecommunications, but the changes were later expanded to include the contracting out of publicly financed welfare services such as child care, primary and secondary education, health care, and elderly care (Ahl & Tillmar, 2015; Brennan, Cass, Himmelweit, & Szebehely, 2012). This chapter will focus on markets in elderly care as arenas for self-employment.

The political arguments for contracting out welfare services have included that this will provide employees in the public sector with the opportunity to start their own small-scale enterprises that will contribute to innovation and improve the quality of public services (Sköld & Tillmar, 2015; Sundin & Tillmar, 2010). As the majority of employees in this field are women, a central argument has also focused on competition creating new business opportunities for women (Government Bill 2008/09:29). Self-employment is assumed to give women more freedom so that they can use their professional skills, influence their work environment, and realise their visions. These arguments can be interpreted as attempts to 'normalise' self-employment by presenting it as a viable and desirable alternative to traditional employment.

However, previous studies show that the elderly care sub-sector in Sweden has undergone structural changes (see, e.g., Meagher & Szebehely, 2013; Trydegård, 2012). These changes include more limited public resources and a more restrictive attitude from municipal authorities towards what initiatives should be approved for the elderly, as well as increased monitoring of care work. Because eldercare services are publicly funded and regulated, private providers end up in a dependent relationship with public welfare institutions. From a critical perspective, it can be argued that women who are expected to establish themselves as entrepreneurs in health care and social services are also expected indirectly to participate in the streamlining of an already streamlined and low-paid sector (Ahl, 2004).

With this in mind, it is important to study how social service providers perceive their potential for running a business in a professional manner and providing high-quality services—especially as access to services is crucial for quality of life among the elderly. Research to date about private business in health care and social services has been described as relatively limited, in both the Nordic and Anglo-Saxon contexts (Anderson & Hughes, 2010; Kovalainen & Österberg-Högstedt, 2013). There is a need for in-depth studies of the various activities within health care and social services, as the conditions for self-employment can vary among the different sub-sectors. Against this background, the purpose of this chapter is to present findings from a research study that examined how individuals who started companies in Swedish elderly care perceive their scope of action and their potential for implementing ideas as professional service providers. The term 'professional' is used to refer to individuals who identify themselves as having a professional role in health care and social services, and who have relevant vocational training and/or extensive professional experience (Kovalainen & Österberg-Högstedt, 2013).

In the next section I review previous research on changes in home care services that affect working conditions in waged and salaried employment, as well as opportunities for private, small-scale enterprise. This is followed by an account of my data and methods, and then two sections in which I address empirical research findings. Based on qualitative interview data, I show that there are large variations in how home care service providers perceive their scope of action and their potential for running a smooth operation. Factors affecting these experiences in both a positive and a negative direction are highlighted. In the final section, I discuss how the results of the study illustrate some larger trends in changing employment and career opportunities in advanced economies.

General trends in home care for the elderly: Marketisation and rationalisation

Home care is the primary form of care provision for the elderly in Sweden, utilised by around 23% of the population aged 80 years and above (Socialstyrelsen, 2016). According to the *Social Services Act* (SFS, 2001:453), individuals who need assistance to stay in their homes because of illness or functional impairment can apply for home care. The needs of the individual are assessed by a municipal care assessor, who may grant applicants home care in the form of services such as cleaning and/or personal care, such as help with showering and getting dressed. The individual pays a minor share of the cost in the form of a fee. Approximately 85% of eldercare funding comes from municipal taxes, while another 10% comes from national taxes (Erlandsson, Storm, Stranz, Szebehely, & Trydegård, 2013).

In the 1960s and 1970s, municipal home care expanded into a huge operation and became an integrated part of eldercare and the Swedish welfare model. The provision of care was based on person-centred organisational models under which each care worker was responsible for a small number of clients (Meagher & Szebehely, 2013). The content of help was not regulated in advance and the time granted was generous, which left room for the care worker to use her (or his) knowledge of the individual care recipients to adjust to the elderly person's needs and wishes on different occasions.

However, since the early 1990s, a number of reforms have led to competition in the provision of welfare services and the creation of publicly funded and regulated markets, so-called 'quasi-markets' (cf. Bartlett, Roberts, & Le Grand, 1998). The reforms were inspired by new public management ideas of greater efficiency in the public services, based on the private sector as a role model. An example of this is the introduction of purchaser–provider models. This means that the municipal care assessors now assess the needs of the elderly and commission the services of a municipal or private home care provider. In this way, a form of buy-and-sell relationship is established, which entails the separation of the assessment and granting of services from the organisations that provide them.

Previously, these tasks were performed within the same municipal unit, usually by a supervisor who assessed needs, approved services, and ensured that they were implemented by the supervisor's own team.

A later stage in the process of marketisation was the introduction of the *customer choice model*, by means of which the elderly can choose a provider once the assessor has granted home care services. Since 1 January 2009, there has been a special law on customer choice, which the municipalities can choose to implement in elder care. Payment terms are predetermined and are the same for all providers within a municipal area (although they can vary between different municipalities, which may design home care markets in different ways). As the individual's choice determines the allocation of public resources, the providers cannot be guaranteed customers. The elderly also have the right to make a new choice if they are dissatisfied with a provider. The political intention of the law was to strengthen citizens' ability to exercise choice and thereby influence public welfare production, but also to facilitate private small-scale enterprise in the public sector.

In parallel with the development towards marketisation there has also been a general trend towards increasing rationalisation in eldercare, including more detailed regulation and increasing time pressure in care work (Eliasson, 1992; Hjalmarsson, 2009; Stranz, 2013). Municipal budgets have generally become tighter (Meagher & Szebehely, 2013). Markets in eldercare were introduced at a time when public finances were hit by recession and economic crisis, leading politicians to search for ways of cutting costs (Jordahl & Öhrvall, 2013). Financial pressures have led to greater restriction on services for the elderly, and especially to downsizing of help with household duties and services that serve to meet elderly persons' social needs (Government Bill 2005/06:115; Sörensdotter, 2008; Szebehely, 2000). The introduction of the purchaser–provider model has also led to more detailed specifications of the services to be provided, which stipulate in advance the tasks that are to be performed in the client's home. This sets limits on how far either the receiver or the caregiver can make decisions about the help that is provided.

It can be argued that the introduction of organisational models that emphasise economic efficiency has undermined care workers' professional discretion and autonomy. In a study of Nordic care workers' experiences (Trydegård, 2012), the figures from Sweden on opportunities for professional development are described as especially noteworthy: '80–85% of the Swedish care workers stated that they only sometimes, seldom or never felt that they had the opportunity to develop in their profession' (Trydegård, 2012, p. 124). This has been attributed to factors such as tight timeframes and the logics of purchaser–provider models, which split up complex caring activities into small components. It has also been noted that care workers feel frustrated when they cannot provide high-quality care, that many reported their work as physically and mentally arduous, and that one out of three care workers declared that they had seriously considered quitting their jobs (Trydegård, 2012; see also Stranz, 2013). According to Wolmesjö (2005), the political prioritising of the economic perspective also affects how managers in eldercare experience their working situation. Demands for cost containment from higher levels in the municipal organisation, combined with organisational factors such as high workload, can lead to managers feeling that their treatment of care workers is inadequate.

Previous research on individuals who have started private enterprises in the health and care sectors suggests that the experience of care workers and professionals in paid employment is important when it comes to their choice to become self-employed. Studies conducted in Sweden and Finland show that subordinate positions and limited scope for applying their professional knowledge can push individuals into leaving employment and motivate them to establish own businesses instead (Hedberg & Pettersson, 2006, 2011; Kurvinen, 2008; Simonen & Kovalainen, 1998; Tillmar, 2004, 2009b). Therefore, the wish to practise their occupation in a more autonomous way and achieve satisfaction in their work has been highlighted as a motive for pursuing entrepreneurship.

These findings point to the significance of professional identities in certain business contexts (Kovalainen & Österberg-Högstedt, 2013; Tillmar, 2004). The wish for independence and to realise personal potential is linked to the wish to provide better quality care (Hedberg & Pettersson, 2011; Tillmar, 2009b). Similar results for the importance of professional motivation in becoming a private provider in the health and care sectors have been found in British research (Kendall, 2001; Matosevic, Knapp, Kendall, Henderson, & Fernandez, 2007; Taylor-Gooby, Sylvester, Calnan, & Manley, 2000).

However, previous findings also suggest that starting one's own business does not always bring better opportunities for realising one's professional vision. Studies from Sweden report the difficulties that small-scale providers, many of them women, have in competing in quasi-markets for health care and social care. In earlier systems characterised by competitive tendering, the tough price competition and short contract periods favoured risk capital investment companies with extensive resources over small-scale providers with limited means (Sundin & Tillmar, 2010; Tillmar, 2004). According to Sundin and Tillmar (2010), it is still an open question whether the new construction of markets in home care, built upon customer choice rather than competitive tendering, will facilitate small-scale entrepreneurship. However, the results from their case study of a Swedish municipality that implemented customer choice in home care are disappointing: large corporations, most often owned and managed by men, accounted for about 97% of the service hours provided by non-public organisations.

Further, both Nordic and British studies point to dilemmas facing self-employed individuals in health and social care. These dilemmas include combining the economic logics of operating a business with the moral and ethical values of care (Andrews & Phillips, 2002; Nadin, 2007; Tillmar, 2004) and dealing with lack of trust in relation to purchasers and authorities (Tillmar, 2009a). Still, the outcomes at a personal level seem to be complex and involve both 'distressed' and 'happy' entrepreneurs, the former experiencing problems with heavy workload and financial issues, and the latter enjoying the freedom of being in charge of their own work (Kovalainen & Österberg-Högstedt, 2013).

Methods and data

This chapter is based on a qualitative and interpretative study that aimed to investigate individual experiences of starting and running a business (Vadelius, 2015). In order to explore the challenges and rewards of working in self-employment from different perspectives, I recruited participants who had built their businesses on different ideas. For example, they had varying views on the desirability of expanding their businesses, and different interests in developing more innovative ways of providing care. Some of the participants had chosen to serve only clients who lived in a limited area of one town, whereas others had established or were trying to establish their businesses in several municipalities within the county.

All the participants were active as owners as well as operational leaders in the daily businesses, which were the central selection criteria for the study, and all described themselves as initiators of their business. Ten were trained in health care or social care, for example as a nurse or social worker, and had previously been employed in large healthcare organisations in the private or public sector. A common denominator was that they had held leadership positions in previous employment, for example, as head of a municipal home care service unit. This proved to be important for understanding both why they had started their businesses and how they perceived the challenges and rewards they met in their self-employed position. At the beginning of the study, three officials in one municipality were also interviewed, but further interviews with officials were not conducted because of limited time, so the research focused on the experiences of providers.

The empirical data comprise interviews with 14 business owners and managers who operated small or medium-sized businesses in the county of Stockholm. Following the classification used by Statistics Sweden (2014), small businesses have a maximum of 49 employees, whereas medium-sized businesses have a maximum of 249 employees. Three participants were interviewed a second time for more information and follow-up; thus, a total of 17 interviews were conducted.

My purpose was to understand how actors engage in and negotiate with a complex phenomenon in a specific context, rather than to quantify trends. The interviews, which were carried out with the help of a thematic interview guide, were open-ended and lasted for 45–160 minutes. The themes treated covered comprehensive aspects of the participants' backgrounds, why they had decided to start a home care service business, its current profile and business idea, the participants' view of what quality in care is, and their opinion of terms and conditions for running a home care business. The interviews were recorded digitally and transcribed as verbatim as possible, except for hesitations and repetitions. In the analysis process, I used coding as the method to conceptualise significant phenomena and identify central themes (Miles & Huberman, 1994). The interviews were conducted in Swedish. The extracts presented here have been translated by the researcher (myself).

Trying to gain control: Reasons to become self-employed

The participants in this study were in a position where they had to combine care with market considerations. In this context, I see rationality as a relevant concept for understanding the values and goals that the participants associated with a business, and also for analysing the contradictions of different logics of action (Brubaker, 1984; Friedland & Alford, 1991). Such contradictions can arise between consideration of human needs and running a business as efficiently as possible. Different concepts of rationality are used to understand different ways to orient action, ranging from narrow concepts in terms of instrumental calculation (Weber, 1983), to wider concepts, which include expressive values and emotions (Engelen, 2006; Waerness, 1984). What is defined and experienced as rational action can vary depending on the situation and relations between the actors involved (Granovetter, 1985). For example, what is rational from a care perspective can be perceived as irrational from an economic perspective, and vice versa.

To understand how the participants experienced their situation as private providers, I first look at how they described their reasons for starting a business. What was noteworthy was that, in the interviews, none of them mentioned the need to earn a living. At the time of starting a business, all the participants already had established careers and incomes. Instead of talking about earning a living, the participants stressed motives related to professional autonomy, such as greater freedom to apply their professional knowledge and the ability to make decisions about both their own daily work and the long-term development of the organisation they had been working for. Some of the participants had previously been employed as managers of municipal home care units. According to their descriptions, however, the possibility of real influence had been limited, because they had been managers at lower levels in large organisations with more senior managers above them. One participant, who was a trained social worker and had long experience of managing local home care units, described how she was dependent on others in the municipal administration for important decisions to be made. As a consequence, she had to wait each time before taking action, which caused feelings of insecurity and frustration.

> I thought that many of the decisions that had to be taken with respect to my unit took [a] very long time, because I was dependent on many bosses outside the unit, outside me. Above me. I had to meet them, I had to inform them, and they in turn had to meet with their bosses. To have a decision go through, I had to wait for two months. That caused me to feel stressed and I knew about the units' economy, I knew how things should be done. And then I wanted to save time. (Interviewee 7)

Against this background, the participant described the decision to start her own small-scale business as the only way to gain a sense of control in her position as manager. One alternative might have been to remain in her former position as employee and try to improve the situation by way of dialogue with politicians and head officials. However, she regarded this possibility as virtually non-existent because, according to her, the home care unit was marginalised within the municipal organisation and its existence sometimes forgotten.

Push factors for leaving a subordinate position were described not only by participants with former employment in public sector organisations, but also by some participants who had held positions as managers in risk capital investment companies. In the latter case, demands from owners and top management to increase profit at the expense of staffing levels and quality of care were described as having impacted on the decision to resign from a corporate career and establish their own business. Whether their background was in the public or in the private sector, the participants emphasised the importance of having insight into the nature of care work for being able to work as managers in home care. For example, they reflected on the fact that their employees often had to perform emotional labour in order to create feelings of comfort and security in the elderly. To achieve this, the employees would often have to manage feelings of anxiety and anger in the elderly at the same time as they suppressed and hid any feelings of stress and frustration they might themselves have (cf. Hochschild, 2003). According to the participants, managers in home care need professional knowledge of occupations such as nursing or social work to be able to support employees in such situations. Some participants even considered such professional knowledge more crucial than knowledge about business administration. In this context, they also expressed a sense of pride. For example, concluding her story about why she had resigned from a career in risk capital investment to start a small business in elderly care instead, one participant said: 'I am very proud in my profession and what I want' (Interviewee 4).

One possible interpretation of the participants' turn to private business is that this enabled them to keep their identity as professionals, thereby creating a positive sense of self. However, they emphasised different elements or components of this identity. Some described themselves more as leaders than as entrepreneurs, in the innovative or risk-taking sense. These participants expressed an interest in quality but did not see any need to develop new methods in care work, or new models for providing care. On the contrary, the main business idea was described as 'customary, traditional home care services'. These participants enjoyed working closely with their employees and being present in the daily operations, and they had chosen to serve only clients who lived in a smaller district of one town. They were not interested in expanding their businesses to other parts of the town or to other municipalities, as this would make it more difficult to maintain preferred leadership styles and personal relations with employees and the elderly clients.

Other participants aspired to ideals of entrepreneurship, and referred to themselves as visionaries or 'entrepreneurs'. They expressed interest in finding new ways to work, developing innovative profiles, and expanding their services to new geographical areas. For instance, one participant expressed a strong professional interest in developing better ways of helping elderly people with dementia, for example by working with methods that would help the individual to remember their life history and important life events. According to this participant, such methods can help to reduce anxiety, which may otherwise turn into aggression. These findings are broadly in line with previous studies (e.g. Kovalainen & Österberg-Högstedt, 2013; Matosevic et al., 2007; Tillmar, 2009b) but they also add to our understanding of different meanings of professional identity in this particular business context.

Being self-employed: Successes and non-successes

A distinguishing feature of home care is that it has the potential to involve care workers in personal and long-lasting relations with clients, as the work takes place in the clients' home and can last for months and sometimes years. A recurrent theme in the interviews was that participants emphasised their contact with elderly clients and their families, for example when making home visits, as emotionally rewarding. To have the opportunity to provide help and improve someone's life contributes to a sense of doing a meaningful job. Some participants also reported that they participated in the care work themselves on a regular, sometimes daily, basis. This provided them with opportunities to observe changes in the elderly person's health status. Help needs were described as complex and changing. According to participants, following standardised templates and orders from care assessors sometimes made it difficult to provide care. They argued that if care is to be of good quality, it has to be flexible and responsive to changing needs.

In this context, issues of control over care work were raised as dilemmas in the interviews. Some participants considered that the instructions from care assessors were too rigid and inflexible, as they stated in detail what kind of help the elderly person should receive and how much time had been approved for the performance of services. For example, an elderly person may have been granted 12 hours of help a month, which should include cleaning every other week, shopping twice a week, and help with showering once a week. If care needs changed in ways that required other kinds of help, or just more of the same help, a new assessment was needed. Sometimes the elderly person had to wait for a new assessment, as municipal care assessors often had a heavy workload. Thus, the institutional framework impacted on how providers perceived their space for manoeuvring and working more innovatively. According to one participant, this space was not very large, as the municipality was exercising legal authority by granting and commissioning services:

> What we do is execute an order. We must do what is stated on that order. The municipal administration is exercising legal authority by saying that

'this individual is now receiving assistance according to the Social Service Act. And he or she has chosen your unit. So you will do the job.' There is not much to choose from. (Interviewee 1)

From a provider perspective, following orders may seem straightforward, but it is not always unproblematic, as care assessors' decisions do not necessarily correspond with the needs and wishes of elderly clients.

In some municipalities, the local authorities also demand that providers should use ICT-based systems, which make it possible to supervise how much time their employees have spent in the elderly person's home and what kind of services they have performed. For example, one participant described a system that involved using a digital pen, which the employees had to use to register their arrival or 'clock in' as soon as they passed through the door into the elderly person's home, register the tasks performed, and then to 'clock out' when they left. If the employees forgot to clock in or out, or if they forgot to register services, the company lost revenue. As the system was not working well, it required substantial corrections from the management group in the company. Solving the technological problems took time and energy away from developing quality in care. The latter was something the participant said she wanted to invest more effort in, for example by working more systematically to increase her staff's knowledge of the importance of nutrition for elderly persons. However, these ambitions seemed hard to fulfil in a market where instrumental steering was permeating professional knowledge and ways of acting. Some participants also viewed the implementation of these and similar ICT-based systems as a sign of distrust from the municipal purchaser.

Low levels of remuneration were described as another problem. For example, in one municipality, levels of remuneration could vary between SEK 280 and SEK 340 (around EUR 28–34) an hour, depending on how many hours of help the elderly person had been granted. According to one participant, the remuneration needed to be around SEK 360 an hour to make it possible for a provider to deliver care according to the agreement and make ends meet. The officials who were interviewed reported that some private providers, known for their quality work, had ended their agreement with the municipality because they regarded the remuneration as too low to enable them to give good quality care.

Some participants perceived the payment to be based only on direct care work performed in the clients' home. They said that not enough consideration was given to expenses associated with owning and managing a home care business, especially expenses connected with operating a business over geographically widespread areas, such as the time employees needed during their working day to travel between the elderly people's homes, and travel expenses, including vehicle repairs and servicing, and fuel. This especially affected providers who tried to develop innovative profiles by specialising in care for elderly clients with particular needs, for example people with psychiatric disorders, as those clients were likely to be dispersed over larger areas.

One provider who was interviewed suggested that there was a relationship between low status, low pay, and the fact that care work is regarded as 'women's work':

> Yes, because this [eldercare] is a woman-dominated kind of occupation. It is unqualified work—it is *regarded* as unqualified work, that is a very subjective judgement. I would like to claim that it is anything but unqualified. /.../.[1] What we are working with here, is life! How can that be unqualified? I don't understand that. I think this is very existential and not at all unqualified work. /.../. But it is public sector, it is part-time work, it is women [who do it], it is low paid. And because of this, it is regarded as unqualified. The status has to be raised. (Interviewee 11)

Further, participants also pointed to a close connection between time and money in the home care business, making control over time a contested area. They said that since clients' health status and help needs could change quickly, this could render the care assessor's decision on service provision obsolete. Providers who were interviewed considered it their responsibility to contact the care assessors and inform them about the need for more time or a new assessment. However, some providers reported that care assessors often reacted with suspicion, regarding the request for allocation of more hours as motivated by greed and profit rather than patient care.

Ultimately, this can be understood as a conflict that is embedded in the organisational split between purchaser and providers: while it is in the interests of the purchaser to control and hold back the amount of time granted, thereby curtailing expenses, it is in the interests of the provider to increase the amount of time allotted. This is a conflict that is not based primarily on personal relations, but has to do with the organising of markets in home care. Providers also reported that they tried to convince care assessors of the need for more time by documenting changes in the elderly person's health status, but these kinds of negotiations often took a long time and sometimes were unsuccessful. In these cases, distrust from the purchaser could have a negative impact on the provider's ability to improve care. (The situation is particularly complex as there are examples of private providers who have been suspected of and indicted for fraud, i.e., getting paid for services not rendered (Vadelius, 2015). Even if these cases are rare, they suggest that distrust from municipal purchasers may sometimes be justified.)

From a provider's perspective, problems of low remuneration and insufficient time allocation leads to conflict between the financial reality of managing a business and the norms of ethics and deference to humans and their needs. Some participants claimed that they were under increasing time pressure, as some municipalities had reduced the time granted by care assessors for the performance of services. Because the remuneration was predetermined and could not be influenced by providers, the only way to create profit was to increase the working pace of employees and make sure that they did not spend more time than had been granted in a client's home—even if the client needed it. As one provider summarised: 'Reality is money and time, even if we don't want to talk about it. We have no time, [and] home visits are becoming shorter and shorter' (Interviewee 8). However, prioritising economic rationality at the expense of elderly people's needs leads to internal conflict, lowering the motivation to remain in the sector. This is illustrated in the following quote:

> This is all wrong. Nobody is there to give care. With this limited amount of time, 10 minutes here, 20 minutes there. Nothing. In earlier days, when I was working as home helper myself, I had time to sit down with the pensioner and have coffee. Nowadays, that time does not exist. Then I don't want to do this anymore. (Interviewee 7)

This participant did not think she could provide a level of care that measured up to her personal and professional standards, causing her to express feelings of defeat and a sense of lost meaning. She also expressed disappointment at the personal consequences of starting a business, saying that it had not put her in a better position than she had had as an employee of the municipality:

> I earn a lower income now, than when I was employed within the municipality. I work more, I have fewer holidays. I can't afford staying away from work because of sickness. /…/. If I close this business, I will never work with care again. It is heavy work, it is badly paid, there's no status. I don't want to be in this sector, I've had enough. /…/. I had a vision and I started, but it was only a vision. There was no reality to it. (Interviewee 7)

Private enterprise is positively associated with the exploitation of opportunities (cf. Tillmar, 2009b), but the situation described here seems to be more about self-exploitation. According to the participant, the financial situation in the company was very strained and it was only a matter of time before the company would go bankrupt. The consequences that the participant foresaw for herself were not only an exit from business ownership, but also an exit from the health and care sector as a whole. As in interviews with other providers, the issue of the low status of care work was brought up as a problem that contributes to her decision not to remain in the sector.

In addition to the question of status and low remuneration, this participant hinted at another obstacle: the problem of insufficient legitimacy, due to divergent standpoints between politicians and local municipal officials on the desirability of private business enterprises in the home care sector. 'The politicians were positive. But in the municipal administration, my bosses weren't happy at all. It [i.e. starting her own home care business] was something of a taboo here.' (Interviewee 7)

The kind of negative outcome described can be summed up with the idiom, 'Out of the frying pan and into the fire'. Other participants described similar experiences of not being able to provide quality care in the way they wanted. They had started their businesses to break free from subordinate positions and realise visions, but had discovered that managing their own organisations did not guarantee professional and entrepreneurial freedom. One explanation for this is that their business activities were being conducted in a quasi-market characterised by institutional conflicts between actors with different interests and competing rationalities.

However, there were also success stories. Some participants were happy with being self-employed workers and largely content with their terms as private providers. For example, one participant had started her career as a home helper, had worked in eldercare almost all her life, and had run a small-scale home care business for just over ten years. She expressed a strong sense of self-fulfilment, which seemed to be related to having created something lasting and being able to realise her visions of how to practise leadership. In her interview, she described the home care company as a lifetime achievement:

> I have always wanted to try and run this company [from the maxim] 'never forget the employees', because it is the employees who are important if the company is to live. That's why I am continuing in this, because I think it's so interesting. To see how different employees react in different situations. I mean, I like taking care of my elderly, of course, but the employees are those who are expected to do the good job. And if the employees feel well, they will do a good job. I am totally convinced about that. /…/. You must give and take all the time, I think that is very important. That is why I continue and that is why I am still here. I feel like this is my lifetime achievement [gives a happy laugh]. (Interviewee 12)

In contrast to the interviews quoted previously, a strong sense of pride permeates this story. The participant also seemed to experience her status as elevated in the eyes of others when they learned that she was the owner of a company and an employer. For example, she described a social occasion when a new acquaintance had been impressed when he had heard how many employees she had.

A situation shared by the more contented participants was that they had concluded agreements with municipalities which had given them the option of serving only clients living in a certain area. If the client base was large enough in this area, there was no economic pressure to expand to other geographic areas. By using this strategy, the providers avoided problems of costly travel time, as described in other interviews. The employees of these contented participants were able to walk or ride a bike from one client to the next. This also meant that these small-scale providers considered the level of remuneration sufficient.

They also shared other characteristics: they had all started their business by taking over municipal home care units in which they had formerly been employed as managers, continuing to provide home care in basically the same way as they had done before. These participants did not describe experiences of being pressured in their former positions as municipal home care managers to the same extent as other participants; instead, they had wanted to free themselves from the municipal red tape. In other respects, they described their relationships with officials in their local administration positively, as based on mutual trust and knowledge of each other. In other words, when they started their businesses, these participants already had established positions and high legitimacy in the municipal context.

Concluding remarks

The results of this study show that there can be large differences in perceived level of success among self-employed providers in home care services. Starting and running a business in this part of the Swedish welfare sector can turn into self-exploitation, but may also lead to a sense of self-fulfilment. According to the data, a sense of self-fulfilment was closely connected to being able to live up to personal and professional norms of what it means to be a good leader and manager in home care. These norms included being present in the daily operations and being able to support one's employees, who often have to perform emotional labour as part of their care work. Some participants argued that they had greater freedom to achieve this as self-employed providers than as managers employed within large organisations (cf. Wolmesjö, 2005). For these participants, leadership seemed to be an important aspect of their occupational identity. This illustrates the importance of values, emotions, and relationships with others. From this perspective, notions of instrumental rationality are too narrow to explain how individuals act in markets. As Friedland and Alford (1991) argue, work provides identities, and participation in markets can be as much an expression of who one is as of what one wants.

However, it is also interesting to note that feelings of success were most clearly expressed by participants who had started out from established positions—positions that were characterised by mutual trust in relations with municipal representatives—and who mainly provided home care services in traditional ways. It seems that their success was due to their continuing to provide care for a general group of elderly instead of specialising to meet the needs of particular groups; that is, rather than developing diversity and innovative business ideas.

Further, this study points to several barriers facing providers who desire to engage in innovation and entrepreneurship. Among these are predetermined levels of remuneration in combination with serving clients who are dispersed over large geographical areas, time-limited orders that stipulate in advance which tasks should be performed, and lack of trust in the relationship with municipal purchasers. For the participants, these barriers contributed to different logics of action and conflicting rationalities; that is, to difficulties in combining economic rationality with meeting the wishes and needs of the elderly.

The results of this study illustrate the importance of studying self-employment in the context of changing labour markets and employment patterns in advanced economies. The traditional role of large organisations in providing stable structures for employment and professional development has been diminished because of restructuring and downsizing. As Hytti (2010) observes, this affects how individuals manoeuvre or manage their careers, for example by turning to self-employment instead of relying on traditional wages and salaried employment. The career without boundaries, created by moving between firms and in and out of self-employment, is becoming more taken for granted.

The shift from a career as something that is managed by the hierarchical organisation to something that is created and managed at the individual level has potentially both positive and negative consequences for the individual (Hytti, 2010). In the context of temporary work and streamlined organisations, self-employment may be perceived by professionals as a means of controlling their own career, thereby protecting their professional identity. By creating their own organisation and becoming their own bosses, self-employed workers may be able to create a sense of power at not having to change who they are in order to please an employing organisation.

However, as for contracted-out service provision in elderly care, the results of this study indicate that successes in self-employment may be limited to particular circumstances. In the empirical context of the study, such circumstances were available when care provision remained local and personalised rather than extending into a larger market, and when business activities were based on trust in relations between purchasers and providers. When these factors were not present, self-employment ran the risk of leading to a precarious and self-exploitative position. Finally, the chapter illustrates the importance of considering the conflicts that arise in the home care business in relation to institutional factors, such as the low value ascribed to work performed by women in the social services and the design of a market that creates inherent contradictions between actors with different interests.

Acknowledgements The author would like to thank Stephanie Taylor, co-editor of this volume, and Clary Krekula, Senior Lecturer at Karlstad University, for helpful comments on an earlier draft of this chapter.

Note

1. /.../ indicates that words have been omitted.

References

Ahl, H. (2004). Företagandets särskilda nytta. In D. Ericsson (Ed.), *Det oavsedda entreprenörskapet* (pp. 108–122). Lund: Academia Adacta.

Ahl, H., & Tillmar, M. (2015). *Swedish welfare state retrenchment and the call for women's entrepreneurship to fill the void.* Paper presented at the 4th European Conference on Politics and Gender 2015, June 11–13, Uppsala, Sweden.

Anderson, N., & Hughes, K. D. (2010). The business of caring: Women's self-employment and the marketization of care. *Gender, Work & Organization, 17*(4), 381–405.

Andrews, G. J., & Phillips, D. R. (2002). Changing local geographies of private residential care for older people 1983–1999: Lessons for social policy in England and Wales. *Social Science & Medicine, 55*(1), 63–78.

Bartlett, W., Roberts, J. A., & Le Grand, J. (Eds.). (1998). *A revolution in social policy. Quasi-market reforms in the 1990s*. Bristol: The Policy Press.

Braunerhjelm, P., Holmquist, C., Larsson, P. J., Skoogberg, Y., & Thulin, P. (2016). *Entreprenörskap i Sverige. Nationell rapport 2016*. Örebro: Entreprenörskapsforum.

Brennan, D., Cass, B., Himmelweit, S., & Szebehely, M. (2012). The marketisation of care: Rationales and consequences in Nordic and liberal care regimes. *Journal of European Social Policy, 22*(4), 377–391.

Brubaker, R. (1984). *The limits of rationality. An essay on the social and moral thought of Max Weber*. London: George Allen & Unwin.

Eliasson, R. (Ed.). (1992). *Egenheter och allmänheter. En antologi om omsorg och omsorgens villkor*. Lund: Arkiv förlag.

Engelen, B. (2006). Solving the paradox: The expressive rationality of the decision to vote. *Rationality and Society, 18*(4), 419–441.

Erlandsson, S., Storm, P., Stranz, A., Szebehely, M., & Trydegård, G.-B. (2013). Marketising trends in Swedish eldercare: Competition, choice and calls for stricter regulation. In G. Meagher & M. Szebehely (Eds.), *Marketisation in Nordic eldercare: A research report on legislation, oversight, extent and consequences* (pp. 23–83). Stockholm: Department of Social Work, Stockholm University.

Friedland, R., & Alford, R. R. (1991). Bringing society back in: Symbols, practices, and institutional contradictions. In W. W. Powell & P. J. DiMaggio (Eds.), *The new institutionalism in organizational analysis* (pp. 232–263). Chicago: University of Chicago Press.

Government Bill 2005/06:115. *Nationell utvecklingsplan för vård och omsorg om äldre*. Stockholm: Regeringen.

Government Bill 2008/09:29. *Lag om valfrihetssystem*. Stockholm: Regeringen.

Granovetter, M. (1985). Economic action and social structure: The problem of embeddedness. *American Journal of Sociology, 91*(3), 481–510.

Hedberg, C., & Pettersson, K. (2006). *Innovativa företagare i vård och omsorg: Genus-och entreprenörskapsperspektiv på företagande kvinnor och män i Stockholms län*. Stockholm: Kulturgeografiska institutionen, Stockholms universitet.

Hedberg, C., & Pettersson, K. (2011). Disadvantage, ethnic niching or pursuit of a vision? Motives of immigrant women care entrepreneurs in the ageing

Swedish society. *Journal of International Migration & Integration, 13*(4), 423–440.

Hjalmarsson, M. (2009). New technology in home help services—A tool for support or an instrument of subordination? *Gender, Work and Organization, 16*(3), 368–384.

Hochschild, A. R. (2003). *The managed heart: Commercialization of human feeling*. Berkeley: University of California Press.

Hytti, U. (2010). Contextualizing entrepreneurship in the boundaryless career. *Gender in Management: An International Journal, 25*(1), 64–81.

International Labour Organization. (2015). *World employment and social outlook 2015: The changing nature of jobs*. Geneva: International Labour Organization.

Jordahl, H., & Öhrvall, R. (2013). Nationella reformer och lokala initativ. In H. Jordahl (Ed.), *Välfärdstjänster i privat regi. Framväxt och drivkrafter*. Stockholm: SNS förlag.

Kelley, D., Singer, S., & Herrington, M. (2016). *Global Entrepreneurship Monitor report 2015/2016*. Global Entrepreunership Monotir. Retrieved June 25, 2017, from http://www.gemconsortium.org/report/49480

Kendall, J. (2001). Of knights, knaves and merchants: The case of residential care for older people in England in the late 1990s. *Social Policy & Administration, 35*(4), 360–375.

Kovalainen, A., & Österberg-Högstedt, J. (2013). Entrepreneurship within social and health care—A question of identity, gender and professionalism. *International Journal of Gender and Entrepreneurship, 5*(1), 17–35.

Kurvinen, J. (2008). *Imitation och omtolkning—entreprenörers identifieringsprocesser ur ett genusperspektiv*. Diss. Umeå: Handelshögskolan, Umeå universitet.

Matosevic, T., Knapp, M., Kendall, J., Henderson, C., & Fernandez, J. L. (2007). Care-home providers as professionals: Understanding the motivations of care-home providers in England. *Ageing & Society, 27*(1), 103–126.

Meagher, G., & Szebehely, M. (2013). Long-term care in Sweden: Trends, actors, and consequences. In C. Ranci & E. Pavolini (Eds.), *Reforms in long-term care policies in Europe: Investigating institutional change and social impacts*. New York: Springer.

Miles, M. B., & Huberman, A. M. (1994). *Qualitative data analysis. An expanded sourcebook* (2nd ed.). Thousand Oaks: SAGE Publications.

Nadin, S. (2007). Entrepreneurial identity in the care sector: Navigating the contradictions. *Women in Management Review, 22*(6), 456–467.

OECD. (2016). *Entrepreneurship at a glance 2016*. Paris: OECD Publishing.

SFS. (2001:453). *Socialtjänstlagen*. Stockholm: Justitiedepartementet.
Simonen, L., & Kovalainen, A. (1998). Paradoxes of social care restructuring: The Finnish case. In J. Lewis (Ed.), *Gender, social care and welfare state restructuring in Europe*. Aldershot: Ashgate.
Sköld, B., & Tillmar, M. (2015). Resilient gender order in entrepreneurship: The case of Swedish welfare industries. *International Journal of Gender and Entrepreneurship, 7*(1), 2–26.
Socialstyrelsen. (2016). *Vård och omsorg om äldre: lägesrapport 2016*. Stockholm: Socialstyrelsen.
Sörensdotter, R. (2008). *Omsorgsarbete i omvandling: genus, klass och etnicitet inom hemtjänsten*. Diss. Göteborg: Makadam förlag.
Statistics Sweden. (2014). *Företagens ekonomi 2012*. Sweden: Statistiska centralbyrån.
Stranz, A. (2013). *Omsorgsarbetets vardag och villkor i Sverige och Danmark: ett feministiskt kritiskt perspektiv*. Diss. Stockholm: Department of Social Work, Stockholm University.
Sundin, E., & Tillmar, M. (2010). Masculinisation of the public sector: Local-level studies of public sector outsourcing in elder care. *International Journal of Gender and Entrepreneurship, 2*(1), 49–67.
Szebehely, M. (2000). Äldreomsorg i förändring—knappare resurser och nya organisationsformer. In M. Szebehely (Ed.), *Välfärd, vård och omsorg* (pp. 171–223). SOU 2000:38. Stockholm: Fritzes offentliga publikationer.
Taylor-Gooby, P., Sylvester, S., Calnan, M., & Manley, G. (2000). Knights, knaves and gnashers: Professional values and private dentistry. *Journal of Social Policy, 29*(3), 375–395.
Tillmar, M. (2004). *Är det möjligt? Om villkor för småföretagande inom vård-och omsorgssektorn*. Stockholm: Nutek.
Tillmar, M. (2009a). No longer so strange? (Dis)trust in municipality–small business relationships. *Economic and Industrial Democracy, 30*(3), 401–428.
Tillmar, M. (2009b). Societal entrepreneurs in the health sector: Crossing the frontiers. *Social Enterprise Journal, 5*(3), 282–298.
Trydegård, G.-B. (2012). Care work in changing welfare states: Nordic care workers' experiences. *European Journal of Ageing, 9*(2), 119–129.
Vadelius, E. (2015). *Paradoxernas marknad—En studie om företagande i hemtjänsten*. Diss. Karlstad: Fakulteten för humaniora och samhällsvetenskap, Karlstads universitet.
Waerness, K. (1984). The rationality of caring. *Economic and Industrial Democracy, 5*(2), 185–211.

Weber, M. (1983). *Ekonomi och samhälle [Economy and society]*. Lund: Argos.
Wolmesjö, M. (2005). *Ledningsfunktion i omvandling—om förändringar av yrkesrollen för första linjens chefer inom den kommunala äldre-och handikappomsorgen*. Lund: Socialhögskolan, Lunds universitet.

Elin Vadelius is Lecturer in Sociology in the Department of Social and Psychological Studies, Karlstad University, Sweden. Her research interests include conditions for entrepreneurship and self-employment in welfare services, and the role of trust and mistrust between actors in quasi-markets. She is also involved in research on senior entrepreneurship and extended working life.

Creating Alternative Solutions for Work: Experiences of Women Managers and Lawyers in Poland and the USA

Ingrid Biese and Marta Choroszewicz

In this age of individualisation and globalisation, the ever-tougher competitive climate and working conditions, defined by financial instability, insecurity, cost-cutting and reorganisation, create a work environment where individuals find it increasingly difficult to create coherent narratives of their lives and work (Elliott, 2013; Sennett, 1998). There is an intensifying and speeding up of globalisation and of how business is done unlike anything experienced before (Elliott & Lemert, 2006; Held, McGrew, Goldblatt, & Perraton, 1999). However, despite this having become the 'new normal' of contemporary working life, organisations continue to idealise linear masculinist career models that have not kept

---

I. Biese (✉)
Department of Management and Organisation,
Hanken School of Economics, Helsinki, Finland

M. Choroszewicz
Department of Social Sciences, University of Eastern Finland,
Joensuu, Finland

up with the changing social climate. The linear career model, which was developed as a result of industrialisation, is still prevalent today, even though it no longer correlates with contemporary individuals' wants and needs (Greenhaus, Callanan, & Godshalk, 2010; Mainiero & Sullivan, 2006). For women in particular, these career models, characterised by continuous and uninterrupted working patterns, are problematic as they struggle to combine a career with care responsibilities, which they continue to be mainly responsible for in society (Crompton & Le Feuvre, 1996). However, even in the current fast-changing economy, mainstream masculinist career models not only persist but also become more rigorous and thus emerge as normalised, especially in male-dominated work environments and job positions. The changing nature of working life makes it increasingly difficult to separate work from other areas of life, with work spilling over into the private sphere (Cahusac & Kanji, 2014).

In 2003, *New York Times* columnist Lisa Belkin published an article about high-powered women who decided to give up their careers to stay home with their children, which started a debate both in the media and in academia on women opting out (Jones, 2012; Williams, Manvell, & Bornstein, 2006). Arguing that what we are seeing is the start of a revolution, Belkin used words like 'balance', 'satisfaction' and 'sanity' to describe what these women lacked in their previous careers and what they were looking for in their new lifestyles. These women wanted to live on their own terms and create their own definition of what it means to be successful. However, the opting out debate has been almost exclusively about women who leave their careers to become stay-at-home mothers, and many have argued that the opt-out revolution is, in fact, a myth; that women are not opting out in any increasing numbers, or if they are, rather than leaving by choice, they are being pushed out of masculinist organisational cultures (Boushey, 2005, 2008; Percheski, 2008; Stone, 2007). There is no statistical evidence that women are leaving their careers to stay home in any large or increasing numbers (Boushey, 2005; Hilgeman, 2010; Percheski, 2008) and, as will be explored further on in this chapter, women most certainly do face issues that make it difficult for them to pursue careers on the same terms as men. However, the opting out debate has been missing two important aspects: the changing nature of working life on the one hand, and the fact that women who opt out do so not to stay at home full-time but to pursue work or a career on different terms. The women, who step off the so-called corporate ladder but stay in the labour force, have simply not been captured in the statistics gathered for the research on women opting out. On the contrary, research has shown that women do not generally leave to stop working altogether, but create different ways of working where they can better combine the different areas of life that are important to them (see e.g., Biese, 2017; Stone, 2007). In this chapter, we will be examining the experiences of women managers from the USA and lawyers from Poland as they opt out of the hectic nature of corporate work—the new normal—as well as career models, which simply are not compatible with the way they want to live their lives. These women did not opt out of the work force altogether, but created new individualised solutions for work that allowed them to combine different areas of life, while also pursuing meaningful careers on their own terms.

Women in Poland and the USA struggle with similar challenges when combining work with family life. The two countries differ considerably in terms of state-provided support of care services and family benefits. Whereas the Polish state provides families with subsidised maternity, paternity and parental leave, in the USA, only some states and employers offer paid or partially subsidised leave (Catalyst, 2013; ZUS, 2014). Still, a similar nanny and stay-at-home mother tradition is prevalent in both countries due to insufficient, unreliable or expensive childcare (see e.g., Plomien, 2009; Still, 2006; Williams & Boushey, 2010). In Poland, parents have a joint right to a one-year parental leave after the birth of a child, yet it is predominantly mothers who are absent from work to care for children. A legislated paternity leave of two weeks has been available to Polish fathers since 2010; however, many do not take this time off as it is generally frowned upon, especially in male-dominated work environments. Gender roles thus remain traditional and established in both countries and women continue to be disproportionately responsible for housework and care.

In this chapter we will start with a discussion of masculinist career models and gender roles. We critically examine the concept of work–life balance, which has been developed to aid women, especially, in combining the competing demands of a career and family. After that we introduce our data, our methodology and the two cases studies of women who opted out to create more sustainable ways of working. We focus on questions of identity that come to the fore as women struggle to 'have it all', and when they come to terms with the alternative views of success and solutions for work that they adopt as they transcend the dualism of work and life. We draw on research and debates, which we interlace with the women's stories to provide the reader with a lens to understand the main issues that these women grapple with, as well as their meanings. Finally we conclude with a discussion of our main findings.

Career models, gender roles and work–life balance

Although working life has become increasingly competitive, with an expectation of 24/7 availability, career models today continue to follow many of the standards created as a result of industrialisation (Greenhaus et al., 2010). Ambitious employees are expected to advance upward in the organisation through promotions in a timely and linear fashion, as well as to be dedicated and available at all hours, which has become possible through technological innovations (Choroszewicz, 2014b, 2016). However, this ideal is no longer compatible with the reality of the workforce today. It has been argued that the linear career model was planned for not one but one and a half people, during a time when a man could concentrate solely on his career, as he typically had a housewife to take care of the children and the home (Beck & Beck-Gernsheim, 2002). Today this is no longer the situation, as women, after decades of feminist struggles, participate in the public sphere. However, despite this, women are still grossly underrepresented in top management positions and on corporate boards (Terjesen & Singh, 2008). Women continue to take the brunt of care responsibilities and household chores and as long as they do so they continue to work double shifts or more (see Hochschild, 1989), which is a major issue making it difficult for many women to have a career on the same terms as men.

Work–life balance as a concept was developed as a rejection of the masculinist notion of the ideal worker (James, 2014). However, as work–life balance has focused mainly on developing solutions for women to combine work and family, it has come to be seen as a 'women's issue' and not the much-needed discussion and critique of prevalent working cultures and ideals (Smithson & Stokoe, 2005). The division that the concept work–life balance creates between work and non-work is, in fact, especially problematic for women (Bourne & Calás, 2013). The idea of two distinct domains has fostered an attitude that the non-paid women's work of the private domain is not as valuable as the paid men's work of the public domain (Lopata, 1993). Thus, the boundaries between the public and the private, which are a central aspect of the discussion of women's careers, need to be questioned (Bourne & Calás, 2013). In addition, owing to technological development and the nature of work in contemporary society, boundaries are becoming increasingly blurred (Choroszewicz, 2014b). However, instead of a scenario where completely blurred boundaries could call for a development of work solutions that enable a transcending of the dualism and the polarisation between the public and the private—work and home—it is more a question of one-way blurring. While work increasingly spills over into private life, children and care responsibilities continue to be best kept invisible at work (Cahusac & Kanji, 2014).

The cases of two women who opted out

In this chapter, we share the stories of two women—Ruth, a US manager, and Hanna, a Polish lawyer—who have opted out of successful corporate careers and adopted alternative mindsets, practices and solutions for work. Their stories originate in two separate studies, one on the opting out experiences of 15 successful women managers in Finland and the USA who have opted out of high-powered careers to adopt alternative lifestyles (Biese, 2017); and one on the career experiences and choices of 25 women attorneys in Finland and Poland, many of whom decided to opt out of careers in large law firms to set up their own solo practices or work for smaller law firms run by friends or relatives (Choroszewicz, 2014a). Comparing our notes from our respective studies, we found striking similarities between both the experiences and choices of these managers and lawyers. For this chapter, we thus wanted to further explore the experiences of the Polish and US women, as their experiences of balancing careers with care responsibilities were especially similar, despite differences in social welfare and state support between the countries.

We have adopted a methodology developed by Susie Orbach (2002) in her book, *The impossibility of sex*, and further developed by Anthony Elliott and Charles Lemert (2006) in *The new individualism: The emotional costs of globalization*. The authors use a fictionalised case method not only to ensure the anonymity of the participators of their studies, but also to capture the most relevant and resonant shared emotional experiences felt by the subjects of a study in a few illustrative narratives. As the narratives and experiences of the women in our studies were so similar, this was an appropriate method to identify and convey the most central and recurrent issues, emotions and struggles discerned among the seven US managers and 15 Polish lawyers in our data sets. We have thus drawn on all these issues and combined them to create two fictionalised case studies—the stories of Ruth and Hanna—to provide two illustrative and representative examples of the main issues with which women from Poland and the USA, who opt out of high-powered careers to opt into alternative careers and solutions for work, grapple. A case study approach follows a long tradition where qualitative inquiry provides an in-depth understanding of a situation or process, as well as insights into enabling factors, and socialisation processes (Miller & Salkind, 2002). Although this methodology does not allow for generalisations, that is not our intention. Through the illustrative stories of Ruth and Hanna we wish to show how opting out and in can be experienced, and thereby add to current debates and understandings of the opting-out phenomenon and new meanings of work.

The Story of Ruth

Ruth is 38 years old, married and has two children—four and six years old. She is very ambitious and when she opted out she was a senior manager at an IT company, with ambitions of being promoted to vice-president. With a degree in creative writing and an MBA from a top university, Ruth started climbing the proverbial career ladder, as she always assumed she would. She had always been taught that she could do and be anything she wanted, anything a man could, and so she did. Then she met her husband, got married, and eventually got pregnant, which she also always assumed she would. However, it never occurred to her that she might give up her career. It was not until she was married with children that she realised how gendered her life really was. Yes, she could compete for top positions, but as soon as she got married, prospective employers would ask of her plans for having children, and after she got pregnant, it was clear that she was no longer taken as seriously at work. This didn't happen to her male colleagues.

After her first child, she went back to work when the child was two months old. She found a wonderful nanny, but was completely unprepared for how she would feel. She hadn't even fully recovered physically, and pumping breast milk in the Ladies Room between meetings was tough. However, most of all she felt a huge ache in her chest over not being around for important things in her child's life. She felt very sad, but she carried on; she had her career to think about.

After about a year she got pregnant again and this time she was simply exhausted. The pregnancy with a small child and a job was tough, but she was also starting to wonder about the incongruence of it all. Why did she have trouble getting it all together when her husband did not seem to? He had a job, he had two kids, and he seemed to be fine; he did not seem to have trouble with the wear and tear of constant transitioning as she did. She constantly felt guilty about not being in any one place enough—at home or at work. Her second child had constant ear infections and she regularly had to take time off work to take her to the doctor. She worked in the evenings after getting her kids to bed, and she constantly felt tired. She kept all this to herself—care responsibilities were just not talked about at work—and she felt like a bad employee and, even worse, a bad mother. She felt completely alone; no one else seemed to be struggling the way she was.

One day Ruth collapsed on the way to work and ended up in the emergency room. It was just exhaustion, but it made her realise that she needed to slow down. She was starting to feel quite disenchanted by her company as it was. She felt she was being mommy-tracked and was not getting the recognition she deserved, and she felt like she just could not be herself. Her children and their needs had to be kept invisible at work and these two parts of her life just seemed completely incompatible. Although she had no plan for what she was going to do next, she resigned the very next day.

(continued)

(continued)

All she knew was that she wanted meaningful work and she wanted to be a good mother; and she wanted to do this in a way that did not make her feel guilty and exhausted all the time. Although scary, quitting was a great relief. She caught up on much-needed rest and was there for her kids. She missed working, however, and when meeting new people, she cringed when asked what she did. She could not see herself as a stay-at-home mom.

Eventually, Ruth became a certified coach. She realised that what she liked the most about her job was coaching her team and she decided she wanted to help others who had difficulties dealing with it all, and she felt she could really make a difference. She gradually set up her own business, together with a woman from her course. They agreed that their organisational culture was going to be different and that children would never have to be kept invisible. Both women were mothers, so if one had to care for her kids, the other would pick up the slack and vice versa. Being able to really be herself brought a great sense of authenticity and coherence. Finally, she felt she was exactly where she was supposed to be. She still got stressed, because being an entrepreneur can be very stressful; it was just a different type of stress. Now she had more control over where, when and how she worked, and it made all the difference.

The challenge of 'having it all'

Like Ruth, many girls today grow up being told that they can and should have it all—both a successful career and a family (Slaughter, 2012, 2015). However, it is especially after having children that women are confronted with just how gendered women's and men's roles in society still are. Although women are increasingly competing with men for top positions, progress in the home has lagged behind. This is not the only issue that makes it difficult for women to combine work and family (see e.g., Acker, 2006 for issues of gender discrimination), but it comes as a surprise for many women, as it did for Ruth, as they are confronted with having to defend and reconfigure their identities after becoming mothers (Beck & Beck-Gernsheim, 2002). Career women with children are also pulled between two contradictory and incompatible schemas: the schema of professional work, which demands individualisation, self-promotion, and single-minded allegiance and dedication; and the schema of motherhood, which is self-sacrificing and which also demands complete devotion (Blair-Loy, 2003; DiQuinzio, 1999). These schemas are culturally and structurally embedded in our lives and consciousness and are difficult for women to reconcile, adding to the difficulty of creating coherent narratives about their lives and their work. However, although it is a structural problem that women deal with, the individualised nature of work in addition to the taboo of talking about private issues, on the one hand, and the risk of seeming weak in an extremely competitive environment, on the other, prevents women from talking openly about this. This makes them, like Ruth, feel very alone in their situations. The problem is greater than the individual woman and her life choices, which makes it very difficult to overcome individually. As Ruth says, she felt guilty no matter what she did, and she could not figure out why she could not seem to get it right. This, in addition to the need to hide certain aspects of oneself and one's life, which also Hanna attests to in her story when she talks about having to hide her pregnant belly to seem professional, adds to a feeling of inauthenticity. The feeling of not being able to be oneself, in turn, adds to the lack of coherence typically experienced during the time before opting out (Biese, 2017).

Maternity is intimately linked culturally to what it means to be a woman (Kristeva, 1985). However, at the same time, for Ruth and Hanna, their sense of self is also clearly linked to their professional identity. Hanna had known she wanted to be a lawyer ever since she was a child and Ruth cringed when having to tell people she did not work. Neither of them wanted to become stay-at-home mothers, even though circumstances had Ruth at home with her children for a period of time. Owing to the nature of her work, Hanna did not even consider this an option.

As a result of the difficulties juggling work and motherhood, the individual solution both women created was to set out on their own, Ruth as an entrepreneur and Hanna as a solo practitioner. Research has shown that women, especially, who set up small businesses without employees gain a greater sense of autonomy and control (Sevä & Öun, 2015), and as we will see in the next section, this is true also for both Hanna and Ruth. Neither of the women gave up on their ambitions; they wanted to continue doing meaningful work, where they could work to their full potential, although in a sustainable way. However, they also wanted and needed to have more control over their work. To do so they had to rethink what it means to be successful as well as what was important to them and what they were willing to give up.

The Story of Hanna

Hanna is 42 years old, married and has two children who are seven and three. Hanna always knew she wanted to be a lawyer; she is carrying on a family legacy—she is a seventh-generation lawyer. The reason she specifically chose to become an attorney was mainly because of the higher prestige associated with this compared to other law professions. However, being an attorney also makes her happy, especially when her clients are satisfied with her work and she feels she is really helping people.

When Hanna obtained her attorney qualifications, she was working at a large international law firm. At the time she had not given having children a thought, but after about three years, she met her husband and they decided to get married and start a family. Her supervisor at work was a wonderful woman who had really supported Hanna since she came to the firm; however, she did not have children herself and she was disappointed when she discovered that Hanna was pregnant. She had high hopes for Hanna, who was talented and driven, but most of the women attorneys who make partner in international law firms simply do not have children as it is difficult to combine the two. Those who do, develop complex systems of assistance from nannies, grandmothers, aunts, and so on.

Establishing a solo practice was always a possibility, but nothing Hanna seriously considered until she and her husband decided to have a second child. She then realised just how detrimental to her career a second child might be. The firm wanted her to continue the way she had, but she felt it was impossible to continue being available at a moment's notice, so she finally decided to start a solo practice. Even with only one child and her mother and two nannies helping her, she is struck by just how tiring her lifestyle was before she left the firm. She did not enjoy it, nor was it a lifestyle she could have kept up with in the long run. Her husband works long hours as well, however, it is Hanna who is in charge of the children, but she also comments that it just is a woman's role. She recognises the societal expectations that her husband deals with; it is harder for him to take time off work to care for the children.

What this meant for Hanna was that she knew that childcare would and did fall on her and she did not want her children to suffer. Although leaving to start a solo practice with a small child was less than optimal, the flexibility it offered made her decide to take the step anyway. The transition was hard, but she drew on her contacts and found a great location for her office, which she shares with six other female solo practitioners. At the time, she tried to hide her pregnancy from clients for as long as possible; she thought a pregnancy would make her look unprofessional and she did not want to risk losing clients, although looking back, she realises how awful that was.

(continued)

(continued)

> Now that her practice is established, things are different. She feels more secure with her clients and does not feel as much of a need to hide certain aspects of her life. She still does two shifts—one at work and one at home in the evening, caring for her children. However, although she works a lot, she is in charge of her schedule—only court deadlines are out of her control. As a solo practitioner, she is the one who sets the pace and decides what cases to take. Sometimes she still has to work at night to get everything done, but she has the freedom to take time off when she wants to or when her family needs her. She wants to be able to spend time with her children when they come home from school, which being a solo practitioner allows her to do. Hanna does not make as much as she did when she worked for the law firm, but this is her choice and she made it so that she can participate in her children's lives and watch them grow. She feels happy; she has the best of both worlds.
>
> To Hanna, being successful does not necessarily mean making lots of money or moving up in the hierarchy. She explains how in a large law firm there will always be problems combining a career with a personal life, because there is simply not enough time or flexibility for both. She does not want to work only for money or prestige, although she does admit that a proper income level is important when doing such demanding work. Today, she gains satisfaction from achieving her personal goals, which is doing work that she loves and having the flexibility to really be there for her children.

Alternative views of success and transcending the dualism of work and life

Traditional or objective views of success are predominantly understood in terms of raises and promotions (Ng, Eby, Sorensen, & Feldman, 2005); however, for both Ruth and Hanna the alternative cost of pursuing a more traditional view of success was too high. As they thought about what was important to them and what they were and were not willing to give up, subjective views of success, based on issues such as career satisfaction and well-being (Ng et al., 2005), came to the fore. For both women, helping people was also important and this became a central aspect of the work they opted into. This was reflected in the working cultures they developed with their new colleagues; working cultures that reflected their values as professionals, women and mothers, creating a sense that they could finally be themselves and that they were exactly where they wanted to be.

Ruth and Hanna developed ways of working that allowed them to have a more balanced life, while allowing them also to have a meaningful career (Choroszewicz, 2014a). For both of them, being able to do what they love most, but also to get the recognition and compensation that they are due, is important. The balance they achieved was mainly thanks to the real flexibility their new setups provided. Flexible time, which is available to employees in many organisations and which has been developed to help women, especially, manage their work–life balance, ironically does not always provide more flexibility. In fact, research has shown that women do not generally feel that flexible hours actually give them more flexibility at all (Rafnsdottir & Heijstra, 2011). As opposed to men, who use flexible time to give themselves more freedom and flexibility, women generally use their flexible time to be on call for their families. As they divide their time between work and home, their schedules simply become too tight (Rafnsdottir & Heijstra, 2011). In addition, women who choose flexible working arrangements easily become stigmatised or 'mommy-tracked', which in turn can have a negative effect on their careers (Choroszewicz, 2016; Epstein, Seron, Oglensky, & Sauté, 1999). However, the solutions that Ruth and Hanna developed provided flexibility not only around when they worked, but also where and how they worked. Although they continued to work hard and long hours, in their new jobs they had real flexibility, which in turn provided them with more coherence, control and balance. In addition, as they no longer had to hide aspects of their lives, a two-way blurring of boundaries between work and family was possible, and as a result, one area of life no longer felt completely at odds with the other. By making compromises and redefining what it means to be successful, they were also actually able to 'have it all', or, as Hanna says, have the best of both worlds. Their new definition of success was thus located somewhere in the juncture of the work and non-work spheres (O'Neil & Bilimoria, 2005).

The stories of Ruth and Hanna illustrate that women who opt out of their high-powered careers generally feel powerless in the masculinist work environment, and it is difficult for them to accommodate the different areas of life that are important to them. The decision to leave was not easy for the two women, nor was it made on a whim. However, these women did not leave their careers altogether. Instead, they rejected the organisational cultures that expect 24/7 availability and a constant striving up the corporate ladder that made it extremely difficult for them to combine a career with motherhood in a sustainable way. It is both of these aspects that, for Hanna and Ruth, added to the difficulty of creating coherent narratives of their lives, and which pushed them to look for and create new solutions for work. For Ruth and Hanna, these solutions go beyond the idea of work–life balance. These solutions transcend the dualism of work and life by allowing for a complete blurring of boundaries, as opposed to the one-way blurring, which is the reality for many working individuals today. This complete blurring was only made possible by having more control over how, when and where they work.

Our findings and the stories of Hanna and Ruth illustrate just how important real flexibility and the ability to create alternative and individual solutions for work can be to one's sense of authenticity, coherence and control; issues that have been found to have a direct effect on wellbeing (see Biese & McKie, 2015). However, more research needs to be done. We know quite a bit about why individuals leave mainstream careers; research on leaving has been carried out long before Belkin (2003) coined the expression 'opt-out revolution' (see e.g., Franks, 1999; Marshall, 1995). Nevertheless, we still do not know enough about the possible alternatives that people choose or would choose if they had the opportunity. When it comes to solutions for work, one size does not fit all. This is something that organisations need to take to heart. As Barrentine (1993) comments, when organisations become toxic, women are the first to leave, and indeed, culturally accepted norms make it easier for women than men to leave. However, previous studies have suggested that it is not only women with children who opt out, but that this is a phenomenon that we may see more of in the future among many different groups (see Biese, 2017; Mainiero & Sullivan, 2006; Wilhoit, 2014). Although prevalent masculinist career models and norms are a remnant of the past, the 'new normal' of the contemporary working climate makes it increasingly difficult for both men and women to create coherent narratives about their lives and work. In order to create more sustainable working cultures and solutions, career models that are more compatible with both wants and needs today need to be developed and adopted.

References

Acker, J. (2006). Inequality regimes: Gender, class, and race in organizations. *Gender & Society, 20*, 441–464.

Barrentine, P. (1993). Introduction: Women as harbingers of business transformation. In P. Barrentine (Ed.), *When the canary stops singing: Women's perspective on transforming business* (pp. 9–21). San Francisco, CA: Berrett-Koehler Publishers.

Beck, U., & Beck-Gernsheim, E. (2002). *Individualization*. London: Sage Publications.

Belkin, L. (2003, October 26). The opt-out revolution. *The New York Times Sunday Magazine, Sec 6*, 42.

Biese, I. (2017). *Opting out and in: On women's careers and new lifestyles*. London and New York: Routledge.

Biese, I., & McKie, L. (2015). Opting out and opting in: Women managers in search of balance, control and wellbeing. In M. Connerley & J. Wu (Eds.), *Handbook on well-being of working women* (pp. 503–516). London: Springer.

Blair-Loy, M. (2003). *Competing devotions: Career and family among women executives*. Cambridge, MA: Harvard University Press.

Bourne, K. A., & Calás, M. B. (2013). Becoming 'real' entrepreneurs: Women and the gendered normalization of 'work'. *Gender, Work and Organization, 20*(4), 425–438.

Boushey, H. (2005). *Are women opting out? Debunking the myth*. Washington, DC: Center for Economic and Policy Research, Briefing Paper, November. Retrieved June 20, 2017, from http://cepr.net/documents/publications/opt_out_2005_11_2.pdf

Boushey, H. (2008). 'Opting out?' The effect of children on women's employment in the United States. *Feminist Economics, 14*(1), 1–36.

Cahusac, E., & Kanji, S. (2014). Giving up: How gendered organizational cultures push mothers out. *Gender, Work & Organization, 21*(1), 57–70.

Catalyst. (2013). *Catalyst quick take: Family leave—U.S., Canada, and global*. Retrieved June 18, 2016, from http://www.catalyst.org/knowledge/family-leave-us-canada-and-global

Choroszewicz, M. (2014a). *Managing competitiveness in pursuit of a legal career: Women attorneys in Finland and Poland*. Joensuu: University of Eastern Finland.

Choroszewicz, M. (2014b). Exposing the myth of equal career opportunities: Women attorneys in Finland and Poland. In M. Virkajärvi (Ed.), *Työelämän*

Tutkimuspäivät 2013. Työn Tulevaisuus [Conference on work research 2013: Future of work] (pp. 5, 15–23). Työelämän Tutkimuspäivien Konferenssijulkaisuja.

Choroszewicz, M. (2016). Women attorneys and gendering processes in law firms in Helsinki. *Sosiologia, 53*(2), 122–137.

Crompton, R., & Le Feuvre, N. (1996). Paid employment and the changing system of gender relations: A cross-national comparisons. *Sociology, 30*(3), 427–445.

DiQuinzio, P. (1999). *The impossibility of motherhood: Feminism, individualism, and the problem of mothering.* New York: Routledge.

Elliott, A. (2013). *Reinvention.* Oxon: Routledge.

Elliott, A., & Lemert, C. (2006). *The new individualism: The emotional costs of globalization.* London: Routledge.

Epstein, C. F., Seron, C., Oglensky, B., & Sauté, R. (1999). *The part-time paradox: Times, norms, professional life, family and gender.* New York: Routledge.

Franks, S. (1999). *Having none of it: Women, men and the future of work.* London: Granta Books.

Greenhaus, J. H., Callanan, G. A., & Godshalk, V. M. (2010). *Career management* (4th ed.). Thousand Oaks, CA: Sage Publications Inc.

Held, D., McGrew, A., Goldblatt, D., & Perraton, J. (1999). *Global transformations: Politics, economics and culture.* Stanford, CA: Stanford University Press.

Hilgeman, C. (2010). *Opting out, scaling back, or business-as-usual? An assessment of women's employment hours in 92 occupations.* U.S. Census Bureau, Working Paper. Washington, DC: US Census Bureau. Retrieved June 8, 2016, from https://www.census.gov/people/io/files/ASAsubmission071610.pdf

Hochschild, A. R. with Machung, A. (1989). *The second shift.* London: Penguin Books.

James, A. (2014). Work–life 'balance', recession and the gendered limits to learning and innovation (or, why it pays employers to care). *Gender, Work & Organization, 21*(3), 273–294.

Jones, B. D. (2012). Introduction: Women, work, and motherhood in American History. In B. D. Jones (Ed.), *Women who opt out: The debate over working mothers and work–family balance* (pp. 3–30). New York: New York University Press.

Kristeva, J. (1985). Stabat Mater. *Poetics Today, 6*, 133–152.

Lopata, H. (1993). The interweave of public and private: Women's challenge to American society. *Journal of Marriage and the Family, 55*(1), 76–90.

Mainiero, L. A., & Sullivan, S. E. (2006). *The opt-out revolt: Why people are leaving companies to create kaleidoscope careers.* Mountain View, CA: Davies Black Publishing.

Marshall, J. (1995). *Women managers moving on: Exploring careers and life choices.* London: Thomson Learning.

Miller, D. C., & Salkind, N. J. (2002). *Handbook of research design and social measurement* (6th ed.). Thousand Oaks, CA: Sage Publications.

Ng, T. W. H., Eby, L. T., Sorensen, K. L., & Feldman, D. C. (2005). Predictors of objective and subjective career success: A meta-analysis. *Personnel Psychology, 58*(2), 367–408.

O'Neil, D. A., & Bilimoria, D. (2005). *Women and careers: A critical perspective on the theory and practice of women in organisations.* Working Paper Series (WP-06-05). Cleveland, OH: Department of Organizational Behavior, Case Western Reserve University.

Orbach, S. (2002). *The impossibility of sex: Stories of the intimate relationship between therapist and patient.* New York: Touchstone.

Percheski, C. (2008). Opting out? Cohort differences in professional women's employment rates from 1960 to 2005. *American Sociological Review, 73*(3), 497–517.

Plomien, A. (2009). Welfare state, gender, and reconciliation of work and family in Poland: Policy developments and practice in a new EU member. *Social Policy & Administration, 49*(2), 136–151.

Rafnsdottir, G. L., & Heijstra, T. M. (2011). Balancing work–family life in academia: The power of time. *Gender, Work & Organization.* https://doi.org/10.1111/j.1468-0432.2011.00571.x

Sennett, R. (1998). *The corrosion of character.* New York: W.W. Norton & Company.

Sevä, I. J., & Öun, I. (2015). Self-employment as a strategy for dealing with the competing demands of work and family? The importance of family/lifestyle motives. *Gender, Work & Organization, 22*(3), 256–272.

Slaughter, A.-M. (2012). Why women still can't have it all. *The Atlantic.* Retrieved November 10, 2016, from http://www.theatlantic.com/magazine/archive/2012/07/why-women-still-cant-have-it-all/309020/

Slaughter, A.-M. (2015). *Unfinished business.* London: Oneworld.

Smithson, J., & Stokoe, E. (2005). Discourses of work–life balance: Negotiating 'genderblind' terms in organizations. *Gender, Work & Organization, 12*(2), 147–168.

Still, M. C. (2006). The opt–out revolution in the United States: Implications for modern organizations. *Managerial and Decision Economics, 27,* 159–171.

Stone, P. (2007). *Opting out? why women really quit their careers and head home.* Berkley and Los Angeles, CA: University of California Press.

Terjesen, S., & Singh, V. (2008). Female presence on corporate boards: A multi-country study of environmental context. *Journal of Business Ethics, 83*(1), 55.

Wilhoit, E. D. (2014). Opting out (without kids): Understanding non-mothers workplace exit in popular autobiographies. *Gender, Work and Organisation, 21*(3), 260–272.

Williams, J. C., & Boushey, H. (2010). *The three faces of work–life family conflict: The poor, the professionals, and the missing middle.* Washington, DC: Center for American Progress.

Williams, J. C., Manvell, J., & Bornstein, S. (2006). *'Opt-out' or pushed out? How the press covers work/family conflict.* WorkLifeLaw Report. San Francisco, CA: UC Hastings College of the Law.

ZUS. (2014). *Social insurance in Poland.* Retrieved June 22, 2016, from http://www.zus.pl/files/Social_Insurance_in_Poland_2014.pdf

Ingrid Biese is an Academy of Finland Post-Doctoral Researcher at the Department of Management and Organisation at the Hanken School of Economics in Helsinki, Finland. Her primary area of research is 'opting out' and sustainable working cultures and career models. Other areas of interest are globalisation, individualisation, identity and gender.

Marta Choroszewicz is a Post-Doctoral Researcher at the Department of Social Sciences at the University of Eastern Finland, Joensuu Campus. Her research interests include gender, progression and integration in the legal profession, work–life reconciliation among lawyers, the professionalisation process of public service interpreting and comparative research.

Beyond Work? New Expectations and Aspirations

Stephanie Taylor

Introduction

In recent decades there have been extensive changes to work and employment in advanced economies, accentuated by the continuing effects of the 2007–2008 downturn. Employment is more precarious and fewer workers anticipate a steady 'age-stage' career progression to retirement. In the UK, where these changes are accentuated by austerity policies and Brexit uncertainty, more people are entering work but many are underemployed, seeking additional hours and income. Increasing numbers work for themselves, freelancing, self-employed, or running businesses. They are part of the trend in advanced economies noted by the International Labour Organisation (ILO) (2015), away from a 'standard employment model' of a 'dependent' relationship between employer and employee, towards 'own account working'. Even for employees, there is pressure to be autonomous and self-managing, engaging with work as a personal responsibility. Digitalisation drives much of the internationalisation and accelerated

S. Taylor (✉)
School of Psychology, Faculty of Arts and Social Sciences,
The Open University, Milton Keynes, UK

© The Author(s) 2018
S. Taylor, S. Luckman (eds.), *The New Normal of Working Lives*,
Dynamics of Virtual Work, DOI 10.1007/978-3-319-66038-7_16

trading which require organisations and employees to be future-oriented and flexible. Digital communication encourages extended working hours and also extends the possibilities for own account working, for example, through the availability of online marketplaces and the possibility of using a digital shopfront instead of physical premises as the public face of a business (Luckman, 2015).

In this context, creative practices have gained a new significance as contemporary labour, as part of the global sector of contemporary cultural and creative work. The figure of the artist or creative maker offers a model for the worker as a self-actualising individual who accepts uncertainty and the requirement to self-manage (McRobbie, 1998; Taylor & Littleton, 2012). There are similarities to the figure of the entrepreneur (Brockling, 2016), another noted model for the contemporary worker that is also associated with creativity. The current revival of craft making similarly has been linked to a different 'social imaginary' for work and working lives (Luckman, 2015).

To explore contemporary understandings of work and creative practice, and the extent to which they may be merging in new norms of work and working lives, this chapter analyses interviews with UK creative practitioners. It investigates the meanings, values, and affect that they attach to their creative practices, and what these indicate about their understandings of work and the new normal of working lives, including their aspirations and expectations, and the difficulties they accept as necessary.

New models of work and the worker

Ursula Huws (2013) suggests that 'the normative model of work has shifted decisively' (p. 5) away from an earlier model of 'continuous, contractually formalised employment' with 'regular holidays, sick pay, pensions and prospects of advancement' (p. 2). She claims, 'Even if [the earlier model] was not a universal reality, it was seen as a legitimate aspiration' (p. 2). This raises the question of whether a new normative model is emerging. Do new workers retain the older expectations for their working lives, or have they formed new ambitions and perhaps also accepted more limited aspirations?

Two idealised and interlinked figures, the entrepreneur and the creative worker, offer a starting point for exploring the emergence of a possible new model for contemporary work. Both supposedly exemplify the qualities of individual responsibility, autonomy, and flexibility required to survive in the contemporary circumstances of work and employment, including own account working. The entrepreneur is understood to be not only a business leader, but also a particular type of person: optimistic, risk-taking, and high-achieving (Ahl, 2006; Brockling, 2016). The entrepreneur realises the 'human potential for creativity and innovation' (Ahl & Marlow, 2012, p. 543) and drives 'social progress' through 'individual aspiration, endeavour and ingenuity' (Royal Society of Arts, 2016). Somewhat similarly, the creative or cultural worker has been celebrated in various countries, but most famously by successive UK governments, for utilising 'individual creativity, skill and talent' (Department for Culture, Media and Sport, 2001) to generate wealth in a global creative sector. The sector was originally defined as industries linked to the arts (e.g., design, crafts, publishing) but subsequently was extended to encompass a much broader range, variously including fashion, retail, the 'cultural industries' (Hesmondhalgh, 2007), and the information economy (Fuller, Hamilton, & Seale, 2013). Through the original link to the arts, the creative association carries an additional promise of creative fulfilment or self-actualisation, which potentially functions as a warrant for managing low earnings and insecurity, on an analogy with the barely surviving artist in the garret (Taylor, 2015; Taylor & Littleton, 2012). A further feature of the creative sector, noted by Mark Banks (2007), is the pursuit of non-economic values and a challenge to the 'rational' and 'acquisitive' aspects of capitalist enterprise (p. 184), for example, through claims to ethical and green business practices and sustainability. Recent media depictions extend the overlapping associations of idealised entrepreneurial and creative figures to people who work for themselves in any occupation, including self-employed workers and those running 'cottage industries' from home (Taylor, 2015).

The entrepreneur and the creative worker therefore suggest the possibilities of a model for work in which contemporary workers experience new demands but also have new rewards to aspire to. Together, the figures suggest the possibility of earning a living and achieving fulfilment or self-actualisation by utilising individual creativity and innovation, while maintaining ethical standards, for example, in relation to sustainability and green values. Celebratory accounts of contemporary work and employment suggest that working autonomously, utilising creativity, and following a personal interest potentially compensate for the difficulties of sustaining economically marginal work activities (e.g., long working hours, uncertain financial return, fewer legal protections or welfare safety nets, and greater isolation). Other accounts are more critical, for example noting that the creative sector's volatile labour markets reinforce and exacerbate gender and other inequalities (e.g., Gill & Pratt, 2008). This chapter will look at the experience of creative practitioners as workers, stepping back from both celebratory and critical accounts to examine how creative activities are pursued and viewed by practitioners themselves, including whether they are linked to the acceptance of a new normal of work.

A research project with creative makers

The research discussed in this chapter is an interview study conducted in a small city in the UK. The city is one of the 'new towns' built within commuting distance of London in the 1960s and 1970s. It is relatively affluent, with strong economic and employment growth (Irwin Mitchell, 2017, p. 13). The research participants are 24 artist-makers from the city and surrounding areas who were interviewed in 2016 as part of a project to celebrate the city. The participants can be described broadly as 'middle class' on the grounds that they have education and qualifications that potentially enable them, if they want, to obtain relatively high-status employment, although some might self-identify as working class because of their family backgrounds.

The participants are creative practitioners who produce made objects (in contrast, say, to conceptual artists). They can be seen as part of the ongoing third wave of craft discussed by Susan Luckman (2015, p. 18), although some describe themselves differently, for example as artists rather than as craft workers. Some were contacted through their use of studio spaces provided by charities or the local government. Other participants were accessed through these initial contacts. After appropriate consents had been obtained, each of the creative makers was interviewed for approximately an hour. The questions focused on making practices, connections with other people, and plans for future practice. The interviews were therefore largely about the making process, with other discussion, including biographical information, linked to that focus. The interviews were audio recorded and transcribed.

The research presented in this chapter adopts a double analytic approach to the interview data set. It combines a broadly ethnographic tradition that approaches talk and other forms of language data as informational accounts (e.g., of speakers' circumstances, experience, and life practices) (Hammersley & Atkinson, 2007), and a narrative–discursive interpretive approach (e.g., Taylor & Littleton, 2012) that analyses language data as evidence of established cultural and discursive resources (e.g., discourses, discursive practices, or narrative structures). The narrative–discursive approach explores the situated take-up and implications of these resources, for instance, as constraints on the tellable claims and biographies of participants. The data extracts that are presented in the following sections illustrate patterns found across the data set. The focus of the analysis is on commonalities in participants' accounts of the details of their creative practices and lives as makers, and on shared associations, values and meanings in their talk. Extracts are therefore presented without reference to individuals or their specific creative practices (Taylor, 2012).

New work or a separate practice?

The creative practitioners introduced in the previous section might be categorised as contemporary workers within the global creative sector, exemplifying the trend of own account working noted by the ILO (2015). Alternatively, they can be seen as people who are following a creative practice that is separate to work, in the long tradition of amateurs or hobbyists. Discussing the problems of the amateur–professional distinction, Luckman notes the frequent denigration of amateur making (e.g., as 'uncritical' (p. 51)), but concludes that it 'continues to play an important role within craft practice', for example by keeping alive skills.

She suggests that when considering the craft economy, the exact location of a maker on an amateur–professional continuum is less important than the quality of the goods produced, especially given the need for many trained practitioners to complement more 'artistic' work with production lines (p. 55). This section begins a fuller exploration of the status of the current participants, considering the status of their creative practice as amateur or otherwise, as part of an exploration of its relationship to work.

From an outside point of view, the creative practitioners in the current study might appear to engage with their creative practice *as* work in that they commit a large amount of time to it on a regular schedule and in a separate dedicated space, and expect to receive some income from it. The practice requires specialist materials and equipment and therefore involves investment. Each practitioner presents a public identity linked to the creative practice, usually through a website and sometimes other online sites like Etsy or, less formally, through membership of specialist groups. In all these respects, the practitioners are similar to many own account workers in both creative and non-creative fields. Their working arrangements correspond to the 'key cultural work models' listed by Luckman (2015), 'micro-entrepreneurialism, self-employment, online selling and working from home around family responsibilities' (p. 60), with the same person sometimes combining several of these.

The most striking respect in which the participants' creative practice appears to differ from conventional understandings of work is in relation to earnings. Although, as noted, the practitioners expect some income from what they do, only a minority make enough to support themselves, and even the most financially successful comment that they cannot charge prices for their work that fully reflect the time and effort of making it. Previously available sources of funding for creative work, such as grants and residencies, have largely disappeared as a result of austerity policies. More positively, the local economy is strong, providing markets for many of the practitioners. They also sell online and through craft fairs and other outlets. Some participants, including women who combine their creative work with childcare, receive extra financial support from their partners, and a small number receive government benefits, for example because of disabilities.

In addition, most of the practitioners supplement their incomes from creative making by following the 'double life' described by Taylor and Littleton (2012), 'in which creative work is sustained alongside, and by, other forms of work or jobs that are undertaken with the specific intention of earning money' (p. 69). The 'other' work of these participants includes teaching their specialist practitioner skills; utilising those skills to make mundane 'un-creative' items that the maker distinguishes from the creative outputs (e.g., plain ceramic objects for other people to decorate); running a business that supplies the raw materials for creative work; and working as an employee in a completely separate occupation. A variation on the double life is the situation of those practitioners who have retired from a conventional career and taken up a creative practice subsequently, rather than concurrently, living off an occupational pension or savings from previous 'other' work.

While the 'double life' initially provides a recognisable description of these participants' life arrangements, the distinction between their creative and 'other' work is not always clear cut. For example, practitioners may depend on income from teaching, which can seem to be an extension of their creative practice, but some claim that teaching leaves them no time for their own making; in other words, it is a separate job. Practitioners who run their own businesses selling their creative outputs may have to devote most of their time and energy to practical management rather than making, so in their case, too, the other work may take over from the creative practice, especially if outputs are replicated following an earlier design. Even those practitioners who sell on a smaller scale or less frequently may devote a large amount of 'un-creative' time to contacts with possible clients, self-promotion, and applications for residencies, grants, and exhibitions. The double-life distinction between creative and other work therefore becomes blurred and this again raises the amateur–professional question. The practitioner's creative identification is potentially challenged if non-creative earning work takes up more hours or days in the week than creative practice. This might mark the practitioner as a hobbyist, and the participants in Taylor and Littleton's (2012) research strongly rejected the 'hobby' label for their creative practice, as if this marked it as lesser quality.

Because of their limited earnings from their creative work, most of the participants experience financial insecurity, although the extent of this varies. The most secure are probably those who do most 'other' work currently or those with pensions or savings from previous employment, while the least secure are those who have dedicated all their working lives to their creative practice and have always survived on a very limited income. Uncertainty about earnings means that many of the practitioners have a precarious hold on their workspaces. Some rent their studios privately and worry about how long they will be able to afford to pay. Other practitioners have council space with lower, subsidised rents but only a limited guaranteed tenancy. In contrast, most of the practitioners seem secure in their living accommodation, whether owned or rented. This may be because most are long-term residents and local property values are relatively low in this city (though rising), especially when compared with London. Several noted that an advantage of living in this city is being able to afford a home space that is large enough to work in.

In summary, even though the practitioners may organise their lives as if their practice is a form of work, for most living on the income from the practice does not appear to be a realistic aspiration. Furthermore, in contrast to the expectations of work linked to Huws' (2013) normative model, most do not look forward to a substantial or steady increase in their incomes over time. Indeed, many said that it is now more difficult for them to survive financially than it was previously, because of the effects of the recession on sales and also because of the austerity policies which have reduced available public funding for grants and studio space. Yet, although there were many expressions of frustration that most of the outputs cannot be priced to reflect the time and materials that have gone into the making, there also seemed to be an acceptance of financial insecurity as a regrettable reality, and it was not cited as a reason for stopping the creative practice. The practitioners do not present earning as a rationale for what they do. One conclusion might be that the earlier normative model of work described by Huws has been superseded, since a sufficient and stable income is apparently no longer regarded as a 'legitimate aspiration' (Huws, 2013, p. 2). Alternatively, the creative practice might be distinguished as 'non-work' that needs to be supported through 'work' or another source of income. To explore these points further, the next section turns to participants' own categorisations of their creative practice and other activities. Through an interpretive analysis of the interview data, it considers what is distinctive about creative practice in these participants' accounts, in what ways they describe it as different to work, and what this indicates about the expectations and aspirations they might attach to work more generally.

The rewards of creative making

Discussing their creative practice, the participants make claims about its distinctive features. One of these is the intense concentration involved. A number of participants refer to this as therapeutic because it apparently offers an escape from ordinary life:

> ... when you're [engaged in the practice] you just concentrate on what you're doing and you forget all your other worries ....

> What I find is that when I'm [engaged in the practice] it doesn't matter what's happening in my life at that particular time everything is just completely cut off because I'm so absorbed in what I'm doing that you know you have no worries everything just kind of disappears into the wind really so it's very very therapeutic ...

> ... And I just I don't know why I just love it I find it so therapeutic it's what I call my bliss once I'm doing it and I'm into it I just love it ...

> ... time just disappears it's very therapeutic there's no thinking about anything else or mind wandering when you're working with this sort of stuff.

These accounts correspond to the 'optimal' or 'flow' experience described by the psychologist Mihaly Csikszentmihalyi (2002). He suggests that all people aspire to this experience as their 'foremost goal'. It can be achieved temporarily, for example by playing games or taking mind-altering drugs, but longer term it is achieved by acquiring skills of concentration and involvement, and setting goals: 'Flow drives individuals to creativity and outstanding achievement. The necessity to develop increasingly refined skills to sustain enjoyment is what lies behind the evolution of culture.' Csikszentmihalyi therefore associates flow with both work and creative activities, although in his account the latter are not necessarily linked to the arts. (He cites examples of production line workers achieving the experience.) For the participants discussed here, however, the concentration is specifically linked to creative practice.

In addition to these accounts of concentration, the participants present their creative practice as unfixed, emphasising ongoing change and development. They continually experiment with new materials and new equipment. They seek advice and learn new skills, attending workshops, demonstrations, and training courses. They utilise the 'affordances of digital technology' (Luckman, 2015, p. 26) in order to research alternative materials and techniques and establish new relationships with other practitioners online, often internationally. Their accounts of their creative practice construct it as a 'quest', but one without an ultimate conclusion. Only one of the participants, who is also one of the most financially successful, refers to retiring or otherwise deciding to end her practice. For the others, their making is presented as an apparently endless project of change and new possibilities:

> I've got some ideas and working out ideas cos as an artist we never stop changing ourselves We keep changing how we're doing things…

This emphasis on an open-ended forward trajectory has parallels with the creative and entrepreneurial models discussed earlier and is in striking contrast to the participants' (mostly) stable living arrangements. They do not refer to plans to change their place of residence or, unless forced, their current studio arrangements, but they anticipate and embrace change in their creative practice.

An additional notable feature in their accounts of creative practice is its relationship to the personal. Conventionally, of course, based on a male 'bread-winner' norm, there was a clear dividing line between the professional or public arenas of work and the other parts of life that are private and personal, usually marked by the strictly enforced boundaries of working hours. There was also a conventional and gendered division between work and home, with the latter the conventional territory of the housewife or homemaker. Her work of social reproduction was essential to the formal workplace, ensuring that the acknowledged workers in the family were available and fit for employment. More recently, theorists have suggested that this is too narrow a conceptualisation of the contribution of the personal to work. Attention has been drawn to all the aspects of so-called personal lives that sustain contemporary industry and contribute to profits, such as social media use and other identity practices and forms of self-presentation, including those involved in emotional labour (Hochschild, 2003). As a consequence, the conceptual separation between work and personal life breaks down.

Somewhat differently, the model of the creative worker draws on 'a particular, intensely individualistic theory of art and how it is made' (Becker, 1982, p. 353) that emphasises 'the maker's special qualities and worth' as the basis of art and therefore, by extension, makes personal involvement central to creative making. Personalisation has also been cited as one of the attractions of contemporary creative work (McRobbie, 1998). In previous research, I noted that for the creative worker, 'her [creative] work is personal in the sense of being unique to her, shaped by who she is, and a product which she owns, as the creative or artistic maker' (Taylor, 2011, p. 364). In the data set discussed in this chapter, there was a similar emphasis on producing something unique, often contrasted with mass produced items, and also an emphasis on ownership. For example, several participants mentioned that they were reluctant to sell particular pieces of work because of this personal ownership:

> … I have a big box upstairs and every now and then my husband will say But you're supposed to be selling that [LAUGHTER] Because I did something I mean this is one of my favourite ones I made this a long while ago and so yes sometimes it's impossible to part with a particular piece…

The participants describe their decision to pursue their creative practice or give more time to it as a prioritising of the personal. In contrast to work (former or current), the creative practice is for themselves:

> I just wanted to do something different I wanted a new challenge I've been teaching for about seven years I've been working [for another

employer] as well. ... And I just wanted something new I wanted something to kind of freshen me up and if I'm not making and creating I get a bit edgy and I want to get my hands dirty and almost although I was [helping other people through my work] but I kind of felt that I was kind of not doing enough for myself...

I was a busy [occupational title] working long hours and doing lots for others and I realised that I wasn't doing anything much for myself

... there was always something missing in my life I think you know because I think I like what I'm doing working in [occupational field] and it's convenient as well and you do get a decent salary and you get a good standard of living and other things But there was always something missing

The distinction made here between doing work for others and doing creative work for yourself was also noted by Taylor and Littleton (2012). Some of their participants criticised themselves for being 'selfish' in pursuing the creative work, but in the current research, this does not appear. Instead, there is a pattern of entitlement, exemplified in the extracts above. Participants present themselves as deserving the personal focus of the creative practice.

In addition, participants present personal connections as integral to the making process. Asked where they gain inspiration (the question itself invoking a classic image of art and artistic making as originating in the individual: Becker, 1982, p. 353), participants present as the starting point a personal experience, such as visiting a special place, or a personal life circumstance or relationship, a preference or feeling, or a tenet of a personal philosophy:

... I was lucky enough to visit [place name] and I try and capture what I saw in the landscape there So I found it such a natural sort of err place wild existence actually people live there It's an incredible landscape. ... Just off the chart really it blew me away. ... And I wanted to try and figure out a way of recapturing that in my [work] when I got back ....

And I've just been quite strong in that way that I'll follow what I really feel I'm very emotional with my art and it has to really resonate with me and that's when I do my most successful work

> ... there are so many fundamental things like I think you know the issue of human beings being fundamentally flawed is something which does actually concern me a lot I do worry that in the present climate there's a sense of loss of moral compass and I think that I'm not saying that what I'm doing is trying to redress that but I think if it makes people aware that these things occur then maybe that's a good thing

The importance of this personal starting point for the making process is sometimes described in terms of almost alchemical conversions or encodings. For example, one participant explains a piece of work as based on a personal typology of life relationships, which she has categorised as significant in terms of 'heart', 'soul' or 'mind', associating specific colours with each:

> ... Now it's a bit complicated it's a bit conceptual Basically what I've done is I've written down all the significant people in my life. ... And some of the relationships that I've had they start off orange because they're heart significant and then they become soul significant for a while and then you break off and then they change to yellow and become mind significant because they're still there in your mind but they're not in your heart anymore they're not as strong

Another notes:

> Normally I work with lots and lots of colour but for some reason I've had this need over the last couple of months to work with far less colour and I don't know why and I don't know how long it will last or whether I can just work through it and then get back into to doing some really you know more colourful things I don't know Strange that how your life things that happen in your life can really affect you

In these accounts, the personal connection is presented as providing meaning and significance (even if these may not be recognisable to others) and as driving the creative making. These encodings constitute a trajectory from the personal starting point to the made object, and potentially beyond, into future making. The forward movement implicit in the trajectory is similar to that of the developmental processes presented in the participants' accounts of experimentation with new equipment and materials.

In addition to the meanings given by personal connections, the participants also claim significance for their work which derives from long established techniques and traditional materials:

> I see myself as a fine artist using a traditional set of craft skills

> … this kind of black clay And I love the kind of the er you know it just looks like something that's been pulled out of the earth and that's what I kind of go for with my ceramics

By describing their practice in these terms which invoke the (extended) past, participants utilise the discursive practice of constructing continuity and additional significance by 'nesting' their personal work narratives with the larger narratives of history (Gergen, 1994, p. 203; Taylor, 2010, p. 66). Some project the narrative into the future and posterity, considering the legacy of their work through its 'vintage' status or simply the lastingness of its materials:

> … when you make something there is a quality about it that you can't get anywhere else It's priceless really If you have got the money and want something unique and different it's well worth it And it's something to treasure as well Because I have boxes that I put my [made objects] in with my name on and it's somewhere to keep them and I'd like to think that one day my [made objects] will be vintage they will get handed down and kept

> … and I just fell in love with working with fire working with the fact that you could take metal and just transform it into anything that you want I mean the only thing that comes close to it is clay and I can guarantee the only things that will survive is metal artefacts and ceramic so in a way some of my stuff's going to last forever hopefully

The extracts in this section exemplify patterns found in the larger dataset in the participants' talk about their creative practice. Their accounts emphasise the process of creative making as intensely concentrated, separating the makers from their ordinary or mundane lives, and as experimental and dynamic, moving them ever onward. Making is presented as personal, in several senses. The creative process starts with aspects of the maker's self and experience and incorporates them within larger histories, constructing a new significance for both the maker and the creative output. It provides something 'for' the maker, compensating for what has been taken away by work. Elsewhere, in their detailed accounts of specific techniques and outputs, participants refer to some of difficulties conventionally associated with work, such as stress, tiredness, and safety issues, but their overviews of creative making are strikingly positive.

Conclusion

Discussing both the creative sector and contemporary work more generally, David Hesmondhalgh and Sarah Baker (2011, p. 17) have called for more 'good work'. They describe this partly in terms similar to Huws' (2013) normative model, as offering 'decent pay hours and safety ... work life balance; security'. However, they combine these features with the 'autonomy; interest and involvement ... esteem and self-esteem' and 'self-realisation' more associated with the creative and entrepreneurial ideals of new work. This is, of course, a version of 'that moral-intimate-economic thing called "the good life"' discussed by Lauren Berlant (2011, p. 2), and Hesmondhalgh and Baker's full list again raises the question of what people now expect and aspire to. Are there new understandings of what work entails and can provide, or is it still understood in terms of the normative model outlined by Huws? And if there has been change, have different expectations simply been added, or have some of those held previously now been relinquished?

This chapter has explored these questions through a discussion of research with UK artist-makers whose working lives diverge sharply from Huws' model and, in many respects, appear to approach an alternative creative/entrepreneurial ideal of work. In the analytic approach adopted in this chapter, the participants' aspirations and expectations are not understood in individual terms but instead as the meanings in play around work in society today, available to be taken up in the talk of individual speakers but not originating with them. In other words, the approach does not present an explanation of the patterns in the participants' talk as evidence of individual psychology or pathology, such as a demand for more personal attention or a rejection of the responsibilities of conventional work. Rather, the analysis explores shared understandings of work, including the affective colouring and associations that have accrued around the working life.

In the contemporary context of work and employment in the UK, these artist-makers could be categorised as own account workers (ILO, 2015), outside the security of the conventional employer–employee relationship. Their talk corresponds to the entrepreneur's optimism and the creative worker's pursuit of self-actualisation through individual and personalised creative practice. Yet their talk refers neither to the integration of the personal into work, which is associated with theorisations of new work, for instance, as involving emotional labour (Hochschild, 2003) nor the exploitation of emotion and personal identity for profit (Conor, Gill, & Taylor, 2015). These academic arguments have apparently not (yet) entered contemporary discourses of work. Instead, the participants' accounts present creative practice as personal and separated from other parts of life, including work. As they characterise it, the creative practice is not work in the terms of Huws' model, because it does not provide a sufficient or steadily increasing income and it is not expected to; the expectation is that other activities ('work') must be undertaken to obtain that.

The earlier normative model of work outlined by Huws (2013) legitimised an expectation of working for others on satisfactory terms. In contrast, both the creative/entrepreneurial ideal of new work and these participants' accounts of their creative practice centre on a personal project. Hesmondhalgh and Baker's (2011) terms for 'good work' imply that the two are compatible. Yet the artist-makers discussed in this chapter aspire to involvement and satisfactions from their creative practice that work supposedly cannot provide. They have apparently relinquished positive expectations of work in a failure of the 'optimism' discussed by Berlant (2011), or perhaps an avoidance of the situation in which an 'optimistic relation' becomes cruel, that is, when 'the object that draws your attachment actively impedes the aim that brought you to it initially' (Berlant, 2011, p. 1). Underlying the artist-makers' organisation of their lives is an acceptance of the limitations of conventional work as not able to provide the positive affect and personal meanings and values that they aspire to and associate with their creative practice. The participants want to escape from work. They expect a more central place in their lives for their creative making than the leisure time made available by 'contractually formalised' work (Huws, 2013) which was the conventional time of hobbies such as craft making (Luckman, 2015). Perhaps confirming the individualism of late capitalism (e.g., Beck & Beck-Gernsheim, 2002), they are claiming a priority for the personal, which is supposedly excluded from work and also other parts of their lives. This emphasis on the personal and on other affect-laden meanings of their creative making, including its place within the extended trajectory of posterity, is a rejection of the anonymity of work as a collective social practice.

These aspirations and expectations of creative making could be dismissed as claims made on life by the privileged, exemplified here by these participants as people who live in a relatively affluent area of an affluent country and are able to support themselves, sometimes with difficulty but without (according to their own accounts) resorting to the truly bad work that must be accepted by the poor. However, as an indication of prevailing assumptions and expectations in society, their talk suggests that the earlier model has not yet been superseded by a 'new normal' of work. In addition, their claim to something more might indicate increasingly negative meanings and affect which are now attached to work. This is concerning, because it seems to amount to a society-wide misrecognition of its possibilities, as if work, all work, is being given a very bad name. Alternatively, and equally negatively, the claim may be the consequence of a more general decline in the quality of work experience and working lives, even for the educated and qualified middle class, who might once have expected to find more satisfaction through their work in once-respected occupations, including self-actualisation and personal reward.

Acknowledgements The author thanks Ann Pegg and Linda Wilks for access to the interviews discussed in this chapter.

References

Ahl, H. (2006). Why research on women entrepreneurs needs new directions. *Entrepreneurship Theory and Practice, 30*(5), 595–621.

Ahl, H., & Marlow, S. (2012). Exploring the dynamics of gender, feminism and entrepreneurship: Advancing debate to escape a dead end? *Organization, 19*(5), 543–562.

Banks, M. (2007). *The politics of cultural work*. Basingstoke: Palgrave Macmillan.
Beck, U., & Beck-Gernsheim, E. (2002). *Individualization: Institutionalized individualism and its social and political consequences*. London: SAGE.
Becker, H. (1982). *Art worlds*. Berkeley, CA: University of California Press.
Berlant, L. (2011). *Cruel optimism*. Durham and London: Duke University Press.
Brockling, U. (2016). *The entrepreneurial self*. London: SAGE.
Conor, B., Gill, R., & Taylor, S. (2015). Gender and creative labour. *Sociological Review, 63*, 1–22.
Csikszentmihalyi, M. (2002). *Flow: The psychology of happiness*. London: Rider.
Department for Culture, Media and Sport. (2001). *Creative industries mapping document*. London: HMSO.
Fuller, G., Hamilton, C., & Seale, K. (2013). Working with amateur labour: Between culture and economy. *Cultural Studies Review, 19*(1), 143–154.
Gergen, K. (1994). *Realities and relationships: Soundings in social construction*. Cambridge, MA: Harvard University Press.
Gill, R., & Pratt, A. (2008). In the social factory? Immaterial labour, precariousness and cultural work. *Theory, Culture and Society, 25*(7–8), 1–30.
Hammersley, M., & Atkinson, P. (2007). *Ethnography: Principles in practice*. London and New York: Routledge.
Hesmondhalgh, D. (2007). *The cultural industries*. London: Sage.
Hesmondhalgh, D., & Baker, S. (2011). *Creative labour: Media work in three cultural industries*. Abingdon, Oxon: Routledge.
Hochschild, A. (2003). *The managed heart: Commercialization of human feeling*. Berkeley, CA: University of California Press.
Huws, U. (2013). Working online, living offline: Labour in the Internet Age. *Work Organisation Labour and Globalisation, 7*(1), 1–11.
International Labour Organisation. (2015). *World employment and social outlook: The changing nature of jobs*. Geneva: International Labour Office, ILO Research Department.
Irwin Mitchell. (2017, April). *UK powerhouse city growth tracker report*. London: Centre for Economics and Business Research. Retrieved June 16, 2017, from http://www.irwinmitchell.com/ukpowerhouse
Luckman, S. (2015). *Craft and the creative economy*. Hampshire: Palgrave Macmillan.
McRobbie, A. (1998). *British fashion design: Rag trade or image industry?* London: Routledge.

Royal Society of Arts. (2016). *A charter for the self-employed*. Retrieved October 11, 2016, from https://www.thersa.org/globalassets/pdfs/reports/rsa-self-employment-charter.pdf

Taylor, S. (2010). *Narratives of identity and place*. London: Routledge.

Taylor, S. (2011). Negotiating oppositions and uncertainties: Gendered conflicts in creative identity work. *Feminism and Psychology, 21*(3), 354–371.

Taylor, S. (2012). One participant said. *Qualitative Research, 12*(4), 388–401.

Taylor, S. (2015). A new mystique? Working for yourself in the neoliberal economy. *Sociological Review, 63*(SI), 174–187.

Taylor, S., & Littleton, K. (2012). *Contemporary identities of creativity and creative work*. Farnham: Ashgate.

Stephanie Taylor is Senior Lecturer in Social Psychology at the Open University, UK. Her research investigates a complex gendered subject and contemporary identification, including identities of creativity, creative work, and own account working. Her recent books are *What Is Discourse Analysis?* (2013) and *Contemporary Identities of Creativity and Creative Work* (2012) (with Karen Littleton), and the co-edited collections *Gender and Creative Labour* (2015) (with Bridget Conor and Rosalind Gill) and *Theorizing Cultural Work: Labour, Continuity and Change in the Cultural and Creative Industries* (2013) (with Mark Banks and Rosalind Gill).

Index[1]

A
Adobe Photoshop, 8, 111, 114–119
Advanced economies, 3, 5, 285, 287, 303, 327
Advantage, 5, 6, 12, 42, 73, 96, 224, 276, 334
Advertising, 65, 67, 88, 92, 136, 144n7, 150, 235
Affect, 12, 117, 143n2, 184, 190, 202–204, 211–214, 229, 267, 274, 286, 287, 290, 298, 303, 328, 339, 343
  affective labour, 4, 65, 73, 202, 214
Agency/ies, 38, 47, 50, 51, 54, 56, 92–96, 98–101, 114, 130, 134, 136, 143n2, 164, 254, 259
Airbnb, 37
Albania, 7, 43, 48

Allon, F., 246, 251
Amateur, 4, 8, 65, 66, 68, 75–79, 82, 152, 331–333
Anthropology, anthropological, 7, 43, 67
Art, arts
  artist, 12, 24, 26–28, 32, 42, 44, 45, 57, 69, 73, 109, 328–330, 336, 340–342
  art school, 110
Artisans, 22
  aspirational, 42, 45, 70, 74
Audience, 9, 68, 138, 148, 149, 151, 153, 156–158, 160–164
Austerity measures, policy, 3, 130, 327, 332, 334
Australia, 25, 27, 28, 30

---

[1] Note: Page numbers followed by "n" refers to note.

© The Author(s) 2018
S. Taylor, S. Luckman (eds.), *The New Normal of Working Lives*, Dynamics of Virtual Work, DOI 10.1007/978-3-319-66038-7

348   Index

Authentic, authenticity, 9, 11, 53, 74, 75, 135, 137–139, 147–164, 204, 222, 316, 321
Autonomy, 41–43, 48, 67, 87, 90, 99, 102, 103, 142, 175, 201–203, 223, 275, 289, 290, 293, 317, 327, 329, 330, 341

B

Balkans, the, 53
Barter, 55, 56, 59
Blogging, 3, 6, 9, 129–144
Boundaries, public-private, 275
Branding, 88, 92, 99
　self-branding, 20, 138, 155–163, 249
Breadwinner, 31

C

Camera phone, 66, 78, 80
Canada, 10, 176, 245, 246, 248, 257, 258
Capitalist production, 87
Career
　career-building, 148
　career changers, 22
　career entry barriers, 6, 35, 37
　careerists, 22
　career models, 11, 309–313, 321
　career path, trajectory, 22, 148
Case study, 8, 91, 92, 101, 111, 123, 231, 265, 268, 270, 291, 314
Celebrity, 148, 157, 160, 161, 163
　micro-celebrity, 155–163
Childcare, 24, 25, 27, 32, 131, 311, 318, 332

Citizen production, 79
Class
　class identities, 70
　middle class, 2, 5, 10, 12, 13, 37, 70, 73, 109, 134, 246, 259, 279, 330, 343
　working class, 51, 67, 68, 70, 330
Clientelism, 44, 53, 54
Coalition building, 8, 87–104
Collaboration, 9, 10, 97, 100, 147–164, 171–173, 176, 179, 182, 185, 191–195, 220, 221, 224, 225, 230, 236, 238
Collectivising, 100
Comedy, 148, 154, 159
Commodity exchange, 88
Communication, 1, 9, 66–68, 81, 88, 100, 101, 112, 113, 131, 150, 157, 163, 171–174, 178–180, 184–187, 189, 191–195, 221, 224, 257, 328
Community, 10, 53, 56, 57, 60, 97, 99, 129, 130, 134, 139, 144n9, 172, 219–221, 223, 224, 228–230, 232–238
Consumer culture, 69–70
Consumption, 11, 67, 68, 75, 119, 162, 219, 265, 279
Context, 1, 3, 4, 6, 9, 10, 38, 44, 47, 55, 57, 74, 91, 96, 138, 140, 144n9, 156–158, 160–162, 164, 172, 178, 181, 191, 192, 204–206, 208, 211, 212, 214, 221–223, 237, 249, 265–267, 285, 287, 290, 292, 293, 295, 296, 302–304, 328, 342
Corporate ladder, 311, 321

Co-working, coworking,
10, 219–238
co-working space, 3, 10, 98–101,
103, 219–238
Craft, craftmaking, 7, 12, 19–38, 75,
80, 102, 104, 136, 150, 162,
328–332, 340, 343
Creative
creative entrepreneur, 20, 75,
341, 342
creative industry, industries, 4, 42,
59, 87, 88, 91–93, 202, 246,
251, 258
creative practice, 4, 8, 12, 22, 23,
73, 74, 81, 123, 201, 328,
331–338, 340, 342
creative practitioner, 21, 29, 32,
57, 119, 328, 330–332
creative sector, 3, 4, 23, 32, 93,
329–331, 341
creative skillset, 149, 150
creative work, 4, 6, 32, 41–47,
53, 55–57, 59, 60, 66, 73, 82,
88, 91, 109, 201–206, 209,
210, 212–214, 328, 332–334,
337, 338
creative worker, 3, 7–9, 32,
41–61, 69, 74, 77, 88,
201–214, 329, 337, 342
Creativity, 4–6, 72–75, 80, 87–89,
91, 92, 96, 100, 101, 103,
109–112, 115, 118–121, 133,
152, 202, 203, 205, 207, 211,
212, 328–330, 335
creativity dispositif, 8, 110, 111,
114, 118–120, 123
Cross-promotion, 159
Cultural
cultural capital, 75, 79
cultural career, 156
cultural geography, 59
cultural industry, industries, 66,
77, 156, 163, 329
cultural intermediaries, 92, 164
cultural production, 44, 82,
109, 111, 112, 115,
119, 155, 162
cultural work, 9, 56, 73, 74, 109,
112, 123, 148–151, 153–158,
164, 202, 332

D
Data, 7, 20, 21, 92, 113, 114, 121,
122, 134, 172, 175–179,
193, 225, 248, 271, 278, 287,
291–293, 302, 312, 314, 331,
335, 337, 340
Debt, 5, 6, 10, 245–260
Design
designer-maker, 20, 25, 31
designers, 7, 20, 25, 28, 30, 31,
43, 50, 51, 56, 73, 92–101,
112, 114–117, 122, 188
design firms, 93, 95
Digital
digital communications, 328
digital image, 114–116
digital media, 73, 114, 134, 150
digital media platforms, 77, 114,
119, 150
digital practice, 129
digital shopfront, 328
digital technologies, 2, 3,
110–113, 172, 266, 270,
274, 336
digital tools, 110
digital working, 3, 4, 6, 9

Discipline, 8, 10, 65–83, 116, 172, 208, 259
Discourse, 4, 8, 10, 21, 71, 73, 76–78, 81, 82, 89, 111, 119, 121, 150, 155, 202, 203, 208, 213, 214, 221–225, 230–236, 246, 249, 252, 259, 331, 342
Domesticity, 3, 35, 66
Double life, 32, 333
Down shifting, 142

Economy, economies
  advanced, 3, 5, 285, 287, 303, 327
  collaborative, 219
  gift, 68
  gig, 37, 88, 89, 95
  information, 329
  micro-, 20, 21, 25
  sharing, 37, 88, 89
Email, 172, 173, 179–187, 189–191, 194, 253, 278
  email overload, 180, 191
Emotional work, 222
  emotional labour, 4, 5, 140, 141, 144n9, 161, 204, 277, 279, 294, 302, 337, 342
Enchantment (at/of work), 213
Entrepreneur
  entrepreneurial activities, 150, 285
  entrepreneurial ethos, 150, 164
  entrepreneurial frame, 73, 75
  entrepreneurialism, 266, 279
  entrepreneurial lifestyle, 10, 131, 135, 268, 272, 278, 279
  entrepreneurial work, 4, 11, 265–280
entrepreneurship, 10, 11, 38, 102, 135, 136, 149, 150, 220, 268, 272, 274, 277, 279, 290, 291, 295, 303
  female entrepreneurs, 35, 279
Equipment, 56, 152, 155, 161, 162, 164, 332, 336, 339
ethical consumption, 68, 75
Ethics, 21, 73, 140, 144n7, 278, 299
ETSY (*Etsy*), 150, 162, 332
Event system theory, 178
Exclusion, 5, 35, 57, 74, 75
Expertise, 5, 8, 9, 65–83, 117, 147–164, 207

Facebook, 71, 138, 270
Family, 5, 7, 11, 20, 25, 27, 29–34, 36, 37, 49, 55, 57, 58, 71–73, 76, 80, 130, 138–140, 179, 184, 186, 190, 234, 247, 255–258, 268, 269, 273, 275, 276, 296, 311–313, 316, 318–320, 330, 332, 337
  neofamilism, 130
Fashion, 7, 43, 50–52, 56, 67, 70, 80, 100, 148, 152, 158–160, 312, 329
Femininity, 70, 74, 134, 135, 137
Feminism, 71
Film and television production, 14
Finland, 9, 11, 130, 143n3, 144n7, 173, 176, 186, 265, 268, 269, 290, 313, 314

Flexibility, 3, 9, 30, 37, 90, 175, 188, 189, 224, 246, 318–321, 329
Fragmentation, 93–97, 172
Freedom, 11–13, 30, 31, 35, 74, 90, 96–97, 147, 150, 163, 202, 278, 279, 286, 291, 293, 300, 302, 319, 320
Freelance, freelancing, freelance work, 4, 8, 37, 87–104, 129, 131, 136, 143n3, 150, 226, 233, 235, 257, 327
   freelancer, 8, 12, 88–90, 92–103, 131, 150, 220, 224, 247, 252, 267
Furniture (making), 25, 33
Future orientation, futurity, 42, 43, 46–48, 54

G

Game development, gaming, video game, 10, 58, 148, 152–154, 202, 205, 206
Gender, 8, 21, 25, 31, 52, 66, 69, 70, 72–74, 78, 82, 174, 266, 267, 316, 330, 336
   gender roles, 267, 311–313
Globalisation, 219, 309
Glut, 8, 109–123
'Good life,' 11, 13, 19, 36, 37, 45–49, 73, 266, 274, 279, 341
'Good work,' 37, 46–48, 75, 341, 342
Google, 132
Graphic design, 88, 92, 122
Guild mentality, 97, 99, 102

H

Health, 11, 48, 49, 51, 60, 245, 286, 287, 290–292, 296, 298–300
Hegemonic ideal, 135, 137
Hobby, 29, 32, 129, 268, 270, 271, 273, 274, 333, 343
Home
   home-based micro-enterprise, 7, 19–38
   home working, home-based working, 3, 5, 7, 11, 13, 19–38, 267–271, 274
Hope, 7, 13, 19, 35, 41–61, 72, 102, 111, 114, 131, 202, 246, 247, 249–255, 259, 266, 318
Housewife, 35, 74, 312, 336
'How to' guidance, texts, literature, materials, 5, 9, 78, 79, 82, 148, 149, 152, 155, 156, 161, 164

I

Immigration, 263
Income, 3, 22, 23, 25, 26, 28, 29, 31–33, 35, 93, 130, 150, 154, 235, 252, 259, 269, 271–273, 293, 300, 319, 327, 332–334, 342
Individualism, individualisation, 102, 119, 161, 246, 309, 316, 343
Inequality, inequalities, 5, 34, 69, 73, 74, 246, 251, 255, 259, 330
Informal work, 54, 58
Information

Information (*cont.*)
　information and communication technologies (ICTs), 100–102, 112, 174, 176, 191, 197
　information economy, 109, 329
Innovation, 11, 68, 73, 111, 113, 155, 220, 224, 228, 286, 303, 312, 329, 330
Insecurity, 38, 210, 211, 247, 258, 267, 271, 272, 294, 309, 329, 334
Instagram, 76, 132, 160
Intellectuality, 67
Internet, 21, 34, 35, 58, 67, 68, 75, 93, 95, 97, 99, 102, 103, 113, 129, 154, 163, 194, 270, 276
Interns, internships, 6, 10, 42, 245–260
Interviews, 7, 9, 12, 21, 23, 25–27, 33, 43, 50–53, 55, 92–100, 117, 118, 131–134, 136–142, 143n2, 143n4, 144n6, 154, 176–178, 193, 205, 208, 211, 225, 231, 233, 247, 248, 253, 254, 268, 270–272, 277, 280n2, 287, 292, 293, 296–298, 300, 301, 328, 330, 335
Intimacy, 45, 137–140, 161, 201, 202, 204, 213, 214, 266
Ireland, 148, 158
Italy, 176, 225, 231

J
Just-in-time learning, 111, 119–123

K
Kodak, 76
Korea, 148

L
Labour
　affective labour, 73, 202, 214
　aspirational labour, 42
　casualised labour, 258
　creative labour, 8, 43–45, 54, 55, 59, 69, 74, 87–104, 202
　cultural labour, 66, 71, 157, 328
　emotional labour, 5, 140, 141, 144n9, 204, 277, 279, 294, 302, 337, 342
　factory labour, 87
　feminised labour, 66
　free labour, 8, 10, 41, 67, 68, 246, 249–252
　hope labour, 7, 41–61, 246, 247, 249–252, 254, 259
　immaterial labour, 8, 65, 67–69, 82, 87, 88, 90, 91, 103
　provisional labour, 42, 45
　relational labour, 157, 160
　sacrificial labour, 42
　self-employed labour, 4, 90, 301, 303, 329
Lawyers, 11, 309–321
Lifestyle, 11, 28, 51, 91, 129, 130, 134, 135, 144n7, 152, 191, 194, 265, 267–273, 277, 278, 310, 314, 318
　lifestyle entrepreneurs, 272, 279
Life writing, 129, 133, 134, 137
Love-work, 8, 65–83
Lynda.com, 119–123

M
Macedonia, 7, 43, 58
Made objects, 330, 339, 340
Make up, 135, 148

Managers, 11, 26, 42, 60, 173, 176, 180–190, 194, 208, 221–237, 258, 290, 292–295, 302, 309–321
Manchester, 57
Masculinity, 70
  masculine activities, 5
Mass worker, 90
Maternalism, 70
Media
  media industries, 65, 67, 164, 247–248
  media production, 67
  media software, 8, 109–123
  media tool, 80
Meetings, 101, 173, 176, 177, 180, 181, 184–186, 188–190, 194, 205, 270, 276, 303, 315, 316
Memex, 113
Memory work, 80
Micro
  micro-celebrity, 155–163
  micro-economy, 20, 25
  micro-enterprise, 7, 19–38
  micro-entrepreneurialism / entrepreneurship, 9, 129, 131, 135, 136, 142, 144n9, 332
Milan, 231
Mobile technology, 79, 173, 177
Mobile work, 175, 177
Mom blogger, 9, 129–132, 135, 144n8
Monetisation, 9, 137, 142, 144n9, 151
Motherhood, mothering, mothers, 9, 26, 27, 33, 70–73, 76, 129–131, 135–137, 140–142, 143n1, 143n3, 190, 234, 258, 270, 274, 280, 280n2, 310, 311, 315–318, 320, 321
Multilocational work, 171, 172
Multipresence, 9, 171–195
Mumpreneur, mumpreneurialism, 72, 73, 144n8

N

Narrative, 9, 24, 41, 46, 78, 110, 114, 129, 164, 205, 225, 233, 234, 309, 314, 317, 321, 331, 340
Neoliberal, 2, 35, 53, 66, 70, 79, 202, 246, 252–254, 278, 280
Netherlands, 8, 92, 99, 104, 176
Networking, networks, 7, 10, 20, 21, 25, 26, 34, 65–70, 72, 78, 81, 94, 97–99, 101, 102, 129, 134, 138, 158–161, 171, 185, 191, 192, 220, 224, 225, 228–235, 237, 249, 254
'New town,' 330
Non-governmental organisations (NGOs), 55–57, 60
Normative model of work, 5, 328, 334, 342
Nostalgia, 45, 47, 49–51, 60, 76, 81, 246

O

Octant Studio, 205–206
Online distribution, online selling, 7, 19–38, 332
Open source software, 68
Operaismo, 89, 90

Opting out, 12, 310, 311, 313, 314, 317
Ordinariness, ordinary lives, 43, 134–137, 139, 162
Organisational culture, 204, 234, 310, 316, 321
Organisational studies, 221
Outlook Calendar, 176
Own account working, 2, 4, 327–329, 331

P

Parental leave, 311
Parenting, 9, 71, 130, 135, 136, 139, 141, 142
Passion, 30, 78, 110, 136, 147, 150–153, 155, 156, 164, 208, 209, 213, 214, 267, 274
Pedagogy, 110, 119, 120
Performance, 53, 57, 70, 81, 138, 150, 152, 157, 159, 162, 164, 222, 224, 296, 299
Personal
  personal identity, 34, 162, 342
  personal interest, 121, 151, 330
  personalization, 4, 337
  personal relationship, 207, 211, 213, 274
Photography, 8, 66, 67, 76–81, 117, 122
Pitches, 94, 95
Platform economy, 38
Poland, 11, 309–321
Portfolio working, 155
Postalgia, 155
Postcapitalist, 87, 89

Post-feminism, 69–72
  post-feminist masquerade, 70, 73
Post-Fordism, 69, 246
Postoperaist tradition, postoperaismo, 8, 87, 89
Post-socialism, 44, 48
Post-socialist nation states, 4
Precariat, precarity, 13, 23, 25, 37, 38, 42, 43, 46, 47, 69, 73, 131, 245, 259
Precarious work, 53, 247
Pregnancy, 315, 318
Private sector, 44, 288, 294
Pro-bono work, 57
Production, 11, 21, 28, 33, 44, 67, 68, 75, 76, 79, 80, 82, 87, 88, 100, 104, 109, 111, 112, 115, 119, 133, 138, 149, 150, 154, 155, 162, 164, 182, 188, 191, 201, 202, 204–206, 219, 221, 251, 265, 266, 274, 279, 289, 332, 336
Productivity, 4, 9, 93, 100, 172, 189, 190, 193–195
Professional
  professionalisation, 70, 76, 137
  professional/ism, 4–9, 11, 12, 20, 21, 24, 27, 30, 34, 43, 45, 60, 66, 70, 74, 77, 79, 82, 98–102, 117, 129–144, 149, 157, 213, 220, 222–224, 226–229, 232, 234–236, 249, 270, 277, 285–304, 316, 317, 320, 336
  professional work, 4, 316
Property values, 334

Q

Quantification (*check: numerical measure*), 134

R

Recession, 289, 334
Redundancy, 37, 93
Returners, 22

S

Sandberg, Sheryl
   Lean In, 71
Science and Technology Studies (STS), 111, 112
Screenwriting, 149
Second-generation autonomous worker, 102, 103
Self
   self-actualisation, 12, 70, 213, 329, 330, 342, 343
   self branding, 20, 138, 155–163, 249
   self-employed, 4, 10, 11, 90, 203, 267, 274, 277, 290–303, 327, 329
   self-employment, 4–6, 11, 20, 24, 34–36, 38, 268, 272, 273, 280, 285–304, 332
   self-exploitation, 2, 10, 11, 45, 213, 247, 251, 285–304
   self-expression, 76, 133, 201
   self-presentation, 148, 157, 337
   self-realisation, 201, 204, 213, 341
   self-valorisation, 67, 88

Sexual contract, 66, 70, 71, 258
Shoemaker, 30
Signalling expertise, 148, 154–158, 160–163
Sites of work, 3
Skills, 2, 5, 9, 10, 12, 20, 21, 46, 59, 93, 110, 112, 117, 119, 121, 122, 148–150, 155–158, 160, 163, 164, 194, 234, 249, 268, 274, 286, 329, 331, 333, 335, 336, 340
Small business, 7, 19, 24, 32, 68, 97, 228, 292, 295, 317
Snapchat, 132
Social
   social identities, 68
   social media, 7–9, 20, 25, 65–83, 100, 114, 134, 148, 150, 154–159, 162–164, 194, 270, 274, 337
   social media account, 158
   social media platform designers, 114
   social media profile, 154, 164
   social networks, 65, 70
   social reproduction, 4, 5, 246, 247, 250, 255–260, 266, 337
Sociology, 43, 45, 46, 59, 220
Soft capitalism, 202
Software inscription strategy, 8, 109–123
Spaces of hope, 49, 51–53, 57, 60
Spa-going, 49–52
Specialisation, 93, 96, 97, 203
Start-up, 153, 206, 235, 285
Stress, 9, 32, 33, 101, 175, 176, 183, 189, 191, 237, 294, 316, 341

Studio, 10, 27, 29, 31, 33, 56, 58, 94, 95, 110, 205–206, 330, 334, 336
Subjectivity, 4, 9, 68, 74, 110, 138, 142, 201, 212, 214, 222, 223, 231, 235
Superannuation, 25
Sustainability, 10, 36, 56, 57, 153, 154, 220, 226, 229, 235–238, 329, 330
Sweden, 10, 11, 176, 206, 265, 268, 285, 286, 288, 290–292

T

Temporality, 54, 59, 133, 246, 254
Third places, 183, 187
Timezone, 171, 182, 185, 187
Trade unions, 52
Training manuals, 8, 66, 120
Twitter, 158–160

U

Uber, 37
UK, the, 3, 8, 12, 22, 70, 78, 92, 104, 148, 149, 159, 162, 163, 176, 258, 327–330, 341, 342
Underemployment, 7, 20

Unpaid (work), 245, 246, 252, 257, 258
USA, 11, 60, 78, 176, 185, 309–321

V

Variety, 161
Video, 10, 117, 120–123, 148–151, 153–155, 157–159, 162–164, 184, 202, 205, 206
Vlogging, 3, 6, 9, 147–164
Vlog Nation, 151, 153

W

Welfare services, 11, 285, 286, 288
Work ethic, 73, 278
Work-life balance, 9, 36, 37, 172, 173, 177, 183, 189–192, 194, 195, 224, 312–313, 320, 321

Y

YouTube, 114, 121, 147–155, 158, 159, 161–164

Z

Zoella, 159, 162, 163

CPI Antony Rowe
Eastbourne, UK
December 04, 2019